Asia Bible Commentary Series

EXODUS

Asia Bible Commentary Series

EXODUS

Chloe T. Sun

General Editor
Andrew B. Spurgeon

Old Testament Consulting Editors
Joseph Shao, Havilah Dharamraj, Koowon Kim

New Testament Consulting Editors
Steve Chang, Finny Philip, Samson Uytanlet

© 2024 by Chloe T. Sun

Published 2024 by Langham Global Library
An imprint of Langham Publishing
www.langhampublishing.org

Langham Publishing and its imprints are a ministry of Langham Partnership

Langham Partnership
PO Box 296, Carlisle, Cumbria CA3 9WZ, UK
www.langham.org

Published in partnership with Asia Theological Association

ATA
QCC PO Box 1454–1154, Manila, Philippines
www.ataasia.com

ISBNs:
978-1-78641-032-0 Print
978-1-78641-094-8 ePub
978-1-78641-095-5 PDF

Chloe T. Sun has asserted her right under the Copyright, Designs, and Patents Act, 1988 to be identified as the Author of this work.

All rights reserved. No part of this publication may be reproduced, stored in a retrieval system, or transmitted in any form or by any means, electronic, mechanical, photocopying, recording, or otherwise, without the prior written permission of the publisher or the Copyright Licensing Agency.

Unless otherwise stated, Scripture quotations are from the New International Version, copyright © 2011. Used by permission. All rights reserved.

British Library Cataloguing in Publication Data
A catalogue record for this book is available from the British Library.

ISBN: 978-1-78641-032-0

ISBN: Cover & Book Design: projectluz.com

Langham Partnership actively supports theological dialogue and an author's right to publish but does not necessarily endorse the views and opinions set forth and works referenced within this publication or guarantee its technical and grammatical correctness. Langham Partnership does not accept any responsibility or liability to persons or property as a consequence of the reading, use, or interpretation of its published content.

CONTENTS

Commentary

Series Preface ix

Author's Preface xi

List of Abbreviations xiii

Introduction...1

Exodus 1:1–15:21 31

Exodus 15:22–18:27 147

Exodus 19–24 183

Exodus 25–40 269

Selected Bibliograpy 339

Topics

The Chinese in America and Anti-Asian Hate 36

Faithful Disobedience in the Context of China's House Churches 45

God's Gender and Pronoun 65

The Multiple Names of God in Chinese 66

The Ten Plagues: The Interaction Between Heaven and Earth 87

The Firstborn Son in Asian Cultures..113

The Chinese Festivals and the Passover 115

The Wilderness Tradition in Chinese Spirituality...........................152

Elim and its Reception: West and East 157

Leadership in Chinese Churches and the Silent Exodus.................180

The Confucian Virtues of Kindness and Righteousness 196

Idol Worship in the Asian Context 202

Law and Immigration in the United States 248

Family and Kinship Relations..266

The Place of Chinese Immigrant Churches in Los Angeles 271

Asian Work Ethics and the False Perception of Rest.......................309

SERIES PREFACE

What's unique about the Asia Bible Commentary Series? It is a commentary series written especially for Asian Christians, which incorporates and addresses Asian concerns, cultures, and practices. As Asian scholars – either by nationality, passion, or calling – the authors identify with the biblical text, understand it culturally, and apply its principles in Asian contexts to strengthen the churches in Asia. Missiologists tell us that Christianity has shifted from being a Western majority religion to a South, Southeastern, and Eastern majority religion and that the church is growing at an unprecedented rate in these regions. This series meets the need for evangelical commentaries written specifically for an Asian audience.

This is not to say that Asian churches and Asian Christians do not want to partner with Western Christians and churches or that they spurn Western influences. A house divided cannot stand. The books in this series complement the existing Western commentaries by taking into consideration the cultural nuances familiar to the Eastern world so that the Eastern readership is not inundated with Western clichés and illustrations that they are unable to relate to and which may not be applicable to them.

The mission of this series is "to produce resources that are biblical, pastoral, contextual, missional, and prophetic for pastors, Christian leaders, cross-cultural workers, and students in Asia." While using approved exegetical principles, the writers strive to be culturally relevant, offer practical applications, and provide clear explanations of the texts so that readers can grow in understanding and maturity in Christ, and so that Christian leaders can guide their congregations into maturity. May we be found faithful to this endeavor and may God be glorified!

Andrew B. Spurgeon
General Editor

AUTHOR'S PREFACE

Writing this commentary has been an exciting and challenging journey. It was exciting because Exodus is such a fascinating and significant book in the biblical canon, laying the theological foundation for the rest of the Bible. It was challenging because the commentary requires a pastoral, contextual, and missional focus. This involved tailoring my writing to a specific kind of readership – those who live in the global Chinese diaspora and embrace the Christian faith in new lands. In this context, leaving home, sojourning, and seeking purpose in new lands are shared experiences, and understanding one's identity is an ongoing quest.

As the Israelites struggled and wrestled with their changing identity – from Hebrew slaves to Yahweh worshipers – they underwent a process of conversion, confusion, construction, and conformation. I have chosen to explore the identity formation process as the lens through which readers can connect with the Israelites' journey of identity formation and find hope for their own journeys of becoming and finding.

Building on the works of Western scholars and integrating and contextualizing their insights in Chinese contexts, my aim is to interpret Exodus for those living in the diaspora – both those who grapple with their identity as sojourners in this world and those who long for a permanent home with God.

I thank the editorial committee of the Asia Bible Commentary Series for allowing me to contribute to this series. The works of several scholars have served as valuable guides and sources of inspiration for this commentary, which has been greatly influenced by Nahum Sarna's exploration of the Hebrew context of Exodus, Terrence Fretheim's insights on creation and order, Avivah Zornberg's reflections on Exodus from a Jewish perspective, Michael Morales's theological perspectives on Exodus, and the methods of contextualization adopted by Athena Gorospe, Kenneth Ngwa, and Jerry Hwang. To broaden the global reading and interpretation of Exodus, it is essential to include more contributions by non-Western scholars and female writers.

While writing this commentary, I had the opportunity to tour Egypt with Egyptologist Dr. James Hoffmeier, whose knowledge and passion for the land's history and culture impressed me and enriched my work. My visits to Sinai, the pyramids at Giza, the tombs in the Valley of the Kings in Thebes, and the Egyptian museum in Cairo enhanced my understanding of ancient

Egypt and its culture. Some insights in this commentary are a result of that trip. Carmen Joy Imes, who is working on her own commentary on Exodus, was also on the same tour, and I have learned a great deal from her work on Exodus. Charlie Trimm, my co-author for another commentary series on Exodus, has been my conversation partner on Exodus. His wealth of knowledge, diligence, and patience have been a constant source of encouragement to me during my writing process.

Special thanks to the general editor of the Asia Bible Commentary Series Dr. Andrew B. Spurgeon, as well as to the anonymous reviewer who made corrections and provided invaluable suggestions for my first draft. Thanks also to the consulting and copy editors for their careful editing, and Bubbles Lactaoen for her coordination in the process of seeing the book in print. I am also indebted to my two script editors: my theologian-pastor brother, Dr. Chun Tse, who edited the first draft and offered invaluable suggestions, and Ulrike Guthrie, who meticulously edited the second draft to ensure precision and clarity of language. Any remaining mistakes are my own. Finally, my thanks to Logos Evangelical Seminary and Fuller Theological Seminary for their role in shaping the writer and the educator I am today and for providing a safe space as I learned to navigate between and integrate the Western and Asian worlds.

Chloe T. Sun
Los Angeles, California
January 2024

LIST OF ABBREVIATIONS

BOOKS OF THE BIBLE

Old Testament

Gen, Exod, Lev, Num, Deut, Josh, Judg, Ruth, 1–2 Sam, 1–2 Kgs, 1–2 Chr, Ezra, Neh, Esth, Job, Ps/Pss, Prov, Eccl, Song, Isa, Jer, Lam, Ezek, Dan, Hos, Joel, Amos, Obad, Jonah, Mic, Nah, Hab, Zeph, Hag, Zech, Mal

New Testament

Matt, Mark, Luke, John, Acts, Rom, 1–2 Cor, Gal, Eph, Phil, Col, 1–2 Thess, 1–2 Tim, Titus, Phlm, Heb, Jas, 1–2 Pet, 1–2–3 John, Jude, Rev

BIBLE TEXTS AND VERSIONS

Divisions of the canon

NT	New Testament
OT	Old Testament

Ancient texts and versions

LXX	Septuagint
MT	Masoretic Text

Modern versions

ASV	American Standard Version
ESV	English Standard Version
ISV	International Standard Version
JPS	The Jewish Publication Society of America Version
KJV	King James Version
NASB	New American Standard Bible
NIV	New International Version
NKJV	New King James Version
NLT	New Living Translation
NRSV	New Revised Standard Version
TLB	The Living Bible

Journals, reference works, and series

ABCS	Asia Bible Commentary Series
AOTC	Apollos Old Testament Commentary
AOAT	Alter Orient und Altes Testament
BSac	*Bibliotheca Sacra*
BASOR	*Bulletin of the American Schools of Oriental Research*
BBRSup	Bulletin for Biblical Research Supplements
BDB	Brown, Francis, S. R. Driver, and Charles A. Briggs. *A Hebrew and English Lexicon of the Old Testament*
BZAW	Beihefte zur Zeitschrift für die alttestamentliche Wissenschaft
CANE	*Civilizations of the Ancient Near East*
CBQ	*Catholic Biblical Quarterly*
CNV	Chinese New Version
COS	*The Context of Scripture*
CurBR	*Currents in Biblical Research*
CurTM	*Currents in Theology and Mission*
CUV	Chinese Union Version
CTR	*Criswell Theological Review*
DDD	*Dictionary of Deities and Demons in the Bible*
DOTP	*Dictionary of the Old Testament Pentateuch*
DOTWPW	*Dictionary of the Old Testament Wisdom, Poetry & Writings*
EBC	The Expositor's Bible Commentary
EBR	*Encyclopedia of the Bible and Its Reception*
ECC	Eerdmans Critical Commentary
EEC	Evangelical Exegetical Commentary
ESBT	Essential Studies in Biblical Theology
HALOT	*The Hebrew and Aramaic Lexicon of the Old Testament*
HBM	Hebrew Bible Monographs
HSM	Harvard Semitic Monograph
Int	*Interpretation*
ISBE	*International Standard Bible Encyclopedia*
JBL	*Journal of Biblical Literature*
JBQ	*Jewish Bible Quarterly*
JSOT	*Journal for the Study of the Old Testament*

List of Abbreviations

JSOTSup	Journal for the Study of the Old Testament Supplemental Series
LH	Laws of Hammurabi
LHBOTS	The Library of Hebrew Bible/Old Testament Studies
NICOT	New International Commentary of the Old Testament
NIDOTTE	*New International Dictionary of Old Testament Theology and Exegesis*
OTL	Old Testament Library
QR	*Quarterly Review*
RevExp	*Review and Expositor*
S&HBC	Smyth & Helwys Bible Commentary
TB	*Tyndale Bulletin*
TDOT	*Theological Dictionary of the Old Testament*
WBC	Word Biblical Commentary
WW	*Word and World*
ZAW	*Zeitschrift für die alttestamentliche Wissenschaft*

INTRODUCTION

A DIASPORIC READING OF EXODUS AS A JOURNEY OF BECOMING

I am a product of the Chinese diaspora. Successive migrations across different countries and cultures have marked my life journey. Born in China, my family later relocated to Hong Kong before I eventually made my way to the United States for college. Throughout my career, I have resided primarily in the United States, where I received my higher education, launched my academic career, raised a family, and am now settling down permanently.

As I have acclimated to my new surroundings, the once unfamiliar terrain has gradually transformed into my new home. Throughout this process, my identity has evolved significantly, transitioning from an international student to an Asian American, broadly defined.[1] I grew up speaking three languages and learned several more through my academic training, reflecting my diverse linguistic and cultural background.

My evolving sense of self, however, is not without its challenges. Questions of belonging and identity continue to pervade my thoughts. Is America my true home, or am I still rooted in my Chinese heritage? Who am I, and where do I belong? Such inquiries are particularly complex for someone like me, a person of "many worlds." At times, the boundaries between home and new land can feel blurry, and notions of ethnic and cultural identity can seem hazy.

The complexities of my identity are further compounded by my religious conversion from atheism to Protestant Christianity, which has introduced another dimension to my sense of self. Does my spiritual or religious identity take precedence over my ethnic and cultural identities? How does my newfound faith shape my understanding of where I belong and with whom I identify?

---

1. The term "Asian American" is a capacious construct encompassing a diverse demographic of Asians in North America. This all-encompassing term includes "all Americans of Asian ancestry and heritage, with their diverse languages, cultures, and traditions." Jonathan Y. Tan, *Introducing Asian American Theologies* (Maryknoll: Orbis Books, 2008), 1. Daniel Lee frames the grammar of Asian American theologies as involving four areas: Asian heritage, migration experience, American culture, and racialization. He calls it the "Asian American Quadrilateral." Daniel D. Lee, *Doing Asian American Theology: A Contextual Framework for Faith and Practice* (Downers Grove: IVP Academic, 2022), 15. My reading of the diasporic condition in this book overlaps with Lee's notions of Asian heritage, migration experience, and to some extent, racialization.

As I navigate these challenges, the quest for meaning and significance in my life has taken on an even greater urgency. Despite the complexities inherent in my situation, I have embraced my newfound identity as a diaspora person, recognizing the richness and depth that this status affords me.[2] The idea of diaspora is multipolar. It involves several destinations, such as involuntary and voluntary migration, fragmentation, hybridity, double consciousness, and settlements that persist.[3]

I am hardly alone in my experience. For over five hundred years, waves of Chinese people have migrated from China to other parts of the world for economic, political, and personal reasons.[4] For instance, in the late 1940s, many mainlander Chinese people under Chiang Kai Shek's nationalist regime "exodus-ed" from China, seeking a new life in Taiwan. Similarly, in 1997, waves of people from Hong Kong "exodus-ed" and migrated to other countries. Under new governance, too, new waves of Hong Kong migrants continue to surge. Furthermore, for decades, people from the Wenzhou area in China have been migrating to Europe.[5] These new waves of migration from China to other parts of the world may aptly be named "the new exodus" of the twenty-first century.

Indeed, diaspora and migration have continued across multiple generations from every corner of the world. As journalist Sonia Shah notes, "More people live outside their countries of birth today than at any time before. The reasons vary: between 2008–2014, floods, storms, earthquakes, and the like sent 26 million people into motion each year."[6] Other factors, such as violence, poverty, and persecution, also drive migration. Shah projects that by 2030, China and India will constitute forty-five percent of the global workforce and that by 2050, there will be two hundred million people on the move. The diaspora has thus become a global phenomenon and a fundamental aspect of

---

2. See my chapter on Job. Chloe Sun, "Reading Job as a Chinese Diasporian," in *T&T Clark Handbook of Asian American Biblical Hermeneutics*, eds. Uriah Y. Kim and Sang Ai Yang (London: T&T Clark, 2019), 295–305. Chloe Sun, *Attempt Great Things for God: Theological Education in Diaspora*. Theological Education between the Times Series, ed. Ted A. Smith (Grand Rapids: Eerdmans, 2020).
3. Kevin Kenny, *Diaspora: A Very Short Introduction* (Oxford University Press, 2013), 11–14.
4. Philip Kuhn, *Chinese Among Others: Emigration in Modern Times*, trans. Li Ming Huan (Taiwan: Shang Wu Yin Shu Guan, 2019), 20.
5. Kuhn, *Chinese Among Others*, 70, 431–432. Wenzhou people live along the Pacific coast and have become the newer wave of migrated people since the twentieth century. Their dialect bears little resemblance to Mandarin.
6. Sonia Shah, *The Next Great Migration: The Beauty and Terror of Life on the Move* (New York: Bloomsbury Publishing, 2020), 10.

Introduction

the human condition.[7] It is not an overstatement to say that "human migration is a fact of history, and the history of humans is one of migration."[8]

This book delves into the concept of exodus, tracing its roots from the biblical exodus to its modern manifestation in the Chinese diaspora – "the new exodus." The term "diaspora" in Greek refers to scattering or dispersion.[9] In Chinese, it may refer to the same notion of scattering (*liú lí*) or have the more neutral understanding of spreading out (*sǎn jū*). According to Fernando F. Segovia, a renowned Hispanic American scholar, a diaspora encompasses all those who have established permanent residence in a country other than their place of birth for various reasons.[10] Hence, a diasporic interpretation of Scripture also recognizes the readers' social locations and contextual backgrounds, which shape and influence their reading.[11] The diasporic experience involves not only upheaval and unsettlement, travel, and resettlement but also cultural, religious, and political displacements.[12] Traditionally, the term "diaspora" has been associated most closely with the exile of the Jewish people; however, it now includes a broader range of experiences.[13] Political scientist William Safran identifies six key characteristics of the diasporic state.[14]

1. Dispersal, either of themselves or their ancestors, from a specific original "center" to two or more "peripheral" or foreign regions.

---

7. Sonia Shah's study has highlighted the global migration of people that includes African migrants escaping from starvation and persecution, Afghan and Syrian refugees fleeing to Europe, and women holding their babies crossing from Honduras and Guatemala to reach the United States border. Sonia Shah, *The Next Great Migration*, 9–10, 34. In 2022, tens of thousands of Ukrainians fled from the war zone of Ukraine to other parts of Europe and the rest of the world. See also the three-volume series on Asian Diaspora Christianity edited by Sam George, *Journeys of Asian Diaspora: Mapping Originations and Destinations*, vol. 1 (Minneapolis: Fortress, 2021).
8. A statement borrowed from Jehu J. Hanciles, *Migration and the Making of Global Christianity* (Grand Rapids: Eerdmans, 2021), 21.
9. The word "*dia*" translates to "in different directions," while "*spora*" signifies "to sow." For different terms on diaspora and its associated ideas in the Bible, see Narry F. Santos, "Exploring the Major Dispersion Terms and Realities in the Bible," in *Diaspora Missiology: Theory, Methodology, and Practice*, ed. Enoch Wan (Portland: Western Seminary, 2011), 21–38.
10. Fernando F. Segovia, "Toward a Hermeneutics of the Diaspora: A Hermeneutics of Otherness and Engagement," in *Reading from this Place: Social Location and Biblical Interpretation in the United States*, eds. Fernando F. Segovia and Mary Ann Tolbert (Minneapolis: Fortress, 1995), 60.
11. Segovia, "Toward a Hermeneutics of the Diaspora," 57.
12. Kay Huguera Smith, "Diasporic Approaches," in *Reading the Bible around the World: A Student's Guide to Global Hermeneutics*, eds. Federico Alfredo Roth, et al. (Downers Grove: IVP Academic, 2022), 118–119.
13. Kenny, *Diaspora: A Very Short Introduction*, 1–3.
14. Cited in Fernando F. Segovia, ed., *Interpreting Beyond Borders* (Sheffield: Sheffield Academic Press, 2000), 16.

2. Retention of collective memory, vision, or myth about the original homeland.
3. Belief that they are not – and perhaps can never be – fully accepted by the host society, leading to feelings of partial alienation and insulation from the host country.
4. View of their ancestral homeland as a true and ideal home and the place to which they or their descendants would or should eventually return under certain conditions.
5. Belief in a collective commitment to the maintenance or restoration of the original homeland and its safety and prosperity.
6. Continued connection, either personally or vicariously, to the ancestral homeland, with ethnocommunal consciousness and solidarity being defined by the existence of such a relationship.

Being diasporic does not necessarily require the presence of all six factors.[15] Rather, it arises from the overarching colonial phenomenon that involved significant European migration to all corners of the globe and the dispersal of non-Western peoples from their ancestral homelands.[16] Concurrently, the global proliferation of Christianity proceeded within the framework of varying colonial configurations, which has had a profound impact on the Asian continent. For instance, Great Britain once ruled Hong Kong, Singapore, Malaysia, India, Pakistan, Myanmar, Bangladesh, and Brunei. Similarly, Portugal colonized Macau; Japan controlled Taiwan; Spain governed the Philippines; the Netherlands administered Indonesia; and France administered Vietnam, Cambodia, and Laos.

In the twentieth century, globalization has caused individuals from the majority world to relocate to the minority world for employment, education, or the prospects of a more promising future. Numerous factors – such as political climates, economic threats or opportunities, climate change, and immigration policies – have contributed to this phenomenon of worldwide migration.[17] Thus, the diaspora has emerged as a contemporary political, economic, social,

---

15. For instance, not all diasporans desired to return to their homeland, just as many Jews remained in Babylon and Persia. The Jews in the Book of Esther are a notable example.
16. Segovia, *Interpreting Beyond Borders*, 18–23.
17. Chan Kwok-Bun, *Chinese Identities, Ethnicity and Cosmopolitanism* (London: Routledge, 2005), 79. For more on the Chinese diaspora in different parts of the world, see Laurence J. C. Ma and Carolyn Cartier, eds., *The Chinese Diaspora: Space, Place, Mobility, and Identity* (Lanham: Rowman & Littlefield, 2003). Kenny, *Diaspora: A Very Short Introduction*, 24–39.

Introduction

and cultural phenomenon that has become the new norm. For the diasporic individual, a "double consciousness" emerges – one where their self-perception is grounded within their own culture while they are also cognizant of how the dominant culture views them. For those who have lived in multiple host countries, this "double consciousness" may evolve into "multiple consciousnesses."[18]

Engaging with the biblical text through a diasporic lens requires an appreciation of the readers' own diasporic experience. This approach brings to the forefront the nuances of otherness, minority status, liminality, and hybridity in a dominant culture, while simultaneously accentuating the transnational, global, and multifaceted roots of such an existence. By contextualizing the readers' experience, a diasporic reading of Scripture seeks to facilitate transformation in their ongoing quest for identity, meaning, and purpose, all within the framework of God's redemptive history.

The abundance of commentaries on Exodus raises a question: Why another one? This commentary distinguishes itself by adhering to the vision of the Asia Bible Commentary Series, which endeavors to furnish biblical, pastoral, contextual, missional, and prophetic commentaries for readers in the majority world. This commentary builds on Western academic scholarship while contextualizing the Chinese diaspora and anchoring it in the identity (trans)formation of God's people. According to the Merriam-Webster dictionary, "identity" refers to an individual's distinguishing character or personality.[19] In sociology, "identity" connotes the qualities, beliefs, personality traits, appearance, or expressions that define an individual or group.[20] Some scholars liken "identity" to "self" and "memory."[21] Identity formation is molded by various factors – both external and internal – and the interpretation of past events. This commentary endeavors to bring hope to the diaspora Christians. To read Exodus in this way is to embark on an exhilarating journey of discovering our place in God's narrative, our commission in God's redemptive plan, and our path to transformation in new lands.

---

18. Smith, "Diasporic Approaches," 120–121.
19. "Identity," https://www.merriam-webster.com/dictionary/identity.
20. Peter Burke, "Identity," in *The Cambridge Handbook of Social Theory: Volume 2: Contemporary Theories and Issues*, ed. Peter Kivisto (Cambridge: Cambridge University Press, 2020), 63–78.
21. For example, John Locke and David Hume, see John F. Kihlstrom, Jennifer S. Beer, and Stanley B. Klein, "Self and Identity as Memory," in *Handbook of Self and Identity*, eds. Mark R. Leary, June Price Tangney (New York: The Guilford Press, 2003), 68–90.

Exodus

READING EXODUS AS A DIASPORIC STORY

The book of Exodus derives its name from the Greek term for "way out" or "exit," and its Hebrew title comes from the word *Shemot*, meaning "names." Exodus tells the story of a migratory people group. It narrates the epic tale of Jacob's descendants who, having been enslaved in Egypt, were ultimately rescued by God and formed into a holy nation, whose destination was the promised land. This intricately woven narrative records the experiences of the Israelites as they undertook a journey marked by unsettled movements, travel, and resettlement.

The journey of the Israelites unfolds as a trajectory that embodies ongoing movement toward a specific destination. This journey epitomizes the Israelites' ambivalence about their collective memory and their concept of home. Many were even unaware of the identity of their God – as in the case of Moses, who did not know God's name when God first appeared to him (Exod 3:13). While in Egypt, the Israelites had been enslaved and deprived of the privileges enjoyed by natives of the dominant society. Since this rendered them outsiders, their sense of belonging had been severely compromised. Furthermore, the concept of Canaan as home seemed distant, especially for those who had been born in Egypt and never seen their ancestral homeland. The country in which they resided was not their own, and this further intensified their feelings of displacement and uncertainty.

As the Israelites entered the wilderness, they began to experience a sense of nostalgia for the only home they had ever known – Egypt (Exod 16:3).[22] However, the lingering question is whether Egypt was indeed their home. The Israelites' journey toward the promised land was far more than just a physical journey; it was also a spiritual journey marked by a deepening understanding of both their identity and their God. It was a journey that enabled them to rediscover their roots, their sense of belonging, and, ultimately, their true home. As we will see, the Israelites' true home is with their God as Moses states in Psalm 90:1.

The phenomenon of migration and displacement is not limited to any particular region, as evidenced by the many Asian contexts in which individuals

---

22. Nostalgia can be defined as the act of "indulging in anachronistic and nostalgic longing of an elapsed time or locality that is recalled abstractly as refined, sublime, and superior." Dominic Meng-Hsuan Yang, *The Great Exodus from China: Trauma, Memory, and Identity in Modern Taiwan* (Cambridge: Cambridge University Press, 2021), 128.

Introduction

travel to other countries and establish permanent residence.[23] Due to various circumstances, some migrants are forced to leave their country of origin, while others choose to make a new home in a new land while still maintaining strong connections to their home country through the practice of transnationalism. Some migrate or immigrate to other countries but never feel quite at home in either place, while others are born in foreign lands but yearn to connect with the home of their parents, leading to what is known as "reverse migration."[24] There are still others who relocate due to coercion – as victims of human trafficking or as refugees – in a phenomenon known as "forced migration."[25] For diasporans, the very experience of belonging to multiple places can perhaps be considered a form of home.

The Asian diaspora is dispersed across the globe, and within this diaspora, Chinese people can be found everywhere in this global village.[26] However, the Chinese diaspora is a diverse and multifaceted community, and the term itself may not do justice to all the particularities that people experience.[27] According to the 2011 data of the Chinese Coordination Center of World Evangelism (CCCOWE), there were 71 million overseas Chinese, a testament to this community's vastness.[28] "Chinese" is an umbrella term encompassing a wide range of ethnic and linguistic identities. For instance, if one encounters Mandarin-speaking Chinese people in the United States or Europe, it is not prudent to assume that they are from China because people from

---

23. For example, an estimated two million Chinese reside in Africa. See Wenhui Gong, *Mission Beyond: Chinese Diaspora Missions* (Paradise: Ambassadors for Christ, 2022), 47.
24. Broadly speaking, in the Chinese diaspora, the general migration pattern is from the East (China or Asia) to the West. The reverse migration refers to those who migrate from the West back to the East, though the term can mean different things to different people depending on where they are and from which angle they are perceiving migration.
25. In the Old Testament, another common description for "forced migration" is exile. Examples of forced migration include Joseph's migration from Canaan to Egypt and Israel's migration from Canaan to Babylon. Both movements are forced and not voluntary.
26. Here, "Asian" includes both East Asians and South Asians. Many South Asians migrate for economic reasons. P. G. George and Paul Swarup, "Exodus," in *South Asia Bible Commentary*, ed. Brian Wintle (Grand Rapids: Zondervan, 2015), 77.
27. Sun, *Attempt Great Things for God*, 84–85. Yang expresses dissatisfaction with the term "Chinese diaspora" due to its connotation with an original locale in China. He regards the term as implying "a homogenous, essentialist, and timeless notion of Chineseness or Chinese culture. This then suggests an everlasting attachment/loyalty of the diasporic communities to the political regime in China and other similar groups worldwide." Yang, *The Great Exodus from China*, 32.
28. See the research by Jeanne Wu, *Mission through Diaspora: The Case of the Chinese Church in the USA* (Carlisle: Langham Academic, 2016), 25. For a history of Chinese migration, see Steven B. Miles, *Chinese Diaspora: A Social History of Global Migration* (Cambridge: Cambridge University Press, 2020).

Singapore and Malaysia also speak Mandarin. Furthermore, some Chinese people who were born and raised in Indonesia, the Philippines, Singapore, Malaysia, Vietnam, or Myanmar identify themselves as *huá qiáo*, a term reserved for ethnic Chinese residing outside China. Some even translate this term as "Chinese sojourners."[29] This identity can be associated with Chinese people who are generations removed from their mainland Chinese ancestors. Many of them speak Mandarin in addition to their native languages, making them multilingual.

My parents, for example, are Vietnam *huá qiáo*, whose ancestors migrated from China to Vietnam in earlier generations.[30] They speak Mandarin, Cantonese, and Vietnamese; some of their friends and relatives who migrated to the United States also speak English, making them quadrilingual. For ethnic Chinese people born and raised in Malaysia, speaking Malay, Mandarin, Cantonese, and Malaysian English is common, and more languages may be added to this list. For millions of Chinese in the diaspora, the ethnic label "Chinese" is a complex matter. Self-identification as a Chinese person may seem natural for those born and residing in mainland China; for many others, however, it is a matter of multifaceted cultural and ethnic identities, not to mention the religious element since migrants often carry with them the gods they worship.[31] Despite these nuances, particularities, and complexities, it is fair to say that being Chinese is a diverse, multicultural, and pluralistic experience.

Several questions arise as we consider the intricate process of identity formation for the Chinese people within the diaspora: Who are we or, more precisely, who are they? Is there a divine design for inhabiting a place that is not one's own? Is this solely for the benefit of securing a brighter future for future generations? Where can one locate the promised land? Does it lie in attaining the "American Dream" or the "European Dream"? But what is this dream anyway? Does it entail assimilation into the dominant culture and succeeding within it? What about the "Chinese Dream"?

The poignant narrative of Exodus, which involves leaving one's homeland, traveling, settling, unsettling, wrestling with identity, seeking a home, and

---

29. Kuhn, *Chinese among Others*, 314.
30. Before the colonized Vietnam, most Chinese migrants in Vietnam were Cantonese. Some escaped from China to Vietnam during the decline of the Ming Dynasty. In 1679, an estimated three thousand Cantonese soldiers fled to Vietnam as the Qing Dynasty attempted to take China. Kuhn, *Chinese among Others*, 117–118.
31. See Juliet Lee Uytanlet, "Hybridity and Chineseness: Finding Meaning in Theories," in *A Hybrid World: Diaspora, Hybridity, and Missio Dei*, eds. Sadiri Joy Tira and Juliet Lee Uytanlet (Littleton: William Carey, 2020), 102–105. Kuhn, *Chinese among Others*, 74.

pursuing aspirations resonates with the present circumstances of the Chinese diaspora. Their story is one of migration, loss, a quest for home, self-discovery, and, simultaneously, self-creation. This self is a blend of diverse identities – national, ethnic, cultural, political, and religious – sometimes converging and at other times overpowering each other. At the heart of this sense of rootlessness and identity struggle lies a yearning for a higher calling and a greater purpose that transcends the limitations of geographical displacement.

The ancient tale of Exodus offers insights into the experiences of diasporans, reminding us to view our own story through the lens of God's larger narrative for his people. By discerning the grander purpose behind our present dispersions and relocations, we can better frame our journey within the context of God's redemptive story.[32]

Our ethnic, cultural, and spiritual identities are intricately woven together, and we cannot fully embrace one without embracing the others. Since people in the diaspora are often on the move, they tend to be more open to spiritual matters, much like the early Christians whose dispersal facilitated the spread of the gospel.[33]

Today, God is using the global diasporic experience to fulfill his grand missional purpose of drawing people from all corners of the world to worship him alone. In this sense, diaspora serves as a hidden link in the "from everywhere to everywhere" missiology.[34] Countries that were once recipients of missionary work are now becoming missionary-sending forces and people scattered across the globe are ultimately gathered together through local churches in anticipation of the ultimate grand gathering in God's eternal home.[35]

---

32. Joseph Shao suggests that if the sojourning experience of Israelites in the land of Canaan situates them in the Patriarchal era, then the diaspora and migration experience occur in the Mosaic era. Joseph Shao, "Hybridity in the Old Testament," in *A Hybrid World: Diaspora, Hybridity, and Missio Dei*, eds. Sadiri Joy Tira and Juliet Lee Uytanlet (Littleton: William Carey, 2020), 4. Roth indicates that the book of Exodus is particularly well suited to diaspora hermeneutics due to its close correlation with the postcolonial lens that involves diversity and difference, homed and unhomed, as well as the inward and the external journey of the traveling Israelites. Federico Alfredo Roth, *Hyphenating Moses: A Postcolonial Exegesis of Identity in Exodus 1:1–3:15*, Biblical Interpretation Series 154 (Leiden: Brill, 2017), 193–196.
33. For seeing diaspora as a missional impetus, see Enoch Wan, *Diaspora Missiology: Theory, Methodology, and Practice* (Portland: Institute of Diaspora Studies, 2011). For missions in the Chinese diaspora of the United States, see Wu, *Mission through Diaspora*. Diaspora is not limited to the Chinese but includes other racial groups. Diaspora studies are closely intertwined with anthropology and missions. See Gong, *Diaspora Beyond*, 42 (especially 90–92 on the four types of Diasporic missions).
34. George, "Diaspora: A Hidden Link," 45–56.
35. George, "Diaspora: A Hidden Link," 46.

For the Chinese diaspora, the new exodus is unfolding through the emergence of Chinese churches around the world. Ultimately, the purpose of this diaspora is to form a community that worships Yahweh, much like the Israelites' journey – from the exodus from Egypt through the wilderness to Sinai, culminating in worship of God through the construction of the tabernacle. As diasporans seek a place to call home, God is inviting us to his eternal home, where his presence dwells.[36] The Exodus narrative invites us to look beyond our present circumstances and discern God's greater purpose at work, finding meaning in our diasporic experiences as we participate in God's grand missional narrative.

READING EXODUS AS ISRAEL'S FOUNDATIONAL MEMORY

The centrality of memory in shaping human identity and informing present actions cannot be overstated. Memory defines who we are as human beings. Memory holds our past, affects our present, and shapes our future. The book of Exodus is a book of memory.[37] By building on the primeval and patriarchal memories in Genesis,[38] Exodus becomes a cornerstone of Israel's collective memory and a foundational story for future generations.[39] At the heart of this memory is the exodus event itself, retold from one generation to the next during the Passover meal. The Jewish tradition writes the Passover Haggadah, a Jewish text that outlines the order of the Passover seder (meal), which includes

---

36. Volf and McAnnally-Linz use the metaphor of the home of God to tell the story of the Bible, which resonates with those who are seeking a home in their Christian journey. Miroslav Volf and Ryan McAnnally-Linz, *The Home of God: A Brief Story of Everything* (Grand Rapids: Brazos, 2022), 2–3.
37. Hendel points out that the rituals, laws, and ethics of Israel are grounded in the memory of Yahweh as the rescuer of Israel (Exod 20:2) and Moses becomes a major part of that memory who ties various strands of the Israelite identity and ambiguity together. Though I may not agree with Hendel's view of the Exodus as a conglomerate of history and myths, his assessment of Moses as a mediator who brings the story of Exodus together I do find insightful. Ronald Hendel, "The Exodus in Biblical Memory," *JBL* 120/4 (2001): 601–622. Nathan Bills has also observed the crucial role of memory in the book of Exodus. Nathan Bills, *A Theology of Justice in Exodus*, Siphrut 26 (University Park: Eisenbrauns, 2020), 23.
38. For example, in Exodus 1:1–7, the descendants of Jacob migrating from Canaan to Egypt when Joseph is already in Egypt recalls the story of Genesis 17–50. In Exodus 2:23–25, God remembering his covenant with Abraham, Isaac, and Jacob recalls God's covenant with them in Genesis (12:1–3; 26:3; 28:13–15; 35:9–12).
39. For example, Psalms 105 and 106 use both positive and negative perspectives to retell the story of Exodus, and so remembering Exodus calls for both praise and repentance, see Richard W. Nysse, "Retelling the Exodus," *WW* 33, no. 2 (2013): 157–165. Hendel indicates that the exodus memory is based not merely on historical events but on "a conflation of history and memory that suits the conditions of different qualities of time. Memory is the result of many pasts that converge together." Hendel, "The Exodus in Biblical Memory," 622.

Introduction

the annual ritual of retelling the exodus narrative during a meal, with children participating in the catechetical format as a way to learn what the exodus from Egypt means for them individually and collectively as the people of God.[40] This ritual serves as a pedagogical tool to inform and form Israel's core identity: to be a Jew is to remember the exodus event.

In this sense, memory serves a pedagogical function.[41] If the book of Genesis marks the beginning of the world and Israel's history, then the book of Exodus can be perceived as its sequel. Some regard Genesis and Exodus as two competing traditions of Israel's "dual origins," combined by the priests into one story.[42] In Genesis, a single family is chosen to be God's instrument of blessing, whereas in Exodus, the process of fulfilling the divine plan of blessing is set in motion through the founding of a nation. Nonetheless, Exodus is not a mere sequel to Genesis but, rather, a significant piece of history – redemptive history or, more precisely, theological history – in its own right. In Exodus, the name of God is progressively and greatly manifested (Exod 3:6, 14; 6:2–8; 34:5–7), and the descendants of Jacob become the people of God (Exod 19:6). In Exodus, God reveals his instructions (laws) for forming a holy nation and establishing his dwelling among his people through the construction of the tabernacle. Nevertheless, the memory of the golden calf serves as a cautionary tale, representing a "primal sin" that becomes part of Israel's later memories as reflected in Jeroboam's idolatry (1 Kgs 12:27–30) and the psalmist's warning (Ps 106:19–23) that reflects Israel's idolatry mentioned in Deuteronomy 9:6–8.

Since the book of Exodus represents Israel's foundational memory, we need to take a bird's eye view of the book's origins, overall design, structure, themes, and significance within the biblical canon. Understanding this history is crucial for the identity formation and transformation of the reader.

---

40. The word "Haggadah" derives from the word "to tell." During the Passover seder, children are commanded to ask four questions: (1) How different is this night from all the other nights? (2) On all other nights, we may eat either leavened or unleavened bread; on this night, why do we only eat unleavened bread? (3) On all other nights, we may eat any vegetable; on this night why are we required to eat bitter herbs? On all other nights, we are not bidden to dip our vegetables even once; on this night we dip them twice. (4) On all other nights we eat our meals in any manner; on this night, why do we sit around the table together in a ceremonial fashion? The leader of the seder will then respond to these questions one by one. Rabbi Nathan Goldberg, *Passover Haggadah*, revised edition (Hoboken: Ktav Publishing House, 1993), 8–9.
41. Nathan Bills, *A Theology of Justice in Exodus*, 28.
42. See, for example, the title of Konrad Schmit, *Genesis and the Moses' Story: Israel's Dual-Origins in the Hebrew Bible*, trans. James D. Nogalski; Siphrut 3 (Winona Lake: Eisenbrauns, 2010).

Authorship

Traditionally, the authorship of the Pentateuch – the first five books of the Bible – has been attributed to Moses. This attribution is reflected in passages in which God instructs Moses to write down what he speaks and Moses obeys (Exod 17:14; 24:4; 34:27; Num 33:2; Deut 31:19–22). However, since Moses could not have written about his own death and burial (Deut 34:5–8), can he truly be considered the author of the Pentateuch? Moreover, it seems unlikely that Moses would have described himself as "a very humble man, more humble than anyone else on the face of the earth" (Num 12:3).[43]

Other internal clues suggest that the Pentateuch was written at a later time, after the death of Moses. For example, Genesis 14:14 mentions a place called Dan, but Judges 18:29 reveals that the city had originally been known as Laish and was renamed Dan, which implies that whoever wrote Genesis 14 would have been aware of this renaming that had taken place during the period of the judges. These clues suggest that while Moses was probably the primary author of the Pentateuch, he might not have been its sole author. Perhaps Moses wrote some parts of the Pentateuch and an editor or editors compiled and edited the work after his death.[44] The possible presence of an editor or editors should not undermine the authority of Scripture since all Scripture is inspired by God (2 Tim 3:16), including the contributions of human editors, who presumably wrote and edited under the influence of the Holy Spirit (2 Pet 1:21). The issue of authorship is also linked to the compositional history of the Pentateuch, where multiple authorship is a possibility.

Compositional History

Questions regarding authorship, dating, and compositional history are interconnected and can be complex because the information available to us is incomplete. Traditionally, source criticism has been one of the major methods used to understand the literary formation of the book of Exodus. This method seeks to discern and analyze the various literary sources that might have been

---

43. The word "humble" (*'anah*) can be translated as "meek," "afflicted," or "poor." It is difficult to determine its precise nuance here in Numbers 12:3. Most translations render it as "humble" (NIV, NASB, NKJV, NLT).
44. The evidence of a later editor after Moses is reflected in the compilation of the Pentateuch as a book, with a beginning, plot, and conclusion. Sailhamer identified the narrative seams in the Pentateuch to demonstrate its literary artistry, form, and unity. John H. Sailhamer, *The Pentateuch as Narrative* (Grand Rapids: Zondervan, 1992), 35–59. For more on the different sources of the composition of Exodus, see Thomas B. Dozeman, *Exodus*, ECC (Grand Rapids: Eerdmans, 2009), 31–35.

Introduction

used in the composition of the first five books of the Bible, known collectively as the Pentateuch. Suzanne Boorer explains the task of source criticism as "identifying the earlier written sources of which the present text is comprised, and, if possible, discerning the date and original historical context of each, and to interpret them in relation to these."[45]

Scholars such as Graf, Vatke, and Wellhausen advanced the following theory, suggesting that four distinct sources emerged over a long period of time.[46] These four sources were named JEDP and also known as the Documentary Hypothesis (DH). J stands for Jahwehist (German spelling), E for Elohist, D for Deuteronomist, and P for Priestly. According to the DH, each source probably had its own author and originated at a different time, with the final author or redactor of the Pentateuch combining them into a single composition.[47]

The criteria used to identify the various sources include the presence of the divine name (Jahweh/Yahweh or Elohim), duplications in the biblical account (doublets), and the distinctive vocabulary used. There are examples of the use of divine names in Genesis 1–2, with Elohim used in Genesis 1 and Yahweh-Elohim in Genesis 2. Examples of doublets include the wife-sister episodes (Gen 12:10–20; 20:1–18) and the manna episodes (Exod 16:2–35; Num 11:4–34). Examples of distinctive vocabulary include the more formal language used in Genesis 1, as opposed to the more fluid and accessible language of Genesis 2.[48] Other examples include two different names for the same person

---

45. Suzanne Booer, "Source and Redaction Criticism," in *Methods for Exodus*, ed. Thomas Dozeman, Methods in Biblical Interpretation (Cambridge: Cambridge University Press, 2010), 95.
46. T. D. Alexander, *From Paradise to the Promised Land: An Introduction to the Pentateuch* (Grand Rapids: Baker Academic, 2002), 3–61. For the evolvement in the Pentateuchal criticism, see Bill T. Arnold, "Pentateuchal Criticism, History of," *DOTP*, 622–631. Childs also provides a succinct overview of the various issues involved in the source, the form, and traditio-critical matters pertaining to the composition of Exodus. Brevard S. Childs, *Introduction to the Old Testament as Scripture* (Philadelphia: Fortress, 1979), 164–170.
47. The proposed time frame for JEDP is J (840 BCE), E (700 BCE), D (623 BCE), and P (500–450 BCE). Alexander, *From Paradise to the Promised Land*, 16. These dates are by no means fixed and are in fact contested in an ongoing scholarly discussion. D. W. Baker, "Source Criticism," *DOTP*, 804. Friedman has separated different sources of the Pentateuch in Appendix B. He used these sources as a piece of evidence supporting the reliability of the story of Exodus. Richard Elliott Friedman, *The Exodus: How It Happened and Why It Matters* (New York: HarperOne, 2017), 227–238. Friedman proposed Levites as the authors of the Pentateuch. For more on this, see pages 32–83. William Propp's commentaries on Exodus include source analysis for each chapter. William H. C. Propp, *Exodus 1–18: A New Translation with Introduction and Commentary*, AB, vol. 2 (New York: The Anchor Bible, 1998) and *Exodus 19–40: A New Translation with Introduction and Commentary*, AB, vol. 2 (New York: Doubleday, 2006).
48. Baker, "Source Criticism," 803.

or place: "Reuel" (Exod 2:18) and "Jethro" (Exod 18:1), as well as "Horeb" (Exod 3:1) and "Sinai" (Exod 19:1–2). The different divine names, the doublets, and the distinct vocabulary used may be explained by the transmission of disparate oral traditions.[49]

Source criticism contributes to one theory about the literary composition of the Pentateuch, but we need other methods to supplement our understanding. The analogy of a rope may help us to better understand source criticism. The Pentateuch is like a rope made up of multicolored strands woven together. Sometimes, one color dominates over others, and each strand might have been added to the rope at different times.[50] For those who view Scripture as God-breathed, divine inspiration is evident in the contributions of multiple authors and in the process by which the Pentateuch was formed.

Dating

Academic discourse on the dating of Exodus is a complex matter, with no clear consensus among scholars. This complexity is due in part to the ambiguous nature of dates and dating in the Bible, where dates are sometimes relative and symbolic rather than precise and literal. Moreover, dates in biblical texts may be presented selectively and are not necessarily intended for calculating precise dates. Adding to the complexity is the challenge of interpreting archaeological evidence to propose possible dates. The relationship between textual evidence and material remains is also uncertain, raising questions about the relative weight that should be assigned to each type of evidence. Such inquiries belong to the "behind-the-text" methodology, which is often fraught with tension and uncertainty. In short, the question of when Exodus was written remains unresolved. Scholarly research has proposed dates ranging from the thirteenth to the sixteenth century BCE, each viewpoint presenting its own merits and difficulties.[51]

T. Desmond Alexander's commentary offers a detailed discussion of the dating of the exodus event and lists three major positions: a) dating the exodus

---

49. For the reliability and limitations of each criterion, see Booer, "Source and Redaction Criticism," 96–98.
50. Alexander, *From Paradise to the Promised Land*, 16–17.
51. For scholarly discussion on the dating of Exodus, see James K. Hoffmeier, *Israel in Egypt: The Evidence for the Authenticity of the Exodus Tradition* (New York: Oxford University Press, 1997). See also Hoffmeier, *Ancient Israel in Sinai: The Evidence for the Authenticity of the Wilderness Tradition* (Oxford: Oxford University Press, 2005). For the difficult discussion of the dating and historicity of the exodus event, see Tremper Longman III, *How to Read Exodus* (Downers Grove: IVP Academic, 2009), 68–82.

Introduction

to the fifteenth century BCE; b) dating the exodus to the thirteenth century BCE; and c) considering exodus event as fictional rather than historical. The basis for this third view that exodus is fictional stems primarily from the lack of archaeological evidence to support the authenticity of the exodus event.[52] However, this lack of archaeological evidence may be due to the Egyptians' reluctance to document or engrave negative or shameful events for public consumption. In the ancient Near East, texts and reliefs depicting warfare were composed to glorify kings and overlook their defeats.[53] The attestation of Egyptian names in Exodus also supports its historicity. However, there are various descriptions and interpretations of the precise way in which the exodus event actually took place and how it was recorded in the Bible.[54] Therefore, we can say that some form of the exodus event has taken place, though the evidence is inconclusive.

The "Stele of Merneptah" (1224–1211 BCE), commonly known as the "Israel Stele," documents the building activities of Pharaoh Amenhotep (Amenophis) III.[55] Of particular interest is the fact that the name "Israel" appears on this stele, marking its earliest mention in an extrabiblical source.[56] This finding lends credence to a thirteenth-century dating of the exodus event. Nonetheless, readers must remember that the biblical narrative is, first and

---

52. T. Desmond Alexander, *Exodus*, AOTC 2, eds. David W. Baker and Gordon J. Wenham (London: Apollos, 2017), 16–30. See also Scott Stripling, James K. Hoffmeier, Gary A. Rendsburg, Peter Feinman, Ronald Hendel, and Mark D. Janzen, *Five Views on the Exodus: Historicity, Chronology, and Theological Implications* (Grand Rapids: Zondervan, 2021).
53. Christopher J. H. Wright, *Exodus, The Story of God Bible Commentary* (Grand Rapids: Zondervan, 2021), 17. Charlie Trimm, *The Destruction of the Canaanites: God, Genocide, and Biblical Interpretation* (Grand Rapids: Eerdmans, 2022), 19–20. In the battle between Muwatallis II of Hatti and Ramesses II (1275 BCE), Ramesses barely won the battle but two great tableaux were carved on the temple walls and recorded in poems and texts. "The Battle of Qadesh – the Poem, Or Literary Record," trans. K. A. Kitchen (*COS* 2.5: 32–38).
54. For the study of names in Exodus, see Richard S. Hess, "Onomastics of the Exodus Generation in the Book of Exodus," in *"Did I Not Bring Israel Out of Egypt?" Biblical, Archaeological, and Egyptological Perspectives on the Exodus Narratives*, eds. James K. Hoffmeier, Alan R. Millard, and Gary A. Rendsburg, BBRSup (Winona Lake: Eisenbrauns, 2016), 37–48. Benjamin J. Noonan, "Egyptian Loanwords as Evidence for the Authenticity of the Exodus and Wilderness Traditions," in *"Did I Not Bring Israel Out of Egypt?"* 49–67.
55. He was the successor of Rameses II. This stele is currently placed in the Carios Museum in Egypt.
56. For more details about the "Stele of Merneptah," see Nahum M. Sarna, *Exploring Exodus: The Origins of Biblical Israel* (New York: Schocken Books, 1996), 7–14. Sarna proposed the thirteenth-century date for the exodus event. Walton also considers the witness of the stele a piece of strong evidence supporting the thirteenth-century date. J. H. Walton, "Exodus, Date of," *DOTP*, 262. However, Christopher Wright leans toward the fifteenth-century date. Wright, *Exodus*, 13–14.

foremost, *theological* history. Its accounts are directed toward communities of faith and conveyed from a theological rather than a purely historical or scientific perspective. Against this backdrop, this commentary concentrates on the text's final form in the Hebrew text and its implications for its readers, especially those living in diaspora communities – that is, those "in front of the text."[57]

Historical Context

A thorough discussion of the historical context is closely linked to the dating of the book. During the Late Bronze Age in Palestine (1550–1200 BCE), Egypt reigned supreme over the ancient Near East.[58] Exodus 1:11 describes building projects that likely correspond to those undertaken by the pharaohs of the nineteenth dynasty (1295–1186 BCE).[59] While these projects may have been the result of the efforts of Pharaoh Ramses II, it is impossible to be certain due to the absence of any specific names of pharaohs in the biblical text. Those who favor the fifteenth-century date base their argument on 1 Kings 6:1: "In the four hundred and eightieth year after the Israelites came out of Egypt, in the fourth year of Solomon's reign over Israel, in the month of Ziv, the second month, he began to build the temple of the LORD." This calculation would date the exodus event to about 1446 BCE.

However, the biblical text lacks some essential dating information necessary to determine its exact historical setting. For instance, it remains uncertain how long the Israelites prospered in Egypt before being subjugated under an unnamed pharaoh.[60] Although the reference to a 430-year period (Gen 15:13; Exod 12:40–41; Gal 3:17) provides an estimate of the Israelites' stay in Egypt, it does not indicate whether this time frame corresponds to four or more generations or if the figure is figurative rather than literal.

---

57. For Chinese Christian traditions, the MT in its translations in the Chinese versions, especially the Chinese Union Version, is deemed the most authoritative text. For a history of the Chinese Union Version and its dependence on the KJV, see Jerry Hwang, *Contextualization and the Old Testament: Between Asian and Western Perspectives*, Logia series (Carlisle: Langham Global Library, 2022), 27–31.
58. The term "ancient Near East" comes from a Euro-centric perspective. For people in Asia, we may call it "ancient West Asia." Since the present commentary addresses the Chinese diaspora and not just readers in Asia, I will retain using the more traditional term "Ancient Near East."
59. The dating is based on James K. Hoffmeier, *Ancient Israel in Sinai: The Evidence for the Authenticity of the Wilderness Tradition* (New York: Oxford University Press, 2005), xxi–xxii. For more on the dating of Exodus, see J. H. Walton, "Exodus, Date of" in *DOTP*, 258–272.
60. The title "pharaoh" in Egyptian means "The Great House." It is similar to Americans using "The White House" as a metonym for the president. Sarna, *Exploring Exodus*, 18.

Introduction

Nevertheless, we do know that the Israelites initially flourished in Egypt before falling under the yoke of slavery under an unnamed Pharaoh. This period of prosperity is thought to have occurred during the reign of the Hyksos – a group whose name means "rulers of foreign lands" – who ruled Egypt for around a century and a half. During this time, there was a significant Semitic presence in high administrative offices, which aligns with Joseph's rise to power in the Egyptian court and the subsequent migration of Jacob's descendants to Egypt. Nahum Sarna explains that a native Egyptian family retained control over Upper Egypt and that their descendants led resistance campaigns against the Hyksos, eventually expelling them from power. Nevertheless, the Semitic population persisted in the region, leading to their later subjugation as slaves under the pharaoh.[61]

From a theological perspective, God had already foretold this enslavement to Abram (Gen 15:13–14). In this sense, since the beginning of time, history unfolds according to God's purpose and his divine plan.

Literary Structure

Scholars structure the book of Exodus in various ways, dividing it into two or three main sections. Among those who prefer the three-part arrangement, one approach is to organize it according to geographical locations:[62]

> Part I: Israel in Egypt (1:1–13:16)
> Part II: Israel in the wilderness (13:17–18:27)
> Part III: Israel at Sinai (19:1–40:38)

Another approach is to divide the book according to the themes of rescue, law, and presence:[63]

> Part I: God rescues Israel from Egyptian bondage (1–18)
> Part II: God gives Israel his law (19–24)
> Part III: God commands Israel to build the tabernacle (25–40)

Through its various themes, the book eloquently portrays the God of Exodus as one who showcases his might through the liberation of his people, unveils his holiness through the law, and demonstrates his graciousness by providing a means of divine fellowship through the tabernacle.

---

61. Sarna, *Exploring Exodus*, 15–16.
62. For example, John I. Durham, *Exodus*, WBC 3 (Waco: Word, 1987), vii–x.
63. For example, Longman, *How To Read Exodus*, 34.

Those who favor a two-part thematic arrangement of the book often regard chapter 15 as a pivotal and transitional chapter that concludes the first section of divine rescue and introduces the subsequent narrative:

>Part I: The power of God (1–15)
>Part II: The presence of God (16–40)[64]

or

>Part I: Restoration of Yahweh to the world through the exodus event (1–15)
>Part II: Restoration of the presence of Yahweh to humanity through the covenant gift of his tabernacling presence to Israel (16–40)[65]

In this commentary, I frame these themes in four distinct sections, viewed through the lens of identity formation of the Israelites:

>Part I: Identity conversion out of Egypt (1:1–15:21)
>Part II: Identity confusion during the in-between space (15:22–18:27)
>Part III: Identity construction at Sinai (19:1–24:18)
>Part IV: Identity conformation to worship (25:1–40:38)

The three locations – Egypt, the in-between space, and Sinai – are pivotal in shaping Israel's journey of identity formation. Conformation signifies both the end goal of forming a community of Yahweh-worshipers who conform to Yahweh's way of worship and the constant reminder of humanity's propensity to fall short of God's expectations, as exemplified by the story of the golden calf. Therefore, the process of identity formation, re-formation, and conformation is an ongoing one for Israel and for all those embarking on the journey of conforming to the image and way of Yahweh.

Selected Themes Related to the Diaspora

As a literary work, Exodus is a masterpiece, with its rich and multifaceted themes that intersect with various disciplines – including theology, culture, ethics, anthropology, sociology, migration studies, postcolonial, and diasporic studies – making it a popular source for theological reflection among

---

64. Dozeman, *Exodus*, 44.
65. L. Michael Morales, *Exodus Old and New: A Biblical Theology of Redemption*, ESBT (Downers Grove: IVP Academic, 2020), 39.

Introduction

individuals of diverse ethnic and cultural backgrounds. In this commentary, I will explore major themes from Exodus that pertain to the experience of living in the diaspora.

Who Is Yahweh?

Exodus is a theological *tour de force*, with God as its central character. God's self-revelation through words and deeds is the salient mark of the book. God reveals his name to Moses and further reveals who he is through the ten plagues, the giving of the law, and the construction of the tabernacle. Throughout this narrative of redemption, God reveals himself as a God who is both transcendent and immanent, a God of glory, truth, holiness, righteousness, compassion, and faithfulness. This multifaceted revelation demonstrates God's desire to be present with his people and guide them on their journey to the promised land.

In the context of the diaspora, God assumes a central role as the constant identity amid the disorienting experiences of migration and displacement. For diasporic communities, the quest for interconnectedness among diverse cultural identities becomes a poignant concern. This search for identity is inextricably tied to questions of faith and spirituality. For example, for a long time, I grappled with the question "Who am I?" and have come to understand that this question is intimately linked to the question "Who is Yahweh?"[66]

The Powerful and the Powerless

The power dynamic between the Israelites and the Egyptians is a central theme in the book of Exodus, which presents the story of seemingly powerless people being empowered by God. Pharaoh, the epitome of power in Egypt, enslaved the Israelites and forced them to serve him. However, his schemes were thwarted by a few seemingly powerless women. God's intervention through the ten plagues – culminating in the death of the firstborn sons of Egypt – and the subsequent parting of the Red Sea demonstrated his ultimate power over Egypt and brought about the redemption of the Israelites. The Israelites were initially powerless but became more powerful over time. The law even instructed them to protect the rights of sojourners, even as they themselves were once sojourners in Egypt (Exod 22:21; 23:9).

In the context of a diaspora, the host country may appear to hold all the power while the diasporans seem powerless and subject to hate crimes and discrimination. For the Chinese diaspora in particular, the struggle often lies

---

66. See Sun, "Reading Job as a Chinese Diasporan," 301–303.

in identity formation and the search for meaning rather than mere survival. The book of Exodus teaches us that even in the face of great power, God has the ability to empower the powerless and bring about redemption and identity formation and transformation.[67]

Home and Foreign Places

In the narrative of the enslaved Israelites, Canaan – not Egypt – was their ancestral homeland. However, those born in Egypt had never seen Canaan, and although Egypt was foreign, it was the only place they understood as home. The Israelites' nostalgia for Egypt during times of hardship (Exod 16:3; Num 11:4–6; 14:2–3) reveals their in-betweenness while journeying in the wilderness. They did not belong to either Egypt or Canaan but were suspended in a state of liminality, a condition that resonates with the experience of many in the diaspora. In contemporary times, with travel back and forth from one place to another becoming more accessible, the concept of home has become more multifaceted and fluid than before.

At a gathering of theological educators, I was asked to lead a worship session according to my "home tradition." This request prompted me to reflect on the meaning of "home" and "tradition." Where is my home? Is it the place where I was born? Is it the place where I grew up? Or is it where I currently live? For diasporans, "home" may have multiple connotations and may be tied to a person or a community rather than to a particular physical location. For instance, the church community may serve as a home away from home for many diasporans, allowing them to preserve and connect with their cultural roots. This explains why many migrants choose their ethnic church as the means of forming a bridge between their birth culture of the past and the present culture where they have settled.[68]

Hence, the idea of a "home tradition" may be problematic for diasporans. I was not a Christian in my previous home countries, raising the question of how I could lead worship according to my "home tradition." In light of the

---

67. For more on this proclivity for identity and meaning-seeking is in contrast to an Africana reading of survival in the context of oppression, see Kenneth N. Ngwa, *Let My People Live: An Africana Reading of Exodus* (Louisville: Westminster John Knox, 2022).

68. Chan quotes from a study on overseas Chinese identities by Wang Ling-Chi, who has identified five types of identities with the word "root" (*gēn* in Chinese): *ye luo gui gen* (fallen leaves return to the roots, the soil), *zan cao chu gen* (to eliminate grass, one must pull out its roots), *luo di sheng gen* (to settle down or "sink roots" in a foreign land and accommodate to the host country), *xun gen wen zu* (search for one's roots and ancestors), and *shi gen li zu* (lose contact with one's roots and ancestors). Chan, *Chinese Identities*, 125.

Introduction

fluidity and complexity of the concept of home, I struggled with whether my current church in the host country should be regarded as my true home. Ultimately, the Israelites' experience in the wilderness demonstrates that the diasporic condition is one of in-betweenness, and the concept of home and tradition for diasporans is similarly multifaceted, fluid, and complex.

Border Crossing

The crossing of the Red Sea marks a decisive point in God's rescue of the Israelites from Egypt. In the literary structure of Exodus, the Song of Moses (chapter 15) is depicted as both the climax of this rescue mission and the bridge that transitions into the wilderness narrative. Without this sea-crossing experience, Israel would still have been under Egyptian rule. Thus, the Red Sea serves as both a physical boundary that separates Egypt from the promised land and a definitive marker that distinguishes between Israel's former identity as servants of Pharaoh and their new identity as servants of God.

For Chinese diasporans – particularly those from China, East Asia, or South East Asia – their sea-crossing experiences often involve crossing the Pacific Ocean, the South China Sea, or some other sea or water body to reach new lands, as indicated by the term "overseas" (*hǎi wài*). Just as the Red Sea serves as a boundary and identity marker, the sea crossing for diasporans represents a border-crossing experience that embodies the motif of re-creation – venturing from a less-than-ideal place to a new and promising place.[69]

The sea-crossing experience is closely associated with the concepts of home and foreign places. Sometimes, one side of the sea is considered home while the other side is not. Other times, even though one side of the sea is regarded as home, there may be political and personal barriers that do not permit people to return home. There are also people who embrace multiple homes and engage in transnational sea-crossing activities.

The Presence and Absence of God

The book of Exodus is an unparalleled testament to the visible, direct, and powerful manifestation of God in the Old Testament. God's self-revelation through his name, miraculous signs and wonders, the giving of his law, and the construction of the tabernacle all attest to his presence. But there are also moments where the absence of God is felt. This is evident at the beginning of

---

69. Bryan D. Estelle, *Echoes of Exodus: Tracing a Biblical Motif* (Downers Grove: IVP Academic, 2018), 109.

the book – when the Israelites were enslaved in Egypt – and after the golden calf incident, when God revealed only his back and not his face to Moses.[70] Nevertheless, despite these instances, the presence of God prevails throughout the narrative until the very end. In fact, even when his presence might have seemed absent, God foreknew the Israelites' four-hundred-year sojourn in a foreign land and their eventual return to their homeland (Gen 15:13–14). The apparent absence of God in the diaspora does not indicate that God has withdrawn from history. The last verse of Exodus aptly summarizes this reality: "So the cloud of the LORD was over the tabernacle by day, and fire was in the cloud by night, in the sight of all the Israelites during all their travels" (Exod 40:38).[71]

For those residing in the diaspora, feelings of disorientation may arise, particularly in the face of discrimination in host countries. However, geographical boundaries do not define or restrict God's presence. The migration of scattered peoples is for a divine purpose. The scattered will be brought together once again through the establishment of local ethnic and immigrant churches in new lands. Indeed, meaning can be forged even while living in the diaspora.

The Significance of Exodus

Exodus makes a profound contribution to biblical theology, OT theology, and Jewish biblical theology.[72] Moreover, it influences both Jewish and Christian

---

70. According to Gowan, Exodus 1–2 can be referred to as "the absence of God." Donald E. Gowan, *Theology in Exodus: Biblical Theology in the Form of a Commentary* (Louisville: Westminster John Knox, 1994), 1–4. The idea of the absence of God is in contrast to "God remembered" in Exodus 2:24, but it does not mean that God is absent from history. Longman also names the movement of Exodus as "from absence to presence," since God is not named until the end of chapter 1. God's absence is notable in the birth narrative of Moses and during his time as a sojourner in Midian. God then made his presence known to Moses in chapter 3. This presence is more profound than what the Israelites experience until the construction of the tabernacle. The ending of the book reveals God's presence with the Israelites on their journey to the Promised Land. Longman, *How to Read Exodus*, 39–44.
71. The cloud in Exodus represents divine presence and glory. It first appears in chapter 13 where God leads Israel in a pillar of cloud by day (13:21–22), then toward the Red Sea and separates the Israelites from the Egyptians (14:19–20). The glory of Yahweh appears in the cloud (16:10) as God comes to Israel in a cloud (19:9, 16) and Moses enters Mount Sinai in a cloud (24:16, 18). Later, the cloud guards the entrance to the tent of meeting (33:9–10; 34:5). Finally, the cloud covers the tabernacle and embodies God's glory (40:34–38). In Exodus, fire is one of the manifestations of God's presence: God appears to Moses in flames of fire within a bush (3:2), God leads Israel with the pillar of fire by night to give them light (13:21), God descends on Mount Sinai in fire (19:18), God's presence is like consuming fire on top of Mount Sinai (24:17), and God travels with Israel accompanied by the fire in the cloud (40:38).
72. The definition of Old Testament theology is unsettled. One issue is whether to include the New Testament when doing Old Testament theology, while Jewish theology does not face

Introduction

thinking and shapes their ways of life and spirituality. Exodus has enduring significance for understanding the nature of God, the pattern of his salvific work, and the presence of God. Its reception history is fascinating, encompassing works of art, plays, movies, music, and literature.[73]

Exodus occupies a significant place in the theological frameworks of the Jewish and Christian faiths, particularly in their understanding of redemption. As this commentary is intended for a Christian audience, the focus will be on the Christian canon. The exodus motif is paradigmatic for subsequent biblical narratives, including those in the New Testament era. On the one hand, the theme of redemption in Exodus recalls the creation narrative – the Israelites' multiplication in Egypt (Exod 1:7; see also Gen 1:28) and their crossing of the Red Sea (Exod 14:21–22) are reminiscent of God's Spirit hovering over the deep and exercising control over the mighty waters (Gen 1:2). On the other hand, the motif of redemption in Exodus resonates throughout Scripture, taking the form of various "new exoduses" and new creations. For instance, Isaiah addresses the exiled Israelites, saying:

> This is what the LORD says –
>   he who made a way through the sea,
>   a path through the mighty waters,
> who drew out the chariots and horses,
>   the army and reinforcements together,
> and they lay there, never to rise again,
>   extinguished, snuffed out like a wick:
> "Forget the former things;
>   do not dwell on the past.
> See, I am doing a new thing!
>   Now it springs up; do you not perceive it?

---

this challenge. Despite sharing similar features, Old Testament theology, and Jewish biblical theology have distinct concerns and themes. For more, see Brittany Kim and Charlie Trimm, *Understanding Old Testament Theology: Mapping the Terrain of Recent Approaches* (Grand Rapids: Zondervan, 2020), 111–127.

73. For a brief account of the reception history of Exodus including its afterlife in Jewish, Christian, feminist, and liberation theology, see John F. A. Sawyer, *A Concise Dictionary of the Bible and Its Reception*, 86–87. Langston sums up the reception history of Exodus in one sentence: "The reception history of Exodus demonstrates that it is a book about power – its sources, expressions, uses, abuses, and management." Scott M. Langston, *Exodus Through the Centuries*, Blackwell Bible Commentaries (Malden: Blackwell, 2006), 8. Hawkins has a chapter on the reception of Exodus in art, architecture, cinema, music, and politics. Ralph K. Hawkins, *Discovering Exodus: Content, Interpretation, Reception, Discovering Biblical Texts* (Grand Rapids: Eerdmans, 2021), 230–255. "The Exodus," in *EBR*, vol. 8, 464–511.

Exodus

> I am making a way in the wilderness
> and streams in the wasteland." (Isa 43:16–19)

The phrase "new thing" in this context pertains to the act of "making ... streams in the wasteland," which represents a reversal and renewal of God's previous act of making "a way through the sea" in Exodus (Isa 43:16; see also Isa 40:3–5).[74] In Jeremiah, the reference to "out of Egypt" in the context of the exile becomes a promise of a new exodus – from the Babylonian exile back to the land of Israel.

> "So then, the days are coming," declares the Lord, "when people will no longer say, 'As surely as the Lord lives, who brought the Israelites up out of Egypt,' but they will say, 'As surely as the Lord lives, who brought the descendants of Israel up out of the land of the north and out of all the countries where he had banished them.' Then they will live in their own land." (Jer 23:7–8)

Ezekiel employs upon a similar analogy, evidenced by multiple allusions to the Exodus paradigm throughout his book (Ezek 11:14–21).[75] Similarly, Hosea speaks of "returning to Egypt" as a new exodus through which the Israelites will be restored from their exile (Hos 8:13; 9:3).

The book of Psalms contains many references to the exodus event (Pss 77:18–20; 81:5–10; 105:23–45; 106:7–33; 114:1–8; 135:8–12; 136:10–22), underscoring the historical and theological significance of God's redemptive work in Israel's history. The Passover, instituted during the final plague in Egypt, serves as a symbol of God's deliverance of his people. Theologians consider the Passover "the heart of the Exodus,"[76] and this significance reverberates from Joshua's time (Josh 5:10) to the religious reforms in the Southern Kingdom (2 Kgs 23:23; 2 Chr 30:1, 18; 35:1, 18), culminating in Jesus the "Passover lamb," whose blood alone holds power to cleanse humanity's sins (1 Cor 5:7; compare John 1:29; Heb 9:12; 1 John 1:7; Rev 1:5).

In Ezra-Nehemiah, the language of "go forth" (*hotz'*) recalls the exodus motif. Of the 277 appearances of the verb "go forth" in the OT, over a quarter

---

74. Isaiah makes extensive references to the new exodus – exiles returning from Babylon to Jerusalem (Isa 4:5; 11:15–16; 40:1–11; 48:21; 49:11–12; 50:2; 51:9–10; 52:10; 63:11–14).
75. See John Frederick Evans, "An Inner-Biblical Interpretation and Intertextual Reading of Ezekiel's Recognition Formulae with the Book of Exodus." ThD diss., University of Stellenbosch, 2006.
76. For example, Morales, *Exodus Old and New*, 66.

Introduction

of them have to do with the exodus.⁷⁷ The phrase "came up" [or "bring up"] from Babylon to Jerusalem" (Ezra 1:11) echoes the idea of God bringing the Israelites from the land of Egypt to the promised land. Thus, the restoration of exile is perceived as a new exodus. In Nehemiah's prayer, he recounts Israel's rebellion and contrasts it with Yahweh's mercy through multiple allusions to the exodus tradition (Neh 9:9–25).⁷⁸

In the NT, Jesus's temptation in the wilderness for forty days parallels the Israelites' wilderness wandering for forty years and pictures a new exodus. Mark's citation of Isaiah, with the words "in the wilderness" (Mark 1:3a, paralleling Isa 40:3a), further affirms this connection.⁷⁹ Moreover, in Matthew, Jesus's flight to Egypt fulfilled Hosea's prophecy: "Out of Egypt I called my son" (Hos 11:1; Matt 2:15). In this sense, Jesus becomes the new Israel, God's firstborn son. After leaving Egypt and crossing the Red Sea, the Israelites faced many trials during their journey through the wilderness. Jesus's baptism at the Jordan evokes the motif of the Red Sea crossing with Moses and the crossing of the Jordan River with Joshua. Jesus's temptations and victories contrast with Israel's temptations and failures. In the letter to the Corinthians, Paul refers to the body of believers as the temple of the Holy Spirit (1 Cor 3:16), likens Jesus to the Passover lamb (1 Cor 5:7), and warns the Corinthians not to repeat the same mistake that Israel made when they built the golden calf (1 Cor 10:6–7). He also affirms that if the Corinthians remain in Christ, the "veil" will be removed and they will be able to see the divine glory in Christ (2 Cor 3:7–18) – here, he is drawing from Exodus 34:29–35.⁸⁰

According to Luke and Paul, the exodus theme serves as a paradigm for the ministry of Jesus and the church, not to mention the significance of the Sinai covenant, the Ten Commandments, and the law, along with the tabernacling presence of God in Exodus, all of which lead to the eschatological presence of God in Ezekiel's temple vision (Ezek 48:35) and, ultimately, to the divine dwelling envisioned in Revelation 21:3. The redeemed people of God will celebrate this new deliverance on the shore of a new sea (Rev 15:2–4), singing a victory song that is "the song of God's servant Moses and of the Lamb" (Rev

---

77. Estelle, *Echoes of Exodus*, 199.
78. Estelle, *Echoes of Exodus*, 203–204.
79. See Augustine Stock, *The Way in the Wilderness: Exodus, Wilderness and Moses Themes in the Old Testament and New* (Collegeville: Liturgical Press, 1969), 70.
80. Hawkins, *Discovering Exodus*, 221–222. For the whole chapter on the echoes of Exodus in the New Testament, see Hawkins, *Discovering Exodus*, 209–229.

15:3; see Exod 15:1–18).⁸¹ Similarly, in 1 Peter, there are several allusions to the exodus motif, particularly with regard to the identity of Christians who have been redeemed from their former way of life by the blood of Jesus and are now a royal priesthood and God's own people (1 Pet 1:18–19; 2:9; see Exod 6:6; 15:13; 19:5–6). Indeed, Exodus encapsulates biblical theology, transcending time, space, and culture.

The book of Exodus holds universal appeal for all Christians, but its migration motif, dynamics of power differentials, depiction of enslavement and oppression, liberation paradigm, and portrayal of God's partnership with women in its early chapters all resonate particularly with Asian readers and biblical scholars of Asian descent.[82] For instance, Chinese pastors frequently preach and draw connections between the three phases of Moses's life – at Pharaoh's house, in the wilderness, and the exodus event – and the typical experiences of Christian leaders. Moses's dramatic life story thus serves as a mirror for spiritual and theological contemplation, making it a rich source of inspiration and guidance for many.[83]

While Israel's formative narrative occurred in the distant past, contemporary readers who connect with this memory and make it a part of their identity can experience a profound transformation.[84] For instance, the Passover instituted in Exodus 12 has evolved into the Lord's Supper, celebrating the new exodus and birth of a new community of God's people, including diasporans worldwide.

---

81. David A. DeSilva, "The Exodus, New Testament," *EBR*, vol. 8, 472.
82. See Chloe Sun, "Recent Research on Asian and Asian American Hermeneutics Related to the Hebrew Bible," *CurBR* 17, no. 3 (2019): 238–265, especially 244–245. For reading Exodus through the lens of liberation theology, see Jorge Pixley, "Liberation Criticism," in *Methods for Exodus*, Methods in Biblical Interpretation, ed. Thomas B. Dozeman (Cambridge: Cambridge University Press, 2010), 131–162. He advocates the exodus event as one of revolution rather than emigration. For a feminist reading of Exodus, see Naomi Steinberg, "Feminist Criticism," in *Methods for Exodus*, Methods in Biblical Interpretation, ed. Thomas B. Dozeman (Cambridge: Cambridge University Press, 2010), 163–192. For a postcolonial reading of Exodus, see Gale A. Yee, "Postcolonial Biblical Criticism," in *Methods for Exodus*, Methods in Biblical Interpretation, ed. Thomas B. Dozeman (Cambridge: Cambridge University Press, 2010), 193–233; Roth, *Hyphenating Moses*; Ngwa, *Let My People Live*.
83. I have preached a sermon on Exodus 2:11–25, framing Moses's life in three stages (the first forty years, the second forty years, and the final forty years) and reflecting on the story's implications for those living in the diaspora.
84. Miroslav Volf powerfully expounds on how memory plays a crucial role in one's identity and how the exodus event is paradigmatic for the Jews precisely because it has much to do with what to remember and what not to remember. Miroslav Volf, *The End of Memory: Remembering Rightly in a Violent World* (Grand Rapids: Eerdmans, 2006), 97, 112, 147.

Introduction

The versatility of the exodus motif is widely known in Asian cultures. One notable example comes from Dominic Yang's research. Yang uses exodus as an overarching metaphor to frame his research on the interconnectivity between trauma, memory, and identity. His research centers specifically on the aftermath of China's civil war that took place in 1949 between the People's Republic of China (PRC) and the Chinese Nationalist Party or the Kuomintang (KMT).

Due to the defeat of the KMT, huge numbers of military personnel, their families, and other civilians were forced to migrate to Taiwan. Yang calls this human migration "The Great Exodus from China."[85] This exodus narrative does not aim to celebrate the victory of the PRC. Rather, it aims to tell the other side of the story – the displacement of a people, their shared experience of trauma in migrating to Taiwan, as well as their shared cultural memory that forged their collective identity as foreigners and sojourners in a new land. The ripple effect of this experience extended to their children who, although born in Taiwan, do not belong to the indigenous people in Taiwan. This traumatic experience of migration also affected the locals – the native people who already lived in Taiwan – because they were forced to receive these exiles from China. Many of these exiles were former soldiers, who had to deal with mental and economic challenges of their own. Therefore, this "great exodus" produced two significant displacements – one for the incoming exiles and the other for the receiving local people in Taiwan.

Continuing the exodus metaphor, Yang describes the phases of the lives of exiles from China to Taiwan first as "wartime sojourning," followed by "cultural nostalgia" when they realized that the possibility of returning home was bleak. When some of them eventually returned home after four decades, there was no home to be found, and they had to learn to live in a new reality as well as negotiate a new identity back in China.[86] This particular contemporary exodus experience has striking parallels to the Israelites' experience in Exodus, although there are also major differences.[87]

---

85. This is reflected in Yang's book title – *The Great Exodus from China*.
86. The social dislocation in this China-Taiwan context includes (1) the mass expulsion from China between 1948 and1955; (2) the moment at which the hope for return began to fade during the late 1950s to the early 1960s; (3) the heartbreaking homecoming in China during the late 1980s to the early 1990s, and (4) the reality of homecoming in Taiwan after the early 1990s. Yang, *The Great Exodus from China*, 6.
87. One such difference is that while the Israelites' former identity was as slaves to Pharaoh, the escapees from China to Taiwan were mostly soldiers and their families, all members of the defeated political party.

READING EXODUS AS A JOURNEY OF BECOMING

Exodus features several dramatic crescendos or shifts in action and identity that propel the narrative forward: Israel's transformation from Pharaoh's disposable slaves to God's beloved children, from building Pharaoh's projects to constructing God's tabernacle, and from serving Pharaoh to worshiping the one true God. In the middle of the book, Israel finds itself in an in-between space – the wilderness. Isolation, rebellion, doubt, tests, and uncertainty mark the wilderness experience. The journey is a difficult one, fraught with struggles and challenges. Even as they near the end of their journey, the Israelites – already God's people by grace – remain in a state of becoming, continually refining themselves as they strive to become the people of God.

Approaching Exodus as a journey uncovers a wealth of insights. Some scholars refer to this journey as a "pilgrimage," with the pilgrimage pattern in Exodus seen as a part of the biblical tradition in which the notion of pilgrimage is not merely a religious practice but "a literary paradigm for expressing future aspirations, present wishes, and past identity."[88] The biblical writer employs the trope of Moses's journey to the holy mountain – where he receives the divine call in God's presence – as a microcosm of this pilgrim pattern, initially alone and then with the Israelites.[89] Others also recognize the journey in Exodus as the archetypal journey of Israel: passing through water, ascending the mountain, and, finally, worshiping God.[90]

Carmen Joy Imes's insightful study reveals the significance of the wilderness stories as a framing device around the central Sinai narrative (Exod 19–Num 10) that depicts the journey of becoming. She notes that the word for "desert" or "wilderness" appears seven times before and after Sinai and that God sustains Israel with food and water before and after the revelation at Sinai (Exod 16–17; Num 11, 20). Israel also fought the Amalekites before and after Sinai (Exod 17:8–16; Num 14:39–45). In this way, the wilderness journey becomes a place of becoming.[91]

---

88. Mark S. Smith, *The Pilgrimage Pattern in Exodus*, JSOTSup 239 (Sheffield: Sheffield Academic Press, 1997), 127.
89. Smith, *The Pilgrimage Pattern in Exodus*, 141.
90. Estelle, *Echoes of Exodus*, 107. For a postcolonial-Africana reading of Exodus, Ngwa identifies the three places – Egypt, Wilderness, and Mountain – as representing the ideological and liberating paradigm for the oppressed. Ngwa, *Let My People Live*, 3.
91. Carmen Joy Imes, *Bearing God's Name: Why Sinai Still Matters* (Downers Grove: IVP Academic, 2019), 14–15. For a classic reading on ritual study, see Arnold Van Gennep, *The Rites of Passage* (Chicago: The University of Chicago Press, 1960). Propp also makes a summary of Exodus from the perspective of the rite of passage. Propp, *Exodus 1–18*, 35–36.

Introduction

Drawing on the studies of anthropologists and ritualists, in particular their understanding of liminality – the Latin word *lim* means "threshold" – Imes locates the Israelites' wilderness experience as a liminal space, a threshold of transition where one's status and identity are transformed. In this space, individuals lack a concrete social and religious status and are dependent on others.[92] For Victor Turner, the pilgrimage itself is a "great liminal experience of the religious life."[93] Moses himself names this in-between status: one is a sojourner or a "foreigner" (Exod 2:22). However, it is precisely in this disorienting experience of feeling like he belonged nowhere that Moses was on the path of becoming God's agent of change. Similarly, the wilderness experience served as a training ground for Israel to become the people of God. The wilderness experience, though temporary, exerted a transformative influence on their identity, shaping them according to God's purpose. For Israel as a whole, the journey from Egypt to the promised land was a journey of becoming. This journey parallels that of Christians – from slavery to sin to worshiping the one true God, and from water baptism to living a transformed life through the redemption of Jesus the Messiah.

Reading Exodus is thus a transformative journey, one that invites us to journey with the Israelites, to empathize with their struggles and challenges, and to seek out meaning in the midst of it all. For those in the Chinese diaspora, this journey mirrors their own journey from their home country to new lands. This is a journey of becoming, marked by the memory of God's redemptive acts and leading, ultimately, to a new identity as part of God's new people. Just like the Israelites on their earthly exodus journey, we embark on a new journey of discovery, one that leads us toward heavenly hope. Exodus invites us to join this transformative and ongoing journey of becoming in which past, present, and future converge to create something new.

Therefore, to read Exodus is to engage with its transformative narrative as one's own and to allow it to shape one's identity for God's purposes. This commentary aims to interweave the themes of diaspora, memory, and journey to present a fresh reading of Exodus that informs and transforms readers within their unique contexts. May this reading and rereading of Exodus in the

---

92. Imes, *Bearing God's Name*, 17. Athena Gorospe's study on the identity of Moses in Exodus 4 also uses this liminal perspective, yielding fascinating insights for identity formation. Athena E. Gorospe, *Narrative and Identity: An Ethical Reading of Exodus 4* (Leiden: Brill, 2007).
93. Victor Turner and Edith Turner, *Image and Pilgrimage in Christian Culture: Anthropological Perspective* (New York: Columbia University Press, 1978), 7.

chapters that follow inspire and guide us on our own journeys of becoming, leading us toward a vision of hope and continuous transformation to conform to the way of God in new lands.

EXODUS 1:1–15:21
IDENTITY CONVERSION OUT OF EGYPT

OVERVIEW

The Chinese people have dispersed throughout the world, and their presence manifests itself in the multitude of Chinese restaurants in communities in the majority and minority worlds. In my youth, I yearned for a better life and a brighter future, and the scarcity of higher education opportunities in the British colonized Hong Kong impelled me to seek knowledge across the ocean in the United States. Similarly, some people went to Taiwan, Australia, the United Kingdom, and the Netherlands for further education. Some returned home to Hong Kong after their studies, while others established new roots in their adopted homelands. Still others ventured to other places to pursue further education and careers. To move to a new land is to embark on a new journey – one filled with adventure and endless possibilities.

When the Israelites migrated to Egypt, they, too, embarked on a new chapter of their journey. Although this beginning was initially marked by freshness and prosperity, things soon turned bitter due to a shift of power in the new land, eventually leading to their enslavement.

Exodus 1 seamlessly continues the story from Genesis 50 and, in this way, preserves the memory of Genesis while extending it into the future. The opening paragraph narrates the Israelites' experiences in Egypt, describing their subjugation under a new pharaoh who schemed to eradicate the Israelites, whom he perceived as a threat to his rule.

The first chapter of Exodus presents a multifaceted exploration of the dynamics between the powerful and the powerless, the interplay between old memories and new experiences, and the theme of divine inactivity alongside human responsibility, as demonstrated by the actions of several named and unnamed women. The birth and early life of Moses in Midian, as depicted in Exodus 2, serves as a prologue to his divine encounter with God in an unexpected locale in Exodus 3, which sets the stage for his commission to return to Egypt in Exodus 4. The identity formation and struggles of Moses permeate the opening chapters of Exodus, laying the foundation for the broader identity formation and struggles of the Israelites as they journey forward.¹ Subsequently, the entanglement between Moses and Pharaoh, recounted in Exodus 5–6, sets the stage for God to exhibit his supremacy through a series of ten plagues, with Moses acting as an intermediary between Israel and Pharaoh, which leads, ultimately, to the downfall of the hard-hearted pharaoh (Exod 7–11). Exodus 12–14 narrates the pivotal exodus event, which includes the institution of the Passover ritual, the consecration of the Israelite firstborn, and the crossing of the Red Sea. Part I of this commentary culminates with two hymns of triumph by Moses and Miriam, respectively. This segment encapsulates the movements from bondage to liberation, from subjugation to victory, from powerlessness to becoming powerful, and from Egypt toward the promised land.

1:1–22: PROSPERITY AND PERIL IN A NEW LAND
1:1–7: Israel Prospers in a New Land

The book of Exodus begins with the phrase "these are the names of," which is the Hebrew title of the book – *shemot*. The author expounds upon these names, referring to them as "the sons of Israel who went to Egypt with Jacob" and going on to name Jacob's 11 sons. The total of Jacob's descendants amounts to 70, symbolizing completeness. This brief account of Jacob's descendants is a recapitulation of Genesis 46:8–27. Though the order of the sons varies, the account's main purpose is to establish Exodus as a sequel to Genesis. Given that Jacob has 12 sons, one may wonder why only 11 are named. The author soon explains, stating that "Joseph was already in Egypt" (1:5) and that he, his brothers, and his generation had died (1:6). The brevity of the description implies that the author assumes that the readers are already familiar with the Joseph story in Genesis 37–50.²

Although Jacob's offspring numbered 70 upon their arrival in Egypt, they soon proliferated, swarming³ and multiplying to such a degree that "the land was filled with them" (1:7). It is noteworthy that the phrasing in verse 7 mirrors

---

1. Some scholars see the whole Pentateuch as a biography of Moses since his birth, life and ministry mirrors the fate of the Israelites. Hendel, "The Exodus in Biblical Memory," 615.
2. The journey of Joseph (characterized by exile, alienation, loss, deception, oppression, and pain) has multiple implications for diasporas and those in exile. For a Cuban reading of Genesis 39–41, see Francisco Garcia-Treto, "Hyphenating Joseph: A View of Genesis 39–41 from the Cuban Diaspora," in *Interpreting Beyond Borders*, ed. Fernando F. Segovia (Sheffield: Sheffield Academic Press, 2000), 134–145.
3. "Swarming" (*sharats*) appears in Genesis 1:21 and 7:21 to describe the aquatics and animals that swarm on earth, as well as in Exodus 8:3 to describe the Nile being swarmed with frogs. As such, the word is used as "zoological imagery" to reflect the danger and uncontrolled growth

the creation mandate given to humankind in Genesis 1:28: "Be fruitful and increase in number; fill the earth."[4] By reusing creation language in a new milieu and at a different time in history, the text intends to demonstrate that the Israelites in Egypt were a new creation.[5] Now, Egypt has become the Israelites' new home, and they are flourishing, as described in Exodus 1:7.

In this opening chapter of Exodus, God is doing a new thing. God's creative work is ongoing and intricately linked to his redemptive plans, manifested this time through the sons of Israel prospering in a new land. Behind the idea of Israelite fecundity lies the role of women in procreation. This subtly points to the role of women in the first two chapters of Exodus.[6] Theologically, the multitude of Israelites signifies that God's promise of a seed to Abraham has been fulfilled, if only partially. What remains to be fulfilled is his promise of a land. The land thus serves as the central thrust of Exodus that propels the plot forward toward the ultimate end – the promised land – through the deliverance of the Israelites from Egypt, the crossing of the Red Sea, and the arduous wilderness experience as a training ground for their identity formation and knowledge of Yahweh.

Entering a new land – whether for work, education, or seeking opportunities for a better future – may result in achieving "model minority" status from the perspective of the host country.[7] Although this status may ring true for some due to their exceptional contributions to a particular field, it is by no means representative of the majority of diasporic experiences in new lands. As the Exodus narrative unfolds, the prosperity of the Israelites soon turns into peril due to the shifting political climate in the new land. This further

---

of the Israelites. See Roth, *Hyphenating Moses*, 65. Kass describes this zoological imagery as "animal-like activity and profusion." Leon R. Kass, *Founding God's Nation: Reading Exodus* (New Haven: Yale University Press, 2021), 24.

4. Also in Genesis 9:1, 7.

5. Fretheim notes that the phrase "the sons of Israel" (Israelites) occurs 125 times in Exodus, marking a shift in language from Genesis and signifying the people of God. The phrase forms an *inclusio* in Exodus 1:1–7. Terrence E. Fretheim, *Exodus, Int* (Louisville: John Knox Press, 1991), 24.

6. Jacqueline E. Lapsley, *Whispering the Word: Hearing Women's Stories in the Old Testament* (Louisville: Westminster John Knox, 2005), 70.

7. The concept of the "Model Minority" is primarily associated with the culture of the United States, though many European countries have concepts of classism that stereotype ethnic groups in a similar manner. The label of the "Model Minority" is perceived from the white Americans and is highly contested by contemporary Asian American scholars. Jonathan Y. Tan, *Introducing Asian American Theologies* (Maryknoll: Orbis Books, 2008), 37. This label only represents a small segment of Asians in America and invites and proves to be inadequate to represent the diverse demographic of this group of people.

underscores the similarities between the experience of Israel in Egypt and that of migrants in the diaspora. Just as the Israelites were subject to the changing political climate of Egypt – their host country – people living in the diasporic state are similarly subject to the political and economic fluctuations of their host countries. As minorities in a dominant culture, identity formation is an ongoing process of understanding who we are and what we are to do in new lands.

1:8–10 Israel Faces Violence in the New Land

As newcomers, the Israelites, although prosperous, were vulnerable to the policies of the host country and the whims of its rulers. As a minority, they were at the mercy of those in power, and their survival and prosperity depended on their compliance with the rules and laws of the host country. After a sweeping recapitulation of why the Israelites were in Egypt, the narrative soon turns in a different direction: "Then a new king, to whom Joseph meant nothing, came to power in Egypt" (1:8). The Hebrew text literally says that this new king did not know Joseph. The Hebrew word for "know" (*yada'*) connotes experiential knowledge or, as in this case, "acknowledgment."[8]

The mention of a "new king" marks the transition of power, a new page in history, a new opportunity, and a new threat. This new king bodes ill for the Israelites because "Joseph meant nothing" to him – meaning that the sons of Jacob could no longer play the "Joseph card" to stay safe in the new land. Furthermore, the new king's lack of knowledge or acknowledgment of Joseph reflects his ignorance of the fate of Joseph, which was an ominous sign for the Israelites in his country. Joseph, a Hebrew who had been forced to migrate to Egypt, became a slave and later rose to power in the Egyptian court. Although this memory could have enlightened this new king in Egypt, it seems that this story meant nothing to him.[9]

According to the book of Genesis, Joseph and his family resided in the land of Goshen (Gen 45:10; 46:28–34; 47:1), living peacefully alongside the Egyptians in the host country. With the emergence of the new king, there was a drastic shift in this situation. Instead of viewing the Israelites as peaceful and non-threatening people in his country, the new Pharaoh perceives them

---

8. *BDB*, 394.
9. That "Joseph was already in Egypt" implies that the journey of the Israelites was a journey of trauma-hope as portrayed in Genesis. Pharaoh's lack of knowledge of Joseph also means that he disregards the history of the community to which Joseph belonged. See the significance of Exodus 1:5 in the context of Exodus 1. Ngwa, *Let My People Live*, 37, 56.

as a threat to Egypt's national security. He fears that they will outnumber the Egyptians, become too powerful, and possibly join Egypt's enemies during times of war (1:9–10). The words of Pharaoh in the Hebrew text reveal his inner psyche. His advice, "Come, we must deal shrewdly with them," reflects the schism between "us" and "them." "Them" in Hebrew is "him," implying that Pharaoh perceived the Israelites as a single unified entity aiming to get "us." Pharaoh's words "Come, let us" (*habah*) echo the words of the people who built the tower of Babel (Gen 11:3, 4), opposing God's intention for humanity to "be fruitful and increase in number and fill the earth" (Gen 9:1). Here, the author reveals Pharaoh's insecurity and pride.

The word "leave" in the phrase "leave the country" (1:10) is literally "go up" (*'alah*) in Hebrew. This word occurs twice in Joseph's speech before his death: "God will take [*'alah*] you up out of this land . . . then you must carry [*'alah*] my bones up from this place" (Gen 50:24–25). Geographically, Egypt is situated in the "lower" area, while Canaan is in the "upper" area. In biblical theology, Egypt embodies the idea of "Sheol," meaning the "underworld."[10] To "leave" (or "go up") is exactly what God intended to do with the Israelites – to bring them out of Egypt into the promised land, thus fulfilling his promise to the patriarchs. In this narrative, Pharaoh is portrayed as failing to realize that he is at war with the God of Israel. His ignorance of Joseph and the God of Joseph continues to be manifested in his resistance to Joseph's God. In hindsight, Pharaoh's plan to deal shrewdly with the Israelites was bound to fail precisely because of his ignorance.

---

10. Morales notices the association of the word "descend" into Egypt and "ascent" out of Egypt, and renders Egypt as Sheol since the verb "descend" is often employed to describe descending into the Underworld (Gen 37:35; 46:4). See Morales, *Exodus Old and New*, 50–51. The Ancient Near Eastern Text – "The Descent of Ishtar to the Underworld" – resembles the notion of descending into Sheol. "The Descent of Ishtar to the Underworld," trans. Stephanie Dalley (*COS* 1.108: 38–84).

THE CHINESE IN AMERICA AND ANTI-ASIAN HATE

The Chinese presence in America dates back over a century, originating with the discovery of gold in California, which prompted a rush of Chinese migrants to San Francisco, seeking a better future for themselves and their descendants.[1] The traditional Chinese name for San Francisco – *Jiu Jin Shan* in Mandarin and *Gao Kam San* in Cantonese – means "Old Gold Mountain." Early Chinese migrants seeking for a better future also worked and settled in New York.

Although life as migrants and minorities in a host country was never easy, the real threat to their existence and human rights came in 1882 with the enactment of the Chinese Exclusion Act, spearheaded by Californian senator John F. Miller. Referring to Chinese immigrants as "inhabitants of another planet," Miller argued that America belonged solely to White people and should be preserved without what he called "oriental contamination." He went so far as to argue, "Why not discriminate? Why aid in the increase and distribution over . . . our domain of a degraded and inferior race, and the progenitors of an inferior sort of men?"[2] His colleagues supported his stance, and the bill was signed and executed. Although this act was eventually repealed, anti-Chinese (Sinophobia) and anti-Asian sentiments still persist in various forms and degrees in several parts of America.

During the COVID-19 pandemic, the rising violence against Asians in Atlanta, San Francisco, New York, and other parts of the country testified to the persistent prejudice and challenges faced by Asians in America. During the pandemic, there was also an increase in instances where even Asians who were not of Chinese descent were wrongly identified as "Chinese" both in America and Europe. Despite occasional perceptions of the Chinese as a "model minority," a more accurate reflection of the Chinese experience in America is the term "perpetual foreigner." Fears of "a Chinese invasion," "a Japanese invasion," or simply "an Asian invasion" echo Pharaoh's nebulous fears about the Israelites in Exodus 1.

---

1. Kuhn, *Chinese among Others*, 190–191.
2. Iris Chang, *The Chinese in America: A Narrative History* (New York: Penguin Books, 2003), 130.

1:11–22: Discrimination and Resistance

In the wake of the perceived threat posed by the burgeoning Israelite population in his land, Pharaoh adopts three successive measures to confront the issue. First, he imposes hard labor upon them (1:11–14). Second, he instructs the Hebrew midwives to kill any male child born to the Israelites (1:15–21).[11] Third, he commands all Egyptians to cast every Hebrew male baby into the Nile (1:22). His death decrees stand in stark contrast to the births of the Israelites. The Nile, a source of life for the Egyptians, becomes an instrument of death for the Hebrew boys.

Pharaoh's first strategy to curb the overpopulation of the Israelites is to impose harsh labor upon them, marking the inception of their enslavement in Egypt. The state organizes and enforces this statewide enslavement, subjecting the forced laborers to grueling and unlimited under inhumane conditions. It treats them as mere objects without basic civil rights, with even less privileges than household slaves.[12] The main purpose of this enslavement was not merely to subjugate them but also to crush their spirits by humiliating, debasing, and degrading them.[13]

This kind of enslavement is reminiscent of the plight of early Chinese immigrants in nineteenth-century America, who labored in mines and on transcontinental railroads like the Central Pacific Railroad, enduring racial discrimination and poor working conditions. While their employers benefited from this new and cheap source of labor, many White workers lost their jobs, leading to the perception of these Chinese laborers as "the yellow peril."[14]

The names of the two cities used for storage, Pithom and Rameses, reflect Pharaoh's domain. In Egyptian, Pithom means "house of (the god) Atum,"

---

11. "Hebrew midwives" can refer to the midwives who were Hebrews or the Egyptian midwives who delivered Hebrew babies. If this phrase refers to Hebrew midwives, it reflects Pharaoh's stupidity in using them to deliver Hebrew babies. If they are Egyptian midwives who deliver Hebrew babies, then it further demonstrates the divided house in Pharaoh's regime. J. Cheryl Exum, "'You shall Let Every Daughter Live': A Study of Exodus 1.8–2.10," in *A Feminist Companion to Exodus to Deuteronomy*, ed. Athalya Brenner (Sheffield: Sheffield Academic Press, 1994), 48. Based on Meyer's study, midwifery was one of the most common women's professions since early human civilization. In Ancient Near Eastern cultures, a midwife was also known as a "wise woman" due to the technical skills and religious functions associated with the act. Carol Meyers, *Exodus*, NCBC (Cambridge: Cambridge University Press, 2005), 40–41.
12. Sarna, *Exploring Exodus*, 23.
13. Kass, *Founding God's Nation*, 29.
14. Tan, *Introducing Asian American Theologies*, 24–25. Rebecca Y. Kim, "*Making Their Mark: Asian Americans and the Californian "Christian" Landscape*," in *Migration, Transnationalism, and Faith in Missiological Perspective: Los Angeles as a Global Crossroads*, eds. Kirsteen Kim and Alexia Salvatierra (Lanham: Lexington, 2022), 94.

while Rameses means "domain of Rameses."[15] Rameses, possibly referring to Ramses II, is the name of the pharaoh who oversaw the construction of a new capital built by Israelite slaves.[16] The place-names Pithom and Rameses are attested in the New Kingdom of Egypt.[17] Both city names reflect the pharaoh's power and authority over those subjugated under his domain. The construction of these storage cities is not merely utilitarian but a means for Pharaoh to impose his own identity upon the Israelites and create a new cultural identity for them as his slaves.[18]

Despite the harsh labor imposed upon them, the Israelites did not decrease in number but "multiplied and spread" (1:12). Since Pharaoh's first strategy to cope with the "Israelite problem" failed, he turns to plan B, ordering the midwives to kill all newborn Hebrew boys. However, Shiphrah and Puah defy Pharaoh's command and let the baby boys live because they feared God (1:15, 17, 21). By preserving the names of these two women, the narrator acknowledges their contribution to the survival of the Israelites and, thus, to the nation of Israel. Their act of disobedience reflects their courage and their obedience to a higher being.[19] The text does not say that God told the midwives to let the Hebrew boys live; we may infer that they acted in accordance with their own conscience and their faith in the God of the Hebrews. In times of injustice and tyranny, one must discern whose voice to obey, as the midwives did when they chose to fear God more than they feared Pharaoh.

In Chinese, the term "fear God" is expressed as a compound word – "respect + fear" (*jìng wèi*), conveying a sense of respect and awe toward someone who holds higher authority and deserves to be respected. This term is a combination of reverence and wonder, underscoring the essential character trait of the wise person in Wisdom books, where the fear of God is said to be the beginning of wisdom and knowledge.[20]

The story of the Hebrew midwives portrays the conflict between the powerful and the powerless, demonstrating how the powerless may resist the

---

15. For more on the etymology and location of these sites, see Hoffmeier, *Ancient Israel in Sinai*, 58–65.
16. For the historical details of Rameses and his reign, see Sarna, *Exploring Exodus*, 18–20.
17. James K. Hoffmeier and Gary A. Rendsburg, "Pithom and Rameses (Exodus 1:11): Historical, Archaeological, and Linguistic Issues (Part I)," *Journal of Ancient Egyptian Interconnections* 33 (March 2022): 1–19.
18. Roth, *Hyphenating Moses*, 73.
19. Fretheim names the midwives' behavior "creative disobedience." Fretheim, *Exodus*, 32.
20. For example, Proverbs 1:7, 9:10; Job 28:28; Ecclesiastes 12:13.

powerful in the face of injustice.[21] As a result of the midwives' action, the Israelites continue to multiply and become even more numerous – a sign of God's blessing. God rewards the midwives with families of their own (1:21), implying his approval of their resistance.

In various political regimes, those in power may act unjustly, causing suffering for the people. Some individuals choose to resist, while others comply or remain silent. In such situations, disobedience often comes at the price of the individual's life, which potentially affects the entire family. While the story of the midwives may not set a precedent for others to disobey their governments, it serves as a reminder that there is a time to resist evil, even when doing the right thing does not guarantee a just outcome. Such is the case in the ever-changing political climate of places like Hong Kong, where civil relations are in flux and larger powers seek to assert control. While God may sometimes reward those who act on behalf of the powerless, this is not always the case. Wisdom is required to discern the times and decide when to act and what actions to take against evil, injustice, and oppression.

In the account of Pharaoh's plan to stem the overpopulation of the Israelites, the conversations between Pharaoh and the midwives are recorded, but the voice of God is conspicuous by its absence. Was God listening? Was God even there, and did God care?[22] Despite the lack of direct evidence of God speaking, the fact that God rewarded the midwives suggests that divine providence was at work behind the scenes. Therefore, God is not entirely absent from the first chapter of Exodus as some may believe.[23]

At this point in the narrative, Pharaoh has exhausted his options and turns to his last resort – plan C. This time, he does not ask the Hebrew people to kill their own. Instead, he turns once again to his people and enlists their help

---

21. Weems's study on the Hebrew midwives provides an ideological reading that intersects with power dynamics related to gender, race, and social status. Renita J. Weems, "The Hebrew Women are not Like the Egyptian Women: The Ideology of Race, Gender and Sexual Reproduction in Exodus 1," *Semeia* 59 (1992): 25–34. It is uncertain whether these Hebrew midwives are ethnically Hebrew or Egyptians who act as midwives to the Hebrews.
22. Kessler has done a sophisticated study on the silence of God. The subject matter is not as simple as it seems. God's silence has diverse implications from alienation to divine punishment or more positively as expressing extreme holiness in Israel's holy sanctuary. Silence expresses a wide range of meanings. John Kessler, *Between Hearing and Silence: A Study in Old Testament Theology* (Waco: Baylor University Press, 2021), 2. The first two chapters of divine silence when viewed from the perspective of the Israelites may seem like silence from a catastrophe, but when seen from the divine perspective, they belong to the category of God's "waiting period" – waiting for the fulfillment of Genesis 15:13–14 and waiting for the birth of Moses.
23. For example, Gowan names Exodus 1–2, "The Absence of God." Gowan, *Theology in Exodus*, 1.

(compare 1:9). He commands "all his people" to cast the Hebrew sons into the Nile upon birth but allow the Hebrew daughters to live (1:22). Twice, Pharaoh commands that the daughters be allowed to live (1:16, 22), little knowing that it is precisely one of the daughters, Miriam, who will save an infant boy, Moses, who will later deliver the Israelites.[24] The opposite situation appears in the South Asian context, where there is violence against girls, and female feticide is also prevalent in some countries, particularly in rural areas.[25] Several commentators consider Pharaoh's edict to be an act of genocide.[26] Even in the twenty-first century, the practice of genocide persists in Asia and other countries. For instance, the Muslim Rohingya people in Myanmar (formerly Burma) faced persecution by Myanmar's military during 2016–2017, forcing over a million Rohingya people to flee to other countries such as Bangladesh, India, and Thailand. This genocide resulted in tens of thousands of Rohingya people being killed and many being raped. The United States has referred to this event as "ethnic cleansing."[27] *Time* magazine featured one of these tragic scenes as its cover image: an elderly woman, wearing sea-soaked clothes, on the shore, her frail hand clinging to a man – possibly her son – as they flee Myanmar's oppressive regime. The cover is titled "Myanmar's Shame."[28]

This broader backdrop of "us" versus "them" sets the stage for the birth of a Hebrew boy – Moses – whose actions in chapter 14 seal the Egyptians' fate as they are drowned in the water, in a dramatic reversal of Pharaoh's edict in chapter 1.

The Hebrew title for the book of Exodus is "Names." Chapter 1 records the names of Jacob's sons and the names of the midwives, yet the name of the pharaoh is notably absent. This omission, while obscuring the historical identity of this pharaoh, allows him to become a potent symbol for all present and future "pharaohs" who seek to oppress, destroy, control birth, and enslave people. In the Egyptian context, a name represents a person. To have a name

---

24. Lapsley, *Whispering the Word*, 73.
25. George and Swarup, "Exodus," 80.
26. For example, Durham, *Exodus*, 9. Moshe Greenberg, *Understanding Exodus: A Holistic Commentary on Exodus 1–11* (Eugene: Cascade, 2013), 30. Fretheim, *Exodus*, 35. For a postcolonial-Africana reading of Exodus that frames the themes of erasure, alienation, and singularity, see Ngwa, *Let My People Live*, 1–12. In this book, Ngwa views empire/imperialism/colonialism through a negative lens while advocating a hermeneutic of liberation for the marginalized and oppressed.
27. "Genocide, Crimes against Humanity and Ethnic Cleansing of Rohingya in Burma," https://www.state.gov/burma-genocide/.
28. See the September 21, 2017 issue of *Time* magazine.

inscribed on a papyrus or a stone signifies the continued existence of that person. If a person's name is erased from a monument, the implication is that this individual never existed and will forever be cast out from the next life.[29] In stark contrast, those who aid in the survival of God's people are blessed, and their names are often preserved in history.[30] The way in which Pharaoh, the very embodiment of power, mistreats the Hebrew slaves in his land serves as a poignant parallel to contemporary contexts where the mistreatment of minority groups such as some Chinese is sadly rampant in foreign lands. The enslaved remain powerless, but between them and the powerful stands God, who unfailingly aligns with those who are oppressed and mistreated.

Though chapter 1 does not feature any explicit physical or verbal manifestation of God's presence, the remarkable growth of the Israelites in Egypt, the dramatic reversal of Pharaoh's edict, and the rewarding of the midwives with families all hint at God's providential care operating behind the scenes. Little wonder, then, that Exodus has been so favorably received by those who are powerless and oppressed. The interplay of life and death, hope and despair, and courage and resistance works wonders in the opening chapter of Exodus, inspiring all who migrate to new lands in search of hope.

2:1–25 THE BIRTH AND THE IN-BETWEEN LIFE OF MOSES

In the Chinese diaspora, people often embody multiple identities, and the concept of "home" is fluid. It is common for those within the Chinese diaspora to migrate from their land of birth and dwell in other parts of the world. Sometimes, this migration entails establishing multiple homes, with no "real home" to which to return. At other times, migration involves seeking a permanent place to settle and call home.

For centuries, the life of Moses has captured the interest of people from various cultures. People are drawn to his experiences as a Hebrew boy raised by the daughter of an Egyptian pharaoh, educated in the Egyptian palace, exiled to Midian, and called by God to lead the Hebrew people out of slavery in Egypt. Moses's experience resonates with those who have migrated and had multiple homes, transcending the boundaries of time, race, class, and gender. The detailed account of Moses's birth mirrors the birth of Israel as a nation.

---

29. Jon Manchip White, *Everyday Life in Ancient Egypt* (Mineola: Dover Publications, 2002), 155.
30. The namelessness of Pharaoh's daughter, the mother, and sister of Moses in Exodus 2 is not part of this generalization.

As we shall see, Moses's identity formation process echoes that of the Israelites, with many parallels between his experiences and those of the Israelites. Moses's journey of identity formation, de-formation, and re-formation prefigures the journey of the nation of Israel – identity formation (out of Egypt), de-formation (in the wilderness), and re-formation (at Sinai).

Moses's life, from his birth to his calling (Exod 2:11–25), took place in an in-between and liminal space. He found himself in a state of limbo, not quite in his home or in his place of residence,[31] yet – perhaps because of this very situation – shaped into a person ready to serve God's purpose. Similarly, the Israelites experienced a steep learning curve while journeying through the wilderness. Despite the challenges they faced, this experience catalyzed their becoming the people of God. For both Moses and the Israelites, the journey of identity formation took place in an in-between space that was fraught with conflict, fear, and pain but also presented opportunities for creativity and hope.[32]

To be in-between means to exist in a state of not fully belonging to any particular world but, rather, being part of multiple worlds simultaneously.[33] According to Peter Phan, to be spatially in-between is to dwell at the borders without a permanent residence.[34] Given the spatial nature of this in-between state, I identify three spatial verbs (going out, settling down, and sojourning) in Exodus 2:11–25 that describe Moses's experience in this transitional state.[35] Ultimately, we will see that living in-between can be both intentional and meaningful when viewed through the lens of God's larger redemptive plan for his people.

---

31. Scholars have noticed the in-betweenness and the liminal phase of Moses and Israel in the wilderness wandering. See the examples cited by Propp, *Exodus 1–18*, 35. Hendel, "The Exodus in Biblical Memory," 620.

32. Jung Young Lee, *Marginality: The Key to Multicultural Theology* (Minneapolis: Fortress, 1995), 47, 62–62, 66, 98. Gorospe, *Narrative and Identity*, 54, 167, 302. An earlier version of this paper was delivered as a message at *1.5 Grand Gathering* on March 8, 2008 at Evangelical Formosan Church of Los Angeles (EFCLA) and later published in "Bridging Past and Future: The In-Between Life of Moses," in *Logos for Life: Essays Commemorating Logos Evangelical Seminary's 20th Anniversary* (Hong Kong: Tien Dao, 2009), 217–237.

33. Jung Young Lee, *Marginality*, 44. Lee equates being in-between with being at the margin. The metaphors of both in-betweenness and marginality have been used to characterize the Asian American experience in North America. Yet those who have more than two identities will experience more intense in-betweenness than a typical Asian American.

34. Peter C. Phan, *Christianity with an Asian Face: Asian American Theology in the Making* (Maryknoll: Orbis Books, 2003), 9.

35. On the subject of using spatial verbs as structural design, see Jan P. Fokkelman, *Reading Biblical Narrative: A Practical Guide*, trans. Ineke Smit (Leiden: Deo Publishing, 1995), 99–111.

2:1–10 A Miraculous Beginning

Subsequent to Pharaoh's decree to throw all newborn Hebrew boys into the Nile, a daughter of Levi gives birth to a son.[36] This presents her with a difficult decision: Will she comply with Pharaoh's order and cast her boy into the Nile, or will she resist Pharaoh as the midwives had done? Will the fate of her son be the same as the rest of the Hebrew boys, or will his fate be different?

When the woman sees that her infant boy is "a fine child," she defies Pharaoh's decree and hides the infant for three months until she can no longer do so. "A fine child" (2:2) is literally "when she saw that he is good (*ki tob*)" – the identical expression (*ki tob*) used to describe God seeing his creation as good.[37] Does this mean that what she saw is comparable to what God saw in his beautiful creation? Does this "good" refer to the boy's physical appearance or to her overall impression? Perhaps this "good" echoes and anticipates a redemptive good like that which Joseph spoke about later in life.[38] Africana scholar Judy Fentress-Williams suggests that the boy is special in his mother's eyes and the eyes of the Creator.[39] The mother puts him in a basket and sets it among the reeds by the bank of the Nile in hopes that he will be found and saved. The word translated as "basket" (*tebah*) is literally the same word translated as "ark" in Genesis 6–9, invoking a memory of rescue from water as well as the motif of creation, de-creation, and re-creation.

Like the two Hebrew midwives, the mother of the boy exercises disobedience by hiding her beautiful baby boy. Her daughter, the sister of the baby boy, is also nameless – like the mother – but plays an indispensable role in preserving the life of her baby brother.[40] "And his sister stationed from afar to

---

36. The mention of the tribe of Levi, together with the detailed birth account of Moses suggests that his biological background is significant. It shows that Moses comes from "pure stock." Song provides an interesting postcolonial reading of Moses and Miriam by entering the text with an emphatic reading strategy. Angeline M. G. Song, *A Postcolonial Woman's Encounter with Moses and Miriam* (New York: Palgrave MacMillan, 2015), 150.
37. Genesis 1:4, 10, 12, 18, 21, 25, 31.
38. In light of his brother's evil deed of selling Joseph to the Midianites which then led Joseph to Egypt, Joseph tells his brothers "God intended it for good" (Gen 50:19). This good anticipates God's covenant to the Patriarchs. Paul Twiss, "Learning God's Redemptive Good: Reading Genesis 50:15–21 as a Last Delay," *JETS* 66, no. 3 (2023): 406.
39. Judy Fentress-Williams, "Exodus," in *The Africana Bible: Reading Israel's Scripture from Africa and African Diaspora*, eds. Hugh R. Page, Randall C. Bailey, Valerie Bridgeman, Stacy Davis, Cheryl Kirk-Duggan, Madipoane Masenya (*ngwan'a Mphahlele*), Nathaniel Samuel Murrell, Rodney S. Sadler (Minneapolis: Fortress, 2010), 82.
40. From a feminist reading, one reason why the narrator withheld the name of the three women (the mother of Moses, the sister of Moses, and the daughter of Pharaoh) may have been to diffuse the perceived female power, but the reader will have no way to verify that. J.

know what will happen to him" (2:4)[41] – to station (*yatsab*) is to take a stand and a position.[42] This verb is later used when Moses instructs the Israelites to station themselves and see the salvation of the LORD at the Red Sea crossing (14:13). The sister is quietly – and we may add curiously – waiting to see what will happen to her brother.

As the story unfolds, the daughter of Pharaoh happens to come down to bathe at the Nile. When she notices the "mini-ark" and the child within, she recognizes him as a Hebrew and is moved to compassion. Her actions – "saw, heard, and took pity"[43] – foreshadow God's action in Exodus 2:24–25.[44] She then adopts him as her own son (2:10).[45] The identity of this Pharaoh's daughter remains a mystery – her name and face, like that of her father, are withheld by the narrator. But her action reflects the "divided house" of Pharaoh. In light of the seemingly lesser status of women in Egyptian culture, her action speaks volumes of her courage and compassion.[46] Her defiance of her own father's edict aligns her with the Hebrew midwives and makes her a strategic instrument in God's rescue plan for the Israelites.[47] Here, she defies multiple boundaries, including ethnic, cultural, social, and class barriers. The sister of the boy then makes a wise suggestion to the daughter of Pharaoh: "Shall I go and get one of the Hebrew women to nurse the baby for you?" (2:7). The daughter of Pharaoh agrees, and so, the boy is nursed by his own mother,

---

Cheryl Exum, "'Second Thoughts about Secondary Characters: Women in Exodus 1.8–2.10," in *A Feminist Companion to Exodus to Deuteronomy*, ed. Athalya Brenner (Sheffield: Sheffield Academic Press, 1994), 83.
41. My translation.
42. *BDB*, 426.
43. In the NIV "She saw . . . he was crying, and she felt sorry" (Exod 2:5–6).
44. Fentress-Williams, "Exodus," 83.
45. The verbs associated with Pharaoh's daughter, "come down," "see," "send," "take pity," and "draw out" are parallel to God's actions in 2:24–25 and 3:7–8. See Bills, *The Theology of Justice in Exodus*, 95. For the concept of ancient adoption, see Martin Noth, *Exodus: A Commentary* (Philadelphia: Westminster, 1962), 26–27.
46. In ancient Egyptian iconography, the women often appear to embrace their husbands in a supportive role and are presented at a smaller scale compared to the men. Though there are female Pharaohs in the later history of Egypt, with Cleopatra VII (51–30 BCE) as a notable example, the action of the daughter of Pharaoh as depicted in Exodus 2 is remarkable. Ann Macy Roth, "Gender Roles in Ancient Egypt," in *A Companion to the Ancient Near East*, ed. Daniel C. Snell (Malden: Blackwell, 2007), 228, 231.
47. Many have discussed the roles of women (the midwives, Pharaoh's daughter, Moses's sister and mother, and Zipporah) in the beginning chapters of Exodus. The ambiguity surrounding their ethnicity has implications for Asian women in an immigrant context. See Esther Hae Jin Park, "Women in Exodus and Asian Immigrant Women: Asian Female Immigrants Bible Reading Strategy on Exodus 1–4," in *T&T Clark Handbook of Asian American Biblical Hermeneutics*, eds. Uriah Y. Kim and Seung Ai Yang (London: T&T Clark, 2019), 220–228.

with compensation also included (2:9)![48] Although the name Miriam is withheld by the narrator at this point, her association with water will resurface in Exodus 15 as she leads the women in singing a victory song after the Israelites cross the Red Sea.

> ## FAITHFUL DISOBEDIENCE IN THE CONTEXT OF CHINA'S HOUSE CHURCHES
>
> In some instances, state laws are intended to safeguard the rights of its citizens, but in other cases, the law is used primarily as a tool by which the state exerts control over its citizens. In regimes where the head of the state has absolute authority to run the country and uses these powers to suppress people's freedom of speech, freedom of religion, and other forms of expression, the state becomes an oppressive regime.
>
> In such contexts, how should Christians relate to the state? When religious freedom conflicts with government policy, what is the Christian response? In China, for example, there are unregistered churches, also known as house churches, and there is also the registered church, known as the Three-Self Patriotic Movement (TSPM), which is the state-sanctioned Protestant church in China. The "three-self" principles are self-governance, self-support, and self-propagation, and the TSPM was founded in 1954 to subsume the practice of Christianity under the Chinese government.[1]
>
> People in house churches use various strategies to deal with the state's control over religion. Some choose to go "underground" and avoid government scrutiny by meeting for worship in inconspicuous locations. Others are more vocal and openly challenge the state. Pastor Wang Yi's story exemplifies the latter approach. He has boldly and openly expressed his views regarding the relationship between state and church, issues of control and freedom, and the ultimate question of lordship and authority over the church. This has made Wang Yi and

---

48. Among the five women securing Moses's life, only Miriam's narrative continues after chapter 2 into the book of Numbers. This suggests her important role in the Pentateuch.

others like him the focus of global conversations about Christianity and the meaning of the way of the cross in the twenty-first century. However, Wang Yi's direct opposition to state's policies regarding house churches has cost him his freedom, and those who disagree with his vocal approach have also distanced themselves from him.

The story of Wang Yi is a modern-day example of civil disobedience. As pastor of a house church in Cheng Du, China, he was arrested and sentenced to nine years in prison for refusing to comply with state regulations on house churches. Prior to that incident, he had spoken and written extensively through blogs, letters, and sermons on various subjects including the relationship of the state and church, the identity of the house church, and the concept of suffering for Christ. Wang Yi has accused the TSPM of submitting to the state and, thereby, failing to submit to Christ. Therefore, he does not recognize the TSPM as a true church. He even cites the worship of the golden calves at Bethel and Dan (2 Kgs 10:29) to describe what he believes the TSPM represents.[2]

Wang Yi believes in nonviolent "faithful disobedience."[3] His intention is not to overthrow the state or change state policy. Rather, he simply believes that the spiritual kingdom of Christ overrides any earthly authorities and regards as Satanic any authority that challenges Christ's lordship over the church.[4] While acknowledging that God's sovereignty allows the communist regime to rule temporarily, he continues to use nonviolent ways to defy human laws that contradict or oppose biblical revelation and God's will. Wang Yi makes it clear that the aim of such disobedience is not to change the world but, rather, to testify to another world. He sees both spiritual disobedience and bodily suffering as ways to testify to this other world of God. He writes, "I will serve my sentence, but I will not serve the law. I will be executed, but I will not plead guilty."[5]

From a position of powerlessness, Wang Yi's conviction about the need for the separation of state and church, his faith in submitting to Christ alone, and his courage in engaging nonviolently with the state and enduring imprisonment offer both those in power and those who lack power a new lens through which to view and rethink global Christianity, liberation theology, and the relationship between state and church. Wang Yi is a contemporary figure who represents the ancient Hebrew midwives, Moses's mother and sister, and Pharaoh's daughter, who also confronted the prevailing regime of their time because of their commitment to a higher authority. There are many other Christians who, like Wang Yi, openly challenge state control over local churches. However, there are also those who deny or lie about their Christian faith in order to preserve their position "in the game" for the long term. Civil obedience

> and civil disobedience cannot be viewed in strict black-and-white terms but depends on the particular context in which these issues arise.
>
> ---
>
> 1. Hannah Nation and J. D. Tseng, eds., *Faithful Disobedience: Writings on Church and State from a Chinese House Church Movement* (Downers Grove: IVP Academic, 2022), 250–251.
> 2. This is from a pastoral letter that Wang Yi wrote to his congregation, dated October 15, 2010. Nation and Tseng, eds, *Faithful Disobedience*, 26–27.
> 3. By that, Wang Yi means civil and spiritual disobedience. He defines "faithful disobedience" as peaceful, meek, actively forbearing, joyful, and inevitable for the progress of the gospel." Nation and Tseng, eds, *Faithful Disobedience*, 222.
> 4. Nation and Tseng, eds, *Faithful Disobedience*, 29, 222.
> 5. Nation and Tseng, eds, *Faithful Disobedience*, 225.

Although born a Hebrew in Egypt, the boy Moses defies the odds and becomes a prince of Egypt, "educated in all the wisdom of the Egyptians" (Acts 7:22). What kind of man will he become as he grows up? How will he perceive his cultural identity? How will the Egyptians regard him? Will he be considered a rightful heir to the throne of Egypt? And how will the Hebrew slaves view him?

The name "Moses" (*mosheh*) embodies a hybrid identity as it is both a Hebrew and an Egyptian name. In Hebrew, it is an active participle deriving from the Hebrew verb "to draw out." In Egyptian, it is based on the Egyptian verb *ms(w)*, meaning "to bear," "give birth to," or "son."[49] "Moses" is a shortened form, similar to other well-known Egyptian names such as Ahmosis or Thutmosis.[50] The Egyptian origin of his name is the result of Pharaoh's daughter, who obviously spoke Egyptian, giving an Egyptian name to her adopted Hebrew son.[51]

The hybrid nature of Moses's name reflects and anticipates the conflicts in his in-between life.[52] Similarly, people living in the diaspora often have

---

49. Kass, *Founding God's Nation*, 44.
50. Peter Enns, *Exodus*, The NIV Application Commentary (Grand Rapids: Zondervan Publishing House, 2000), 63.
51. Roth argues that the naming of Moses entails identity implications for both Moses and the daughter of Pharaoh. Roth, *Hyphenating Moses*, 112.
52. The birth narrative of Moses forms a striking parallel to the birth narrative of the *Legend of Sargon*, and at the same time is different from it. Thus, the differences point to the author's interest in exploring the identity of Moses. This theme of identity continues in Moses's

hybrid or hyphenated names. For instance, many Chinese diasporans use both Chinese and English or other non-Chinese names to adapt themselves to multiple cultures and contexts. Some choose to retain their Chinese names but use English spellings, while others have two or more entirely different names in both Chinese and English. These names may offer clues to their cultural contexts and multiple consciousnesses.

2:11–22 A Conflicted In-betweenness

The biblical text offers only limited information regarding the time period between Moses's birth (2:1–10) and his call (Exod 3), as well his life in Egypt and his return to that land. A mere 12 verses (2:11–22) cover a span of 40 years in Moses's in-between life (Acts 7:30). Within these verses, the author employs three spatial verbs imbued with geographic and liminal connotations to describe Moses's experiences during those 40 years. These three verbs, along with their derivatives, are repeated twice: going out (2:11, 13), settling down (2:15b, 21),[53] and sojourning (2:22).[54]

Going Out

In the first part of Moses's in-between life, he is depicted as "going out" (*yatsa'*), also translated "went out" (NIV). Upon reaching the age of 40 (Acts 7:23), Moses goes out (*yatsa'*) to his brothers and witnesses their grueling labor. Upon seeing an Egyptian beating one of his own Hebrew brothers, Moses takes justice into his own hands by striking down the Egyptian (2:11–12). This incident where an Egyptian is beating a Hebrew captures the tension between these two groups of people at the time.[55] The following day, Moses goes out (*yatsa'*) again and, much to his surprise, sees two fellow Hebrews fighting each other. He confronts the perpetrator, asking, "Why are you hitting your fellow Hebrew?" The perpetrator retorts, "Who made you ruler and judge over us?

---

encounter with God in Exodus 3. Thomas B. Dozeman, "Creation and Environment in the Character Development of Moses," in *Character Ethics and The Old Testament: Moral Dimensions of Scripture*, eds. M. Daniel Carroll R. and Jacqueline E. Lapsley (Louisville: Westminster John Knox, 2007), 27–36. For a translation of the birth account of Sargon, see Hays, *Hidden Riches*, 113–114. Sargon of Akkad was a historical figure (2340–2284 BCE). Later, a Neo-Assyrian king took Sargon's name and become Sargon II (722–705 BCE).
53. The word "sit" in 2:15 shares the same root as the word "settle." It signals the author's wordplay. The root thus occurs three times in Exodus 2:11–23.
54. In Hebrew *yatsa'* (in the NIV "went out," vv. 11, 13), *yashav* (in the NIV "sat down," v. 15, "stay with," v. 21), and *hayah ger* (in the NIV "become a foreigner").
55. Stephen later assumed that Moses thought the Hebrews knew that Moses was God-sent as a rescuer of the Israelites (Acts 7:25).

Are you thinking of killing me as you killed the Egyptian?" Fearing that the matter had been revealed, and having learned that Pharaoh was seeking to kill him, Moses flees from the presence of Pharaoh (2:13–15).

"Going out" implies a transition from one place or state to another.[56] Moses's two experiences of "going out" are marked by going out from the grand Egyptian court and entering the humble Hebrew slave field, as well as going out from his royal position as Pharaoh's adopted son and joining his suffering Hebrew brothers. Although the narrative does not disclose why Moses went out to his people precisely at this time, it is evident that he was acutely conscious of his Hebrew roots and identified with the Hebrew people. This is underscored by the author's repetition of the phrase "his own people" in the same verse (2:11).

The significance of the verb "going out" becomes apparent when we consider God's later command to Moses to "bring out" the children of Israel from Egypt.[57] The Hebrew word *hotsa'* ("to bring out") comes from the same root as "to go out," but it emphasizes divine rather than human initiative.[58] In other words, Moses had first "gone out" to his own people before God called him to "bring out" his people. Without "going out," there could be no "bringing out." Twice, the verb "going out" is associated with the verb "to see" and "behold" (2:11b, 13), suggesting that Moses's going out was deliberate and purposeful. He went out to see to the well-being of his people. Moses's character was marked by a strong sense of justice and compassion even before he was called by God.[59]

Unfortunately, when Moses takes matters into his own hands and acts independently, the outcome is disastrous and the exact opposite of what he had expected. In the first scene, upon witnessing an act of injustice against his fellow Hebrew, Moses responds by killing the Egyptian perpetrator. In the second scene, after seeing two fellow Hebrew brethren fighting each other, Moses intervenes by questioning the aggressor, only to be humiliated and accused of being an unqualified judge.

---

56. *BDB*, 422.
57. For example: Exodus 3:10; 13:3, 9, 14, 16; Deuteronomy 26:8.
58. Eugene H. Merril, יצא in *NIDOTTE* II: 499.
59. Kass thinks that the compassion of Moses is associated with the women in his life (his Egyptian mother, his Hebrew mother, and his Hebrew sister). While this is possible, the narrator does not provide any explicit reasons to support such a reading. Kass, *Founding God's Nation*, 44.

In these two scenes, the conflicting aspects of Moses's life are reinforced at several levels. He was brought up in the Egyptian court but identifies with his Hebrew brothers who are slaves. He was a prince of Egypt but became a traitor by killing a "fellow" Egyptian. He demands justice by defending his own Hebrew brothers, yet they reject him. He was Pharaoh's adopted grandson, yet he became a fugitive from Pharaoh. He goes out from home but cannot return. At this point, Moses is suspended somewhere between the Hebrews and the Egyptians. He is neither a Hebrew slave nor an Egyptian prince, and he has no clear sense of his identity or purpose. At this juncture, Moses is a conflicted individual, unaware that God will use his two "going out" experiences to anticipate Israel's future exodus.[60] In hindsight, it is clear that God later transforms Moses's seemingly disastrous "going out" experiences into a redemptive "going out" experience for Israel. Little does Moses know that the rejection and pain he feels during these "going out" events will later enable him to identify with Israel's need for an exodus.

Settling Down

Moses's life enters a new chapter, marked by the verb "settling down" (*yashav*). After Pharaoh discovers that Moses has killed an Egyptian, he seeks to kill him, leaving Moses with no choice but to flee and take up residence in Midian (2:15). Moses's going out results in his entering an unfamiliar and unknown in-between space, mirroring his conflicted self. The "land" of Midian is emblematic of Moses's in-between life since Midian lacked defined borders, symbolizing his own unclear identity.[61] While some commentators suggest that entering Midian was a homecoming of sorts for Moses since it was where God had appeared to him and called him, and where he later met his wife and fathered a son,[62] Moses himself describes Midian as "a foreign land" (2:22).

The term "settle down" can be translated as "dwell," expressing an extended stay.[63] This sedentary connotation stands in stark contrast to the preceding movements of "going out." Even as Moses goes out twice on two consecutive days, he "settles down" twice in two consecutive actions. He first settles in Midian and then sits by a well (2:15). The word "sat" (*yashab*) is the same word as "settles down," emphasizing Moses's sedentary state. In subsequent

---

60. Fretheim, *Exodus*, 42.
61. Durham, *Exodus*, 22.
62. For example, Durham, *Exodus*, 24.
63. Gorg, יָשַׁב *TDOT*, 426–427.

verses, Moses not only settles down in Midian but also stays in Midian with a man named Reuel, his father-in-law (2:21). How does Moses end up with Reuel? It all begins with Moses's earlier experiences of "going out." When Moses sits by the well, the seven daughters of the Midianite priest, Reuel, arrive to draw water for their father's flock.[64] When a group of shepherds drive the daughters away, Moses comes to their rescue and even waters their flock for them (2:16–17).

Moses assumes the role of defender of the weaker party in three scenes, standing up for the oppressed Hebrew slave, the beaten Hebrew, and the daughters of Reuel. This concern for justice reflects God's divine concern for justice. Nevertheless, it is only in God's time and God's way that Moses's sense of justice finds its rightful place. After hearing of Moses's heroic rescue, Reuel tells his daughters to invite Moses to dine with his family (2:18–20). As the narrator says, "Moses agreed to stay with the man" (2:21). The verb "agreed" encompasses a range of volitional force, ranging from "pleased" and "resolved" to "willing" and "consent."[65] Considering Moses's remark about being a sojourner in a foreign land, it seems more fitting to interpret "agreed" as expressing "consent" rather than signifying determination or excitement.[66] We might view this consent to stay with Reuel as Moses's second adoption, marking a transformation in his identity from a refugee to a sojourner.[67]

Hence, his settling down in Midian with Reuel, his father-in-law, characterizes the second part of Moses's in-between life.[68] Now, Moses has a place to settle, a wife to love, a family on whom to depend, and a job to do.[69] But

---

64. So far in Exodus 1–3, twelve daughters appear (two midwives, a daughter of Levi, Moses's sister, Pharaoh's daughter, and the seven daughters of Reuel). Scholars have noticed that these twelve daughters play crucial roles in the founding of the nation of Israel with twelve tribes. By including twelve daughters in the beginning chapters of Exodus, the author may hint at the counter-cultural way of God – using unlikely means to achieve rescue. See Meyers, *Exodus*, 37. Roth, *Hyphenating Moses*, 132.
65. *BDB*, 383–384. Other translations include: "ready to stay" (Noth, 28); "consented to stay," Nahum M. Sarna, *Exodus: The JPS Torah Commentary* (Philadelphia: The Jewish Publication Society, 1991), 12; "Delighted to live," Durham, *Exodus*, 21; "Agreeable to stay," Brevard S. Childs, *The Book of Exodus: A Critical, Theological Commentary*, (OTL; Philadelphia: Westminster, 1974), 27. Walter Brueggemann, *The Book of Exodus*, New Interpreter's Bible, vol. 1 (Nashville: Abingdon, 1994), 702. Enns, *Exodus*, 72.
66. The same volitional force is evident in Joshua 7:7; Judges 17:11; 19:6.
67. Ngwa, *Let My People Live*, 107.
68. Reuel's hospitality toward Moses is reflected in his wise counsel to Moses in chapter 18. While the friendliness of Reuel to Moses in Exodus 2 stands in contrast to Pharaoh's discrimination against the Hebrews, Reuel's friendliness to Moses in Exodus 18 forms a contrast to the Amalekites' hostility toward the Hebrews.
69. Exodus 3:1 reveals Moses as a shepherd in Midian.

is Moses truly at home with himself in this new setting? How will he make sense of his dual upbringing as both Egyptian and Hebrew? And the husband of a Midianite woman or even a Midianite shepherd? What will become of his passion for justice? And what about the fate of his fellow Hebrew slaves in Egypt? Does Moses view Midian as an in-between space, or has he found his permanent home?

It is from the narrator's viewpoint that the phrase "settle down" is used of Moses (2:15b, 21). This represents how a third party perceives Moses and does not necessarily reflect Moses's own perspective. At times, the distinction between a "settler" and a "sojourner" can become obscure; without personal identification, it may be challenging to classify individuals into either category.[70]

Sojourning

The narrative does not disclose Moses's own perception of himself and his life while dwelling in Midian. Does he perceive himself as an Egyptian, a Hebrew, a Midianite, or perhaps as a Hebrew-Egyptian residing in Midian? To which community does he feel a sense of belonging? With which people does he identify? Where will he go from there? The sole lens through which to gain insights into Moses's inner thoughts and feelings during this in-between phase is his naming of his son, as recounted in Exodus 2:22: "Then she bore a son and he called his name 'Gershom' for he said, 'A *ger* I have been in a foreign land.'"[71]

Through the naming of his son, Moses reveals his sense of cognitive dissonance. The name "Gershom" is composed of two Hebrew words – *ger* (which means "sojourner") and *sham* (which means "there") – that together mean "sojourner there." Furthermore, the name is also a wordplay, with the verb *garash* meaning "to drive out." This verb appears earlier in the narrative, describing the shepherds driving out (*garash*) the daughters of Reuel from the well where they were drawing water for the flock (2:17). Therefore, we can infer that Moses regarded himself as a *ger* in a foreign land. In the Hebrew Bible, a *ger* is someone who is disconnected from their original social context and now lives in a new setting where they lack the same privileges as the natives. A *ger* resides

---

70. Hanciles categorized the migrants into four groups: settlers, sojourners, itinerants, and invaders. "Settlers" includes captives, slaves, diasporas, and refugees. "Sojourners" are those who plan to return to their home country, which includes seasonal laborers, merchants, diplomats, exiles or deportees, refugees, and asylum seekers. See Hanciles, *Migration and the Making of Global Christianity*, 25–26. The social status of Moses while he was in Midian fits the category of "settlers," though he may also fit the category of "sojourners."
71. My translation.

permanently among the members of the new society, yet does not become fully one of them and lacks a sense of belonging to any particular social group.[72] In other words, to be a *ger* is to be in-between – in this case, in-between a free Israelite citizen and a slave, in-between a native and a foreigner.[73]

In the Hebrew Bible, a *ger* is classified along with widows and orphans as someone in need of social justice.[74] Thus, to be a *ger* is to exist in a vulnerable state with a conflicted identity because one is neither fully one thing nor another. Similarly, people living in the diaspora – depending on their socio-economic or political situation – can easily become nonresident persons or undocumented migrants, who are often marginalized in society and do not enjoy proper rights. In American terminology, such individuals are referred to as "nonresident aliens." The term "alien," by definition, denotes their foreign and outsider status.

Moses identifies himself as a *ger*, one who is in between the Hebrews, the Egyptians, and the Midianites, without fully belonging to any of these cultures. He is not a free Egyptian since he is a fugitive. He is not a Hebrew slave as he does not suffer with them as a slave. He is not a free Midianite because he is in a dependent relationship with Reuel while living in Midian. A *ger* is how Moses sees himself – a nobody who belongs nowhere and is going nowhere. While an observer may view Moses's stay in Midian as a time of "settling down," he himself interprets it differently – as evident in the naming of his son – as the in-between state of a temporary and transient sojourn.

Feeling like a *ger* must have been a devastating experience for Moses, yet little did he know that there were profound historical and theological implications of being a *ger*. The motif of *ger* dates back to God's promise to Abram: "You shall surely know that your seed [collective] will be a *ger* in the land not theirs" (Gen 15:13).[75] Abram was himself a *ger* (Gen 23:4; 35:27). According to later law codes, having been a *ger* in the land of Egypt becomes the motivation for the Israelites to protect the *gerim* (plural of *ger*) in their land.[76] God reminded the Israelites not to oppress the *gerim* when they entered Canaan because the Israelites themselves had once been *gerim* in Egypt; similarly, God

---

72. Gorospe, *Narrative and Identity*, 162.
73. Christiana Van Houten, *The Alien in Israelite Law* (JSOTSupp 107; Sheffield: Sheffield Academic Press, 1991), 59. D. Kellermann, גֵּר *TDOT* I:443.
74. Van Houten, *The Alien in Israelite Law*, 35, 94. The laws regarding the protection of the sojourners include Leviticus 25:35, 47; Deuteronomy 10:18; 24:17, 19. These laws are all apodictic laws, indicating their absolute nature.
75. My translation.
76. For example, Exodus 22:20; 23:9; Leviticus 19:34; 25:23; Deuteronomy 10:19.

intended Moses to experience what it was like to be a *ger* so that he could understand the *gerim* experience of the Israelites later on. The "*ger*" status of Moses thus points backward to God's promise to the patriarchs and forward to Israel's experience as *ger* in Egypt before the exodus event. This concept of *ger* is fundamental to Israel's self-understanding and identity formation.[77] For Moses, being a *ger* was like experiencing another "exodus in person," but this time, it is a "*ger* in person" experience.

The status of a *ger* is, by definition, linked to land matters. When Moses says, "A *ger* I have been in a foreign land," to which land is he referring? Is it Midian, Egypt, or both? Some scholars posit that it is Midian because Moses stayed in Midian, expressing his feelings of displacement.[78] Some scholars think that Midian is a place of sojourn and a settled home because of a loving wife and son.[79] Others suggest that it is Egypt, since the name of Moses's son, *gershom*, means "sojourner there." "There" is in contrast to "here." If "here" refers to Midian, then "there" means Egypt.[80] Since Moses uses the perfect tense "I have been" instead of the imperfect "I am," I suggest that he is referring to his past in Egypt. The reference to "there" also supports this interpretation. However, given that Moses consented to settle in Midian, the foreign land can also allude to Midian since he was not a full citizen in Midian but was in a dependent relationship with his father-in-law.[81] Therefore, it is more likely that he felt like a *ger* in both Egypt and Midian. He felt like a *ger* among the Egyptians in Egypt and among the Hebrews in Egypt. Moses was indeed a "threefold *ger*."

Moses's experience of being in-between was not solely due to being a migrant or a minority in a foreign land but could also have been a result of his conflicted identity.[82] The name "Gershom" encapsulates Moses's experiences in this in-between space. Moses experiences an "exodus" event by going out

---

77. R. J. D. Knauth, "Alien, Foreign Resident," in *DOTP*, 26.
78. For example, Enns, *Exodus*, 84, n. 17.
79. Durham, *Exodus*, 24. Childs interprets this along the same lines, considering Midian as Moses's home. See Brevard S. Childs, *The Book of Exodus: A Critical, Theological Commentary*, (OTL; Philadelphia: Westminster, 1974), 32.
80. For example, Sarna, *Exodus: The JPS Torah Commentary*, 13; Brueggemann, *The Book of Exodus*, 704.
81. Moses's relationship with his father-in-law is the focus of his life in Midian. His marriage is secondary to that relationship.
82. See Gorospe's insightful analysis on Moses's identity that involves ambivalence in the text as well as in the geographical location of Midian that symbolically marks Moses's lack of identity. The loss of a sense of identity results in the sense of being lost between two worlds and present in both worlds at the same time. Gorospe, *Narrative and Identity*, 278–280.

from Egypt. Then he embodies Israel's *ger* status by becoming a *ger* himself. This *ger* experience enables Moses to identify with Israel's suffering. His journey in Midian evokes memories of the patriarchs as narrated in Genesis 24 and 29, which include stories of sojourners, women at the well, an invitation to a family feast, a marriage, and a child.[83] This type-scene once again reflects Moses's identity formation as both a continuation of Israel's ancestral memory and a prefiguring of Israel's future identity formation.

In the contemporary diaspora context, people frequently migrate, settle down, and move back to their countries of origin or relocate elsewhere. Where is home? At each new residence, one may feel like a *ger* – not fully belonging but not intending to leave either. This in-betweenness may embody the vulnerability inherent in a liminal state. For Moses, this liminal existence during his time in Midian was not the end of his journey.

2:23–25 A Purposeful In-betweenness

The passing of Pharaoh signifies a new epoch in history. Verse 23 introduces a new scene: "During that long period, the king of Egypt died" (2:23). The Israelites were groaning under the bondage of slavery, and their plea for help ascended to God.

Within the broader context of the Exodus narrative, the birth of Moses and his period of in-betweenness occurs in the midst of Israel's period of slavery in Egypt. In other words, Moses's birth takes place amid Israel's suffering. Therefore, the trio of spatial verbs – "going out," "settling down," and "sojourning" – symbolize the phase between Moses's birth and his call, and positions Moses between Israel's past and future, between God's promise and his rescue, and between the Abrahamic and Sinaitic covenants. These three spatial verbs evoke God's covenant with Abraham while also foreshadowing the grander purpose of the Pentateuch – the exodus of the Israelites to form a holy nation that will be a Yahweh-worshiping community who will dwell in the land of Canaan and be governed by the Sinaitic covenant.

God's covenant with Abraham focuses on two key themes and promises: the land and the seed. In one way or another, the three spatial verbs discussed earlier revolve around these two covenantal themes. For instance, when God makes the promise regarding the seed, he tells Abram, "One who shall go forth [*yatsa*] from your own body, he will be your heir" (Gen 15:4).[84] The same

---
83. Bills, *The Theology of Justice in Exodus*, 103.
84. My translation.

verb is also used to describe God's deliverance of the Israelites from Egypt, which is the first step toward forming a holy nation. The verb "settling down" (*yashav*) – "stayed" and "had been living" in the NIV – is employed when Abram dwells in the land of Canaan (Gen 13:6; 16:3). Later, it is used to describe God's desire to dwell with the Israelites (Exod 25:8; 29:45–46; Num 5:3; 35:34; Deut 12:11) and the Israelites' future dwelling in Canaan (Lev 20:22; Deut 12:29; 30:20).

In addition, Moses's sojourning experience points backward to God's promise to Abram that his descendants would be *ger* in a foreign land (Gen 15:13) and forward to Israel's experience of living as *ger* in Egypt. The Sinaitic covenant specifically exhorts the Israelites to treat the *ger* in their midst with justice and compassion. For instance, God instructs Moses to remind the Israelites not to wrong or oppress sojourners (Exod 22:21; 23:9), to pay them their wages (Deut 24:14–15), to ensure they receive justice (Deut 24:17), and when reaping the harvest to deliberately leave the gleanings for them to gather (Lev 19:10; 23:22; Deut 24:19–22).

Moses goes out, settles down, and sojourns. The Israelites also go out, settle down, and sojourn. In this sense, Moses's experiences prefigure Israel's future experiences. Being in this in-between state places one in a dialectical relationship between God's past promises and future deliverance. Four active verbs mark God's response to the cry of his people: God heard; God remembered; God saw; and God knew (2:24–25).[85] God's hearing and seeing both trigger memories, and memories result in empathy,[86] prompting God to remember his covenant with Abraham, Isaac, and Jacob. In response, God calls Moses to return to Egypt to bring the Israelites out of that land of bondage (3:7–10). In the larger purpose of God's redemptive plan, Moses stands between the Abrahamic covenant and the Sinaitic covenant.[87] In retrospect, we can see how Moses plays a key role in transforming the nation of Israel from slaves in Egypt to a holy nation marching toward the promised land, moving forward in fulfillment of God's promises to Abraham.[88] The idea of "God knew" reflects

---

85. In the NIV, "God heard . . . he remembered . . . God looked . . . and was concerned."
86. Volf and McAnnally-Linz, *The Home of God*, 37.
87. Commentators generally agree that the Sinaitic covenant was subsumed under the Abrahamic covenant. Bernhard W. Anderson, *Contours of Old Testament Theology* (Minneapolis: Fortress, 1999), 137.
88. Phan states that being betwixt and between can bring about personal and societal transformation and enrichment. Phan, *Christianity with an Asian Face*, 235.

his keen awareness and empathy toward the suffering of his people, and this awareness precedes his plan of redemption.[89]

God's call is decisive in transforming Moses's experience in Midian, making it a mere in-between state rather than a permanent condition. This divine call forges a new identity and purpose for Moses in his mission to lead the Israelites out of Egypt.[90] "God saw" (NIV, "looked on") in Exodus 2:25 forms an *inclusio* with "Moses saw" (NIV, "watched") in Exodus 2:11. Nevertheless, what transforms the plight of the suffering Israelites is what "God saw" rather than what "Moses saw." What defines Moses's purpose during his in-between existence is God's call rather than his inner desire for justice. Moses's initial attempt to take justice into his own hands failed. Only after going through the in-between experience did God call Moses to seek and practice justice among his people, as reflected in the Deuteronomic and priestly laws that emphasize the importance of safeguarding the rights of sojourners.[91]

God does not call Moses while he is still a prince of Egypt but only after he has become a *ger* in the land of Midian, which suggests that Moses's in-between status signifies his divine selection as God's servant.[92] This experience of in-betweenness is part of God's plan since Moses is meant to undergo the exodus as an individual before Israel undergoes this experience as a nation. Through his personal exodus from Egypt to Midian, Moses becomes the embodiment of "incarnation," he serves as the mediator, conveying God's word to his people and bringing the people back to God.[93]

Moses's experiences of going out, settling down, and sojourning have profound significance. In his in-between space, Moses embodies the Israelites' future journey and binds them to God's covenant. In God's grander desire to honor his promises to Abraham, Moses emerges as the critical mediator

---

89. Avivah Gottlieb Zornberg, *The Particulars of Rupture: Reflections on Exodus* (New York: Schocken Books, 2001), 35.
90. Gorospe, *Narrative and Identity*, 230. Dumbrell points out that the call of Abram is an "elective call," as is the call of Moses. William J. Dumbrell, *Covenant and Creation: A Theology of Old Testament Covenants* (Nashville: Thomas Nelson, 1984), 57. Roth sees God's call of Moses as God's avowal of Moses's liminality. Roth, *Hyphenating Moses*, 152.
91. Van Houten traces these laws pertaining to sojourners from the Pre-Deuteronomic laws, to the Deuteronomic laws, and the Priestly laws. Van Houten, *The Alien in Israelite Law*, 52–57.
92. Jung Young Lee, *Marginality* (113), drawn from Sang Hyun Lee, "Called to Be Pilgrims: Toward a Theology within the Korean Immigrant Context," in *The Korean Immigrant in America*, eds. Byong-Suh Kim and Sang Hyun Lee (Montclair: AACS, 1980), 48. Jung Young Lee and Sang Hyun Lee seem to use the terms "marginality" and "in-betweenness" as synonyms.
93. Anderson, *Contours of Old Testament Theology*, 154.

between Abraham and Israel, between God and Israel, and between slavery and rescue.[94]

In the Chinese diaspora, identity is closely intertwined with a person's migration experience, and there is fluidity in the boundaries between one's "homeland" and one's place of residence. Many diasporans have accepted this fluidity as a reality. Around the world, many in the diaspora have embraced Christianity. Through their conversion experiences amid migrations, God has a grander purpose for the Chinese diaspora: their very dispersion serves as a means for spreading the gospel, and drawing people to God. For example, many of my students come from China or other parts of Asia. After graduating, some of them serve as pastors in Chinese immigrant churches within the United States, and Christianity has spread through these migrants. While some opt to return to Asia, bringing their experiences and resources back home, others travel between the United States and Asia, establishing connections that serve the spread of the gospel.

In today's Chinese diaspora, people "go out," "settle down," and "sojourn." Like Moses, in each of our unique in-between spaces, we can find hope in knowing that being in-between may be part of God's redemptive purpose, a purpose that extends beyond ourselves. The identity of a sojourner – as a migrant and a minority within the diaspora – takes on a redemptive significance when viewed from God's macro and missional perspective.

God's heart for liberation and his saving actions do not apply to any one people or to just the Chinese diaspora but are relevant to all people. Throughout history, the exodus narrative has been a story of hope for African Americans, whose lives of slavery, oppression, and discrimination led them to identify with the Israelites in the Bible. "A story of redemption and liberation, freedom and hope, and the promise of God's faithfulness – became their story."[95] Historically, the people of Africa identified closely with the enslaved Israelites. In their context, Pharaoh symbolized the slave master, Moses represented a freedom fighter, and God was seen as being on the side of the

---

94. Hendel expands the role of Moses as a mediator into other areas such as the ruling authority between Pharaoh and Yahweh and linage relations as Moses is a Levi who has no land and thus becomes a mediator of all the other tribes. Hendel, "Exodus in Biblical Memory," 618–619.
95. David W. Kling, "Let My People Go": Exodus in the African American Experience," in *The Bible in History: How the Texts Have Shaped the Times*, ed. David W. Kling (Oxford: Oxford University Press, 2004), 193–230. Historically, Pharaoh has been identified with white slave owners, racists, and general oppression, and the oppressed identify themselves with the Hebrew slaves.

oppressed. The Exodus narrative becomes a "taproot of liberation theology in its varieties of expressions."[96]

3:1–4:31 MEETING GOD IN UNEXPECTED PLACES

Many people in Asia may either identify as atheists or adhere to various local and folk religions. When they migrate to new lands, their old ways of life may adapt to accommodate new ways of living and different perceptions of the world, including the practice of faith. Having identified as an atheist before coming to the United States, I have encountered numerous individuals who, like me, have encountered God unexpectedly while in a new land, causing them to abandon their atheism or former religion and embrace the Christian faith. Physically relocating to a new land often initiates a new intellectual or spiritual journey that opens doors to meet God in unexpected ways.

Moses's identity struggle as a *ger* in Midian takes a dramatic turn in chapters 3 and 4 through his divine encounter. This identity struggle of finding oneself a "sojourner" (*ger*) can be resolved only when a person views it through the divine lens of God relocating people for his own purposes. Augustine of Hippo (354–430 CE) beautifully stated in his *Confessions*, "Because you made us for yourself, our hearts find no peace until they rest in you."[97] For those in the diaspora, their dispersion from their homeland is often not simply a physical displacement but represents a search for a larger purpose beyond oneself. Many Chinese diasporans have found this purpose through their conversion to Christianity while studying, working, or living abroad. Like me, many of them became Christians in the United States, especially in college or graduate school, an experience that decisively altered the trajectories of our lives. I turned from being an atheist to teaching Scripture at a seminary, while many others serve faithfully in their local churches, engage in missions, or are involved in various forms of ministry to spread the gospel so that more people will become Yahweh worshipers. During my travels to different parts of the world, I have witnessed Chinese churches and Christians actively engaged in the propagation of the gospel. This global propagation of Christianity by Chinese diasporans reflects the adventures and unexpected divine encounters that make up life's journey, particularly for those living far from their homeland.

---

96. Fentress-Williams, "Exodus," 83–84.
97. Augustine, *Confessions*, trans. R. S. Pine-Coffin (New York: Penguin Classics, 1961), 21.

3:1–6 The Burning Bush Encounter

Chapter 3 marks a new chapter in Moses's life as he tends the flock of his father-in-law, the priest of Midian. "Tending the flock" stands in stark contrast to his previous life as a royal prince in Egypt. Relocating to a new place, whether by choice or necessity, often entails a shift in one's profession, identity, and status. For 40 years, tending the flock was Moses's new job. On this particular day, Moses probably went about his usual routine, anticipating another ordinary day with the sheep. However, he happened to lead the flock into the wilderness and eventually arrived at Horeb, the mountain of God. "Horeb" means "wasteland" in Hebrew, yet this apparent "wasteland" becomes the site of God's rich self-revelation and divine encounters. From a divine perspective, what may appear to be a wasteland can become holy ground. It was there in this wasteland that the angel of God appeared to Moses in a blazing fire from within a bush.[98]

This extraordinary sight piques Moses's curiosity and holds his gaze. While Moses is observing this strange sight, God calls out to him from within the burning bush: "Moses, Moses!" Moses responds, "Here I am" (3:4).[99] God then commands Moses to remove his sandals because the ground he stood on was holy. God alone demarcates what is wasteland and what is holy ground. The place where we reside may appear to be a wasteland, but it could also be holy ground where God's presence dwells. God introduces himself to Moses: "I am the God of your father, the God of Abraham, the God of Isaac and the God of Jacob" (3:6a).

Many Asians, including Chinese people, remove their shoes when entering their own or another's home, regardless of whether they are residing in their own Asian culture or a Western culture. Shoes are seen as carrying "dirt" and "dust," and stepping into someone's home is considered entering a "new domain" at the invitation of the host. Therefore, removing one's shoes is a gesture of respect for the host and the home one enters. Most Chinese people automatically remove their shoes upon entering another's home unless the host insists that they need not do so.[100] The ancient Hebrew culture shares this

---

98. "Bush" (*seneh*) in Hebrew sounds like "Sinai," a foreshadowing of what Moses will see at the appearance of God on Mount Sinai in Exodus 19. God later will appear as a pillar of fire in Israel's journey to the Promised Land (13:21; 40:38).
99. In Hebrew, "Here I am" (*hinneni*) means "yes, I am here." It connotes a sense of alertness to respond to the one who calls but it does not imply the person will obey and do what he hears.
100. First-generation migrants usually keep this shoe-removing practice. It may not be the same for the second or third generation American-born Chinese. Removing shoes or not then would depend on each person's ethnic identification and family tradition.

custom with the Asian people, a practice that God clearly regards as significant. When God instructs Moses to remove his sandals, it signifies that the place where Moses is standing is God's temporary home. The symbolic gesture of removing one's sandals shows absolute respect for God's "house rules."

In God's self-revelation to Moses, he chooses to establish a connection with Moses through his familial lineage: "I am the God of your father" (3:6a). The mention of Abraham, Isaac, and Jacob also recalls God's covenant with the patriarchs (see also 2:25). Earlier, in chapter 2, Moses identified with his Hebrew kinspeople despite living in the Egyptian palace (2:11), which suggests that his Hebrew mother probably played a role in shaping his ethnic identity.[101] Moses's initial reaction upon encountering God was that he "hid his face because he was afraid to look at God" (3:6b). This response parallels that of Adam and Eve in the garden of Eden after eating the forbidden fruit (Gen 3:8). Moses's fear probably did not stem from wrongdoing but, rather, reflects the sense of awe experienced when encountering the mysterious, superior, and transcendent Other. This encounter with the transcendent profoundly alters the trajectory of Moses's journey.

3:7–12 The Divine Call

God reveals that his purpose in meeting with Moses is to appoint him as the deliverer who will lead the Israelites out of Egypt. This divine calling gives Moses a sense of purpose and a reason to align his life with God's overarching narrative. From a micro perspective, Moses's calling may seem significant only to him and the Israelites. From a macro perspective, however, it reflects a God who is on a mission – a mission that begins with creation and continues despite the fall, working toward redemption and hope, for the ultimate glory of God's name that is exalted above all else.[102] Realizing God's grand purpose becomes a defining moment in one's identity formation and transformation.

A call narrative usually includes the following elements:
1. Theophany (3:1–4a)
2. Introductory word (3:4b–9)

---

101. Jochebed's name (the mother of Moses) is not mentioned until Exodus 6:20. Jochebed has received a warm reception in the Chinese Christian context as pastors credit Moses's spirituality and his affection for his Hebrew brothers to his Hebrew mother. Jochebed appears as one of the female characters in sermons delivered on Mother's Day.
102. For a detailed mapping of God's grand narrative for Israel and for humanity, see Christopher J. H. Wright, *The Mission of God: Unlocking the Bible's Grand Narrative* (Downers Grove: IVP Academic, 2006), 64.

3. Divine commission (3:10)
4. Objection (3:11)
5. Reassurance (3:12a)
6. Sign (3:12b)

The call of Moses reflects a variation of this basic structure, suggesting that the narrator portrays the call of Moses within the framework of the prophetic tradition.[103]

In Exodus 3:1–9, God speaks directly using the first-person "I" voice, reflecting God's innermost emotions and persona within his divinity.[104] This "I" voice "humanizes" God, enabling us as humans to relate to him. God emphatically declares, "I have indeed seen," repeating the first-person pronoun twice – by the pronoun "I" and the verb "I have seen" in the Hebrew text. God has seen, heard, and known the suffering of the Israelites – echoing the narrator's third-person remarks in Exodus 2:24–25. Therefore, God declares, "I have come down" to rescue the Israelites from the Egyptians and bring them to a good and spacious land, flowing with milk and honey (3:8). Here, God's deep concern for the affliction of the Israelites (Exod 3:9–10) and his plans for their rescue replace the long silence of God in chapters 1–2. The cry of the Israelites (3:9) parallels their earlier cry for help in Exodus 2:23, while the Egyptians' oppression harkens back to and echoes Exodus 1:11–22.

God's plan for Israel was to bring them to a good land, which we now know to be Canaan. Deuteronomy provides further details about the goodness of this land:

> "a land with large, flourishing cities ... houses filled with all kinds of good things ... wells ... and vineyards and olive groves" (Deut 6:10–11);

> "a land with brooks, streams, and deep springs gushing out into the valleys and hills; a land with wheat and barley, vines and fig trees, pomegranates, olive oil and honey; a land where bread will not be scarce and you will lack nothing; a land where the rocks are iron and you can dig copper out of the hills" (Deut 8:7–9);

---

103. Fretheim, *Exodus*, 51.
104. Leung Lai provides a critical methodology for the interdisciplinary study of this "I" voice in the Hebrew Bible. Barbara M. Leung Lai, *Through the "I"- Window: The Inner Life of Characters in the Hebrew Bible* (Sheffield: Sheffield Phoenix, 2011), 16–18.

and, above all, a land chosen by God – "a land the LORD your God cares for; the eyes of the LORD your God are continually on it from the beginning of the year to its end" (Deut 11:12).

While in Egypt during Joseph's time, Israel lived in a good land called Goshen, where they prospered, acquired property, and increased greatly in number (Gen 47:6, 27). However, Goshen was not their permanent home, and they were subject to the shifts in the political and socioeconomic conditions of the host country. But Canaan, God's promised land, was intended as their permanent home on earth – on the condition that they obeyed God's covenant. God intended to lead Israel to a place they could call a true home. Though we may encounter "Goshens" in our own migration journeys, these places are not meant to be permanent homes and cannot fully satisfy our deeper need for belonging. Only when we settle in a place that meets our spiritual, emotional, and physical needs can we truly call it home. For Israel, Canaan was that home.

Then God says to Moses, "So now, go. I am sending you to Pharaoh to bring my people the Israelites out of Egypt" (3:10). Despite the clarity of this call, Moses struggles to accept it. After being a shepherd for 40 years, Moses is no longer an Egyptian prince living in a palace. He has become a "commoner," busy with mundane chores and managing his family business. He no longer has big dreams for the future. His passion for justice and compassion belong to the distant past. Moses's first response reflects his self-doubt: "Who am I that I should go to Pharaoh and bring the Israelites out of Egypt?" (3:11). This question may reveal Moses's uncertainty and his doubts about God's choice of himself. Perhaps Moses wonders: Who am I to lead the Israelites out of Egypt? I am a despised shepherd, a nobody of whom no one will take notice. How could someone like me possibly lead the Israelites out of Egypt? Quite apart from Pharaoh, will even the Israelites listen to me?

God then assures Moses of his presence, which resolves Moses's self-doubt. As a sign of his promised presence, God tells Moses, "When you have brought the people out of Egypt, you will worship God on this mountain" (3:12). "This mountain" refers to Mount Horeb – also known as "the mountain of God" (3:1). The ritualist would identify this mountain as a sacred pilgrimage site.[105] The word "worship" (*'abad*) can also be translated as "serve" or "work" and is the same word used to describe the Israelites "working" on Pharaoh's building

---

105. Victor and Victor, *Image and Pilgrimage*, 22.

projects (1:13–14). This double entendre in God's call is an invitation for the Israelites to transition from serving Pharaoh and laboring on his building projects to serving God and working on God's project – the construction of the tabernacle. God's call marks a pivotal moment in transforming both Moses and the plight of the Israelites. God's call interrupts Moses's ordinary experience in Midian and infuses a sense of purpose into a seemingly meaningless existence. In other words, God's call beckons Moses to become the person God intended him to be, forging his new identity as a divine messenger, a mediator between God and Israel, and a servant of God. This encounter with God in the wasteland at Horeb catches Moses by surprise, demonstrating that God can manifest himself in unexpected places and that turning points in our lives may occur when we least expect them.

3:13–4:17 Doubt and Decision

Upon encountering God, Moses does not react with excitement and awe but, instead, expresses doubts and offers excuses. Having questioned his own identity with the question "Who am I?" (3:11), he then proceeds to inquire about God's identity, asking, in effect: "Who are you? What is your name? What should I tell the Israelites about your identity?" (see 3:13). The Hebrew text presents Moses as constructing a hypothetical dialogue in his mind, anticipating the questions that the Israelites might ask him. Exodus 3:13 records Moses's words to God: "Suppose I go to the Israelites and say to them, 'The God of your fathers has sent me to you,' and they ask me, 'What is his name?' Then what shall I tell them?" In response, God reveals his name to Moses: "I AM WHO I AM . . . This is my name forever, the name you shall call me from generation to generation" (3:14–15).

Though its exact etymology is unclear, this name of God originates from the Hebrew word *hayah*, meaning "to be" or "to become."[106] The statement "I AM WHO I AM" reveals God's nature as the one who was, is, and will be. In the Chinese translation, this phrase is rendered as the "self-existing, forever existing one" (*zì yǐu yóng yǐu*), underscoring God as a transcendent, uncreated, omnipresent, and everlasting being.[107] All these attributes are inherent in the

---

106. Charlie Trimm and Chloe T. Sun, *Exodus 1–18*, NICOT (Grand Rapids: Eerdmans, forthcoming).
107. Goldingay states that "God is the eternal, self-sufficient, all-sufficient one, not a god who comes into being or can die, like other Middle Eastern gods, but one who simply 'is.'" This resonates well with the Chinese translation of the name of God (*zi yiu yong yiu*). John Goldingay, *Old Testament Theology: Israel's Gospel*, vol. 1 (Downers Grove: IVP Academic, 2003), 336.

verb "to be." Therefore the name of God as "to be" or "to become" implies that God "is" or "will be" whoever we need him to be, in the way in which he determines.

> ## GOD'S GENDER AND PRONOUN
>
> In the twenty-first century, the issue of gender identity confronts both Christians and non-Christians. The prevailing secular view challenges traditional family and societal norms and holds that gender is not God's creation but, rather, a matter of personal choice and social construct. Advocates of women's rights and gender equality question the notion of God as a male and protest against such a simplistic view. Similarly, individuals who identify with a gender different from their biological gender find it problematic to regard God simply as male. This gives rise to several questions: Is God male? Can God be defined by gender? Does God even have a gender? Given that most languages have only two or three pronouns to denote gender (male, female, and neuter), God is often referred to as "he" or "him."
>
> The use of masculine pronouns to refer to God is a matter of ongoing academic debate, especially in theological circles. This is because there also exists within Godhood feminine elements such as God's compassion (Exod 34:6) – compassion being a word that is also used for a woman's womb. Consequently, to refer to God simply as "he" or "him" is to oversimplify, failing to accurately reflect the nature of God. Moses, using the Hebrew language, addresses God using masculine pronouns. But can God be defined solely by masculine attributes?
>
> The Chinese language offers a solution to this theological and cultural dilemma. In Chinese, the pronoun "he" or "him" (Mandarin: tā) can be expressed in five different ways: a) He/him: a male, with the particle "man" in the character "he/him" (他); b) She/her: a female, with the particle "female" in the character "she/her" (她); c) It: an inanimate object with a particle resembling a cover (它); d) It: an animal with a particle meaning "cow," with Satan also included in this category (牠); and e) God-self: with a character element for God (祂). Therefore, the Chinese language reserves a specific pronoun for God alone, preserving God's unique status and position. The five different ways of expressing the third-person pronoun (tā) demonstrate that God is neither male nor female according to human concepts of gender. Neither is God an inanimate object or an animal. God is God. Therefore, we might

translate God's pronoun as God-element, God-particle, or God-self. According to this perspective, the God-self transcends human concepts of gender, rendering the debate over God's pronoun – if not God's gender – less significant in the Chinese mind that understands that God is simply God.[1]

---

1. For this commentary, I will use "he/him" to describe God due to the limitation of the English language. However, I understand God as neither male nor female, but Godself. Peeler's book on the gender of God raises an interesting question about the Christian perception of equating God with the male gender. Yet, in the Chinese mind, God is often conceived as a spirit and "beyond" gender confinement. Her argument that God the Father is not male is based on the annunciation narrative, where Mary was impregnated by the Holy Spirit, and no male penetration was involved in that act. Therefore, the virgin conception defies attributing God as male. The western idea of gender and the Chinese conceptual idea of God may generate fruitful discussions. See Amy Peeler, *Women and the Gender of God* (Grand Rapids: Eerdmans, 2022).

THE MULTIPLE NAMES OF GOD IN CHINESE

In the Chinese Christian tradition, there are multiple ways to address God. For example, Shén (a generic term for God), Zhǔ (the Lord), Shàng Zhǔ (the Lord above or the high Lord),[1] Shàng Dì (the emperor above), Tién Fù (the heavenly father), Yē Hé Huá (Jehovah), and the less commonly used Yahweh. Among these, Yē Hé Huá is the most popular name for God. While these names and epithets are often used interchangeably, there are sometimes disagreements about which name should be used. For example, in the 1919 Chinese Union Version of the Bible, two versions emerged with differing terminology – one version used Shàng Dì, while the other used Shén.[2]

This history of different – and sometimes competing – names for God stems from Western missionaries' efforts to translate the Bible into Chinese. These missionaries can be categorized into four groups, each with differing views about which Chinese name should be used for God: Roman Catholics (including Jesuits, Franciscans, and Dominicans) in the seventeenth and eighteenth centuries, British and American Protestants, British Anglicans, and Scottish Presbyterians in the nineteenth century. Roman Catholics used the terms Zhēn Zhǔ (True Lord), Tián Zhǔ (Heavenly Lord), and Sháng Zhǔ (High Lord). Some translators interpreted the notion of Tián (sky) as divine providence, with the character used to denote it conveying ideas of both oneness and greatness, while others rejected the syncretism of using *dì* (the Chinese term for emperor) in Shàng Dì.[3] Among the Protestant missionaries, Robert Morrison (1782–1834) favored the use of Shén as the name for God, while others – including James Legge from the London Missionary Society – supported the use of Shàng Dì. Both terms met with linguistic and cultural opposition.[4]

In Exodus 3:15, God reveals his name as "the Lord." In Hebrew, this is represented by the four capital letters YHWH, traditionally referred to as the "tetragrammaton." By adding the vowels of the word "Lord" (Hebrew: Adonai) to YHWH, the name of God becomes YaHoWaH, which is rendered Yē Hé Huá in Chinese. Although this name does not accurately reflect the Hebrew name of God, it has become the preferred name for God in China and the Chinese diaspora, popularized by the Chinese Union Version of the Bible. Perhaps it is because the syllable "Huá" also refers to the Chinese people (Huá Rén) that Yē Hé Huá is the preferred translation of the name of God in the Chinese language.[5]

In 2022, the Worldwide Bible Society, a Christian organization based in Hong Kong, launched an event inviting global Chinese Christians to vote on the best Chinese translation of God's name. Within a month, over a thousand participants from over 20 countries had cast their votes. The final result showed that fifty-four percent of voters favored Yē Hé Huá, twenty percent voted for "the Lord (zhǔ)," fifteen percent voted for "Yahweh," while the rest proposed various other options.[6] This result is not unexpected since Yē Hé Huá has become almost synonymous with the name of God in the Chinese Christian tradition, and few new Chinese translations of the Bible would attempt to challenge this status quo.

---

1. "Shang" can mean "above" or "high."
2. Jerry Hwang, *Contextualization and the Old Testament*, 67.
3. Sung-Deuk Oak, "Competing Chinese Names for God: The Chinese Term Question and Its Influence upon Korea," *Journal of Korean Religions* 3, no. 2 (2012): 90–91.
4. Oak, "Competing Chinese Names for God," 93–97.
5. *Hua Ren* is reserved mostly for the Chinese living in the diaspora or in multicultural contexts of Asian countries such as Singapore and Malaysia.
6. The form produced by the Worldwide Bible Society lists the pros and cons of each translation of God's name in Chinese. https://docs.google.com/forms/d/e/1FAIpQLScTvydOVL31HJmhNeXDE4W7pOy9yh/_Snymn7-DdZMg-1BkR_Q/viewform.

The emphatic "I have watched over [*paqad*] you" (3:16) is literally "I have indeed taken notice of you." The Hebrew term for "watched over" (*paqad*) is "I have visited you." When God visits someone, it is either to execute judgment or to care.[108] Joseph uses this same word on his deathbed when he tells his brothers that God will care for them and bring them out of Egypt to the land God had promised to their forefathers (Gen 50:24–25). The idea of visitation is also familiar to Chinese people. In the eyes of many Chinese Christians, pastors have a responsibility to visit their congregations and show care. Here, God, like one of these Chinese pastors, has seen the affliction of his people and personally visits them. But God does not stop at a pastoral visit. He intends to deliver them from their affliction. Verse 17 reiterates what God had already told Moses in verse 8. God's ultimate goal is not merely to rescue his people from their affliction but also to bring them into a land flowing with milk and honey. This promise of land is an integral part of God's covenant promise to the patriarchs, and God is determined to fulfill it.

God then tells Moses to go to the king of Egypt, along with Israel's elders, and say to Pharaoh, "The Lord, the God of the Hebrews, has met with us. Let us take a three-day journey into the wilderness to offer sacrifices to the Lord our God" (3:18). This concept of a "three-day journey" is familiar to Chinese Christians as it is similar to the idea of a "three-day retreat" that most Chinese churches conduct annually. During these retreats, the congregation typically travels to a secluded site, resides there for three days, listens to messages by a guest speaker, and engages in fellowship with one another in between sessions. This "three-day retreat" is a time for renewal and reflection as it reorients believers' lives toward God and one another. God tells Moses to lead the Israelites into the wilderness so that they can sacrifice to God – that is, worship him. The wilderness retreat symbolizes space and time for renewal and preparation for a new journey in life, marking their departure from their former life in Egypt.

In Exodus 3:19–22, God reveals to Moses what would happen to Israel, as previously made known in Genesis 15:14. God begins by declaring emphatically, "But I know that" (3:19). The omniscient God foreknew that Pharaoh's heart would be hardened.[109] God knew that Pharaoh would not release the Israelites unless compelled by a strong hand – God's mighty hand. In Hebrew

---

108. *BDB*, 823.
109. "Strong" in 3:19 is the same word to describe Pharaoh's hardened heart (Exod 7:13, 22; 8:15; 9:35).

anatomy, "hand" and "arm" signify strength and power. In the Egyptian context, the pharaohs are often depicted as having a raised hand to defeat their enemies.[110] Here, it is God's strong hand that will be raised against Pharaoh's strong hand. God promises to stretch out his hand to strike Egypt with great wonders until Pharaoh relents and releases the Israelites. Later chapters detail how God's wonders are displayed. God also tells Moses that Israel will plunder the Egyptians when they leave Egypt (3:22) and explains that this will happen because God will grant Israel favor in the eyes of the Egyptians so that they will give the Israelites articles of silver and gold, as well as clothing. Therefore, Israel will, after all, receive "wages" for their hard labor.[111] Furthermore, the silver and gold will be used to construct the tabernacle. The underlying message here is that, ultimately, history unfolds according to God's divine purposes.

Despite God's eloquent and persuasive arguments, Moses remains unconvinced and poses another question: "What if they do not believe me or listen to me and say, 'The LORD did not appear to you'?" (4:1) To address this concern, God instructs Moses to perform two signs as proof that he was sent by God. The first sign was to turn his staff into a serpent (*nakhash*) and then back into a staff (4:2–5).[112] The Egyptians venerated the goddess Wadjet, whose cobra image appears on the pharaoh's crown. Her name means the "green one," which refers both to the serpent's color and the color of the Delta's papyrus swamps, which the Egyptians believed this goddess had created. The royal uraeus on the head of the pharaoh conveys a dual message of sovereignty and destruction, as if the serpent is rising up in anger, ready to spit flames in defense of Pharaoh.[113] In the Hindu religion, the deity Shiva also has a cobra around his neck.[114] This first sign would have been a familiar one to Moses. If the Israelites still did not believe him, then, says God, Moses should perform

---

110. In the Narmer palette housed in the Egyptian Museum in Cairo, pharaoh Narmer from the First Dynasty, is depicted with a raised right hand against a prisoner. A photo can be seen from White, *Everyday Life in Ancient Egypt*, 21.
111. These articles of silver and gold can be seen as Israel's "booty." Fretheim, *Exodus*, 67.
112. The word in Exodus 7:9–10 is *tannin*, a serpent or dragon-like creature. In the Old Testament, a serpent (Gen 3:1; Num 21:9; Ps 140:3 [Hebrew 140:4]; Isa 27:1; Jer 46:22) or *tannin* (Gen 1:21; Ps 91:13; Jer 51:34) often symbolizes chaos. Sometimes the words are used interchangeably, both denoting serpents (Job 26:13; Ps 91:13). In the ancient Chinese context, the dragon is perceived as a mythic creature. The motif of slaying the dragon permeates the Old Testament. See Morales, *Exodus Old and New*, 54–59.
113. George Hart, *The Routledge Dictionary of Egyptian Gods and Goddesses*, 2nd ed. (London: Routledge, 2005), 161. See also the drawing of the uraeus on the same page.
114. George and Swarup, "Exodus," 84.

the second sign – turn his healthy hand leprous ("white as snow") and then restore it to its original state (4:6–7).

Tradition says that the Chinese people are the "descendants of the dragon" (*lóng de chuán rén*) and that the Chinese emperors themselves embody the dragon, which has long been considered a positive symbol of royalty. There is even a well-known Chinese song titled *lóng de chuán rén*, that has been popular since the 1970s. Images of dragons appear in ancient Chinese architecture and traditional Lunar New Year decorations. The Chinese zodiac even has a year of the dragon, and the dragon is a popular logo on Chinese people's business cards. However, Chinese readers should not confuse the negative portrayal of the biblical serpent or dragon with the seemingly positive connotation of the dragon (*lóng*) in the Chinese context.[115] Unlike in ancient Near Eastern iconography, images of dragons rarely appear in fight or combat scenes in Chinese royal contexts.[116]

God gives Moses additional instructions about what to do in case the Israelites refuse to believe the first two signs. He instructs Moses to take water from the Nile and pour it on the ground, saying that this water will turn into blood (4:8–9). In short, God has anticipated every possible scenario to persuade Moses to accept the task. Despite God's efforts, Moses remains reluctant and seems determined to evade the call by coming up with a variety of excuses.

Moses now appeals to his own perceived weakness, claiming that he is "slow of speech and tongue" (4:10). The expression is literally "heavy of speech and heavy of tongue," which could mean that he lacks fluency or has a speech impediment, or perhaps that his Hebrew and Egyptian language skills have become rusty during his 40 years as a shepherd in Midian. Living in the diaspora can cause people to lose touch with their homeland and their mother tongue. The way they speak may differ from the speech of those currently residing in their countries of origin. In addition, their newly acquired language – for example, British English, American English, Australian English, German, or French – may carry an accent that distinguishes them as non-native speakers. This accent can make them feel like "perpetual foreigners," regardless of how

---

115. The dragon appears in the book of Revelation, which alludes to the serpent in Genesis 3 and Satan. The appearance of the dragon shifts from being a reference to the primordial chaos at creation to the eschaton where it will be defeated (Isa 27:1; Rev 12:9). See J. W. Van Henten, "Dragon," in *DDD*, 266.
116. Some of the Ancient Near Eastern dragon images in combat appear in Othmar Keel, *The Symbolism of the Biblical World: Ancient Near Eastern Iconography and the Book of Psalms*, trans. Timothy J. Hallett (Winona Lake: Eisenbrauns, 1997), 52–54.

long they have lived in their host countries. Whether Moses is genuinely deficient in speech or is simply making an excuse, God uses his "deficiency" for a good purpose. Later, God uses Moses's "heavy tongue" (in Hebrew, 4:10) to combat Pharaoh's "heavy heart" (in Hebrew, 7:14; 8:15, 32; 9:7, 35). God reminds Moses that he created the human mouth and reassures him with this promise: "I will help you speak and will teach you what to say" (4:11–12).

Up to this point, Moses has, in essence, voiced three objections to God's call: What is your name? What if they don't believe me? I don't know how to speak. These objections encompass his concerns about God, the Israelites, and Moses himself. Although God has patiently addressed each of these concerns, Moses remains unconvinced. It appears that he had already made up his mind that he was not the right person for the job. After exhausting all possible excuses and reasons, Moses makes a final plea: "Pardon your servant, Lord. Please send someone else" (4:13). This blunt statement reveals what had truly been in his heart all along – Moses had never wanted to do what God had asked him to do.

In Chinese culture, not all Christians aspire to become ministers or pastors. Even when called by God to enter full-time ministry, some may be reluctant to follow through for various reasons such as the difficulties of supporting their families financially, feelings of unworthiness, a perceived lack of abilities, or fear of public speaking. People in such situations can certainly empathize with Moses's struggles.

Since first appearing to Moses, God has shown remarkable patience with him, but when Moses refuses to yield, God's anger burns against him (4:14). In response to Moses's reluctance, God revises his plan. Previously, God intended Moses and the elders of Israel to go to Pharaoh and speak to him (3:18). Now, instead of the elders, God announces that Aaron will serve as Moses's mouthpiece. God reassures Moses, using an emphatic first-person pronoun as he declares, "I, I will be with your mouth and with his mouth"[117] (4:15). In the future, Aaron will function as Moses's mouthpiece, while Moses will function like God in relation to Aaron. They will be ministry partners as well as siblings.[118] God's reassurance leaves Moses speechless, with no more excuses to offer. Sometimes, as we seek to discern God's call, the lack of further excuses may signal that it is time to answer that call.

---

117. My translation.
118. This relationship suggests that "the priest is under the prophet." Victor P. Hamilton, *Exodus, An Exegetical Commentary* (Grand Rapids: Baker Academic, 2011), 76.

4:18–31 Returning to Egypt

With God's assurance of his presence with Moses, the promise to make Aaron his mouthpiece, and the powerful staff that could perform miracles (4:14–17), Moses has no further excuses. He leaves Mount Horeb and returns to Jethro, his father-in-law, seeking permission to return to Egypt and visit his "people" or his "brothers" there (4:18).[119] The term "my brothers" refers to Moses's Hebrew kin, emphasizing his ethnic origin and identity, as distinct from non-Hebrews such as the Midianites or the Egyptians. The phrase "return to my brothers who are in Egypt" (4:18 NASB) is significant, evoking memories of Moses's earlier visit to see the suffering of his Hebrew brothers (2:11–12). Moses probably wondered: Are my people still alive and well? Will they accept me as one of them now that I have been away for 40 years? How will Pharaoh and the Egyptians react to my return? How will I fit in in Egypt since I am no longer the person I once was?

For Moses, the prospect of returning to Egypt must have stirred up a flood of memories and mixed feelings. The repetition of the term "return" (*shub*) five times in Exodus 4:18–21 signifies that this is a key concept in this passage. Returning to one's home country is a complex and emotional experience, filled with longing, nostalgia, fear, excitement, and apprehension about the uncertain outcome and the reception by family and friends.

The experience of returning home is familiar to those living in the diaspora and influences an individual's identity formation and kinship relations. In my own situation, I arrived in the United States alone while my parents remained in Hong Kong. For about three decades, I have traveled between the United States and Hong Kong as a transnational person, feeling as though I have two homes. Whenever I return to Hong Kong, although everything seems familiar, my extended absence often makes me feel like an outsider among the local Hong Kongers. In addition, my Cantonese has become rusty, which heightens my sense of not belonging. Like Moses, many diasporans find themselves in a state of limbo, not fully belonging in either country but living in an in-between space. The notion of "returning to one's home country" does not necessarily equate to "returning home" or "returning to where one belongs" or "experiencing a sense of belonging." For many diasporans, the concept of home is a complex issue; and for some, there may be no home to which to return.

In obedience to God's directive to return to Egypt, and with Jethro's blessing, Moses takes his wife and sons and returns to Egypt. The passage also

---

119. NIV: "Let me return to my own people in Egypt."

notes that "he took the staff of God in his hand" (4:20). The staff of Moses has now been transformed into "the staff of God," mirroring how Moses himself has been transformed from a shepherd into God's agent of change. Whatever "staff" we possess – our gifts, strengths, resources, or relationships – can similarly become God's instruments to serve God's purposes.

In Exodus 4:21–23, God instructs Moses to "perform before Pharaoh all the wonders" he had been empowered to do, but God also says, "But I will harden his heart so that he will not let the people go" (4:21). Readers often puzzle over this idea that God hardens Pharaoh's heart. How are we to reconcile the idea that God hardens Pharaoh's heart with the fact that Pharaoh is still responsible for his actions? To address this question, we must recognize that God knew beforehand that Pharaoh himself would harden his own heart (3:19) and that God then allowed this hardening to continue. In Exodus 4–14, the motif of the hardening of the heart occurs 20 times, with 10 instances describing Pharaoh hardening his own heart and 10 instances stating that God hardened Pharaoh's heart. In the ten plagues, it is not until the sixth plague that Scripture says that God hardens Pharaoh's heart (9:12), which seems to suggest that in the first five plagues, Pharaoh willfully chose to harden his own heart. God then uses Pharaoh's own natural proclivity toward evil to accomplish God's deliverance. In light of Pharaoh's cultural and religious context of seeing himself as a god, God beats him at his own game.[120]

The plague narrative uses three Hebrew words in reference to Pharaoh's heart: strong (*khazaq*), heavy (*kabed*), and difficult (*qashah*).[121] The first two words focus on the stubbornness of the heart, while the third word focuses on the unyielding aspect of the heart. Together, they convey the idea of the hardening of the heart as the tendency to adhere to strict preconceived ideas and the inability to change course.[122] Since the word "strong" (*khazaq*), when associated with the word "heart" (*leb*), often connotes a positive condition, it is possible to view it somewhat positively from the perspective of Pharaoh to suggest that he remained strong regardless of outside forces. In this reading, the narrative presents a colored spectrum of Pharaoh's heart depending on which

---

120. Sarna, *Exploring Exodus*, 64–65. Charlie Trimm also conducts a detailed study on the topic of divine control. Charlie Trimm, *"YHWH Fights for Them!" The Divine Warrior in the Exodus Narrative*, Gorgias Biblical Studies 58 (Piscataway: Gorgias, 2014), 206–222.
121. *Khazaq* (4:21; 7:13, 22; 8:19; 9:12, 35; 10:20, 27; 11:10). *Kabed* (7:14; 8:15, 32; 9:7; 10:1). *Qashah* (13:15). NIV translates the first word "hard" or "hardened" and the second word "unyielding" (NIV 7:14; 9:7), "hard" (8:15) and "hardened" (8:32; 10:1). NIV translates the third word "stubbornly refused" (13:15).
122. Trimm, *"YHWH Fights for Them,"* 204–206.

perspective as well as the irony that it is precisely this "strength" of Pharaoh that God challenges.[123]

Matthew McAfee helpfully summarizes the stages of Pharaoh's and Yahweh's involvement in the hardening of the heart:[124]

a. Yahweh tells Moses that Pharaoh will be unwilling to set the Israelites free and will only do so by the strong arm of God (3:19).

b. Yahweh tells Moses that, at an unspecified time, he will strengthen Pharaoh's heart (4:21; 7:3a) and, subsequently, multiply his signs and wonders in Egypt (7:3b).

c. As the contest between Yahweh and Pharaoh unfolds, the narrative describes Pharaoh's heart as being strong and heavy or stubborn (8:19, 32).

d. At a critical point, the narrative reveals Yahweh directly strengthening ("hardens" in NIV) the heart of Pharaoh (9:12) and acknowledging his role in hardening the heart of Pharaoh (10:1).

e. In the final stage of hardening, the narrative describes the exclusive strengthening activity of Yahweh (10:20, 27; 11:10).

f. The final stage of Yahweh's strengthening activity motivates Pharaoh and his army to pursue the Israelites to the Sea of Reeds ("Red Sea" in NIV), where they are dealt the final blow (13:15).

Since the "heart" – in both Hebrew and Egyptian – often connotes an individual's volition and will, the condition of the heart determines the direction of a person's life and the choices they make. The expression "acting according to one's heart" implies that the gods reside in the heart and guide human behaviors while following the *ma'at* (order) of the cosmos.[125] God does not impose the hardening on Pharaoh. Rather, it is Pharaoh's own choice. At the same time, Pharaoh's heart is not solely under his own control but under God's control. On a different note, the hardening of Pharaoh's heart serves a specific purpose in God's plan for salvation history. Without this hardening, God's power would not have been manifested in such miraculous ways. This fact may bring comfort to those currently living under oppressive regimes or

---

123. Matthew McAfee, "The Heart of Pharaoh in Exodus 4–15," *BBR* 20, no. 3 (2010): 335–336.
124. McAfee, "The Heart of Pharaoh in Exodus 4–15," 352–353.
125. Trimm offers a helpful study on the meaning of the heart in the Hebrew and Egyptian context. Trimm, *"YHWH Fights for Them!"* 202–203.

in countries that suppress democracy. Under such circumstances, Christians can pray to God to soften the hearts of those in authority. As Proverbs 21:1 affirms, "In the Lord's hand the king's heart is a stream of water that he channels toward all who please him."

God also tells Moses, "Israel is my firstborn son" (4:22), a concept that appears here for the first time in the Bible. In Genesis, God often rejects firstborn sons – among them Ishmael, Esau, and Reuben – and, instead, chooses the younger son – for example, Isaac, Jacob, Judah, and Joseph – to fulfill his covenant promises. For instance, although Esau was the firstborn son, he showed disdain for this privilege by trading his birthright for Jacob's "red stew" in a moment of hunger and, as a result, firstborn status passed to Jacob. Later, following his time of wrestling with the angel of God, God renamed Jacob "Israel" (Gen 32:28). From that moment, Jacob (Israel) enjoyed the status of firstborn due to a complex interplay between divine and human actions.

In the ancient Near East, the firstborn son enjoyed a privileged position in the family, enjoying a double portion of the inheritance and acting as head of the household in the absence of the father.[126] Similarly, Israel collectively enters into a covenantal relationship with God, enjoying the privileged position of the firstborn son. As Jeremiah declares, "Israel was holy to the Lord, the firstfruits of his harvest" (Jer 2:3).

Foundational to the status of the firstborn son is the concept of divine election, where God chose Israel as his firstborn son because of his love for them (Deut 7:8). God instructs Moses to say to Pharaoh, "I told you, 'Let my son go, so he may worship me.' But you refused to let him go; so I will kill your firstborn son" (Exod 4:23). The principle of "an eye for an eye" is at work here. This command anticipates the tenth plague – where God struck down the firstborn sons of Egypt because Pharaoh did not let Israel go – and emphasizes Israel's special status as God's firstborn son.

In Chinese culture, as well as in many other Asian cultures, the firstborn son (*zhǎng zǐ*) often holds a privileged position in the family. The firstborn is viewed as the "bloodline" who will carry the family name through his own children. Parents often place higher expectations on the firstborn son, who is expected to take care of his siblings and shoulder heavier financial

---

126. For more on the identity of the firstborn son and its pattern in Genesis and the Pentateuch, see Roger Syren, *The Forsaken Firstborn: A Study of a Recurrent Motif in the Patriarchal Narratives* (JSOTSup 133. Sheffield: Sheffield Academic Press, 1993). Joel S. Kaminsky, *Yet I Loved Jacob: Reclaiming the Biblical Concept of Election* (Nashville: Abingdon, 2007). Isaac Mendelsohn, "On the Preferential Status of the Eldest Son," *BASOR* 156 (1959): 38–40.

responsibilities. Therefore, Chinese parents will understand and relate to God's disposition toward Israel – God's firstborn son.

Exodus 4:24–26 is one of those enigmatic OT passages. Some scholars suggest that some text between verse 23 and verse 24 might have been lost in the transmission of the original manuscript. The scene where God seeks to kill Moses for no apparent reason makes no sense to readers. Given that Moses had already agreed – even though somewhat reluctantly – to return to Egypt, why would God seek to kill him? The original Hebrew text adds to the confusion with vague pronouns in the phrases "his feet" and "he let him alone" (4:25–26). Whose feet are these? Who is to let whom alone? The most troubling question is why God would desire to kill Moses and how this episode is related to circumcision.

A study by Athena Gorospe, a Filipina scholar, provides a compelling interpretation of this cryptic passage. In a nutshell, her study focuses on the central issue of circumcision, its association with rites of passage, and Moses's ambiguous identity at this point in the narrative. When God commissioned Moses to return to Egypt, although Moses himself was already circumcised, his son was not. This left Moses and his family in a liminal state, without clear identification with any group. Although a Hebrew by birth, he was not clearly accepted in his spheres of influence – he was not a full-fledged Hebrew, Midianite, or Egyptian. Since circumcision is a sign of the Abrahamic covenant (Gen 17:11), as an uncircumcised male, he stands outside of his ethnic identity as a Hebrew, alienated from the covenant between God and Abraham. That it is Zipporah who serves as the circumciser only heightens the ambiguity surrounding this enigmatic passage. Traditionally, it was a male who performed the rite of circumcision, not a female. Zipporah, who is neither a Hebrew nor an Egyptian but a Midianite woman assumes the role of circumciser, during this transitional phase of Moses's life. In this sense, Zipporah becomes a "marginal mediator" in Moses's transition from a liminal state to a more "settled identity" as a messenger of God.[127]

Discussing familial relationships in the diaspora is complicated. For instance, when migrants relocate to a new country and marry someone of a different race, their children become a mixed-raced generation (*hùn xŭe ér*). This raises questions about their identity – for example, are they Chinese, American, Chinese American, Chinese French, Chinese Mexican, or Chinese-Japanese? The multiethnic nature of Moses's family parallels many diasporic

---

127. Gorospe, *Narrative and Identity*, 165–182.

families worldwide and also demonstrates that racial, ethnic, and cultural identity formation can be messy and sometimes confusing. Returning to one's homeland or former places of residence can further complicate matters. Amid all this confusion, the call of God becomes a deciding factor in the journey of self-discovery.[128]

In Exodus 4:27–31, Moses meets Aaron at the mountain of God and, together, they gather all the elders of Israel. Aaron serves as Moses's mouthpiece, conveying what God had told Moses, while Moses performs signs before the Israelites. The final verse in this passage states that "they believed" and – upon hearing that God had visited his people and seen their afflictions – "bowed down and worshiped" (4:31). God's visitation to Israel fulfills Joseph's prediction to his brothers on his deathbed – that God would surely visit them (Gen 50:24–25). The dramatic encounter between Moses with God – despite involving a difficult and challenging process of negotiation – concludes on a positive note.

Identity formation in the diaspora is an ongoing process of negotiating and renegotiating with oneself, family, community, and God. Just as Moses wrestled with accepting God's call, our own struggles to follow God's call provide an opportunity to reexamine our place and mission in God's world.

5:1–6:30 ENCOUNTERING PHARAOH AND GOD'S PROMISE OF RESCUE

When the mainlanders arrived in Taiwan due to the defeat of the Nationalist Party in 1949, they came to a new island with the hope of eventually returning to China to reconnect with their cultural roots and the family members they had left behind. It was not until four decades later that this dream finally came true. However, to their surprise and dismay, the homes and families they had so longed to see in China were nowhere to be found. Their loved ones had died; their homes had been destroyed or confiscated; the once-familiar landscapes had changed drastically; and worst of all, after decades of separation, their surviving relatives and friends had become strangers.[129]

Those returning home after a long sojourn must often make multiple adjustments to reconnect with family members, old friends, and once-familiar places, while also meeting new people and adapting to the changing social

---

128. This is not to say that we should privilege our spiritual identity over our ethnic, racial, and cultural identities, but that we should embrace all of our identities as people living in diaspora.
129. Yang, *The Great Exodus from China*, 18.

and political landscape of their homeland. These returnees may be perceived as "outsiders" by the locals, and they may discover that their emotional bonds with those they once knew have changed even if their economic status remains the same. Some returnees may have come home with the intention of helping their family financially, while others may be seeking to reconnect with their roots before embarking on new journeys in other places. However, the experience of returning home may not always unfold as anticipated by returnees. The unpredictable nature of transnational relations bears witness to the multifaceted nature of identity formation between old and new lands.

This section commences with the initial encounter between Moses and Pharaoh, continues with the Egyptians' mistreatment of the Hebrew slaves, and concludes with the genealogy of Moses and Aaron.

5:1–9 The Initial Encounter with Pharaoh

Exodus 5 marks the beginning of a new scene, in which Moses and Aaron have returned to Egypt from the wilderness. When they go to see Pharaoh and ask him to send the Israelites out so that they may offer sacrifices to God, Pharaoh scornfully replies, "Who is the Lord, that I should obey him and let Israel go? I do not know the Lord and I will not let Israel go" (5:2). Here, "the Lord" is the four-letter word that spells out God's name – YHWH.[130] In the Egyptian context, Pharaoh sees himself as a deity,[131] and his rhetorical question, "Who is the Lord?" accentuates his refusal to acknowledge the divinity of God. His subsequent statement, "I do not know the Lord," further reinforces this refusal. This pharaoh is just like the previous one who refused to acknowledge Joseph and God's work in Joseph's life (1:8). Once again, the author of Exodus places the pharaohs in the category of those who do "not know," in contrast to the all-knowing God who already knew this pharaoh's response ahead of time (3:19).

Moses and Aaron then reiterate God's identity by specifying that he is "the God of the Hebrews" and warn of the consequences should Pharaoh refuse to comply – "or he may strike us with plagues [pestilence] or with the sword" (5:3). As the story unfolds, a "terrible plague" or pestilence does indeed come upon the livestock of the Egyptians (9:3). The emergence of COVID-19 and

---

130. Henceforth in this commentary, the four upper case letters, the Lord, refers to YHWH in Hebrew.
131. Pharaoh is regarded as the incarnation of the Egyptian god Re, who is the god of creation, the sun, and the state who rules the whole universe. J. Assmann, "Re," *DDD*, 689.

its variants on a global scale has prompted questions about the possibility of plagues being a divine instrument of justice. However, although Scripture frequently depicts God's judgment as being administered through plague or sword,[132] this does not necessarily signify that God will use these methods to judge people in the present time.

The warning delivered by Moses and Aaron falls on deaf ears. Pharaoh shifts the blame onto them, saying, "Why are you taking the people away from their labor?" (5:4). He then commands the slave drivers and overseers to immediately stop supplying the Israelites with straw for brick-making, forcing them to gather their own straw while still fulfilling their usual quota of bricks.[133] Pharaoh also accuses the Israelites of being "lazy" and attributes this as their motivation for wanting to leave Egypt. By imposing additional hardships, Pharaoh seeks to prevent the Israelites from hearing what he terms "lies" (5:5–9). Moses's initial encounter with Pharaoh ends in disaster. Following God's call does not guarantee that everything will proceed as planned or expected. There will often be opposition and roadblocks, but that does not mean that what we are doing is wrong. Rather, such opposition may well be a sign that we are on the right path.

5:10–19 The Harsh Treatment

This passage describes the results and consequences of Pharaoh's command to the Egyptian slave drivers. Through two incidents consisting of "speech and action," the author illustrates the cruelty inflicted upon the Israelites by these slave drivers. In the first incident, the slave drivers announce that while the Israelites will not be given straw to make bricks, they will still be required to produce the same quota of bricks (5:10–13). In the second episode, the slave drivers beat the Israelite overseers for failing to meet their quotas (5:14). Similar mistreatment of workers occurs in many parts of the world, including South Asia, where child labor is prevalent. These child workers often do not receive the promised wages, and some of them even end up committing suicide.[134]

---

132. For instance, Numbers 14:36–38; 16:46–50; 25:9; 2 Samuel 24:15; 1 Chronicles 21:14; Jeremiah 14:11–12; 21:7; 27:8; Ezekiel 5:12; Luke 21:11; Revelation 6:8.
133. For details regarding brickmaking in Egypt and the function of straw in the brickmaking process, see Sarna, *Exploring Exodus*, 22–24 and 65. Basically, the straw or stubble gathered from the fields, when chopped and mixed with the water-soaked clay, can function as a binding element and strengthen the plasticity of the bricks. Without the straw, the bricks would shrink and lose their shape. Thus, straw is essential in the brickmaking process.
134. George and Swarup, "Exodus," 86.

As a result of the harsh treatment meted out to them, the Israelite overseers come to Pharaoh and cry out, "Why have you treated your servants this way? Your servants are given no straw, yet we are told, 'Make bricks!' Your servants are being beaten, but the fault is with your own people" (5:15–16). Pharaoh replies by again accusing them of being "lazy" – literally, "lazy, you are lazy!" – and reiterates his order to not supply any straw while insisting that the Israelites still produce the same quota of bricks (5:18). The Israelite overseers realize that they are in deep trouble (5:19). The word "trouble" is literally "evil" or "disaster" (*rah*). The aftermath of the initial encounter between Moses and Pharaoh is indeed catastrophic.

Throughout chapter 5 and up to this point, the narrator has included the voices of Moses, Aaron, Pharaoh, the Egyptian slave drivers, and the Israelite overseers. But the voices of the Hebrew slaves are never heard, as if the narrator is making a sharp distinction between the voice of the oppressors and the deafening silence of the powerless slaves. The constant repetition of the theme of no straw but the same quota of bricks only serves to reinforce the disparity between the powerful and the powerless. Those under oppressive regimes often find themselves without a voice, but God hears their cries and advocates for them (2:24). Even in their darkest moments, when it seems as though God is absent or silent, he is at work, actively guiding history forward in the direction that he intends.

5:20–23 Two Confrontations

The Israelite overseers – probably realizing the futility of confronting the Egyptians – choose the easier option of confronting their own leaders, Moses and Aaron. They meet with Moses and Aaron and express their frustration: "May the Lord look on you and judge you! You have made us obnoxious to Pharaoh and his officials and have put a sword in their hand to kill us" (5:21).[135] One can imagine the intensity of their emotions as they charge Moses and Aaron with what they perceive as a betrayal. Scripture does not reveal how Moses and Aaron responded or how they felt about this accusation. However, it does describe Moses going to God and asking God why this was happening. Moses finds himself caught in the difficult position of being both an agent of God and a leader of his people.

---

135. "May" can also be translated as "let." The latter fits better in light of the anger of these overseers.

The verb "returned" (*shub*) echoes Moses's return (*shub*) to Egypt (4:20). However, this time, it is not a physical return but a spiritual "return" to God for answers. Moses confronts God, saying, "Ever since I went to Pharaoh to speak in your name, he has brought trouble on this people, and you have not rescued your people at all" (5:23). Moses emphatically stresses the word "rescue."[136] When confronted and challenged by his own people, Moses, in turn, confronts God and charges him with the "crime" of failing to fulfill his promise. In Moses's eyes, the outcome of his obedience to God's call seems disastrous. Moses's return to God also establishes a pattern for his future interactions with God in his role as mediator and intercessor for the Israelites. Throughout the Israelites' journey, Moses repeatedly returns to God to intercede on Israel's behalf.[137]

6:1–13 Divine Reassurance

In response to Moses's question, God reiterates what he had previously revealed to Moses (3:19) – that Pharaoh will let the Israelites go only because of the strong hand of God (6:1). The phrase "by a strong hand" ("because of my mighty hand" in NIV) is repeated twice for emphasis. God then shifts the focus to the subject of his own name, revealing that although he had appeared to the patriarchs as "God Almighty" – *El Shaddai*[138] – "by my name the LORD I did not make myself fully known to them" (6:3). This name YHWH ("the LORD") reflects God's nature, character, and actions. Although the book of Genesis shows that the patriarchs knew God in some capacity, they had not known and experienced God as fully as the Israelites in Exodus, who witnessed God's signs and wonders – including the ten plagues – received God's law through Moses on Mount Sinai, witnessed the revelation of God's attributes after the incident with the golden calf, and experienced God's presence through the pillar of cloud by day and the pillar of fire by night. Only in Exodus does God reveal the covenantal obligation of Yahweh to deliver his people from their oppression.[139]

---

136. In Hebrew, the verb "rescue" has been repeated twice for emphasis (hiphil infinitive absolute + hiphil perfect).
137. Exodus 19:8; 32:31.
138. Genesis 17:1–8; 35:11–12.
139. Blackburn notes that nowhere in Genesis does God demand exclusive worship or assert his incomparability to other gods, while in Exodus this exclusivity and polemic against other gods are prevalent. W. Ross Blackburn, *The God Who Makes Himself Known: The Missionary Heart of the book of Exodus* (NSBT 28, Downers Grove: InterVarsity Press, 2012), 57.

In Exodus 6:2–8, God repeats to Moses his earlier words that focus on God's covenant promise to the patriarchs to give them the land of Canaan (3:7–9, 16–17). God describes this land as "the land of their sojournings in which they sojourned in it" (6:4).[140] The twice repeated "sojourn" highlights the patriarchs' liminal status and the fact that Canaan was not their home. However, God had promised to give them the land as their future home. The phrases "I have heard," "I have remembered," and "I will free you . . . I will redeem you" (6:5–6) reinforce God's good intentions and purposes for the people of Israel.

Verse 7 captures the essence of the covenant: "I will take you as my own people, and I will be your God. Then you will know that I am the LORD your God, who brought you out from under the yoke of the Egyptians." The relationship between God and Israel is based first on his covenantal promise to the patriarchs and then on God's loving election of Israel.[141] God desires that Israel be his own people. The identity of the people of God is intimately tied to the God who claims them as his own. "I will take you" signifies God's deliberate action, which is not dependent on any merit of Israel. This phrase also emphasizes the sense of belonging that God offers to Israel in their liminal state, where they do not yet fully belong anywhere.

The clause "Then you will know that I am the LORD your God" is a signature statement in Exodus, indicating that God fulfills his promises, and when he does, people will come to know God in his full manifestation.[142] The word "know" (*yada*) recalls the earlier declaration that God *knew* Israel[143] (2:25), as well as Pharaoh's "do not know the LORD" (5:2). Through the ten plagues, Pharaoh will eventually come to know God. Our knowledge of God is gained and deepened both by experiencing God's rescue and by witnessing the fulfillment of his promises.

God concludes by reaffirming his promise: "I will bring you to the land" (6:8). In Exodus 6:2–8, God establishes a redemptive paradigm for Israel – a framework that serves as a crucial lens through which to comprehend the story of salvation in the OT. Some scholars view this passage as a manifestation of "God's Design."[144]

---

140. My translation.
141. The idea of God's election of Israel is later revealed as out of God's love (Deut 7:7–8).
142. For example, Exodus 10:2; 16:12.
143. "God looked on the Israelites and was concerned about them" (NIV).
144. For instance, Elmer Martens considers Exodus 6:6–8 as a paradigm for God's purposes in Exodus and in his later work of redemption, which includes the four-fold designs: Deliverance

Although Moses conveys God's promise of a glorious, splendid, and inspiring plan for their future, the Israelites remain unmoved. Their "shortness of spirit" on account of their hard labor has robbed them of hope.[145] Suffering tends to dishearten people and obscure their vision of hope, while oppression drains and saps their energy, leaving them feeling powerless. When God urges Moses to speak to Pharaoh and seek freedom for the Israelites, Moses is reluctant, offering the excuse of his "faltering lips" (6:12) – literally, "uncircumcised lips" or "foreskinned lips" – which echoes the earlier reference to Moses being "slow of speech and tongue" (4:10). However, God quickly dismisses Moses's excuse and commands Moses and Aaron to bring the Israelites out of Egypt (6:13). Those who are called to do God's work must learn to see things from God's perspective. Moses's self-diagnosed "heavy tongue" problem turns out to be an exaggeration of his own limitations. In Deuteronomy, Moses speaks to the new generation of Israelites with eloquence and fluency, demonstrating that he had overcome his self-diagnosed speech impediment.

6:14–30 The Genealogy of Moses and Aaron

The narrative now shifts from the dialogue between God and Moses to a genealogy focusing on the family of Levi (6:14–25). Thereafter, the narrative returns to Aaron and Moses's collaboration in pleading with Pharaoh to let them bring the Israelites out of Egypt (6:26–30). The genealogy serves as a bridge between Israel and their forefathers, while also setting the stage for the ensuing plagues. Sarna observes that since genealogies symbolize vigor and continuity, the presence of a genealogy here injects a note of reassurance into an otherwise despondent mood.[146]

The narrator begins the genealogy by stating, "These were the heads of the households of their fathers,"[147] where the term "their fathers" refers to "Moses and Aaron" who are mentioned in the preceding verse. The narrator then traces the lineage of the sons of Reuben – Israel's firstborn – and the sons of Simeon, but only one generation is mentioned in respect of each of them. Verse 16 introduces another genealogical section, which opens by stating, "These were

---

(6:6), God's community (6:7a), knowledge of God (6:7b), and abundant life (6:8). Elmer A. Martens, *God's Design: A Focus on Old Testament Theology*, 4th ed. (Eugene: Wipf & Stock, 2015), 4.

145. "Shortness of spirit" is the literal translation of the original Hebrew in Exodus 6:9. NIV renders it as "discouragement."

146. Sarna, *Exodus*, 33.

147. My translation. The NIV has "These were the heads of their families." In Hebrew, the words "their families" are literally "the households of their fathers."

the names of the sons of Levi according to their records" and concludes with a similar statement, "These were the heads of the Levite families, clan by clan" (6:25). This section of the genealogy includes five generations, ending with Phinehas, who represents the sixth generation from Aaron's line (6:25).[148] This arrangement suggests that the events described in Numbers 25 had already occurred by the time this genealogy was composed and that the writer wanted readers to pay particular attention to Phinehas, who later played a significant role in continuing the Aaronic priesthood.

By tracing the genealogy of Levi and, thereby, Aaron's lineage to Phinehas, the narrator sought to emphasize both Levi's prominence among his brothers and Aaron's unique status among the Levites. This genealogy culminates in Aaron's grandson, Phinehas, to whom God later grants a "covenant of peace" and a "covenant of an eternal priesthood" (Num 25:12–13).

Another unique feature of this genealogy is the inclusion of women's names: Jochebed, Elisheba, and the daughter of Putiel (6:20, 23, 25). However, the name Miriam, the sister of Moses and Aaron, is conspicuously absent (6:20).[149]

In the genealogy of Levi, Aaron is given more prominence than Moses. While the descendants of Moses are omitted, the lineage of Aaron's wife and all her sons is included (6:23). The pairing of "Aaron and Moses" (6:20, 26), rather than "Moses and Aaron," suggests that the primary purpose of this genealogy is to trace the bloodline of Aaron, establishing him as the legitimate heir to Israel's priesthood.

The inclusion of Jochebed, the mother of Aaron and Moses, and mention of her close relationship to Amram – the grandson of Levi – alerts the reader to the fact that this marriage took place before the institution of Mosaic law, which forbids marriage between close relatives – in this case, the father's sister (Lev 18:12; 20:19).

Exodus 6:23 reveals that Aaron married Elisheba, whose lineage links her father and brother to the line from Judah to David and, ultimately, to Jesus.[150] This connection shows that Jesus's ancestry includes both Levi – symbolizing the priesthood – and Judah – symbolizing the prophetic line. Although the genealogy of Levi is the main focus of attention, the narrator also includes the

---

148. Hamilton provides a helpful table of this genealogy. Hamilton, *Exodus*, 108.
149. Though the name Miriam is included in the Septuagint, Syriac, and Samaritan texts. See Sarna, *Exodus*, 34.
150. Ruth 4:20; 1 Chronicles 2:10–11; Matthew 1:4; Luke 3:32–33. See Hamilton, *Exodus*, 109.

names of Levi's descendants who had failed to honor their privileged position within this priestly line. For example, Levi's great-grandson Korah (6:21) and Aaron's sons Nadab and Abihu (6:23) are mentioned by name. Korah and his followers, the Korahites, rebelled against Moses's authority and were severely punished (Num 16), while Nadab and Abihu died because they offered unauthorized fire upon the altar of the Lord (Lev 10:1–2).[151]

This genealogy tells the story of God's providence and demonstrates the fulfillment of God's prediction to Abraham that his descendants would be enslaved in a foreign country for four hundred years and that they would return to the promised land in the fourth generation (Gen 15:13, 16). In Exodus 6:25, Eleazar, Aaron's son, the fourth generation of Levi, does enter the land of Canaan and later dies there.[152] At least twice in Scripture, "the fourth generation" conveys a redemptive meaning – first, in the return of the Israelites from Egypt to Canaan, and second, in the return of the exiles from Babylon to Canaan.[153] History does indeed move forward according to God's purposes.

In Exodus 6:26–30, the narrator revisits an earlier passage (6:9–12) and reaffirms that it was Moses and Aaron whom God had chosen to lead the Israelites out of Egypt. The expression "by their divisions" (6:26) – literally, "by their armies" – is a military term, implying that the entry into Canaan was a military act.[154] Earlier, Moses had cited the unlikelihood of Pharaoh listening to him and offered the excuse of his own uncircumcised or "faltering lips" (6:12). Here, Moses reverses the order, mentioning his uncircumcised or "faltering lips" before asking, "Why would Pharaoh listen to me?" (6:30).

A Genealogy of Diaspora

The genealogy of Levi and his descendants spans five generations and multiple locations. Levi's descendants resided in various geographical locations: Canaan, Egypt, the wilderness, and then Canaan once again. Throughout their journey, they experience multiple dislocations and disruptions in identity. Although Canaan initially serves as their place of sojourning (6:4), upon their arrival in Egypt, they find themselves in a new land that ultimately becomes a place

---

151. This subtly suggests that the writing of this genealogy may have occurred after the events of Numbers 16 and Leviticus 10.
152. Numbers 20:25–29; Joshua 14:1; 24:33.
153. Hamilton, *Exodus*, 110.
154. For more on the nature of the Israelite conquest, see John H. Walton and J. Harvey Walton, *The Lost World of the Israelite Conquest: Covenant, Retribution, and the Fate of the Canaanites* (Downers Grove: IVP Academic, 2017).

of suffering and enslavement. Later, their 40 years in the wilderness places them in yet another state of liminality. Eventually, in the fourth generation, they return to Canaan – their original land of sojourning – but this time, as possessors of the land. This genealogy tells the story of the Levites' journey – from traveling to sojourning, from sojourning to traveling, and, finally, back to their ancestral home. It is both a tale of diaspora and a story of the migrant experience – similar to the stories of migrants from China or East Asia who journey to other parts of the world. Some migrants return to their country of origin, others settle in their host countries, and still others travel back and forth as transnationals.

This genealogy recounts the struggles of multiple generations. Yet through it all, God forms these individuals into his people. The Levites are appointed to serve in the tabernacle and bear the sacred responsibility of Israel's priesthood. Levi, an imperfect and ordinary human being (Gen 34), becomes a special vessel of God's grace. Similarly, in the context of the Chinese diaspora, people migrate and relocate for different reasons. Every land in which these diasporans reside may be seen as a land of sojourning. If we were to trace our family's genealogy, where would we begin and with whom? How many geographic locations and people would be involved, including those our children and grandchildren will marry and their geographic locations and races? Throughout this journey of becoming, what disruptions, formations, and re-formations in identity will take place?[155] Yet through it all, God's grace manifests itself in unexpected places. For instance, I came to know God and embraced Protestant Christianity in the United States, a land that is neither my birthplace nor the place where I grew up. However, it is in this new land that my life was transformed to serve God's purposes. As the first Christian in my family's lineage, God has done a new thing in my family that shapes subsequent generations to become part of God's household. There are valuable lessons to be gleaned by understanding our ancestry and discerning the intricacies of God's purposes in the diaspora.

---

155. The broken genealogy due to migration is a common narrative shared by South Asians, who often call family gatherings to attempt to write their genealogy. George and Swarup, "Exodus," 87.

THE TEN PLAGUES: THE INTERACTION BETWEEN HEAVEN AND EARTH

The Confucian concept *tiān rén gǎn yìng* denotes the belief that the human condition is closely intertwined with heaven and that the relationship is characterized by reciprocity. The term "heaven" in this context refers to a higher power or God, who exercises sovereignty over humanity and earthly events. It is reasonable to identify this heaven as heaven. Another related concept, *zāi yì tiān qiǎn*, asserts that disasters and calamities are sent by God or heaven to warn and punish wicked rulers on earth and give justice to the oppressed. Therefore, natural disasters are perceived as heaven's sign of disapproval, while calamities signify more severe disasters that serve as evidence of heaven's judgment of offending emperors or rulers. In this view, there is no such thing as "natural disasters" since all these calamities originate from heaven's will. For those lacking power to voice their grievances over injustices done to them, heaven serves as a divine judge, providing the checks and balances necessary to maintain moral order in the world.

Viewing the ten plagues through this lens suggests that the first nine plagues, which involve natural disasters, can be regarded as heaven's warnings to Pharaoh. In contrast, the tenth plague can be seen as a calamity in which heaven unleashes its divine fury upon Pharaoh and the Egyptians because of their wrongdoing, particularly their enslavement of the Israelites. Through the ten plagues, divine justice is meted out.

Asians are familiar with plagues. In 2003, the outbreak of Severe Acute Respiratory Syndrome (SARS) in China – which eventually spread to other Asian countries – caused widespread panic. Similar to COVID-19, the SARS virus is airborne and is transmitted through small droplets of saliva or indirectly through contact with contaminated surfaces. The World Health Organization (WHO) describes SARS as "the first severe and readily transmissible new disease to emerge in the 21st century."[1] However, the effects of SARS pale in comparison to the impact of the highly infectious respiratory disease COVID-19, which broke out in early 2020.

Although COVID-19 originated in Asia, it swiftly escalated into a global pandemic that affected the entire world, with its variants continuing to spread even in years that followed. Within a period of less than a year, the COVID-19 death toll far surpassed that of World War II and continued to rise for a further two years. In the wake of COVID-19, some Christians wonder whether this pandemic is purely a natural disaster or whether it has some religious significance. They speculate whether this could be a sign of the end times or whether God is using this plague to execute judgment on a sinful world. The pandemic has thrust the world into a liminal state, characterized by an anti-structural existence or disorder.[2]

During the pandemic, diaspora people – living away from their original homes – were deeply concerned about the safety of their families and loved ones back home. Many families with members scattered across the globe were unable to see one another in person. Countless elderly parents passed away alone, without their adult children by their side. Plagues devastate lives, and human efforts often seem impotent to help. In ancient times, people attributed plagues to the actions of gods and believed that only a more powerful deity could offer protection from such disasters. In the twenty-first century, scientists are able to develop vaccines to combat viruses, a possibility that was not available during the time of the exodus.

From a ritualistic standpoint, natural disasters are often perceived as a form of liminality.[3] Since a liminal experience describes a transitional stage, it can manifest at individual, communal, or societal levels. Disasters such as earthquakes, floods, and pandemics are both dangerous and disruptive, with potentially severe consequences at all these levels. However, they may also open up a new way of seeing and living.

---

1. "Severe Acute Respiratory Syndrome (SARS)," https://www.who.int/health-topics/severe-acute-respiratory-syndrome#tab=tab_1.
2. The terms "structure" and "anti-structure" are used in ritual studies to denote society's basic structure that governs human communities. The anti-structure is the chaotic state one finds oneself in. Turner and Turner, *Image and Pilgrimage in Christian Culture*, 93, 174.
3. Bjørn Thomassen, *Liminality and the Modern: Living Through the In-Between* (London: Routledge, 2014), 90. Other moments that count as liminality include sudden invasions, carnivals, revolutionary moments, wars, prolonged political instability, and prolonged intellectual confusion.

7:1–11:10 THE TEN PLAGUES

Exodus 7:1–11:10 recounts the stories of the ten plagues, emphasizing the themes of the hardening of Pharaoh's heart and God's demonstration of signs and wonders to accomplish his plan of rescuing the Israelites. The first nine plagues are structured in cycles of three, with the first sign in each cycle mirroring one another (7:15; 8:20; 9:13) and a consistent pattern of Moses and

Aaron approaching Pharaoh in the morning during his ritual bath in the Nile.[156] The first two plagues in each cycle involve warnings, whereas the third does not.[157] On the one hand, the ten plagues display God's creative order being imposed upon chaos; on the other hand, they demonstrate God's judgment upon the gods of Egypt through signs and wonders (12:12). The Egyptians believed in the created order (*ma'at*) that is present in nature,[158] but God's confrontational display of power through the dramatic intensity, timing, and selectivity of the first nine plagues establishes his sovereignty over nature, over the Egyptian gods, and, ultimately, over Pharaoh himself.[159]

Through these events, God demonstrates his sovereign power to all – the Israelites, the Egyptians, and the whole world. The recurring phrase "you will know that I am the LORD" acts as a refrain underscoring God's supremacy over the obstinate Pharaoh who considers himself a god incarnate.[160] Some scholars argue that the phrase "Ten Strikes" better captures the essence of the ten plagues, emphasizing both God's power and the use of Moses and Aaron's staff to strike Egypt with divine judgment.[161]

Before we move on to the plagues, a basic understanding of Egypt's worldview helps to comprehend the conflict between Pharaoh and God as the contest of two mindsets. Addressing the question "What is Egypt?" Kass underscores 10 features, which are summarized below:[162]

---

156. Morales, *Exodus Old and New*, 59–60.
157. For an analysis of the ten plagues and their literary structures, see Sarna, *Exploring Exodus*, 76–77. For the recounting of the Ten Plagues in the Psalms, see Psalms 78:43–51 and 105:27–36.
158. *Ma'at* is an Egyptian word from the root "be straight (in conduct)." Thus, its meaning includes truth, justice, rightness, and right order, and it is a foundational value guarding the relationship between humans and the divine. See K. A. Kitchen, "Maat," *DOTWPW*, 447. *Ma'at* encompasses not only the natural order in creation but also the moral order, and the gods and Pharaohs are believed to be the ones upholding this order. When a king practices justice and righteousness, he is upholding the *ma'at*. *Ma'at* also functions as a judge in the netherworld to establish one's righteousness upon a scale. See D. A. D. Smelik, "Ma'at," in *DDD*: 534–535. The opposite of *ma'at* is chaos. See Bills, *The Theology of Justice in Exodus*, 35–40.
159. My reading rejects seeing the ten plagues as a result of natural disasters because then it would not manifest the signs and wonders of God. For the three ways of reading the ten plagues – natural disaster, a demonstration of the impotence of the Egyptian gods, and the undoing of creation, see Ziony Zevit, "Three Ways to Look at the Plagues," *Bible Review* 6, no. 3 (June 1990): 16–23.
160. For example, Exodus 7:5; 8:22; 9:14, 16; 10:2. Compare 15:11; 18:11.
161. Alexander, *Exodus*, 146–147.
162. Kass, *Founding God's Nation*, 136–139. The worldview of Egypt helps us to understand why the heart of Pharaoh is so strong/stubborn to let the Israelites out of his country. As "Egypt

Exodus

1. Egypt's fertility stemmed from the seasonal flooding of the Nile – in contrast to other regions which depended on the rain – and attracted people seeking agricultural prosperity.[163]
2. The Egyptians revered the sun and the sun god Ra (sometimes spelled Re).[164]
3. The Egyptians believed that nature was cyclical, dependable, eternal, friendly to humans, and worth revering.
4. Throughout their lives, the Egyptians were preoccupied with the inevitability of decay and death.
5. The Egyptians worshiped nature and natural elements as gods.
6. The Egyptians did not usually place great value on human life.
7. Change was generally unwelcome in Egyptian culture.
8. For Egyptians, "seeing is believing," as evidenced by their picture writing.[165] Drawing and painting their deities on the reliefs and tombs reinforces their belief in them.
9. The Egyptians trusted in technology, and their wise men attempted to use their knowledge to manipulate nature.
10. Politically, Egypt was an autocracy ruled by one man, and slavery was a natural consequence of this system.

Given this understanding of Egypt and, by extension, Pharaoh, the contest between the God of Israel and Pharaoh can be viewed as a contest involving both physical aspects and symbolic meanings of the Nile, nature, the sun god, and, ultimately, Pharaoh's attitudes and beliefs. Below is a table setting out the first nine plagues and their effects on Pharaoh's heart.

---

was an absolute dictatorship," its king needed to be strong. Cyrus H. Gordon and Gary A. Rensburg, *The Bible and the Ancient Near East* (New York: W. W. Norton & Company, 1997), 64.
163. In this sense, for Egypt the Nile is reminiscent of the early rain and the latter rain that God sent for Israel.
164. The Egyptians' reverence for the Sun god plays a significant role in the ninth plague of darkness.
165. A visit to the tombs in the Valley of the Kings, the Valley of the Queens, and the tombs of Egyptian noblemen in Thebes will testify to the "seeing is believing" way of life. The Egyptian hieroglyphics also reflect this sentiment. White, *Everyday Life in Ancient Egypt*, 176–177.

Table 1: The First Nine Plagues and Their Effects on Pharaoh's Heart

Plague	Scripture	Content	Outcomes
1	7:14–25	Blood	"He turned and went into his palace, and did not take even this to heart" (7:23).
2	8:1–15	Frogs	"When Pharaoh saw that there was relief, he hardened his heart" (8:15).
3	8:16–19	Gnats	"Pharaoh's heart was hard" (8:19).
4	8:20–32	Flies	"But this time also Pharaoh hardened his heart" (8:32).
5	9:1–7	Pestilence affecting livestock	"His heart was unyielding" (9:7).
6	9:8–12	Boils	"The LORD hardened Pharaoh's heart" (9:12).
7	9:13–35	Hail	"Pharaoh's heart was hard" (9:35).
8	10:1–20	Locusts	"The LORD hardened Pharaoh's heart" (10:20).
9	10:21–29	Darkness	"The LORD hardened Pharaoh's heart" (10:27).

Throughout the first nine plagues, the narrative provides an increasingly detailed account of how Pharaoh and his court officials respond, showing the gradual hardening of Pharaoh's heart – initially by his own choice and later by God's action of hardening. The chronological sequence of the first nine plagues progresses from the waters, to the land, to animals, to human beings, and culminates in an upward movement to the sun.[166] The knowledge of God (1:8; 5:2; 6:7; 7:17; 9:29) progresses as the story unfolds. Several key themes reemerge, emphasizing the narrative's coherence: the command to "send my people out"[167] for the purpose of worshiping God, the sharp distinction between Goshen and the rest of Egypt, Pharaoh's appeals to Moses for prayer, and the repeated use of "hand" and "staff" as symbols of power.[168]

---

166. This upward direction shows that the power of God covers all domains from water, land, to the entire cosmos. Kass, *Founding God's Nation*, 142.
167. Most readers are familiar with the phrase "let my people go," but the words more literally mean "send my people out."
168. Alexander, *Exodus*, 151–153.

7:1–7 Prelude to the Plagues

In this scene, God instructs Moses and Aaron, clarifying their respective roles, reiterating their common mission, and restating what God himself would do to Pharaoh. Moses is to function as a god to Aaron, while Aaron will function as a prophet, who will be a spokesman for Moses (compare 4:16). God's declaration in verse 3 – "But I will harden" – underscores Pharaoh's hardened heart and his resistance to the message delivered by Moses and Aaron, leading, ultimately, to the achievement of God's mission to rescue the Israelites from Egypt. The missiological purpose of God – "the Egyptians will know that I am the LORD" (7:5) – forms a stark contrast to Pharaoh's "I do not know the LORD" (5:2).[169] God names two events by which the Egyptians will know God: a) "when I stretch out my hand against Egypt" and b) "when I . . . bring the Israelites out of it" (7:5). In hindsight, the Egyptians did indeed come to know God for who he is.[170] The obedience formula in verse 6 echoes Noah's obedience to God's command to build the ark (Gen 6:22; 7:5). Both these incidents involve rescue.

This scene concludes with a side note about the ages of Moses and Aaron: "Moses was eighty years old and Aaron eighty-three when they spoke to Pharaoh" (7:7). Moses and Aaron were in their eighties, which we may view as old age. But their actions of speaking and leading the people tells us they were in their prime when they served God. Similarly, today, when God calls us to serve him, our age does not matter; all that matters is our willingness to serve him.

7:8–13 The Sign before the Plagues

While some scholars view this scene as the first plague, a closer examination reveals that it is merely an introduction to the plagues that will follow. The word used for "snake" or "serpent" in Exodus 7 differs from the word used in Exodus 4. In Exodus 4:3, it is a snake (*nakhash*), whereas in Exodus 7:9–12, it is a serpent or a sea dragon (*tannin*). Although the latter connotes a "chaos monster," the narrator uses the two words interchangeably as synonyms.[171] The imagery of Aaron's staff "swallowing up" the staffs of the Egyptian magicians

---

169. See the helpful chart tracing the curriculum of Pharaoh's education in Wright, *The Mission of God*, 94.
170. Exodus 8:19; 9:20; 10:7; 12:33–36. In the eschaton, God calls Egypt "my people" (Isa 19:25). The Egyptians are also in God's grand narrative of redemption.
171. See Hamilton, *Exodus*, 117–118. Kass reads *tannin* here as "crocodile," which often appears in the Nile. Its nature to be hidden in the reeds, silent (being tongueless), invisible to the

is a recurring motif that reappears in the Red Sea crossing, where God's right hand "swallows" the Egyptians (15:12), and in Babylon's conquest, where Israel is "swallowed" up by the Babylonians (Jer 51:34).[172] This scene establishes a pattern that foreshadows Pharaoh's ultimate fate, when the power of God metaphorically "swallows" him in the Red Sea (Exod 15:12). The uraeus, a sign of Pharaoh's power that struck the enemy with lethal force, was also viewed as the eye of Horus, who symbolizes power and virtue. Since the serpent-diadem on Pharaoh's forehead represented absolute monarchy, its swallowing up by Aaron's staff would have been alarming to anyone familiar with its significance and symbolism.[173]

Other key themes surface in this brief introduction. First, it was Pharaoh who asked for a miracle – and he got one! – and further demonstrations of God's miraculous power would follow. Second, the staff takes center stage as an instrument and weapon of God (compare Exod 7:19; 14:16). Moses and Aaron were not only able to replicate a feat that the Egyptians took pride in – the manipulation of the serpents – but the staff-turned-serpent also swallowed the magicians' serpents. Third, the presence of the Egyptian wise men echoes Pharaoh's intention to "deal wisely"[174] with the Israelites (1:10), but these wise men prove to be no match for Moses and Aaron. The episode concludes with Pharaoh's hardened heart, and this pattern of a hardened heart persists throughout the first nine plagues.[175] There is a saying among the Bangala people of the Democratic Republic of the Congo: "You cannot kill an elephant with a single spear." Pharaoh is that elephant who had to be struck ten times

---

eyes, and it is the emblem of Sobek, the god of crocodiles whom Egyptians believed to be the one who created the Nile. That the staff of Aaron becomes a *tannin* is no small matter. Kass, *Founding God's Nation*, 134.

172. The use of *tannin* can also be interpreted as a symbol of Pharaoh (Ezek 29:3). Sarna, *Exodus*, 37. The motif of "dragon-slaying" in chapters 7 and 15 is confirmed by Morales, *Exodus Old and New*, 58–60.

173. Hart, *The Routledge Dictionary of Egyptian Gods and Goddesses*, 161. Curid regards the serpent confrontation in Exodus 7:8–13 as a paradigm for the rest of the plague narratives because it foreshadows Yahweh's humiliation of Egypt through the plagues and at the Red Sea. John D. Currid, *Ancient Egypt and the Old Testament* (Grand Rapids: Baker Books, 1997), 85, 89, 91.

174. NIV translates it as "shrewdly."

175. Fretheim rightly names this power struggle between Pharaoh and God "a battle of wills." Fretheim, *Exodus*, 113.

before he yielded to God.[176] The phrase "just as the LORD had said" (7:13) emphasizes God's foreknowledge of Pharaoh's hardening heart and his fate.[177]

The outcome of the serpent confrontation was that Pharaoh's heart became hard (Exod 7:13). Heart typically refers to mind or will; but in the Egyptian context, heart carried another layer of meaning. The Egyptians believed that the heart played a critical role in a person's afterlife. The Book of the Dead records that the deceased enter the hall of judgment, where the judge calls for the hearts of the dead to be weighed against the feather of truth and righteousness – this feather is considered the emblem of *ma'at*. If the heart is found to be too heavy, then its owner is deemed to have been a sinner.[178] If the heart is as light as a feather, then the person is rewarded with eternal life. Therefore, the condition of a person's heart determines whether or not they will enter the afterlife. The frequent mention of Pharaoh's heavy (or "hardened") heart points to this Egyptian custom and suggests that Pharaoh was not a virtuous person. Consequently, the assertion that God hardened Pharaoh's heart suggests that God, functioning as a judge, weighed Pharaoh's heart and deemed it too heavy or unworthy.[179]

The power struggle between Pharaoh and God follows a distinct pattern: God performs a miracle, which Pharaoh then attempts to replicate using his own methods. However, when Pharaoh fails, he still refuses to yield.

7:14–25 The First Plague: Blood

Scholars estimate that the ten plagues took place over the course of one year.[180] The first plague strikes at the very heart of Egyptian life and culture – the Nile. This vital water source was integral to Egyptian daily life and was used for drinking, washing, and bathing (see Exod 2:5). The desert areas surrounding the Nile depend on its waters, which surge northward into the valley and eventually flow into the Mediterranean Sea.[181] The shape of the Nile resembles

---

176. Abel Ndjerareou, "Exodus," in *Africa Bible Commentary*, ed. Tokunboh Adeyemo (Grand Rapids: Zondervan, 2006), 96.
177. See my discussions on Exodus 4:21.
178. White, *Everyday Life in Ancient Egypt*, 75–76. E. A. Wallis Budge, trans., *The Egyptian Book of the Dead: The Complete Papyrus of Ani* (New York: Clydesdale Press, 2021), xliv, cxxix. Originally published in 1895 by order of the Trustees of the British Museum.
179. Currid, *Ancient Egypt and the Old Testament*, 96–103. The paintings of the weighing of the heart are prevalent in Egypt, in museums, papyrus stores, and tombs.
180. Greenberg, *Understanding Exodus*, 122.
181. Sarna, *Exploring Exodus*, 78–79.

the spreading head of a lotus flower set on a long stalk. The Nile is like "a garden in a wilderness."[182]

To the ancient Egyptians, Egypt was synonymous with the Nile.[183] Because of its life-giving qualities, they revered the Nile as a local deity. The Egyptian god Hapi (or Hapy) personified the yearly flooding of the Nile rather than the Nile itself. Depicted with pronounced breasts and a prominent stomach, Hapi symbolized abundance and fertility.[184] The overflowing of the Nile was also associated with the Egyptian deity Osiris. His dying symbolized his reign in the underworld, and his rebirth through his son Horus after his death represented his power.[185] Thus, the ancient Egyptians perceived the Nile as the transformed lifeblood of Osiris.

The Nile was vital for Egypt's sustenance. As historians say, "The Nile is the gift of Egypt."[186] Pharaoh himself claims the Nile as his own creation: "The Nile belongs to me; I made it for myself" (Ezek 29:3). Therefore, turning the Nile into blood symbolizes God's victory over the god of the Nile and demonstrates his superior status over the Nile and all that it represents.

The first plague brings about poetic justice by its striking reversal of the earlier narrative where Pharaoh commanded the Hebrew boys to be thrown into the Nile. The once life-giving river is now non-functional and becomes a deadly weapon in God's hands. The frequent use of the word "struck" (*nakah*) echoes "Moses struck (*nakah*; "killed" in NIV) the Egyptian" (2:12) and anticipates "God struck (*nakah*) down all the firstborn in Egypt" (13:29; see also 12:12–13).[187] Throughout history, God has often partnered with human agents to accomplish his redemptive plans.

Initially, God commands Moses to meet Pharaoh in the morning at the Nile with his staff in hand (7:15) – the same staff that had recently transformed into a serpent and swallowed the staffs of the Egyptian wise men (7:9–12). God instructs Moses to speak to Pharaoh and identify himself as being sent by the "God of the Hebrews" (7:16). Since Pharaoh had refused to release the Israelites (7:14), Moses was to strike the water with his staff, turning it into blood to demonstrate God's power. This sign was intended to reveal God's

---

182. White, *Everyday Life in Ancient Egypt*, 15–16.
183. White, *Everyday Life in Ancient Egypt*, 15–16.
184. Currid, *Ancient Egypt and the Old Testament*, 109. Hart, *The Routledge Dictionary of Egyptian Gods and Goddesses*, 61.
185. M. Heerma Van Voss, "Hathor," *DDD*, 650.
186. Sarna, *Exploring Exodus*, 79.
187. The same verb also appears when Moses struck the rock from which water flowed (17:6).

identity – "By this you will know that I am the LORD" (7:17). Turning the water into blood would have dire consequences for the Egyptians: the fish would die, the Nile would stink, and the water would be undrinkable (7:18). These consequences disrupted the daily life of the Egyptians, making things inconvenient, to say the least.[188]

God then instructs Moses, "Tell Aaron, 'Take your staff and stretch out your hand over the waters of Egypt . . . and they will turn to blood'" (7:19). This remarkable event is witnessed by Pharaoh, his officials, and Moses and Aaron themselves (7:20). The repeated description of the consequences, including the death of the fish, the stench of the Nile, and undrinkable water, confirms God's earlier warning to Moses (7:18). The "stink" (or "foul smell") echoes the word "obnoxious" that the Israelite overseers had used in their complaint to Moses: "You have made us obnoxious to Pharaoh" (5:21).[189] Now, God had turned the tide, making the Nile "obnoxious." That "blood was everywhere in Egypt" (7:21) – literally, "blood was in all the land of Egypt" – foreshadows the blood of Egypt's firstborn during the tenth plague and the blood on the Israelites' doorposts as a sign of protection (12:12–13). The phrase "everywhere in Egypt" (7:21) parallels the cry of the Egyptians "throughout Egypt" (11:6). The repetition of "all" emphasizes the extensive nature of the plague.

As in the prelude to the first sign (7:11), Pharaoh once again summons his magicians to perform the same "trick" (7:22). Despite the magicians' ability to replicate the sign, Pharaoh hardens his heart, just as God had predicted. God sees and knows the thoughts of human hearts, and the narrator paints a vivid picture of Pharaoh by revealing what was in his heart – Pharaoh "turned and went into his palace, and did not take even this to heart" (7:23), reflecting his obstinance and desensitized heart. Pharaoh did not even consider whether this sign might have come from a higher power or care about the impact of unclean water on his people. He simply ignored the sign and carried on with his life as if nothing had happened. The Egyptians, however, suffered from this first sign and had to dig around the Nile to find potable water. The duration of the plague – "seven days" (7:25) – emphasizes the suffering the Egyptians endured

---

188. Sarna remarks that the first plague is the result of the extreme intensification of a phenomenon that occurs periodically in the Nile valley. The Nile is filled with the tropical red earth from the highlands of Ethiopia, carried by snow and rain. In this sense, the "blood" referred to by God is not human blood but a blood-like color. Sarna, *Exodus*, 38.
189. The words, stink, smell bad, odious, and obnoxious all originate from the same Hebrew word (*ba'ash*).

while people may live without food for some time, the idea of surviving for an entire week without clean water is unimaginable. Pharaoh's callousness toward his own people reflects his perception of himself as supreme and superior to everyone else.

8:1–15 The Second Plague: Frogs[190]

The second plague is likely connected to the first since the frogs emerge from the Nile, which is the focal point of the first plague. While the realm of the first plague is water, the domain of the second plague is land. The amphibious nature of frogs also highlights the transition from water to land. Interestingly, the ancient Egyptians worshiped a goddess named Heqt (or Heket, Hekhet) – often depicted with a frog's head – who was thought to assist women during childbirth, much like a midwife.[191] Egyptian women often wore amulets and scarabs bearing the image of this frog-goddess to protect them during childbirth.[192] Thus, the second plague might be associated with Pharaoh's decree to drown the Hebrew baby boys in the Nile.

In ancient Egypt, Heqt was believed to have authority over frog multiplication and power to protect the frogs from frog-eating crocodiles. However, her failure to control this frog infestation of the second plague demonstrated God's supremacy over the domain she represented.[193]

The first plague of turning water into blood inconvenienced the daily life of the Egyptians; the second plague makes their situation worse, with frogs invading all indoor spaces, including ovens and kneading bowls. Although the frogs do not endanger human life, they do make people's lives miserable. To simply describe the invasion of the frogs as a "huge nuisance" would be an understatement. The word "smite" (8:2)[194] concerning the plague of frogs foreshadows the smiting or striking down of Pharaoh's firstborn in the future (12:23, 27).

As in the previous plague, Aaron's staff serves as God's instrument in bringing the frogs from all water sources in Egypt. Although the magicians are also able to summon the frogs from the Nile, they are unable to remove them from people's houses. One can only imagine the impact – including the problem of noise – of two consecutive waves of frog invasions. However, the

---

190. Hebrew text, 7:26–8:11.
191. Sarna, *Exodus*, 40. Kass, *Founding God's Nation*, 137.
192. Hart, *The Routledge Dictionary of Egyptian Gods and Goddesses*, 67.
193. Currid, *Ancient Egypt and the Old Testament*, 110.
194. NIV simply translates it as "send," which reduces the nuance of the word.

magicians' ability to replicate the frog invasion causes Pharaoh to mistake this second plague for a work of magic.

As a result of the frog infestation, Pharaoh summons Moses and Aaron, pleading with them to entreat Yahweh to remove the frogs. Pharaoh even promises to let the Israelites go to sacrifice to God. This is the first time Pharaoh uses the name of God – Yahweh – thereby acknowledging, at least outwardly, that Yahweh is the true God and recognizing that God has the power to rid Egypt of the frogs. When Moses asks Pharaoh when he wants the frogs removed, Pharaoh responds, "Tomorrow."

God removes the frogs according to Pharaoh's timeline but not exactly as Moses had requested (8:10–11) – Moses had asked God to let the frogs depart, but God let the frogs die. As a result, "the land reeked of them" (8:14) – the Hebrew word used means "obnoxious," "stink," or "smelled" (5:21; 7:21). If Moses's request had been granted, the frogs would simply have left the homes of Pharaoh and the Egyptians and returned to the Nile, causing no foul stench. The smell from the dead frogs must have served as a strong warning to this powerful Pharaoh and posed a serious threat to public health and the environment. However, having experienced relief from the frogs, Pharaoh hardens his heart and refuses to heed Moses and Aaron. The narrator adds, "just as the Lord had said" (8:15), reasserting God's foreknowledge of the condition of Pharaoh's heavy heart and stubborn will.

8:16–19 The Third Plague: Gnats

In the third plague, as in the first two, Aaron's staff once again serves as a tool through which God demonstrates divine authority over nature and challenges the Egyptians' beliefs in their gods and the concept of *ma'at*. When Aaron stretches out his staff and strikes the dust of the earth, gnats descend upon people and animals. Gnats are small insects, typically found in Egypt during October and November, that can transmit diseases and move between land and air.[195] The mention of "dust" recalls the "dust" in Genesis 3:19 and its association with death. Dust can be seen as "a sign of human mortality and abject humility."[196] The statement "all the dust throughout the land of Egypt became gnats" (8:17) captures the intensity and extent of this plague. Gnats are winged insects that make buzzing sounds as they fly. One can only imagine

---

195. Sarna, *Exodus*, 41. Other translations for "gnats" include mosquitos, vermin, insects, and lice.
196. Fretheim, *Exodus*, 118.

the overwhelming sight and sound of this vast swarm of insects all through the land of Egypt. The magicians try but fail to replicate this plague. The waning power of the Egyptian magicians stands in sharp contrast to the mighty power of the God of Israel.

This plague can be seen as a direct challenge to the Egyptian god Khepri, believed to be a sun god associated with creation. Egyptian iconography depicts Khepri as a scarab beetle pushing the sun disk upward from the underworld to make his daily journey across the sky. As they observed scarab beetles rolling balls of dirt on the ground, the ancient Egyptians might have interpreted this activity as symbolizing the sun's journey across the sky.[197] The plague of the uncontrollable gnats would have been viewed as a direct confrontation of Khepri and *ma'at*, once again demonstrating God's sovereignty over both nature and this Egyptian deity.

Tracing the evolution of the magicians, we see a gradual shift from relying on their own magical abilities to recognizing the limitations of their magic and, ultimately, to acknowledging the supremacy of God's "magic." Before the first plague, the magicians turned their staffs into serpents, but Aaron's staff swallowed theirs (7:11–12). During the first plague, the magicians mimicked Moses and Aaron by turning the water of the Nile into blood (7:22). In the second plague, they brought forth frogs from the Nile but were unable to remove them (8:7). In the third plague, the magicians were unable to bring forth gnats (8:18). By confessing to Pharaoh that "this is the finger of God" (8:19), they attribute this work to God. The term "finger" refers to a direct action of God,[198] as when God would later use his "finger" to inscribe the Ten Commandments on the tablets of stone (Exod 31:18; Deut 9:10). Ironically, the magicians' testimony to God's might stands in sharp contrast to Pharaoh's unrelenting hardness of heart.

Since the magicians were able to turn the Nile into blood and bring forth frogs from it, one may wonder why they could not replicate the plague of gnats.

---

197. Hart, *The Routledge Dictionary of Egyptian Gods and Goddesses*, 84. Sculptures or paintings of scarabs often appear in Egyptian tombs and coffin covers. Scarab is one of the three charms to be placed in the embalming process of mummification. White, *Everyday Life in Ancient Egypt*, 141.
198. Some suggest that the finger of God is an anthropomorphic language. See David L. Baker, "The Figure of God and the Forming of a Nation: The Origin and Purpose of the Decalogue," *TB* 56, no. 1 (2005): 5. In the Old Testament, the finger of God appears thirty-one times, of which three times are used in connection with God's giving of the law. The motif of the finger of God should be seen in the larger narrative of the power struggle between Pharaoh and God. See Gerald A. Klingbeil, "The Finger of God in the Old Testament," *ZAW* 112 (2000): 409–415.

The explanation probably lies in the fact that the Nile belonged to the domain of the Egyptians, whereas the gnats originated from the dust of the earth. The first two plagues are concerned with the Nile, the realm of Egyptian power,[199] whereas the dust of the earth represents a realm that is beyond human control. The magicians' inability to produce gnats demonstrates God's sovereignty over all realms of life, which include both water and land. The next plague will show that God also rules over the realm of the air. While the first triad of plagues merely causes disruption and disturbance, the second triad causes destruction.

8:20–32 The Fourth Plague: Flies

In the fourth plague – which marks the beginning of the second triad of nine plagues – Pharaoh goes to the river, probably as part of his morning bath ritual (8:20; compare 7:15). God instructs Moses to warn Pharaoh that if he does not release the Israelites, swarms of flies will invade Egypt, affecting Pharaoh, his officials, and all the Egyptians, including their houses and land.[200] Flies, being creatures of the air, may not pose a direct threat to life, but they are a tremendous source of annoyance, like the frog invasion and the gnat attack. Flies, like gnats, are winged insects that buzz loudly when flying. In Egyptian thought, flies were probably seen as belonging to the domain of the god Khepri.[201] Many people find even the presence of a single fly irritating; a swarm of flies would have been intolerable. The devastating impact of this plague on daily life and livelihood would have been compounded by the disturbing noise produced by the flies, which could even be regarded as a form of torture.

God also declares, "But on that day I will deal differently with the land of Goshen, where my people live; no swarms of flies will be there, so that you will know that I, the LORD, am in this land" (8:22). Amid the plagues, Goshen becomes a refuge for Israel – a "safe house" or sanctuary of sorts.[202] This is the first plague in which God distinguishes between the Egyptians and the Israelites, separating the ground where the Egyptians stood from the land where Israel lived. This distinction is directly tied to God's foreknowledge and creative power since God uses separation to bring about the differentiation of

---

199. Enns, *Exodus*, 210.
200. Some understand "flies" as insects. In Hebrew, *'arob* means swarm. It may refer to a swarm of insects. If they are indeed blood-sucking insects, they would transmit diseases and cause environmental concerns. Sarna, *Exodus*, 42.
201. Currid groups the gnats and the flies together. Currid, *Ancient Egypt and the Old Testament*, 111.
202. Compare Exodus 9:26.

water and land, as well as day and night (Gen 1:6–7, 14, 18). Through each plague, God reveals a new aspect of his nature that has not been manifested before. In other words, God's power is manifested through transcending nature – for instance, sending the flies – and distinguishing between physical and geographical realms. The purpose of this distinction is "so that you will know that I, the Lord, am in this land." In a land where Pharaoh was worshiped as a deity, God asserted his divinity over Pharaoh and demonstrated his superiority to Pharaoh.

God sends the flies as promised, and the land of Egypt was "ruined" (8:24) or "laid waste" (NASB) by the flies. This is the same term (in Hebrew) used to describe the corruption that prevailed in the land during the time of Noah (Gen 6:11), thus invoking the language of creation and painting a picture of utter destruction – which one might call de-creation. Visualize the incredible sight of Goshen, untouched by flies, while the rest of Egypt is plagued by them. Imagine the sight and sound generated by swarms of flies, affecting all the Egyptians. Although this extraordinary scene may seem more appropriate for science fiction or digitally generated film, this was a stark reality for the people of Egypt.

Exodus 8:25–29 describes a negotiation between Pharaoh and Moses. Initially, Pharaoh agrees to permit Moses and Aaron to sacrifice to their God but stipulates that they can only do so within the land of Egypt. However, Moses counters this proposal, explaining that the sacrifices offered by the Israelites would be offensive to the Egyptians and could lead to them stoning the Israelites. Therefore, Moses insists that it is imperative that they go on a three-day journey into the wilderness to sacrifice to their God. Then, Pharaoh says, "I will let you go . . . only you shall not go very far away. Plead for me" (8:28, my translation).[203] Pharaoh's words, which contain both a condition and a plea, send mixed signals – asserting his authority while also asking for prayer. Moses agrees to intercede for Pharaoh by asking God to remove the swarm of flies from Egypt. However, Moses also adds a caveat: "Only do not let Pharaoh deal deceitfully again in not letting the people go to sacrifice to the Lord" (8:29b, my translation).

Unfortunately, although Moses upholds his end of the agreement, Pharaoh does not, and his heart remains hardened. The phrase "not a fly remained" (8:31) connotes another miracle since such a situation can only be attributed

---

203. This is emphatic in the Hebrew with the presence of *anoki* at the beginning of the sentence (MT 8:24a).

to God's intervention. This phrase also uses a literary tool known as hyperbole,[204] emphasizing the complete removal of every single fly. Interestingly, the term "hardened" (8:32) comes from the Hebrew word *kabed*, which is the word for "heavy," and this same word is also used to describe the "dense" or "thick" (*kabed*) swarms of flies in Exodus 8:24. This suggests a measure-for-measure (*kabed* for *kabed*) approach, where God employs the same measure of intensity to combat Pharaoh, and Pharaoh in turn employs the same measure of intensity to harden his heart.

9:1–7 The Fifth Plague: Plague on Livestock

The fifth plague affects the animals of Egypt. In Bible times, since livestock and humans shared the same physical environment, outbreaks of disease among animals would have had serious effects on human beings. According to the US Department of Agriculture, a deadly pig disease called African swine fever is highly infectious.[205] Though it would not threaten human health, it would devastate the economy and quality of life for humans.

As in previous plagues, God instructs Moses to demand that Pharaoh release the Israelites. Should Pharaoh refuse, God warns that his hand will unleash a "terrible plague" upon all Egyptian livestock, including horses, donkeys, camels, cattle, sheep, and goats (9:2–3). The Egyptians worshiped these creatures and considered them deities. For instance, Hathor, the Egyptian sky goddess, was depicted as a cow,[206] and the Egyptian god Apis is associated with a bull.[207] Therefore, this plague struck at the core of the religious and conceptual worldview of the Egyptians and underscored Yahweh's superiority over the Egyptian gods and goddesses.[208] Although the pestilence itself would have struck silently, its effects would have been noisy – with animals whimpering, whining, and groaning in pain.

Similar to the fourth plague, God distinguishes between Egyptian and Israelite livestock, ensuring that no animal belonging to an Israelite is affected

---

204. Hyperbole is a literary device, a figure of speech that contains an exaggeration for emphasis. J. A. Cuddon, ed., *A Dictionary of Literary Terms and Literary Theory*, 5th ed. (Oxford: Wiley-Blackwell, 2013), 346.
205. See https://www.aphis.usda.gov/animal-disease/swine/protect-pigs?gad_source=1&gclid=CjwKCAjw_ZC2BhAQEiwAXSgClqD0tFqk2r4OU2Et4SSkolFzjBaodvbLu1TVfJ0bRge6d15h-WgiZRoCIsQQAvD_BwE. Accessed August 20, 2024.
206. M. Heerma Van Voss, "Hathor," *DDD*, 385–386. Erik Hornung, "Ancient Egyptian Religious Iconography," in *CANE*, 1716–1717.
207. Hart, *The Routledge Dictionary of Egyptian Gods and Goddesses*, 29.
208. See Herman Te Velde, "Theology, Priests, and Worship in Ancient Egypt," in *CANE*, 1736.

by the plague. This repeated emphasis on not a single animal belonging to the Israelites dying (9:4, 6, 7) may be seen as a hyperbole that accentuates the miraculous nature of this plague. God's warning, along with a day's notice before execution of the plague, demonstrates his leniency toward Pharaoh, giving Pharaoh time to relent and obey God's command (9:5). Each plague is an opportunity for Pharaoh to soften his heart and release the Israelites, but Pharaoh stubbornly refuses to relent.

Despite investigating and verifying that not even one of the Israelite livestock had died, Pharaoh's heart remains "unyielding" (9:7). Here, the narrator uses wordplay to highlight the dynamic confrontation between God and Pharaoh. God used a terrible or severe (*kabed*, 9:3) plague of pestilence to combat Pharaoh's hardened (*kabed*) heart, but Pharaoh's heart remained hardened (*kabed*, 9:7). A similar wordplay is apparent when God sent a dense or great (*kabed*, 8:24) swarm of flies into the Egyptian houses, but Pharaoh's heart remained hardened (*kabed*, 8:32). In the struggle between God and Pharaoh, God chose a measure-for-measure military strategy to battle Pharaoh's obstinate heart.[209]

9:8–12 The Sixth Plague: Boils

The escalation of the plagues is evident: they begin as a mere nuisance with the first four plagues (blood, frogs, gnats, flies), then intensify with the fifth plague that affects livestock, and now target humans in the sixth plague. These plagues create chaos in an otherwise orderly world, roughly mirroring the creation order outlined in Genesis 1, which moves from water to animals to human beings. Each subsequent plague also increases in intensity and the severity of its impact on human lives.

The outbreak of boils on human skin resembles symptoms of anthrax, a disease that results in skin ulcerations and malignant pustules.[210] This disease attacks both the internal and external systems of the body, impairing basic physical functions like walking and sitting. In the context of the Egyptian pantheon, this plague might have been associated with the Egyptian goddess Sekhmet, depicted as a lion-headed deity of plagues. Her name means "the powerful one,"[211] and in ancient Egypt, she was perceived as being responsible

---

209. There are many wordplays in the plague narrative. For example, in 9:7, Pharaoh "sent" people to investigate the plague, as opposed to "sending" the Israelites out of Egypt as God told them to do.
210. Sarna, *Exodus*, 45.
211. Hart, *The Routledge Dictionary of Egyptian Gods and Goddesses*, 138.

for plagues as well as being the healer of plagues. The priests of her cult were often medical doctors or veterinary surgeons.[212]

The boils were so severe that the Egyptian magicians could not even stand (9:11), suggesting that the boils had also affected their feet. The phrase "could not stand before Moses" carries an additional layer of meaning, implying that these magicians were powerless against Moses and his God. In Deuteronomy, having painful boils on the body is listed among the covenant curses that Israel would experience if they disobeyed the covenant (Deut 28:35);[213] here, however, the boils afflict the Egyptians. Like the plague on the livestock, the boils in themselves are silent but can provoke moans, cries, and even screams of pain. As in the fifth plague, the staff of Moses is not mentioned. Instead, God instructs Moses and Aaron to take handfuls of soot from a furnace and throw it in the air before Pharaoh. Initially, the soot turns into fine dust, but soon after, boils erupt, affecting both humans and animals throughout Egypt. The narrator then states that "the LORD hardened Pharaoh's heart" (9:12) – the first occurrence of such divine hardening in Exodus. God had given Pharaoh five chances to respond favorably (7:23; 8:15, 19, 32; 9:7), but each time, he had refused. Now, in this sixth plague, God allows Pharaoh's heart to remain hardened.[214]

9:13–35 The Seventh Plague: Hail

This plague, which marks the beginning of the third triad of plagues, resembles the earlier pattern where Moses confronts Pharaoh in the morning and warns him of the impending plague. The description of this plague is one of the longest among the ten plagues and includes meticulous details about the impact of the hail on vegetation (9:25). The severity of the plague reaches new levels of destruction, afflicting not only the Egyptians but also their land, animals, plants, and trees. The narrative introduces new assertions such as "so you may know that there is no one like me in all the earth" (9:14) that emphasize God's incomparability and his supremacy over Pharaoh and the created order.

God declares that although he could have used a plague to strike down Pharaoh and the Egyptians, he has chosen to spare Pharaoh's life so that God's power might be demonstrated and his "name might be proclaimed in all the

---

212. Currid, *Ancient Egypt and the Old Testament*, 111.
213. Although the boils reflect one of the covenant curses, there are always exceptions, as seen in the story of Job whose boils, despite covering him from head to toe (Job 2:7), were not due to his violation of divine moral codes.
214. See my comments on Exodus 4:21.

earth" (9:16). The God who rescues works once again to achieve that end. "All the earth" (9:14, 16) accentuates God's kingship over all nations, not just his precious Israel. God's power over "all the earth" forms a striking contrast to the hail's devastation that struck "all the land of Egypt" (9:24) and "everything in the fields" (9:25).[215] The recurrent use of "all" emphasizes the magnitude and scope of the plague of hail on Egypt. The thunderous sound of hail pouring down from the heavens would have been deafening and would have inflicted vast devastation on land, houses, and other structures. The size and weight of hail can range from tiny pellets to golf-ball-sized chunks. I have witnessed pebble-sized hail falling, and the sound was loud. How much louder and more destructive it would have been if the hail had been the size of golf balls? Throughout the OT, hail often serves as God's instrument of destruction and judgment.[216]

The plague of hail confronted several ancient Egyptian deities, including the sky goddess Nut, god Shu – the sky god's supporter – and Tefnut, the goddess of moisture, rain, and water.[217]

Once again, God gives Pharaoh one day's advance notice of the plague of hail. Had Pharaoh paused to reflect on the state of his nation or recognized his own limitations, perhaps this plague could have been averted, sparing him and his people. God's warning is explicit: "At this time tomorrow I will send the worst hailstorm that has ever fallen on Egypt . . . bring your livestock . . . to a place of shelter . . . every person and animal that has not been brought in . . . will die" (9:18–19). Now, Pharaoh's officials are split into two camps: those who feared God's word and brought their livestock into the house, and those who disregarded the warning and left their animals in the fields. Within Egyptian society, one can discern a gradual shift – from standing with Pharaoh to recognizing the "finger of God" to fearing God and obeying his commands. This process of change reflects God's intention for all people, including the Egyptians, to come to know him (9:14). However, Pharaoh shows no inclination to join this group of Egyptian "converts" – at least not yet, and probably never.

---

215. The NIV translates "all" as "everything."
216. Joshua 10:11; Psalms 78:47; 147:17; Isaiah 28:2, 17; 30:30; Ezekiel 13:11, 13; 38:22; Haggai 2:17.
217. Currid, *Ancient Egypt and the Old Testament*, 112. The Egyptians depicted her as human in form but she can appear as the Sky Cow. Hart, *The Routledge Dictionary of Egyptian Gods and Goddesses*, 110.

After the hailstorm subsides, Pharaoh and his officials "hardened their hearts" (9:34). When Moses stretches out his staff toward the sky, God sends thunder, hail, and lightning. As the narrator plainly states, "the LORD rained hail on the land of Egypt" (9:23). The assertion that "it was the worst storm in all the land of Egypt since it had become a nation" (9:24) captures the severity of the plague. Never, since the founding of Egypt, had the Egyptians faced disaster on such a monumental scale. The devastation of hail struck everything in the field, affecting humans, animals, plants, and trees. The repetition of "everything" and "every" in verse 25 highlights the totality and completeness of the destruction.[218] The dramatic intensity of this plague on the Egyptians stands in stark contrast to the Israelites' experience in the land of Goshen, where not a single hailstone fell (9:26). This geographical separation evokes the creation story, where God uses separation as a way to bring order out of chaos (Gen 1:6–7, 14, 18).

Verses 27–35 recount, in great detail, the consequences of the seventh plague, particularly in relation to Pharaoh's reactions and his dialogue with Moses. For the first time in the narrative, Pharaoh confesses to Moses and Aaron, saying, "This time I have sinned . . . the LORD is in the right, and I and my people are in the wrong" (9:27). Subsequently, Pharaoh begs Moses and Aaron to plead with God to stop the hail, promising to release the Israelites. Although Pharaoh's confession might seem genuine, only his actions would prove its authenticity. Remarkably, this is the third occasion on which Pharaoh requests Moses's intercession and promises to release the Israelites. Going by the outcomes of the first two instances and this current one, it is clear that Pharaoh's word does not carry much weight.

Moses agrees to Pharaoh's request, adding that when the thunder and hail stop, Pharaoh will know that "the earth is the LORD's" (9:29). However, Moses also states that he knows that Pharaoh and his officials "still do not fear the LORD God" (9:30). It is not clear how Moses discerns this, whether through intuition, observation of Pharaoh's attitude or tone, or some other means. Nevertheless, Moses keeps his promise and leaves the city, spreading out his hands toward God and causing the thunder and hail to cease (9:33).

Egyptians are familiar with wheat and barley because they are used to making beer – the national drink of Egypt. Wheat and barley are also vital ingredients for bread and cake, which were essential parts of everyday life in

---

218. Hamilton notes that the word "all" or "every" appears twelve times in this plague. Hamilton, *Exodus*, 149.

ancient Egypt.²¹⁹ The information about the flax and barley (9:31–32) serves a dual purpose. First, it creates suspense regarding how Moses will respond to Pharaoh's request in verses 27 and 28. Second, it sets the stage for the next plague of locusts because if all the plants had been destroyed by hail, there would be nothing left for the locusts to consume. The use of "all" and "every" in describing the eighth plague is, therefore, hyperbolic – an exaggerated figure of speech not meant to be taken literally.

When Pharaoh sees that the plague has ceased, "he sinned again: He and his officials hardened their hearts" (9:34). The term "hardened" is literally "heavy" or "severe," the same expression used in describing the "heavy hail" (9:18) and the "very severe" hail (9:24).²²⁰ The battle between God and Pharaoh continues, with measure-for-measure responses by both Pharaoh and God. This section concludes by reiterating the hardness of Pharaoh's heart, as foretold by God (9:35). The motif of hail raining down from the heavens often symbolizes the judgment of God.²²¹ Unfortunately, Pharaoh and his officials refuse to take this warning to heart. Once again, God's hardening of Pharaoh's heart (9:12) and Pharaoh's own hardening (9:35) form a dynamic interplay between divine sovereignty and human volition.

10:1–20 The Eighth Plague: Locusts

The narrator introduces fresh elements in the eighth plague (10:7) and provides details about the interaction between Pharaoh and Moses. Starting immediately where the preceding chapter ended, this section reiterates divine action, reinforcing that God has hardened Pharaoh's heart and he will perform miraculous signs and that Moses will later recount how God had "dealt harshly"²²² with the Egyptians and performed his signs among them so that they "may know that I am the Lord" (10:1–2). Here, God continues to teach the Egyptians who he is through signs and wonders that the Egyptians could not replicate.

Moses and Aaron approach Pharaoh and convey God's message to him: "How long will you refuse to humble yourself before me?" (10:3). The Hebrew term for "humble" (ʿanah) denotes a state of suffering and affliction.²²³ Thus,

---

219. White, *Everyday Life in Ancient Egypt*, 107.
220. NIV translates it as "worst storm."
221. For instance, Joshua 10:11; Psalms 18:12; 147:17; Isaiah 28:2; 30:30; Ezekiel 13:11; Haggai 2:17.
222. NASV and JPS render the phrase as "made a mockery." By performing the signs against what Egyptians honored as their gods, God humiliated Pharaoh and made him a joke.
223. Later, the text describes Moses as a man of ʿanah (Num 12:3). The word ʿanah carries a wide range of meanings including "to be bowed down, afflicted, humble, to become low, to

humility requires enduring hardships such as swallowing one's pride or repressing a desire for self-exaltation. Throughout the first seven plagues, Pharaoh has exhibited a hardened heart that refuses to yield to God's power. Moses and Aaron warn Pharaoh, giving him a day's notice and cautioning him about the consequences of not releasing the Israelites – God will bring locusts to Egypt (10:4). Locust plagues, which were common in the ancient Near East, frequently functioned as signs of divine judgment and covenant curses in the OT.[224] The ancient Egyptians worshiped the god Senehem, whom they believed could protect people from pests. This time, however, Senehem could not help them.[225]

The scope of the devastation caused by the locust plague is evident from its impact on vegetation and human livelihood: the locusts will cover the surface of the land so completely that it cannot even be seen. They eat whatever vegetation was left after the hailstorm. They will eat every tree in the field and invade every Egyptian home. The narrator stresses the unprecedented impact of this plague: no one – including their ancestors – had ever seen something so devastating from the day they had first settled in Egypt until now (10:5–6).

Upon hearing this proclamation, Pharaoh's officials respond with the question, "How long will this man be a snare to us?" (10:7), echoing God's earlier question to Pharaoh through Moses: "How long will you refuse to humble yourself before me?" (10:3). They then urge Pharaoh to release the Israelites, concluding with another question: "Do you not yet realize that Egypt is ruined?" (10:7) Pharaoh had previously declared, "I do not know the Lord and I will not let Israel go" (5:2). Even Pharaoh's own officials could discern his blind spot, yet Pharaoh remains unyielding.

As a result, Moses and Aaron are brought back to Pharaoh. The passive voice here subtly reflects Pharaoh's unyielding heart despite his slight openness to compromise under the circumstances. Pharaoh agrees to allow the Israelites to leave but poses a question: "But tell me who will be going" (10:8). It is not clear why Pharaoh asks this question. Judging from what follows, Pharaoh intended to exert control over who departed from his country. Moses replies that all Israelites, regardless of age or gender, will go. Pharaoh then imposes a condition, stating that only the men could depart, leaving behind the women

---

be downcast, to be weakened." *BDB*, 776. In Pharaoh's case, to be humble is to place himself under God's sovereignty and acknowledge God as the higher authority.
224. For example, Deuteronomy 28:38; Judges 6:5; 1 Kings 8:37; Jeremiah 46:23; Joel 1:2–4; Amos 4:9; Nahum 3:5–17.
225. Currid, *Ancient Egypt and the Old Testament*, 112.

and the children – perhaps as hostages to ensure the return of the men. Moses and Aaron are then dismissed from Pharaoh's presence.

Pharaoh's tactics will resonate with those in the diaspora since the diasporic lifestyle often involves families being separated across continents. Frequently, a breadwinner – typically the father or mother – will relocate to a foreign country for work, leaving family members behind with the hope of reuniting in the future when economic circumstances improve. It seems that Pharaoh's intention in saying he would only allow the men to go with Moses was to prevent the Israelites from leaving Egypt permanently.

Just as God had said, when Moses stretches out his staff over the land of Egypt, the locusts come (10:12–13). The narrator describes the arrival and spread of the locusts in Egypt in this way: a) God sends an east wind that blows across the land throughout the day and night; b) By morning, the east wind carries in the locusts; and c) The locusts invade all Egypt and settle down in every area of the land. The narrator then remarks that "never before had there been such a plague of locusts, nor will there ever be again" (10:14). By using an element of nature (the east wind) to influence another element of nature (the locusts), God demonstrates his sovereignty over nature and the revered Egyptian principle of *ma'at*. The east wind reemerges in Exodus 14:21, where God employs it to drive back the Red Sea and turn it into dry land, allowing the Israelites to pass through. Nature lies under God's control, beyond the domain of Pharaoh and the Egyptian gods.

The locust invasion is described in meticulous detail, with repeated use of "all" or "every" to portray the devastating scale of the plague.[226] The locusts cover the surface of the entire land to the extent that the land turns black (*khashaq*), evoking the darkness (*khosheq*) at the beginning of creation (Gen 1:2)! This covering foreshadows the water that will engulf the Egyptians at the Red Sea (14:28; 15:5) and anticipates the next plague – the plague of darkness, a motif of decreation. The locusts devour all the plants and all the fruit of the trees that had survived the hailstorm, leaving nothing green in all the land of Egypt (10:15). Since locusts are winged insects – larger than smaller insects like gnats and flies – their presence creates a resounding noise as they fly and devour vegetation. The sights and sounds, as well as the extent of the destruction, intensify during the eighth plague.

---

226. Fretheim notices that "all" (*kol*) appears seven times in 10:12–15. The repetition stresses the absoluteness of the devastation left by the locusts. Fretheim, *Exodus*, 127.

Pharaoh hurriedly summons Moses and Aaron and confesses, once again, "I have sinned against the LORD your God and against you" (10:16). He implores them to forgive his sin "once more" and intercede to God on his behalf to "take this deadly plague away" (10:17). The devastation of all vegetation in Egypt forces Pharaoh to swallow his pride, even though temporarily. New vocabulary such as "quickly summoned" and "once more" in Pharaoh's response indicates his growing desperation and recognition of his powerlessness to get rid of the plague. In hindsight, it is clear that Pharaoh's apparent humility was shallow and insincere. Moses grants Pharaoh's request, and God causes a strong west wind to blow the locusts into the Red Sea,[227] effectively removing them from Egypt. Where previously the locusts had "invaded all Egypt," now "not a locust was left anywhere in Egypt" (10:14, 19). The phrase "not a locust was left anywhere" (10:19) reflects the same concept and rhetoric as "not one of them survived" – referring to the Egyptians – in Exodus 14:28. The locust plague serves as a precursor to the greater miracle of the Israelites' crossing of the Red Sea.

The description of this plague concludes with the statement that God hardened Pharaoh's heart and, therefore, Pharaoh did not let the Israelites go (10:20), thus forming an *inclusio* with the opening line of this section (10:1).

10:21–29 The Ninth Plague: Darkness

The blackened sky in the eighth plague sets the stage for the darkness in the ninth plague. This darkness might have been caused by the scorching sirocco wind that blows in each spring from Saharan Africa or Arabia, carrying thick sand and dust. This wind, which can last for several days, darkens the sky.[228] This darkness could also have been caused by a solar eclipse. In traditional Chinese thinking, natural phenomenon like an eclipse of the sun – which is regarded as an astronomical abnormality – were viewed as a form of divine punishment. Legend has it that during the Han Dynasty (206 BCE–220 BCE), a solar eclipse was seen as an omen of impending disasters and even the death of the emperor.[229]

For the Egyptians, who worshiped the sun god Amon-Re (or Amun-Re or Amun-Ra) as a supreme deity with power over darkness and demons, the darkening of the sky must have been petrifying. The rising of Amon-Re in the

---

227. The "West wind" is literally the "wind of the sea."
228. Sarna, *Exodus*, 50.
229. Lee, "The Plague of Darkness and the Creation of Light," 443.

east symbolized new life and resurrection, whereas his going down in the west symbolized death and the underworld.[230] Some even believed that Pharaoh was the sun god incarnate,[231] and so the darkening of the sky directly challenged the Egyptian sun god, rendering him impotent. The darkness must have been a heavy blow to the Egyptian ethos and religiosity. This darkness was the kind "that can be felt" (10:21), which may refer to its intense physical presence or the heavy sand and dust carried by the scorching wind.[232] In Psalm 105, when the psalmist recalls the exodus event, he names the darkness first among the plagues in Egypt.[233] Given the context of Egyptian worship of the sun god, the plague of darkness must have made the strongest impression on the personal and collective memory of both Egypt and Israel. This plague, while dealing with natural elements, also relates to religious aspects such as God's power over the Egyptian gods.

Similar to the third and sixth plagues, the ninth plague strikes suddenly, without any warning from God, such as "Tomorrow, I will . . ." (9:18). Moses obeys God's command and stretches out his hand toward the sky, causing thick darkness to descend upon all Egypt for three days. In contrast, the Israelites continue to experience light in their homes during this time of darkness (10:23).

The phrase "darkness covered all Egypt" (10:22) brings to mind the statement "darkness was over the surface of the deep" (Gen 1:2). In this sense, Egypt experiences chaos similar to the primordial waters at creation. The three-day period recalls several biblical accounts involving the number three: the third day of creation when God separated the waters and formed dry land (Gen 1:9–13), the Israelites' "three-day journey" to sacrifice to God (Exod 3:18; 8:27), the three hours of darkness during Jesus's crucifixion (Matt 27:45; Mark 15:33; Luke 23:44–45a), and Jesus's resurrection on the third day.[234] The reference to the Israelites having "light" (10:23) echoes "let there be light" and

---

230. Currid, *Ancient Egypt and the Old Testament*, 112. In a hymn to Amun-Re, the opening lines read: "Adoration of Amon-Re, the bull resident in Heliopolis, Chief of all the gods, the good god, the beloved, who gives life to every warm being and to every good herd." It expresses the benevolent and powerful nature of the Sun god who was considered the "God of gods and a good shepherd" in the Egyptian religious milieu. "The Great Cairo Hymn of Praise to Amun-Re," trans. Robert K. Ritner (*COS* 1.25: 37).
231. For more on Re, the Sun god, see J. Assmann, "Re," *DDD*, 689–692. Enns, *Exodus*, 228–229.
232. Sarna, *Exodus*, 51.
233. Psalm 105:28.
234. For the prediction and prefiguration of Jesus's resurrection on the third day from the Old Testament to the New Testament, which involves the motif of rising up out of the water

"there was light" in the creation account (Gen 1:3). The ninth plague combines the themes of creation, darkness, light, order, and chaos, which anticipate the emergence of a new creation. This creation motif will resurface in an even more pronounced way when the Israelites cross the Red Sea.

Although Pharaoh agrees to release the Israelites, including the women and children, he imposes a condition: their flocks and herds must remain in Egypt (10:24). This is Pharaoh's third attempt to negotiate a compromise. Moses rejects Pharaoh's proposal, insisting that "not a hoof is to be left behind" because the animals are necessary to offer sacrifices to God (10:26). The narrative concludes by stating that God hardens Pharaoh's heart and that Pharaoh is no longer willing to release the Israelites. One can imagine Pharaoh's fury as he shouts, "Get out of my sight!" and declares that he never wants to see Moses again (10:28). The plague ends with Moses echoing Pharaoh's sentiment.[235] The final and most devastating blow to Pharaoh and the Egyptians is still to come.

11:1–10 The Tenth Plague: Firstborn

It is only after the tenth plague that Pharaoh finally relents and permits the Israelites to leave Egypt. The tenth plague is closely linked with the firstborn son, the institution of the Passover, and the actual exodus event, which includes the crossing of the Red Sea. The narrator skillfully interweaves these three themes to present this final plague as the ultimate blow to Pharaoh's heart. Simultaneously, the connection between the tenth plague and the Passover becomes a significant marker of Israel's identity formation. The God of Israel is the one who led Israel out of slavery in Egypt and also the one who passed over death to give Israel a new identity and a new life with God.

The firstborn son was the heir to the throne of Pharaoh. By killing the firstborn sons of Egypt, God forces Pharaoh to confront God's sovereign power that strips him of his self-declared divinity. In ancient Egypt, Pharaoh was considered a son of the sun god Amon-Re. Therefore, the attack on the firstborn sons can be viewed as a direct attack on Pharaoh's perceived deity and authority, which ultimately exalts the God of Israel as the one true God.[236] Ironically, the killing of the firstborn sons serves as poetic justice for Pharaoh's

---

(Exod 14–15; Jonah 2:10) and rising up out of the ground (John 12:24), see Nicholas P. Lunn, "'Raised on the Third Day According to the Scriptures': Resurrection Typology in the Genesis Creation Narrative," *JETS* 57, no. 3 (2014): 523–555.

235. The motif of seeing, ironically, contrasts with the darkness in the land of Egypt where "no one could see anyone else" (10:23).

236. Enns, *Exodus*, 245.

earlier killing of Israel's infant boys at birth (1:22). As the first nine plagues are interconnected from water to land and air and from affecting the animals to human beings, so too the tenth plague of killing the firstborn son is closely linked to the plague of darkness, a sign of decreation and chaos. While the first nine plagues conclude with the hardening of Pharaoh's heart, the tenth plague leads to a different outcome. As Dozeman rightly notes, "The death of the Egyptian firstborn is an epiphany of darkness."[237]

THE FIRSTBORN SON IN ASIAN CULTURES

The status of the firstborn or eldest son holds great significance in many Asian cultures. Typically, the firstborn son is considered the "second in command" after the father and bears the responsibility of demonstrating filial piety, which includes conducting mourning rites after the death of the father. He is also entrusted with the family name and the care of younger siblings. In families that lack financial resources, the firstborn son is expected to work to provide for the family. In well-to-do families, the firstborn usually inherits the family businesses and properties and is given authority over his siblings. Similarly, in ancient Israel, the firstborn son enjoyed an elevated status, received a double portion of the inheritance (Deut 21:17), and was a symbol of his father's strength (Gen 49:3). Israel, as God's treasured possession, is considered God's firstborn son (Exod 4:22). Therefore, the tenth plague reflects God's measure-for-measure principle – that is, "a son for a son." As God tells Pharaoh, through Moses, "'Let my son go, so he may worship me.' But you refused to let him go; so I will kill your firstborn son" (Exod 4:23). The tenth plague was not an afterthought; on the contrary, it was part of God's plan from the outset, from the time he called Moses.

---

237. Thomas B. Dozeman, *God at War: Power in the Exodus Tradition* (New York: Oxford University Press, 1996), 19.

First, God speaks to Moses, cautioning him about the impending plague. He then instructs Moses to tell the Israelites to ask their Egyptian neighbors for articles of silver and gold. In addition, God grants favor to the Israelites in the eyes of the Egyptians (11:1–3). The asking for silver and gold, along with granting the Israelites favor in the eyes of the Egyptians, had already been on God's mind during Moses's commissioning (3:21–22) and as far back as God's promise to Abraham (Gen 15:14). As always, history unfolds according to God's plan. Verse 3 serves as a "sidebar" for readers about the elevated status of Moses, who was "highly regarded" in Egypt by both Pharaoh's officials and among the Israelites.[238] The threefold repetition in verse 3 (highly regarded in Egypt, by Pharaoh's officials and by the people) stresses Moses's honorable position within both the Egyptian and Israelite communities.

Continuing from where Exodus 10:29 left off, Exodus 11:4–8 highlights the crucial phrase "go out" (*yatsa*).[239] Moses relays God's instructions to Pharaoh: "I will go out to Egypt, and all the firstborn in Egypt will die, from Pharaoh's firstborn to the firstborn of the slave girls to the firstborn of cattle. There will be a great cry in Egypt. By contrast, not even a dog will bark among the Israelites. That's how I will make a distinction between Egypt and Israel."[240] Dogs are known for their barking, so the phrase "not even a dog will bark" implies absolute silence.[241] The contrast between the great cry – the "loud wailing" (11:6) – in Egypt and the complete silence in Israel could not be more striking. Consequently, all Pharaoh's officials would beg Moses and all the Israelites to leave Egypt, and Moses confirms that he would then "go out" or "leave" (NIV). Having said this, Moses, "hot with anger," departs from Pharaoh's presence (10:8). The repetitive use of "go out" subtly hints at the impending exodus – "exodus" in Greek, Latin, and English means "to go out."

The exchange between Pharaoh and Moses concludes with God informing Moses that Pharaoh will not listen to him and that because of this, God will multiply his wonders (11:9) – and one such wonder will be the parting

---

238. The last phrase, "Among the people," can refer to the Israelites or the Egyptian people. I've understood it as the Israelites.
239. NIV translates as "go throughout" (11:4).
240. My paraphrase.
241. Kessler's study on silence provides insights into the diverse ways in which it is used in the Old Testament context. Silence can denote the state "when everything falls apart," as in divine judgment (Zeph 1:7; Hab 2:20; Zech 2:13) or in the context of death, *Sheol*, and the grave. Kessler, *Between Hearing and Silence*, 33–34, 87–96. "Not even a dog will bark" can simply refer to the condition of absolute quietness or it can also point to the anticipation of God's impending judgment.

of the Red Sea. God hardens Pharaoh's heart, and he stubbornly refuses to release the Israelites (11:10). Commentators note the tragic-comical fact of Pharaoh's inability to control his own heart.[242] The tenth plague is interwoven with the narratives of the institution of the Passover and the consecration of the firstborn sons, which take place before the execution of the tenth plague in Exodus 12:19–30. There is, therefore, an inextricable link between the killing of Pharaoh's firstborn, the Passover, and the consecration of Israel's firstborn sons. This interweaving of narratives recalls God's words in Exodus 4:22–23.

THE CHINESE FESTIVALS AND THE PASSOVER

The Chinese people celebrate a variety of festivals and traditions throughout the year, and they often continue to practice these rituals even when living abroad as a way to preserve their ancestral roots and cultural heritage. For instance, during the Mid-Autumn Festival (*zhōng qīu jié*) – which takes place in early autumn when the full moon is at its brightest (typically in September) – the Chinese people eat mooncakes or gift these to loved ones. In cities like Los Angeles or San Francisco, wherever there are significant Chinese communities, local bakeries sell beautifully packaged mooncakes. The Mid-Autumn Festival is a time to gather with family and enjoy the full moon. It is also a time to remember those family members who are far from home or unable to join the rest of their family. As family members who reside in different places gather together and gaze at the full moon, this evokes a sense of belonging, knowing that family members in different geographical regions are also looking at the same full moon and thinking of one another. The roundness of the full moon symbolizes unity, and gazing at it evokes memories and a yearning for the family to be reunited.

The Lunar New Year (*xīn nían or chuēn jié*) holds great significance for the Chinese, the Chinese diaspora, and many Asian cultures. It is their most popular festival, typically falling between late January and mid-February in the lunar calendar and marking the beginning of a new year. In China, the Lunar New Year is a three-day national holiday that

---

242. For example, Hamilton, *Exodus*, 169.

is celebrated throughout the country, much like Independence Day or Thanksgiving in the United States. Festivities during this period include splendid fireworks displays and delicious food. The Chinese diaspora honors this tradition by gathering with their families to share meals, presenting red envelopes with cash to their unmarried children as a token of blessing, and exchanging or giving gifts. For those who have lost touch with these traditions, their Chinese immigrant church will often remind them of these customs and practices.

The Passover ritual is strikingly similar to the traditions of the Lunar New Year. Traditionally, the celebration of the Lunar New Year is referred to as *gùo nián*, which means "pass over nián." Whereas *nián* usually means "year" in Chinese, in this context, *nián* refers to a mythical beast that allegedly attacks people during the New Year. This beast is said to fear loud noises, bright lights, and the color red. Therefore, people engage in activities such as playing loud music, holding firework displays, tying red ribbons on doorposts, and wearing red clothes to ward off this mythical monster.[1] To this day, Chinese people worldwide write words of blessings in Chinese calligraphy on red posters and hang them on their doors or as decorations in churches.

At the heart of the Lunar New Year festivities is a focus on food, feasts, and banquets. There is a certain power in eating together as a family or community since this not only forges kinship bonds but also affirms a shared communal identity. Within the Jewish tradition, Passover is literally a meal or feast enjoyed by faith communities. In the NT, this ritual is superseded by the Lord's Supper, which Jesus instituted during a Passover meal to commemorate his death (1 Cor 11:23–26). There are striking parallels between the traditional Chinese customs of celebrating with food and red decorations and the Christian identity centered on Jesus's redemptive work through his shed blood.

While our cultural, ethnic, and religious identities may sometimes merge and intertwine, the parallels between Passover and the Lunar New Year are striking. For those living in the diaspora, individuals may reframe their identity, viewing themselves as pilgrims or sojourners, and redefine their identity by participating in the broader narrative of the people of God. We can all experience a new beginning that is grounded in the redemption of God through the blood of Jesus while also respecting and honoring one another's ethnic and cultural identities.

---

1. Adam Augustyn, "Chinese New Year," https://www.britannica.com/topic/Chinese-New-Year.

Exodus 1:1–15:21

12:1–14:31 THE PASSOVER AND THE EXODUS

Observing the Mid-Autumn Festival and the Lunar New Year helps people remember their ethnic and cultural identity. Similarly, for Jews, observing Passover commemorates God's historical acts that define their identity as a people redeemed by God, influencing how they are to treat the marginalized in their midst.[243] In observing these rituals, memory plays an integral role in identity formation – "no memory, no human identity."[244] Therefore, Passover and its observance perpetuate the memory of God's rescue of Israel from Egypt. It is significant that the Passover ritual is conducted within a family setting, offering parents an opportunity to teach their children about the significance of this event (Exod 12:25–27).

Exodus 12–14 move God's redemptive story forward, beginning with instructions about the first Passover and moving on to their Red Sea crossing. This section comprises detailed regulations for observing the Passover (12:1–28), the initiation of the exodus event (12:29–42), Passover instructions for non-Israelites (12:43–51), a call to remember the exodus for future generations of Israelites (13:1–16),[245] and an account of how God led his people through the wilderness (13:17–22), culminating in the climactic moment of the ten plagues – the Red Sea crossing (14:1–31).

The Passover ritual is intertwined with the broader narrative of the tenth plague, the exodus event, and the consecration of the firstborn sons. Chapter 12 is a complex composition, comprising several literary units that each deal with different aspects of the exodus event. The word "keep" or "observe" (*shamar*) appears seven times in the chapter, emphasizing the command to observe the Passover.[246] Given its complex structure and the overlapping of various literary units, this chapter reflects multiple layers of tradition, suggesting that it might be the result of an extensive redaction process.[247]

Chapter 12 opens and closes with the Passover, with the exodus event described in the middle, thus forming an *inclusio* or sandwich structure as shown below: This section comprises detailed regulations for observing the

---

243. Deuteronomy 15:12–15 and 24:17–18.
244. Volf, *The End of Memory*, 147.
245. Volf indicates the importance of memory and community. The sacred memories of both Jews and Christians are communal memories as well as pointing toward the future through looking at the past. The future is made present in their shared communal memories. Volf, *The End of Memory*, 99–101.
246. The root word (*shamar*) is translated differently in NIV: Take care (12:6), celebrate (12:17, 2x), obey (12:24), observe (12:25), kept vigil (12:42, 2x).
247. Sarna, *Exodus*, 53.

Passover (12:1–28), the initiation of the exodus event (12:29–42), Passover instructions for non-Israelites (12:43–51)

Table 2: The Structure of Exodus 12

The Passover 12:1–28
The exodus event 12:29–42
The Passover for the others 12:42–51

The detailed descriptions of the Passover attest to its significance in Israel's identity formation. Israel is a people rescued by God precisely because he passed over the Israelites' homes marked by blood on their doorposts. The influence of the Passover stretches from the exodus event to religious reforms during critical moments in Israel's history.[248] Later, there developed within Jewish liturgy the "Passover Seder" as a remembrance of God's deliverance of their ancestors from Egyptian bondage. "Seder" means order, and observing the Passover became a time to symbolically reorder or realign one's life according to God's will. Tamara Prosic views the Passover as a rite of passage that signifies passing over from an old order to a new order of life.[249] The Jewish Passover also influenced the Christian practice of the Lord's Supper or Eucharist, which remembers the sacrificial death of Jesus and affirms believers' unity in Christ (1 Cor 11:23–26). Both the Passover meal and the Lord's Supper are sacred rituals that symbolize a transformation in believers' identity – from past to the present, from chaos to order, and from creation to new creation.

Just as observing the Mid-Autumn Festival and the Lunar New Year contributes to identity formation and reinforces cultural identity in the Chinese context, observing the Passover rite is pivotal in forging Israelite identity – from their origin as slaves of the Egyptians to becoming God's redeemed people. In essence, the Passover ritual provides Israel with a framework that distinguishes

---

248. While the first Passover takes place during the tenth plague in Egypt, the next recorded Passover occurs forty years later under the leadership of Joshua when Israel is about to take Jericho (Josh 5:10). The observance of this Passover follows after the circumcision, which aims to connect the second generation of the children of Israel with the covenant (Josh 5:2–7). Observing the Passover is perceived as a key ingredient in the religious reforms of Josiah and Hezekiah. See 2 Kings 23:21–23; 2 Chronicles 35:1–19; 2 Chronicles 30:13–27.

249. Tamara Prosic, "Passover in Biblical Narrative," *JSOT* 82 (1999): 48–49, 53.

insiders from outsiders and invigorates the collective memory of the in-group by linking past experiences with the present.[250]

12:1–28 The Passover

Chapter 12 begins with instructions about the specific time to observe the Passover (12:1–3a), followed by instructions about preparing and eating the Passover lamb (12:3b–11), and concludes with God's rationale for these instructions (12:12–13).

God tells Moses and Aaron that "this month is to be for you the first month, the first month of your year" (12:1). "This month" refers to the month of Abib.[251] Abib means barley, designating springtime, which can also refer to the entire three-month-long season.[252] By designating "this month" as the inaugural month of the year, God introduces a paradigm shift in Israel's religious and cultural identity. This shift breaks away from their past and forges their new identity as God's redeemed people, an identity that is grounded in the exodus event.[253] God's redemption marks the beginning of a new chapter in Israel's collective consciousness, akin to a new creation and a new order. Similarly, in Christianity, by accepting Jesus as one's Savior, a person enters a new realm of reality and becomes a new creation (2 Cor 5:17).

The instructions for carrying out the Passover ritual are recorded in detail, as illustrated by the following table:

---

250. Ritual belongs to the realm of anthropology but is now explored in other disciplines, including biblical studies. For seeing ritual as a cultural framework, see Mary Douglas, *Purity and Danger: An Analysis of Concept of Pollution and Taboo* (London: Routledge & Kegan Paul, 1966), 78–79.
251. In the book of Esther, it is called Nisan (Esth 3:7).
252. The first spring harvests as the beginning of the year marks a deliberate break from other practices among Israel's neighbors, which regard the autumn equinox as the beginning of the year. Michael LeFebvre, *The Liturgy of Creation: Understanding Calendars in Old Testament Context* (Downers Grove: IVP Academic, 2019), 22, 40.
253. The specification of "in the land of Egypt" (Exod 12:1) is meant to indicate that the rite of Passover, unlike other laws, was not instituted in the wilderness.

Table 3: Instructions for the Passover

Date of the rite	On the tenth day of this month (12:3)
What to eat	Take one lamb for each household (12:3)
Instructions for small households	Gather the right number of people to share the lamb (12:4)
Quality of the lamb	Unblemished, one-year-old male; either sheep or goats (12:5)
Further instructions	• Keep the lamb until the fourteenth day of the same month; kill it at twilight (12:6) • Take the blood of the lamb and put it on the sides and tops of the doorframes of their houses (12:7)[254]
How to eat the lamb	• Eat the flesh that very night; roasted over the fire; eat it with unleavened bread and bitter herbs (12:8) • Meat should not be eaten raw or boiled in water; eat the roasted head, legs, and entrails (12:9) • Leftovers should not be eaten the next morning; any leftovers should be burned (12:10)[255]
Dress code and manner of eating	With loins girded, sandals on your feet, staff in your hand; eat in haste (12:11)

The detailed instructions, particularly the emphasis on blood, indicate that the Passover ritual was seen as a form of sacrifice (12:7, 22),[256] while the association with eating signifies its nature as an act of worship.[257] The lamb was to be unblemished and kept under careful watch from the tenth until the fourteenth day. The instructions conclude by emphasizing that this is "the LORD's Passover" (12:11). The exhaustive instructions in this chapter heighten the significance of the Passover rite and emphasize that the Israelites must adhere to all God's requirements.

---

254. Doorposts are the entrances to a room or a house, and they mark the extremities where one would strike first. Another example of such extremities are the earlobe, the right thumb, and the big toe of the right foot (Exod 29:20; Lev 8:23–24). See Hamilton, *Exodus*, 181.
255. In the Old Testament, burning is a way of disposing of impure products (Lev 13:52, 55, 57) or idolatrous impurities (Exod 32:20). Hamilton, *Exodus*, 183.
256. Alexander, *Exodus*, 231.
257. Hamilton notes that in the Old Testament, worship and eating are often associated with each other. This can be seen in the repetition of the word "eat" in Exodus 12:1–20, which appears thirteen times, and in Exodus 12:43–49, where it appears five more times. Hamilton, *Exodus*, 180.

In verses 12–13, God provides the theological rationale behind the Passover ritual. On that fateful night, God would pass through (*'abar*) Egypt, striking down all the firstborns and executing judgment against all the gods of Egypt. The blood of the lamb applied on the doorposts would be a sign for the Israelites, and when God saw this sign, he would pass over the houses of the Israelites and "no destructive plague will touch you when I strike Egypt" (12:13).

In this narrative, God uses a destroyer to exact vengeance for Israel, while the blood serves as a sign of rescue and protection.[258] In biblical history, the concept of a "sign" is significant, and is often tied to remembrance. For instance, the rainbow served as a sign of God's covenant with Noah (Gen 9:12–17), circumcision as a sign of the covenant with Abraham (Gen 17:9–14), and the Sabbath as a sign of the Sinaitic covenant that God expects Israel to observe throughout their generations (Exod 31:16–17).

In verses 14–20, God continues with instructions about the Feast of Unleavened Bread. This feast might have originated from a different tradition but evolved to become part of the Passover observance.[259] Unleavened bread (Hebrew: *matsah*) is a type of bread made with only flour and water, much like pita bread, flatbread, Indian roti, naan, or chapatti. Since this kind of bread has no yeast, it can be made quickly. This haste in preparation symbolizes the Israelites' hurried departure from Egypt (12:39). The sacredness of this feast is reflected in its observance for seven days, the command that it be "a lasting ordinance" for future generations, the prohibition of work, and the warning that non-compliance – whether one was a sojourner (*ger*) or a native – would lead to being cut off from the community (12:14–19). The inclusion of sojourners in this ritual reflects the inclusive nature of this feast. Later, however, a new regulation is imposed requiring that sojourners who want to partake must be circumcised (12:48–49), thus ensuring the ritual integrity of the rite.[260] The repetition of "you are to eat bread made without yeast" or "eat nothing

---

258. In the biblical tradition, the "Destroyer" is used to designate someone who functioned as a supernatural messenger from God who performed the task of annihilating large numbers of people, usually by means of a plague. In Exodus 12:23, the Destroyer acted by God's command and used restraint in killing by passing over the doorposts with the blood of the lamb. Another text that links the Destroyer to the plague is 2 Samuel 24. See S. A. Meier, "Destroyer," in *DDD*: 240–244.
259. Jeffrey H. Tigay, "Exodus," in *The Jewish Study Bible*, 2nd ed., eds. Adele Berlin and Marc Zvi Brettler (Oxford: Oxford University Press, 2014), 118.
260. This ritual integrity recalls the incident in Exodus 4 where Zipporah circumcised the son of Moses so that God would not kill Moses upon his family's return to Egypt (Exod 4:24–26).

made with yeast" (12:15, 18, 20) emphasizes the prohibition against eating leavened bread.

In verses 21–27, Moses gives instructions to the elders of Israel on how to conduct the Passover ritual, including directions about using hyssop to apply blood on the top and both sides of the doorframes (12:22). The identity of the destroyer mentioned in verse 23 is unclear but seems to refer to someone other than God – possibly God's agent or angel, though some scholars consider that God *is* the destroyer.[261] Moses does not merely reiterate God's instructions verbatim but places great emphasis on the lasting significance of the Passover ordinance by instructing the elders to teach it to future generations. The mention of children and the imaginary dialogue where children ask, "What does this ceremony mean to you?" (12:26) and parents respond by explaining the significance of the Passover ritual creates a tradition of remembrance that is rooted within a family context.

The memory of the exodus lives on, primarily through the families in each generation. God's action in passing over and sparing the firstborns of the Israelites while striking down the Egyptians has become central to Israel's identity as a people rescued by God. Each subsequent generation of Israel is called to see themselves "as though he or she had personally come forth out of Egypt."[262] Similarly, observing ethnic festivals and rites such as the Mid-Autumn Festival and the Lunar New Year strengthens kinship ties and ethnic and cultural identity in foreign lands or host countries. Such celebrations typically involve family traditions and church activities in communities where there is significant presence of Chinese migrants.

While most Chinese festivals do not have religious significance, the Passover is closely linked to the national identity of Israel as a people rescued by God. In the era of the monarchy, one of the qualities that characterized a good king was his leadership in religious reform, which included the observance of the Passover. Hezekiah, for instance, reinstituted the Passover during his reign, and many who had not purified themselves were able to partake in the Passover meal because Hezekiah prayed for their forgiveness and God mercifully healed them (2 Chr 30:1–3, 13–20). Similarly, in Josiah's time, when the book of the Law was found, Josiah led the people in renewing their

---

In the Jewish tradition, circumcision and Passover are intimately linked. The word "strike" or "touch" appears in Exodus 4:25, connecting circumcision with Passover. Morales, *Exodus Old and New*, 74–75.
261. Tigay, "Exodus," 119. Compare 1 Corinthians 10:10.
262. Morales, *Exodus Old and New*, 73.

covenant with God and recommitting themselves to observing God's law. This religious reform included the removal of idolatrous objects and priests, as well as the reinstatement of the Passover (2 Kgs 23:4–25).

In later Jewish tradition, the Song of Songs became associated with the Passover because Jewish allegorists interpreted it as a parable portraying the love between God and Israel. Therefore, the Song was seen as the key to unlocking the meaning of the Torah, particularly Exodus. For instance, in Song 2:9, the man standing behind the wall of the woman's house and gazing through the windows is allegorized in the Targum's Song of Songs 2:9 as God, depicted as a gazelle standing behind the wall of the Israelites' homes and seeing the blood of the Passover sacrifice on their doors.[263]

In the NT, Jesus is identified as the Passover lamb sacrificed for sinners (1 Cor 5:7). In Christian tradition, Jesus is seen as having transformed the Passover ritual into the Lord's Supper or Holy Communion. Through this sacrament, Christians commemorate the sacrifice of Jesus, examine their own hearts, and reorient themselves to God (1 Cor 11:23–26).

Upon hearing Moses's words, the people bow down in worship, mirroring their response when they first heard that God had seen their afflictions and cared for them (Exod 4:31). God's concern for his people had been demonstrated through his dramatic actions against the Egyptian powers. Verse 28 serves as an obedience formula, stressing the importance of obedience to God's instructions given through Moses and Aaron.

12:29–42 The Exodus

This passage describes the execution of the final plague. The narrative states that "the LORD struck down all the firstborn in Egypt," from the highest-ranking – that is, the firstborn of Pharaoh – to the lowest, which included the firstborn of prisoners and even cattle. The intensity of this tragedy, which caused Pharaoh and all the Egyptians to get up in the middle of the night, leads to "loud wailing in Egypt" (12:30). While this may be the first specific mention of sound in the plague narrative, sound had played a significant part in the earlier plagues related to frogs, gnats, flies, hail, and locusts, reflecting the devastation and disturbance they caused. Although the plagues

---

263. Philip S. Alexander, *The Targum of Canticles: Translated with a Critical Introduction, Apparatus, and Notes*, Aramaic Bible 17A (Collegeville: Liturgical, 2003), 106. Chloe T. Sun, *Conspicuous in His Absence: Studies in the Song of Songs and Esther* (Downers Grove: IVP Academic, 2021), 206, 210–212.

of livestock, boils, and darkness did not directly involve sound, the pain and inconvenience they caused probably resulted in cries of distress from both animals and humans. The thunderous cries that must have resounded on that darkest night in Egypt's history are difficult to imagine. The fact that Pharaoh called for Moses and Aaron in the middle of the night reflects the urgency of the situation. His tone must have reflected absolute horror as he commanded, "Up! Leave my people, you and the Israelites! Go, worship the Lord as you have requested. Take your flocks and herds, as you have said, and go. And also bless me" (12:31–32). "Up! Leave my people" is literally "Arise! Go! From the midst of my people," which we may rephrase as "Go and get out!" Pharaoh's heart had been hardened, he could no longer control his own heart and keep the Israelites in his land. God had struck at the very core of Pharaoh's being, demonstrating that Pharaoh had not only failed to act as a god but could not even save his firstborn son, the heir to his throne. In the contest between God and Pharaoh, Pharaoh had lost.

The exodus from Egypt is described in Exodus 12:33–39. The Egyptians, fearing for their own lives, urgently demand that the Israelites leave their land, prompting the Israelites to depart hastily,[264] carrying unleavened dough and kneading bowls wrapped in their clothes. Moses also instructs the Israelites to ask the Egyptians for articles of silver and gold and clothing; surprisingly, the Egyptians willingly comply with their request. This was because "the Lord had made the Egyptians favorably disposed toward the people" (12:36), which literally means "the Lord gave grace in the eyes of the Egyptians." The verse concludes by saying, "So they plundered the Egyptians." The basic meaning of "plunder" (*natsal*) or stripped off is "to rescue." Ironically, God rescued the Israelites by making the Egyptians "rescue" their silver and gold for the Israelites. This silver and gold would later play a crucial role in the construction of both the tabernacle and the golden calf!

The Israelites' journey from Rameses to Sukkoth was about one day's distance.[265] The narrative notes that there were "six hundred thousand men on foot" and that this number excluded women and children. This number may be a hyperbole to emphasize the vast number of God's people (compare

---

264. The word "urge" (*khazaq*) is actually the same word used to describe Pharaoh's hardened heart. Alexander remarks: "Whereas Pharaoh was resolute in not releasing the Israelites, his people are determined to do otherwise." Alexander, *Exodus*, 238.
265. Tigay, "Exodus," 120.

1:7), or it could mean "six hundred clans or tribes."²⁶⁶ The "many other people" who accompanied the Israelites might have been non-Israelites residing in Egypt (12:38), some of whom might have been sojourners. This incident shows that God is on the side of the marginalized, the enslaved, and those lacking governmental protection – similar to the situation of undocumented migrants in our own society.

The exodus event represents a salvific act not only for God's people but also for those who are yet to become God's people. By leaving Egypt with the Israelites, these non-Israelites identified themselves as those who desired freedom and a better future for themselves and their descendants. However, not all host countries view the "mixed multitudes" within their borders positively. The issue of immigration in today's world is complex, with attitudes toward refugees and asylum seekers varying from country to country. Still, the biblical vision is clear – God intends for all people to be included in his grand narrative of redemption.

The passage concludes with an editorial note stating that the Israelites lived in Egypt for 430 years and that at the end of this period, "all the Lord's divisions left Egypt" (12:41). "Division" is a military term that refers to an "army" or a "host" (*tsibe'oth*). This editorial comment reflects the situation in a later time, when the Israelites were organized into military ranks to conquer Canaan. In God's agenda, these former slaves would serve as his armies in conquering the land, thereby fulfilling God's covenantal promise to Abraham (compare Ps 105:42–45).

Finally, verse 42 is a command to observe "this night" in honor of God. Although this night was dark, it was the very night that God rescued and released the Israelites from the dominion of darkness that had plagued them in Egypt for four centuries.

12:43–51 The Passover for the Others

In the final scene of the tenth plague, the focus returns to the Passover ritual, introducing seven additional rules concerning foreigners and sojourners living

---

266. The land of Goshen would not have been able to sustain six hundred thousand men, plus children and women. For more information on the issue of this number, see Alexander, *Exodus*, 242–243. The number of 600,000 men is unsustainable based on archaeological findings. The issue could be explained by the translation of the word "thousand" (*'leph*), which can also mean "tribe" or "clan." Six hundred clans or tribes as a military unit would be a more realistic number. See Hoffmeier, *Ancient Israel in Sinai*, 157–159.

among the Israelites.²⁶⁷ The repetition of the word "eat" emphasizes the key point that these rules are not about "where to eat, or what to eat, or how to eat or when to eat, but . . . who may eat."²⁶⁸ These regulations, which had not been stated previously, are now included because "many other people" (12:38) who joined the exodus needed to know the requirements for participating in the Passover.

These regulations are as follows:

1. No foreigner is to eat the Passover meal (12:43).
2. Any purchased slave may participate in the meal after being circumcised (12:44).
3. A sojourner or hired worker is not permitted to eat this meal (12:45).²⁶⁹
4. The meal must be eaten inside the house (12:46a).
5. No one is to break any of the bones of the lamb (12:46b).
6. The whole community of Israel must celebrate this ritual (12:47).
7. A *ger* (foreigner) must be circumcised – along with the males in his household – if he wishes to celebrate the Passover; the same rules apply to both foreigners and natives (12:48–49).

These rules are directed at the "outsiders" among the Israelites. In Chinese, one concept of "outsiders" is often expressed through the designation *"wài,"* which means "outside" or "others." For instance, a Caucasian might be called a *"wài rén"* or *"wài gúo rén,"* meaning an outsider or a person from another country. In Cantonese, a Caucasian might be called a "white person" or even a "ghost person."²⁷⁰ Though these terms may not be used in a derogatory sense, such "name calling" and labeling reveal the perception of the foreignness and otherness of those who do not belong to one's ethnic group. In contrast, God's perspective on foreigners, sojourners, and outsiders is quite different. While God chose Israel as his people, he is not a racist, and he does not show

---

267. "A foreigner" (*ben nekar*) refers to an individual who came to the land temporarily, usually for work. It is distinguished from "a sojourner" (*ger*) who resides with the native on a permanent basis. Tigay, "Exodus," 121. Sarna, *Exodus*, 63.
268. Hamilton, *Exodus*, 197.
269. The "sojourner" (*toshab*) here is not the same as the sojourner (*ger*) in Exodus 2:22. When compared with the latter, *toshab* appears to be more temporary and dependent. See *BDB*, 444. The different terms for the outsiders point to the diversity of "many other people" in the midst of Israel.
270. In the United States, permanent residents are also known as "resident aliens" – highlighting their "alien" status.

partiality. God desires that all people be part of his family. In this case, God permits outsiders to join the Israelites in celebrating the Passover together as one community, provided they meet certain conditions. In God's economy, there is no strict dichotomy between insiders and outsiders; however, the order of inclusion is the Israelites first and then the non-Israelites. The ultimate aim is that everyone should know and worship God as one community.[271]

Circumcision, as the sign of the covenant between God and the Israelites (Gen 17), becomes a prerequisite for non-Israelites who wish to participate in the Passover meal. Within any marginalized group, there are also those who are even more marginalized than others in the group. I remember attending a predominantly White academic conference and lamenting my own social status as an ethnic minority woman in academia. While I sat in my hotel room feeling marginalized and invisible, a maid of Asian descent knocked on my door and asked for permission to clean the room. It struck me then that as a woman of Chinese descent teaching at a seminary in the West, I held a privileged position and enjoyed honored status within my own community, while countless others, like that maid, were struggling to make ends meet or did not have the legal status to work or remain in the country. Being or feeling marginalized is relative. God's concern for the enslaved Israelites demonstrates the breadth of his compassion and mercy. By including non-Israelites alongside his people, God demonstrates that his regulations are not intended to exclude but to include.

The warning not to "break any of the bones" (12:46) is significant because it prefigures Christ's death, during which none of his bones were broken.[272] God's instructions may sometimes seem tedious, but God knows what he is doing. Israel's obedience to God's instructions was absolutely crucial for becoming the people God intended them to be. Ever since its institution, the Passover has remained a foundational memory and a core element of Israel's identity.[273]

The concluding obedience formula – "All the Israelites did just what the Lord had commanded Moses and Aaron" (12:50) – echoes Exodus 12:28.

---

271. Sometimes I am asked why God chose the Israelites and not the Chinese. I always point to God's purpose – regardless of whom God chooses first, God desires that the chosen people (whether Jews, Chinese, or another group) bring knowledge of God to others. God's purpose remains the same.
272. Compare Psalm 34:20; John 19:36.
273. LeFebvre observes that no date is recorded in Exodus until Passover night, stressing its significant and symbolic value to the Israelites. LeFebvre, *The Liturgy of Creation*, 60.

By reiterating God's mighty act of bringing the Israelites out of Egypt on that very day, the formula emphasizes that obedience to God's instructions leads to blessings. Observing the Passover as God has commanded defines the identity of his people. Israel's identity is not determined by race or ethnicity but by identification with the God of Israel and his redemptive work. Thus, this observance plays a crucial role in Israel's identity formation both now and in the future.

The Passover ritual illustrates anthropologist Van Gennep's three stages of the ritual process: separation, transition, and incorporation.[274] Through participating in the Passover, the Israelites separate themselves from their prior identity as slaves to Pharaoh. The observance of the Passover ritual process marks the transitional stage, which might be likened to a rite of passage. Finally, by completing the Passover ritual, Israel is incorporated or reconfigured into the family of God as servants and worshipers of Yahweh. The amazing grace evident through this entire process is that any non-Israelite who is willing to be circumcised is also invited to join the larger family of the people of God.[275] Thus, religious affiliation, rather than ethnic or cultural origin, defines the people of God. As a Chinese or as any non-Israelite who has accepted Jesus as Savior, we are invited to be part of God's family and to participate in a new exodus, leaving behind the slavery of sin to embrace our new identity as the people of God. Though by no means we become perfect in God's sight, we are all on the journey of becoming.

13:1–16 Memory for the Future

This section revisits the theme of the firstborn, giving further instructions for the observance of the Passover ritual by future generations of Israel. The recurrence of this theme reinforces the interconnectedness of various elements in the tenth plague, including the death of the firstborn sons in Egyptian households, the institution of the Passover, the exodus event, and the redemption and consecration of God's firstborn son – Israel. This postscript on the firstborn refers back to Exodus 4:22–23, where God identifies Israel as his firstborn son and declares that if Pharaoh refuses to release Israel, God would kill Pharaoh's own firstborn son. Therefore, the death of Pharaoh's firstborn son is closely linked to the redemption of God's firstborn son – Israel.

---

274. Van Gennep, *The Rites of Passage*, vii.
275. Some church traditions have a similar "requirement" that Christians must be baptized to participate in the Holy Communion or the Lord's Supper (Eucharist).

God initially commands Moses, "Consecrate to me every firstborn male" (13:1), meaning that they were to be set apart and made holy.[276] This command applies to all firstborn males, whether human or animal. Since God claims the firstborn as his own, they hold a special status in the divine realm. In Exodus 13:3–10, Moses reiterates the instructions already given in Exodus 12:14–20, emphasizing that the people must "commemorate this day" or, in the Hebrew, "remember this day" and tell their children about it. The focus of this remembrance is not the painful suffering Israel endured as slaves but God's mighty hand that rescued them from Egypt (13:3, 8, 9, 14, 16). By remembering their past, Israel integrates it into their present and future identity. By their annual observance of the rite of the unleavened bread, Israel embraces its new identity as a people God redeemed by his mighty hand.

The act of consecration was to take place in the month of Abib, which was later called Nisan. "Abib" means "new ears of grain" or "young ears of barley." It refers to the period when vegetation turns green, symbolizing springtime.[277] This month symbolizes a new season of rebirth in nature, marked by the start of the new barley harvest and the reproductive cycle of animals.[278] Therefore, the timing of God's redemption of Israel coincides with new beginnings in nature. Israel's new identity as God's firstborn son corresponds to this renewed creation.

Moses's instructions are forward-looking, as seen in phrases such as "when the Lord brings you into the land" (13:5; see also 13:11), "on that day tell your son" (13:8; see also 13:14), and "this observance will be for you like a sign" (13:9; see also 13:16). He instructs the Israelites to consecrate their firstborn sons after God fulfills his promise and brings them into the land of Canaan, the land he swore to their forefathers (13:11–12), which reflects Moses's confidence that God will accomplish what he had promised. All firstborns, whether human or animal, had to be consecrated because they belonged to God. With regard to a donkey, which was an unclean animal, its firstborn was to be redeemed with a lamb (13:13; compare Lev 27:27). If this was not done, the donkey's

---

276. Sarna indicates that the act of consecration involves a purification rite and an induction ceremony. The purification rite involves bathing, laundering of clothes, and abstaining from any defilement. The induction rite involves an investiture. Sarna, *Exodus*, 65.
277. *BDB*, 1.
278. Sarna, *Exodus*, 64. It is not surprising that the early rabbinic tradition regards the Song of Songs as a divine love song about God and Israel and that love originates in the Spring as Song of Songs 2:8–14 is named "A Poem of Spring." Tremper Longman III, *Song of Songs*, NICOT (Grand Rapids: Eerdmans, 2001), 116.

neck was to be broken, which is a non-sacrificial way of killing an animal.[279] Later, during the wilderness wandering, God selected the Levites in place of the firstborns. These Levites would serve as his priests (Num 3:12; 8:16–18). Nevertheless, the firstborn continues to enjoy a special status with God in both spiritual and ritual contexts.

13:17–22 God Leads the People

Following Moses's address to the Israelites, this section describes how God leads them on a longer route out of Egypt toward Canaan. This was because God knew that a shorter route was likely to take them to areas where they would encounter warfare, which could have led to the Israelites desiring to return to Egypt. God knew the Israelites well and understood their strengths and weaknesses. Therefore, he chose the more arduous but safer route to prevent their demoralization.[280] Verse 19 mentions that Moses carried the bones of Joseph with him, honoring Joseph's deathbed request to be buried not in Egypt but in God's promised land (Gen 50:25). After four hundred years, Joseph's final wish to join his ancestors is on the way to being realized. In this way, the narrator once more links the exodus story with Genesis and shows that Israel's fate is closely bound up with Joseph's life and legacy. Ultimately, it is Joshua who buries the bones of Joseph in Shechem, in the land that Jacob purchased and gave to Joseph and his descendants as their inheritance (Josh 24:32). Today, the tomb of Joseph is believed to be located in the modern city of Shechem, near Mount Ebal and Mount Gerizim, as a testament to God's faithfulness in fulfilling his covenant with Abraham to give his descendants the promised land.

This section concludes with an affirmation of God's continual presence with his people. God was present with them day and night, guiding them with a pillar of cloud by day and a pillar of fire by night (13:21–22). The cloud

---

279. Tigay, "Exodus," 124.
280. The route of the exodus has generated much discussion. While the "way of the land of the Philistines" (13:17) can be located on the map, "the way of the wilderness" (13:18) and the location of Etham (13:20) are not clear. What adds to the difficulty in identifying the exact route is that place names often change over time. Egyptologist Hoffmeier provides a detailed study of the different names and possible locations of Succoth and Etham. Hoffmeier, *Ancient Israel in Sinai*, 65–71. Durham, *Exodus*, 185. Furthermore, the Bible's references to the route of the exodus are fragmented. What is most likely is that God leads Israel on a more difficult but less guarded route through the marshy lake-land of the eastern delta to Sukkot rather than on the shorter route (possibly "the ways of Horus") where Egyptian forces were stationed. For details on the longer and the shorter routes on the maps, see Sarna, *Exodus*, 68; Sarna, *Exploring Exodus*, 103–106. Tigay, "Exodus," 125.

offered relief from the burning sun during the day, while the fire illuminated the darkness and warmed the people on cold nights. Despite the difficulties of the wilderness journey, God's leading presence ensured the safety and well-being of his people. This tangible and caring presence accompanied Israel throughout their journey in the wilderness to the promised land. For Christian diasporans, their exodus experience from their homeland could be liberating or traumatic. It is the continuing presence of God that provides comfort and assurance in their journey of becoming a new and freed people.

14:1–31 The Exodus

This scene recounts the epic story of the exodus event: Israel flees Egypt in haste, pursued by Pharaoh through the Red Sea; God miraculously turns the Red Sea into dry land for the Israelites to walk through; and the Egyptians drown when they pursue the Israelites into the sea. In this pivotal event, Egypt symbolizes death and Sheol, and later in Israel's history, Egypt was also seen as a metaphor for their exile.[281] The reference to the Red Sea also evokes memories of the drowning of the Hebrew baby boys and Moses's rescue from the water (Exod 1:22; 2:1–10). The waters of the Nile and the waters of the Red Sea form a literary *inclusio*, symbolizing death in watery chaos. Furthermore, the crossing of the Red Sea echoes the creation story, where God separates the waters and makes the dry land emerge (Gen 1:7–9).

The crossing of the Red Sea thus manifests the cosmic dimension of God's activity, in which redemption and creation are closely interconnected.[282] Through the waters, the Israelites experience God's rescue and emerge as a new people – God's people. In Exodus 14, the Israelites' journey appears to be moving through the waters and to the mountain for worship.[283] Exodus 14 recounts this pivotal event in prose, while Exodus 15 retells, memorializes, and celebrates this story in poetry. These two chapters recall the creation motif, celebrate God's rescue of the Israelites, and anticipate the future reign of God (15:18).

In Exodus 14:1–4, God instructs Moses about the strategy the Israelites are to adopt, while forewarning them about the conflict they would face and the events that would soon take place. He instructs them to camp at a specific

---

281. The frequent repetition of descent into Egypt parallels the language of death as in descent into the underworld (Gen 37:35; 46:4). See Morales, *Exodus Old and New*, 50–51.
282. Fretheim, *Exodus*, 153.
283. L. Michael Morales, *The Tabernacle Pre-Figured: Cosmic Mountain Ideology in Genesis and Exodus*, Biblical Tools and Studies 15 (Leuven: Peeters, 2012), 1. Estelle, *Echoes of Exodus*, 107.

location to create a false sense of security for Pharaoh and reveals that he would harden Pharaoh's heart, which would prompt Pharaoh to pursue the Israelites, but that all this would ultimately bring honor and glory to God.[284] The ultimate purpose of God's rescue of his people is to demonstrate his sovereignty to the Egyptians – "The Egyptians will know that I am the Lord" (14:4). The remainder of the chapter is a detailed account of the unfolding of the plan that God outlined in Exodus 14:1–4.

Michael Morales offers an insightful interpretation of the Red Sea crossing, relating it to the motif of creation and re-creation. He highlights the significance of time – namely, the darkness, light, and dawn – during this event. Entering the sea and coming out from it symbolize a movement from death to life, from chaos to order. Using this framework of the time of day, Exodus 14 could be divided as follows: moving toward the sea at dusk (14:1–14), traversing the sea at night (14:15–25), and emerging on the other side at dawn (14:26–31).[285] This threefold structure and theme will guide our reading of this chapter.

When the king of Egypt is informed of the Israelites' escape, he exclaims, "What have we done?" (14:5)! He immediately mobilizes six hundred of his best chariots of war and pursues the Israelites. The narrator emphasizes that "the Lord hardened the heart of Pharaoh king of Egypt" (14:8). Though Pharaoh might have believed that he was acting of his own accord in pursuing the Israelites, he had no control over either his own heart or the fate of the Israelites. Eventually, Pharaoh and his army catch up with the Israelites, who are camping by the sea near Pi Hahiroth, opposite Baal Zephon (14:9). This incident is narrated from the perspective of the Israelites: they see the Egyptians before their eyes and are terrified. At first, they cry out to God for help, but soon fear takes over and they begin to blame Moses, complaining, "Was it because there were no graves in Egypt that you brought us to the desert to die? What have you done to us by bringing us out of Egypt?" (14:11). They preferred to be enslaved in Egypt rather than to die in the wilderness, failing to recognize that Egypt was a place of oppression and death. This is not the first time that the Israelites turned against Moses when faced with threats or danger (compare 5:21).

---

284. The root word for "honor" or "glory" (*kabed*) is the same as that used for Pharaoh's hardening of the heart (*kabed*). Therefore, God's honor is gained through Pharaoh's hardening heart.
285. Morales, *Exodus Old and New*, 49. Dozeman also draws attention to the place of darkness, light, and dawn in the plague narratives. Dozeman, *God at War*, 17–18, 24–26.

Moses responds not with anger or agitation but with calmness and comforting reassurance, saying, "Do not be afraid. Stand firm and you will see the deliverance the Lord will bring you today. The Egyptians you see today you will never see again. The Lord will fight for you; you need only to be still" (14:13–14). God then instructs Moses to lift his staff to divide the waters so that the Israelites can cross the sea on dry ground. The narrative goes into great detail about how God will be honored through this remarkable event: "I will harden the hearts of the Egyptians . . . I will gain glory . . . The Egyptians will know that I am the Lord" (14:17–18a). Crossing the Red Sea is not about demonstrating Moses's power but about showcasing God's supremacy over chaos so that God would be glorified in the eyes of the Egyptians.

Exodus 14:19–20 presents an interesting scenario involving three groups: the angel of God, the camp of Israel, and the camp of Egypt. Initially, the text states that the angel of God had been leading the camp of Israel. However, almost immediately, it says that the pillar of cloud moved from its position at the front of the Israelites. Exodus 13:21 makes it clear that it was God himself who led Israel in the pillar of cloud. The convergence of the angel of God, God, and the pillar of cloud suggest that these are all different divine manifestations of the same God.[286] The angel of God then stands between the camp of Israel and the camp of Egypt, creating a barrier that prevents these two groups from coming near each other. The distinction between light and darkness echoes and evokes the memory of the creation story. However, God's ultimate victory over the forces of chaos is seen in the Red Sea crossing.

The Sea Crossing

This section narrates the pivotal moment in Israel's history: the crossing of the Red Sea. The narration is action-packed: Moses stretches out his hand over the sea, and God causes a strong wind to blow over the sea all night, turning it into dry land and dividing the waters. The Israelites then enter the sea on dry land, with walls of waters on their right and their left, while the Egyptians pursue them into the sea. The act of entering and crossing the sea demonstrates Israel's faith in God's power to rescue them.[287] Just as God had separated the waters and let the dry land emerge on the third day of creation (Gen 1:9) and

---

286. Sommer's study argues that divine manifestation can take many forms. In that sense, God has many "bodies" including his glory, the pillar of cloud, and the ark. Benjamin D. Sommer, *The Bodies of God and the World of Ancient Israel* (Cambridge: Cambridge University Press, 2009), 60, 85.
287. Fretheim, *Exodus*, 159.

caused a wind to pass over the earth so that the waters subsided in Noah's time (Gen 8:1), here God divides the sea and makes dry land emerge. This creation and re-creation motif reminds us that one of the purposes of God's rescue is to bring about a new creation and establish a new order. The symbolism of the sea as the realm of death points to God's battle with and victory over the forces of chaos.[288]

Exodus 14:24 states that "at the morning watch"[289] God looks down on the Egyptian camp and causes disruption within it, causing their chariot wheels to be locked.[290] The Egyptians' response, "Let's get away from the Israelites! The LORD is fighting for them against Egypt" (14:25), demonstrates that God's earlier prophecy – "the Egyptians will know that I am the LORD" (14:4) – and Moses's promise that "the LORD will fight for you" (14:14) are now being fulfilled. The divine intervention in the sea crossing depicts God as a divine warrior doing battle against evil forces. This warrior motif continues in Exodus 15:3: "The LORD is a warrior." The sea crossing also demonstrates that God's intervention involves both judgment and redemption.

Exodus 14:26–29 describes the aftermath of the Israelites' crossing of the Red Sea. Moses stretches out his hand over the sea, and the waters return to their normal state by daybreak. Meanwhile, the Egyptians are fleeing right into the sea, and God defeats and destroys them. The waters cover Pharaoh's entire army and "not one of them survived" (14:28), echoing earlier references to "not a fly remained" (8:31), "not even one of the animals" (9:7), and "the only place" (9:26).[291] In contrast, the Israelites walk on dry land through the sea "with a wall of water on their right and on their left" (14:22, 29), a dramatic portrayal of the event from their vantage point. The return of the waters to their normal state signifies the restoration of both the creational and the moral

---

288. The sea in the Bible denotes chaos and death. Although there is no mention of the sea monster in the Red Sea crossing event, based on the Old Testament and Ancient Near Eastern contexts, the reader may understand God defeating chaos by his slaying the sea dragon (Job 9:8, 13; 26:12–13; Pss 74:12–17; 89:9–10; Isa 51:9–10). See Morales, *Exodus Old and New*, 54–65.
289. Literally, in the night watch of the morning or "during the last watch of the night" (NIV), i.e. dawn. Sarna indicates that this morning watch lasts from two to six in the morning. Sarna, *Exodus*, 74.
290. "Locked" in the sense of "stuck in the mud." See Tigay, "Exodus," 127; Sarna, *Exodus*, 74.
291. In Egyptian consciousness, death by drowning was considered one of the worst ways to die because the Egyptians were preoccupied with bodily burial as a way to ensure life after death, the difficulty of recovering one's corpse from the depths of the sea made it impossible to hope for a life beyond this earthly life. See Leonard H. Lesko, "Death and the Afterlife in Ancient Egyptian Thought," *CANE*, 1766.

order. As the Israelites come out on the other side of the sea, this signifies a new birth, a new order, and, most significantly, a resurrection from the dead.[292]

The final verses of the chapter reiterate God's rescue of Israel from the clutches of the Egyptians. During the sea crossing, the Israelites witness two contrasting images: the lifeless bodies of the Egyptians on the seashore and the powerful hand of God working against their pursuers.[293] Both point to one reality of God's triumph over the enemy. This evidence led the Israelites to fear the Lord and place their trust both in God and in his servant Moses.

In a diasporic context, what might a sea crossing mean? People often cross seas to reach new lands that they believe will provide more opportunities or an escape from poverty or a hostile regime. For example, when people in Asia migrate to the United States or Canada, they often cross the Pacific Ocean by plane – or, in earlier times, by ship. Similarly, others may cross the Atlantic Ocean to reach new lands. While "the sea" does not always symbolize death, it often has connotations of both danger and thrill, obstacles and hope. When people cross over to the other side, hope abounds, opportunities arise, and a new journey begins. Therefore, "sea crossing" is an in-between state, in which the old is left behind and a new beginning is coming. In the contemporary context, some diasporans are also transnationals, and the sea crossing experience often connotes the global reality in which people live. What constitutes "home" depends on each person's particular context.

Spiritually speaking, Israel's crossing of the Red Sea can be viewed as a kind of baptism with water (compare 1 Cor 10:1–2), marking their emergence as a new people of God. Identity formation involves entering into the sea of chaos, allowing God to do his refining and redemptive work, and then emerging as someone who has been made new.

---

292. The motif of "resurrection from the dead" describes Israel's former identity as slaves to Pharaoh and their new identity as the people of God.
293. Sarna notices that "hand" (*yad*) is a keyword in Exodus 14. "Hand" symbolizes power and authority (Exod 3:19–20; 7:4–5; 9:3, 15; 13:3, 14), and appears seven times in the chapter. Sarna, *Exodus*, 75. Trimm indicates that the hand of Yahweh is an anthropomorphic term that involves warriors holding their weapons with their hands. Trimm, *"YHWH Fights for Them!,"* 16. The indiscriminate killing of the Egyptians has caused some scholars to question God's character. Though some justify the incident using the idea of "corporate responsibility" or see the deliverance from a theological rather than an ethical perspective, the killing of the firstborn of the Egyptians and then of the Egyptian army poses a lingering question on the part of the reader. See a lengthy discussion on this topic in Bills, *The Theology of Justice in Exodus*, 155–158.

15:1–21 TWO SONGS OF THE SEA

In the Chinese diaspora, people are scattered across the globe. Some become Christians in their homeland and later migrate to other places, continuing their worship in local churches. Others become Christians elsewhere and join local churches for worship. These churches become social and religious spaces where people of similar ethnicities gather for fellowship and worship. I have taught and preached in different cities across the Chinese diaspora – Paris, London, Edinburgh, Barcelona, Rome, Auckland, Sydney, Melbourne, Sao Paolo, and Amsterdam. In all these places, local Chinese churches sing the same praise songs during their worship services.[294] These songs bridge geographical divides and unite diaspora communities into one spiritual body. Praise songs play an important role in perpetuating and reinforcing social and spiritual identities. Similarly, singing the two "Songs of the Sea" serves to remind the Israelites of their identity as a people who had been rescued by their God from the power of the Egyptians.

In biblical narratives, it is a common literary practice to juxtapose poetry with prose, as seen in passages such as Judges 4–5, 1 Samuel 1–2, and some Psalms – for example, Psalms 105 and 106, which are poetic reworkings of earlier prose accounts set against the backdrop of the exodus event.[295] While there is some overlap in content in the prose and the poetry, this literary construction highlights the distinctiveness of each version and illuminates their meanings, with each version enriching the other. The prose and the poetry thus complement each other. Exodus 15 not only serves as a summary of the events of Exodus 14 but also offers an interpretation of these events, placing greater emphasis on God's power than on the role of Moses as God's agent.[296] The Song of Moses interprets God's rescue as both an exodus from Egypt and a conquest, whereas the Song of Miriam focuses on the destruction of the Egyptian army in the sea.[297]

---

294. For example, Xiao Mei's (a well-known Chinese songwriter and singer) songs and the songs by Streams of Praise (a famous Christian worship band) are being sung in the diaspora.
295. Sarna, *Exploring Exodus*, 75.
296. Estelle, *Echoes of Exodus*, 109–110. For example, the staff of Moses is not mentioned, and the "strong east wind" in Exodus 14:21 becomes the "blast of God's nostrils" in Exodus 15:8. Sarna notices that intermediaries such as the angel, the cloud, and the darkness are absent in the Song of Moses yet present in Exodus 14. This reflects the fact that the Song of Moses celebrates God's direct intervention in the exodus event and his personal incursion into human history. Sarna, *Exodus*, 75.
297. Dozeman, *Exodus*, 331.

The genre of poetry or song serves to memorialize the exodus event for future generations. Both the narrative prose and the songs help contemporary readers understand how Israel's oral culture worked and how it shaped their understanding of their identity as God's people. As successive generations of Israelites retell the exodus event and repeatedly sing the Song of Moses and the Song of Miriam, both the story of the exodus and the Songs of the Sea reinforce their national identity.

In Exodus 15, there are two Songs of the Sea. The first song has 18 verses (15:1–18), while the second song has just one verse (15:21). Despite their differing lengths, both songs share the themes of God's exaltation and his victory over Pharaoh's army. Both songs are part of the larger narrative that depicts God's deliverance of Israel from Pharaoh's power. After the Red Sea crossing, Moses leads the Israelites in singing a song that celebrates God's victory at the sea. The song begins, "I will sing to the LORD" (15:1). Then, Miriam – who is described as a "prophet" (15:20) – joined by a group of women, follows with a song of her own, which begins with the words, "Sing to the LORD" (15:21).

While Moses uses the first-person pronoun "I will sing to the LORD," Miriam uses the imperative "Sing to the LORD!"[298] Who writes the song and who sings it first? It appears that first, Moses sings on behalf of Israel and then, Miriam responds by leading the congregation of Israel in song. The fact that only one verse is attributed to Miriam may indicate that the rest of the lyrics of the Song of Miriam are similar to those of the Song of Moses and that the narrator chose to retain just the first verse and omit the rest. Another possibility is that both Moses and Miriam led the congregation of Israel in a duet or antiphonal singing that alternated between men and women.[299]

Both songs belong to the genre of triumph or victory songs – essentially, songs of praise.[300] Their function was to ritualize and immortalize the exodus event in Israel's national history. In a contemporary context, we may refer to these as songs of praise that celebrate what God has accomplished for his people. Given that most South Asian countries suffered under colonial rule,

---

298. Carmen Joy Imes indicates that by using an imperative Miriam does not only exhort the community to sing, she leads them to sing. Carmen Joy Imes, "Can I Get a Witness?: Miriam's Song in the Literary Design of Exodus," *BBR* 33, no. 4 (2023): 435, 426–440.
299. For diverse understandings of the relationship of the two songs of the sea, see Dozeman, *Exodus*, 326–333. Sarna, *Exodus*, 76. For the redaction of the two songs, see Dozeman, *God at War*, 153–170.
300. Estelle, *Echoes of Exodus*, 95, 111. Frank Moore Cross, *Canaanite Myth and Hebrew Epic: Essays in the History of The Religion of Israel* (Cambridge: Harvard University Press, 1973), 121.

much of the literature arising from this colonial context contains a blend of history and national pride, reflecting similarities with the Song of Moses.[301]

The two "Songs of the Sea" in Exodus 15 are among the earliest Hebrew songs.[302] The archaic features of these songs include a mixed metrical structure, repetitive parallelism, internal rhyme, and assonance, which conform to the literary patterns of the Late Bronze Age. Cross dates the song to the late twelfth or early eleventh century BCE.[303]

Another interesting aspect of the song that points to its early tradition is that while the prose account in Exodus 14 mentions the splitting or dividing of the waters – enabling the Israelites to walk on dry ground through the sea, with the waters like a wall on their right and left (14:21–22) – this memory is absent in the songs of the sea and in other texts. Instead, the Song of Moses says that the blast of God's nostrils makes the waters pile up and stand up like a wall and that when God blew with his breath, the sea covered the Egyptian soldiers and they sank like lead in the mighty waters (15:8, 10). It does not mention the splitting of the sea, the Israelites walking on dry ground, or the waters returning and covering the Egyptians. These motifs do, however, appear in later texts (Neh 9:11).[304] These clues suggest that the song in Exodus 15 originates from a much older tradition than the prose account and that the narrator of Exodus incorporated and reworked an older hymn to complement and fit the present literary arrangement.

The purpose of the Song of Moses is to exalt God as the only king (15:18). The image of God as a warrior appears for the first time in this song, along with the combat motif that is often present in other ancient Near Eastern creation myths.[305] Some scholars view the Song of Moses as Israel's national anthem, while others see it as a pivotal point that links God's display of power in Exodus 1–14 with his continued presence in Exodus 16–40.[306] Kevin Chen summarizes the structural significance of the Song of Moses in this way:

---

301. George and Swarup, "Exodus," 98.
302. Much has been written about the Song of Sea regarding its dating, linguistic features, and literary artistry. For example, Frank M. Cross, Jr. and David Noel Freedman, *Studies in Ancient Yahwistic Poetry* (1975; reprinted Grand Rapids: Eerdmans, 1995), 1–45.
303. Cross, *Canaanite Myth and Hebrew Epic*, 121–124.
304. Cross, *Canaanite Myth and Hebrew Epic*, 131–134. Cross also uses the book of Joshua as an example to illustrate the dialectic as well as the evolution of different traditions in Israel's memory of the sea-crossing.
305. Estelle indicates that the song's praise of God as the king seems to function as a polemic against Pharaoh's self-proclaimed deity. The song not only evokes creation but also looks to the future. Estelle, *Echoes of Exodus*, 112–116.
306. Dozeman, *Exodus*, 332.

The Song of the Sea is located not only at a compositional seam of the Pentateuch but at a climax of one of its central themes – faith. This convergence of compositional and thematic climaxes distinguishes this song from the other poetic seams and suggests that it has a unique contribution to the eschatological message of the Pentateuch.[307]

Indeed, the Song of Moses not only crystallizes the exodus event but also points toward the future reign of God.

15:1–19 The Song of Moses

Some scholars divide the Song of Moses into four units,[308] while others see it as having three units. I will structure it into three units: introductory praise (15:1–3), the celebration of God's victory at sea (15:4–16), and the concluding exaltation of God's eternal kingship (15:17–18). The introductory praise extols God's supremacy and power over the sea. Moses acknowledges God as "my strength," "my defense" (or "my song"), and "my salvation" (15:2). Then, in verse 3, he calls God "a warrior" (literally, "man of war"), whose name is "the Lord" (YHWH). "Name" represents one's character and actions. The association between "warrior" and God's name reinforces this essential aspect of God, which the patriarchs never encountered in Genesis. This image of God as a divine warrior also appears elsewhere in the OT (Pss 24:8; 74:12–14; Isa 42:13). This image is rooted in the ancient creation combat myths in which the gods are said to have created the world by defeating the forces of chaos.[309]

---

307. Kevin Chen, *Eschatological Sanctuary in Exodus 15:17 and Related Texts*, Studies in Biblical Literature (New York: Peter Lang, 2013), 68.
308. For example, Sarna, *Exodus*, 76, says it:
    1. Celebrates God's great triumph over the Egyptian foe (15:1–10);
    2. Tells of the incomparability of God (15:11–13);
    3. Describes the impact of the extraordinary events upon the surrounding people (15:14–16);
    4. Is forward-looking and anticipating future development (15:17–18).
Tigay, "Exodus," 127 identifies:
    1. Introduction (15:1–3);
    2. The defeat of Pharaoh's forces (15:4–12);
    3. God's guidance of Israel and people's reactions (15:13–17);
    4. Acclaiming God's eternal rule (15:18).
309. For more on God as a warrior and its cosmic implication, see Theodore J. Lewis, *The Origin and Character of God* (Oxford: Oxford University Press, 2020), 428–453.

The second part of the song is a detailed portrayal of God as a warrior, which is a significant aspect of his attributes and actions in the OT.[310] Although discussed extensively in academic circles,[311] this divine warrior motif may not be familiar in church settings. We can understand this motif in the context of Holy War, where God engages in warfare against his enemies or the enemies of his people to demonstrate that victory belongs solely to him and not to any human agency. Moses alternates between third-person and first-person pronouns to depict God's actions – which is also a common literary feature of the Psalms.[312] God's military actions against the Egyptian army are described in anthropomorphic terms: God hurls them into the sea (15:4), throws down those who oppose him (15:7a), unleashes his burning anger (15:7b), piles up the waters by the blast of his nostrils (15:8), covers them with the sea by blowing with his breath (15:10), and stretches out his right hand for the earth to swallow his enemies (15:12).

All these actions depict God as a warrior who fights on behalf of his people against the Egyptian army. The Song of Moses uses vivid poetic imagery to describe Pharaoh's chariots and army drowning in the Red Sea and sinking to the depths like a stone (15:5) or like lead (15:10).[313] The image of the surging waters standing up like a wall (15:8) recalls the descriptions given in Exodus 14:22 and 14:29.

Even the words of the enemy are included to heighten the dramatic effect:[314]

> The enemy boasted,
> "I will pursue, I will overtake them.
> I will divide the spoils;

---

310. For a detailed study on the definition of YHWH as a warrior, including the divine warrior texts and patterns as well as divine weapons, see Trimm, *"YHWH Fights for Them!,"* 35–42.
311. See, for example, Patrick D. Miller, Jr., *The Divine Warrior in Early Israel*, HSM 5 (Cambridge: Harvard University Press, 1973); Tremper Longman III and Daniel G. Reid, *God is a Warrior*, Studies in Old Testament Biblical Theology (Grand Rapids: Zondervan, 1995). Trimm, *"YHWH Fights for Them!,"* 43–75. Sa-Moon Kang, *Divine War in the Old Testament and in the Ancient Near East*, BZAW 177 (Berlin: W. de Gruyter, 1989).
312. Such as Psalms 23, 27, 30.
313. The word "sink" is literally "descend" (*yarad*). The motif of "descending into the depths" (Exod 15:5) recalls a Mesopotamian myth, "The Descent of Ishtar into the Underworld." See "The Descent of Ishtar to the Underworld," trans. Stephanie Dalley (*COS* 1.108:38–84). Depths and waters symbolize *sheol*, the realm of death.
314. Sarna thinks that the poet is imagining what went on in the mind of Pharaoh to show his arrogance and self-confidence. Sarna, *Exodus*, 79. The Hebrew in verse 9 presents a series of literary devices called alliteration, in which the first word of each sentence is almost identical. In the song of Deborah, she also imagines what goes on in the mind of Sisera's mother using the first person pronoun (Judg 5:28).

> I will gorge myself on them.[315]
> I will draw my sword
> and my hand will destroy them." (Exod 15:9)

The use of the first-person singular "I" presents the enemy as speaking with one voice and symbolizes their unity or depicts the voice of Pharaoh. Employing the first-person "I" voice also helps the reader to directly hear the enemy, thereby bridging the gap between the reader and the enemy while also contrasting the perceived power of the enemy with the true power of God.

In the Song, Moses repeatedly extols the power of God's right hand (15:6, 12). He also poses a rhetorical question, "Who among the gods is like you, Lord? Who is like you – majestic in holiness, awesome in glory, working wonders?" (15:11), to magnify God's incomparability and his supremacy over all other gods, especially the Egyptian gods.[316] This verse is sometimes considered the pivot of the Song, highlighting God's authority over nature and his sovereignty over all creation.[317] Nature is portrayed as being obedient to God's will and serving as God's weapon. Fretheim notes the connection between God as a liberator of his people and as the Creator. In the Song of the Sea, the Creator God piles up the waters and engulfs the Egyptians with floods. God blows on the water and the earth swallows them up.[318] By defeating the forces of chaos in creation, God upholds justice for his people. The word "swallow" was introduced earlier in the narrative, where Aaron's rod becomes a serpent and swallowed up the staffs of the Egyptian magicians (7:12). This image is revisited in Exodus 15:12, where God stretches out his right hand and the earth "swallows" the Egyptian army. Isaiah also echoes this warrior imagery of the Song of the Sea but in a new context – as the exiles return from Babylon to Jerusalem (Isa 51:9–11).[319]

---

315. Literally, "my desire/appetite (*nephesh*) will be filled with them." This image evokes a Ugaritic text. In the Ugaritic Baal Cycle, Mot invites Baal to eat and drink where Mot describes his unsated appetite (*nephesh*) and his attempt to swallow Baal in his throat (*nephesh*). "One lip to Hell, one lip to Heaven, a tongue to the Stars. Baal will enter his innards, into his mouth he will descend, like a dried olive, produce of the earth, and fruit of the trees." Mark S. Smith, trans. "The Baal Cycle" in *Ugaritic Narrative Poetry*, SBLWAWS, ed. Simon B. Parker (Atlanta: Scholars Press, 1997), 143.
316. Compare Exodus 12:12.
317. For example, William Johnstone, *Exodus 1–19*, S&HBC (Macon: Smyth & Helwys, 2014), 303.
318. Fretheim, *Exodus*, 167, 169.
319. For more on the "slaying the sea dragon" motif in Exodus and Isaiah, see Morales, *Exodus Old and New*, 54–61.

Verse 13 indicates that God's rescue of Israel was not an end in itself but a means to lead them to their ultimate destination – God's holy dwelling. God's leading (*nakhah*) recalls his earlier leading in the wilderness (13:17). The word "dwelling" (*naveh*) denotes the abode of shepherds or flocks, evoking pastoral imagery – God is like a shepherd leading his flock to his dwelling place.[320] This dwelling place is further described in verse 17 as God's mountain-sanctuary or the "new Sinai."[321] God's desire is to lead his people to his home, and he welcomes them to this home. Being home with God is what God wants. For many diasporans, the concept of home may be fluid and unclear; yet coming home to God gives them a sense of permanence as they look forward to their eternal home. This journey to God's home can become a new identity formation in the diaspora.

Exodus 15:14–17 describes the fearful reactions of Israel's enemies. These enemies include Edom, Moab, and Canaan, which anticipates the future conquest of Canaan. This is a distinctive feature of the Song of Moses but one that is absent in the Song of Miriam as we have it.

The final verse of the Song of Moses proclaims, "The LORD reigns for ever and ever" (15:18), beautifully depicting the salvific pattern of "through the waters to the mountain for worship," which has been accomplished by God's mighty power.[322] This underscores the idea that "deliverance is for worship," echoing God's words to Moses in Exodus 3:12: "When you have brought the people out of Egypt, you will worship God on this mountain." In this way, the Song of Moses anticipates the construction of the tabernacle – and later the temple – where God desires to dwell among his people and be present

---

320. *BDB*, 627.
321. With hindsight, this holy dwelling refers to Mount Sinai and later to Mount Zion. The motif of mountain-sanctuary recalls a common theme in the Ugaritic Baal Cycle in which Baal after his victory builds a temple for his enthronement. "The Baʻlu Myth," trans. Dennis Pardee, *COS* 1.86: 273. Cross proposes several possible historical sites for this mountain-sanctuary including Sinai, Qadesh, and Shittim. Cross, *Canaanite Myth and Hebrew Epic*, 141–142. Durham, *Exodus*, 209. Based on the generic descriptions of the Song such as "horse and chariotry" (15:1b), "enemy" (15:9), "God's people" (15:13, 16), the choice of the word for "dwelling" (15:13), and the reactions of the nations that do not appear in the Pentateuch, Chen makes a case for the eschatological fulfillment of this Song. Chen, *Eschatological Sanctuary in Exodus 15:17*, 48–52.
322. Morales, *The Tabernacle Pre-Figured*, 1. This salvific pattern can be traced from Genesis: The earth is delivered through the primal waters and Adam is brought to the Eden mount (Genesis 1–3); Noah is delivered through the flood and brought to Mount Ararat (Genesis 6–9); Israel is delivered through the sea waters and brought to Mount Sinai (Exodus 14–24). Morales, *The Tabernacle Pre-Figured*, 4.

with them.[323] The declaration "The Lord reigns" echoes Psalms 93–99, which celebrate God's eternal rule. The alternating use of present tense, future tense, and past tense[324] in the Song of Moses provides a theological framework within which to understand that God's past actions compel worshipers to praise and adore him in the present and exult in his reign in the future.[325]

Verse 19, which serves as a transitional verse between the Song of Moses and the Song of Miriam, is a brief prose statement that reiterates the poetic content of Exodus 15:1.

15:20–21 The Song of Miriam

Compared to the Song of Moses, the Song of Miriam is given relatively little space, which has led to various scholarly discussions about Miriam's role in the larger narrative of the exodus story. Some scholars see her as a highly venerated prophet while others view her as an insignificant figure whose story ends badly later on in the wilderness.[326] One way to read the Song of Miriam is to consider the role of women in the tradition of victory songs such as the song of the prophet Deborah in Judges 4–5. In Exodus, Miriam is first introduced as a prophet and as the sister of Aaron. Her prophetic role also points to her later confrontation of Moses's authority in Numbers 12, and her song likely contained prophetic elements.[327]

Among the three siblings, Miriam was the first to die in the wilderness, followed by Aaron and, finally, Moses. Miriam's death might have been a foreshadowing of the fate of her brothers.[328] The name Miriam has several

---

323. The author of 1 Kings indicates that the building of the temple starts after the exodus event and ties the purpose of Exodus to the temple (1 Kgs 6:1).
324. For example, "I will sing" in 15:1a is in the future tense (imperfect tense in Hebrew), and "he has hurled into the sea" (15:1b, perfect tense in Hebrew) is in the past tense. "The LORD is a warrior" (15:3a is a verbless clause, judging by the context, is understood as in the present tense) is in the present tense, connoting a statement and "The best of Pharaoh's officers are drowned in the Red Sea" (15:4b, perfect tense in Hebrew) is in the past tense. For more on the verbless clause, see C. L. Seow, *A Grammar for Biblical Hebrew*, revised edition (Nashville: Abingdon, 1995), 59. For the uses of perfect and imperfect in Hebrew, see S. R. Driver, *A Treatise on the Use of the Tenses in Hebrew and Some Other Syntactical Questions* (Grand Rapids: Eerdmans, 1998), 13–49.
325. Johnstone, *Exodus 1–19*, 301.
326. See Imes, "Can I Get a Witness?" Janzen proposes Miriam's priority of the authorship of the Song of the Sea over Moses. J. Gerald Janzen, "Song of Moses, Song of Miriam: Who Is Seconding Whom?" *CBQ* 54 (1992): 212. See Dozeman, *God at War*, 160.
327. Other examples of prophets confronting leaders include Nathan rebuking David (1 Sam 12:1–12) and Elijah confronting Ahab (1 Kgs 21:17–19).
328. Dozeman, *Exodus*, 343.

meanings, including bitter (*mar*), water (*mayim*), sea (*yam*), or, in Egyptian, beloved (*mryt*).[329] The narrator portrays Miriam somewhat ambiguously, depicting her both as a heroine and prophet who served as a witness to the rescue of Moses and a song leader of the Israelites over the Red Sea in Exodus, and as a humiliated leader in Numbers 12.[330] All three siblings – Moses, the servant of God, Aaron, the first high priest, and Miriam, a prophet of God – become prominent leaders in Israel's exodus and deliverance history.

Exodus 15:20–21 depicts Miriam as a worship leader, leading a group of women with timbrels and dancing[331] and calling upon them with the imperative "Sing to the Lord."[332] This imperative indicates that Miriam led and sang with authority. Some scholars interpret this imperative as indicating that the song that Moses and the Israelites sang in Exodus 15:1–18 was a response to the Song of Miriam and the other women even though it precedes it in the narrative sequence.[333]

Although Miriam's song is similar to the opening line of the Song of Moses, it serves a different function. The Song of Miriam refocuses the reader's attention back to the event that took place at sea, whereas the Song of Moses moves from the sea to the conquest of the land and God's future dwelling place.[334] This prophetic function underscores Miriam's role as a prophet – she

---

329. It is alarming that the next episode in Israel's journey is the encounter with bitter water (Exod 15:23). Hamilton indicates that the first part of Miriam's name *mir* has a sonant parallelism with the story of Marah in Exodus 15:25–26, but he does not elaborate further on other possible connections. Hamilton, *Exodus*, 236.
330. Ngwa associates Miriam with water. She is a woman who gives voice to the waters. Her name, which means "water" or "beloved" in Egyptian, suggests that Miriam is a beloved one who carries the bitter experience of the oppressed, and who generates and sustains the flow of water. Her death in Numbers 20 signifies a drying up of community life. Ngwa, *Let My People Live*, 136–138.
331. The word "dance" comes from the root "to turn or writhe" (*hul*). It involves the turning and the movement of the body with music or rhythm, a verb that implies writhing or making a circle. The noun form was also used to describe a woman's "turning and twisting" during the pain of childbirth (Isa 13:8; 23:5). Dancing, music, and singing comprised three key elements in Israel's worship and celebration. Chloe Sun, "Dance," *EBR* 6:65–66. Dancing can be taken as a "voiceless singing with the whole body." Kass, *Founding God's Nation*, 215.
332. Literally, "them" includes both men and women. Miriam is not just leading the women in singing, but the whole congregation of Israel.
333. Janzen, "Song of Moses, Song of Miriam," 215. Raymond Apple, "*Shirat Hayam*: Miriam's Song?" *JBQ* 45, no. 2 (2017): 100. For an objection to the Song of Miriam preceding the Song of Moses on the ground of canonical arrangement of the Song of Miriam and other literary features (*ki*, *'az*, and the inter-dynamics of Exodus 14:22–15:21), see Hannah S. An, "A Canonical Reconsideration of the Song at the Sea (Exod 15:1–21): The Song of Moses or the Song of Miriam? *Canon & Culture* 10 (2016): 7–35.
334. Dozeman, *Exodus*, 343.

reinterprets the exodus event and emphasizes the crossing of the Red Sea as central to God's rescue of Israel.

The two "Songs of the Sea" teach the people of God that the proper response to God's rescue is praise and worship, which points forward to the final section of the book of Exodus – the construction of the tabernacle as a sacred place for worship.

In Exodus 1:1–15:21, women form an *inclusio* that frames the story of the founding of the nation of Israel. The *inclusio* begins in Exodus 1, with two midwives who courageously protect the Hebrew babies, and ends in Exodus 15:21, with Miriam leading the women in a song of victory. This framing device accentuates the significant role and contribution of the oppressed groups, not least women, in the broader narrative of God's redemptive action in the history of Israel. Miriam's presence in Exodus 15:20–21 also forms an *inclusio* with her presence in Exodus 2:4–8, with both episodes centering around water, which also echoes the meaning of Miriam's name. This literary framing suggests that the Song of Miriam is best seen as following the Song of Moses in the present canonical arrangement.

In the first part of the exodus narrative, Israel's identity underwent a significant shift – from being enslaved under Pharaoh to becoming a free people in the household of God. Through the powerful manifestation of God's power during and through the ten plagues, they witnessed God's strong hand and his determination to bring them out of Egypt. The institution of the Passover marked a shift in their allegiance from Pharaoh to God, while the consecration of the firstborn sons reminded them of their own firstborn status in God's eyes. Finally, the Red Sea crossing marked their departure from Egypt and the beginning of their journey to a new land. This process of identity conversion – from slavery in Egypt to freedom in a new land – was a dramatic journey toward a new hope and a journey of becoming the people of God in a new land.

People in the diaspora also travel from place to place seeking new lands, new opportunities, and new homes. For people who consider China or East Asia their ancestral home, the crossing of the sea – the Pacific Ocean, the South China Sea, or some other sea – to journey to some other country symbolizes a border crossing that leads to a new identity: a newfound sense of self, a migrant in a host country, a transnational person, or someone living in perpetual liminality. In such a context, identity formation is an ongoing process of seeking to understand one's place in the new community, and an ongoing process of becoming.

EXODUS 15:22–18:27

IDENTITY CONFUSION DURING

THE IN-BETWEEN SPACE

Most people in the diaspora are familiar with the term "overseas" (*hǎi wài*) and what it entails. From the perspective of home, "overseas" describes the state of "not being home" – that is, being "out there." For people in East Asia, "overseas" may signify crossing over to the other side of the Pacific Ocean, the South China Sea, or some other sea. This border crossing involves grief over what has been lost in the former home – such as family members or friends one has left behind – and apprehension about what lies ahead. According to Daniel Lee's study, approximately three-quarters of the Asian American population was born overseas, making the experience of migration and its losses personal for many of this generation. These losses include the loss of their Asian heritage, the loss of family members, and the loss of a sense of self – since our personhood is closely connected with our past and places of origin – country, culture, and people group.[1]

The experience of sea crossings or border crossings becomes an integral part of the diasporan's identity formation and re-formation. Whenever we move from one geographical location to another, transition from a previous social status to a new one, or enter a different cultural context, we experience liminality. Since sea crossings place us in a liminal space, our old and new identities intermingle and, at times, conflict with each other. In addition, the sea represents a space of connection, linking lands, places, and homes. Thus, the experience of sea crossing also means traveling, border crossing, connecting, and reconnecting with one's former home and new home(s).

The Israelites have now crossed to the other side of the Red Sea, out of Egypt, out of slavery. However, they have not yet entered the promised land. Instead, they enter the wilderness. They are free from the bondage of slavery, but they have now become homeless. They have exchanged the stability of

---

[1]. Lee, *Doing Asian American Theology*, 115, 117–121. Though Lee uses the term "Asian American" as an umbrella term, it overlaps and includes what I define as the diasporan – one who is scattered, away from home, and is often rootless. This is different from some Asian Americans who consider America as their home but experience racism in America and live as perpetual foreigners.

slavery for the uncertainty of the wilderness.[2] The wilderness represents an in-between space, one that is neither here nor there[3] – it is neither Egypt nor Canaan but a transitional space. As a result, the wilderness can be a dangerous place, placing those who pass through it in a liminal state.[4] What is on the other side of the sea? It may not be the promised land but, rather, a new state of isolation, confusion, uncertainty, and displacement. When the Israelites first entered the wilderness, their initial reaction was to yearn for Egypt. They felt the "pull" of Egypt while resisting the "push" into a new land.[5] They preferred the familiarity and perceived stability of slavery over the unpredictability and risk of life with God and Moses in the wilderness.[6]

In Isaiah's adaptation of this wilderness tradition, the wilderness is closely associated with "the way of the LORD" (Isa 40:3). The "wayless wilderness" is juxtaposed with the way toward which God points his people. Though this "way" motif is less prominent in Exodus, it is prominent in Isaiah and in the Gospels.[7] The Babylonian captivity is depicted as the new wilderness experience, with the return from captivity symbolizing Yahweh's return to his people (Isa 40:5). In addition, Isaiah also uses the exodus motif to describe the deliverance of the exiles, urging Israel to forget the former things and assuring them that Yahweh, who made a way in the sea, promises to do a new thing, making a way in the wilderness and rivers in the desert (Isa 43:16–21). This notion of "the way" resonates with the Chinese understanding of *Dao* (which

---

2. Fentress-Williams, "Exodus," 84, 85.
3. Many have recognized this liminal theme in Israel's wilderness journey. Ann Fritschel, "Exodus 16 as an Alternative Social Paradigm," *CurTM* 41, no. 1 (February 2014): 35–38.
4. Drawing upon Mary Douglas's study on ritual purity, unclassifiable elements that are difficult to fit into any category are considered marginal and dangerous. This seems to apply to the wilderness transition. Douglas, *Purity and Danger*, 118–119.
5. The theory of "push and pull" is well-known in migration studies. Here is the excerpt from the *Dictionary of Race, Ethnicity and Culture*, "The study of the causes of migration traditionally considers push factors to be those elements in the place of exodus which determine the choice to leave. Pull factors are those elements in the area of arrival which also influence the decision to emigrate, as well as the duration and character of the emigration process." Guido Bolaffi, Raffaele Bracalenti, Peter Braham, and Sandro Gindro, eds., *Dictionary of Race, Ethnicity and Culture* (London: SAGE Publications, 2003), 233–234.
6. Dozeman, *Exodus*, 349.
7. Estelle, *Echoes of Exodus*, 150–152. Augustine Stocks summarizes Isaiah's use of the exodus tradition, which includes the flight from Egypt, the deliverance at the Sea, the march through the wilderness, and the triumphant journey toward Canaan. Augustine Stock, *The Way in the Wilderness: Exodus, Wilderness and Moses Themes in Old Testament and New* (Collegeville: Liturgical, 1969), 14.

means "way").[8] Dao – a branch of philosophical thinking with its origins in ancient China – advocates humility and religious piety.[9]

OVERVIEW

Israel's identity formation is rooted in God's rescue of them from Egyptian slavery. While their transition from serving Pharaoh to serving God begins with the Red Sea crossing, time, education, and reinforcement is necessary to fully internalize this new reality. Therefore, the wilderness experience plays a critical role in shaping Israel as the people of God. The wilderness journey is not merely a transitional phase for Israel on their way to the promised land but, rather, a journey marked by tests, temptations, and challenges. It is in this sense that the wilderness serves as the "workshop of Israel's becoming."[10]

A Chinese proverb illustrates this idea: "It takes ten years to grow a tree, but it takes a hundred years to form a person." The journey of becoming takes time. Although it did not take a hundred years for the Israelites to become who God wanted them to be, 40 years in the wilderness is still a long time.

For Israel, their wilderness experience is marked by a pattern of "lack and complaint," whereas for God, it involves testing, instruction, provision, and protection. While God provides, Israel whines. The contrasts between the two could not be more pronounced. Exodus 15–18 narrates Israel's journey through the wilderness, where the people face various scarcities and grumble against Moses and Aaron. In each instance, God teaches them more about who he is.

Through this repetitive pattern of human whining and divine provision, Israel learns who they are in relation to God. Moses later affirms this God-Israel relationship by saying, "Man does not live on bread alone but on every word that comes from the mouth of the LORD" (Deut 8:3), which emphasizes that God's provision and Israel's obedience are inseparable. Israel's survival in the barren wilderness depends entirely on whether or not they obey God. In this formative process through the wilderness, Israel experiences de-formation and re-formation. God teaches Israel who he is: their healer (15:26), their God (16:12), and their provider of water (15:25; 17:6), meat (16:13), and bread from heaven (16:15). These experiences in the wilderness form the basis of Israel's theological education – effectively a field education – laying

---

8. An alternate spelling is *Tao*.
9. A comparison between "the way of the LORD" and Dao in Chinese thinking is beyond the scope of this book, but for those who are interested, it could yield fruitful results.
10. Imes, *Bearing God's Name*, 17. Dozeman also uses Arnold Van Gennep's rite of passage to define Israel's wilderness journey. Dozeman, *Exodus*, 347–348.

the foundation for their knowledge of God's ways, their relationship to God, and their role among the nations. These lessons learned in the wilderness were the prerequisites for God's giving of the law in Exodus 19–24. Although the wilderness journey represents a liminal experience for Israel, it is only the beginning of their liminality, with the law-giving at Sinai marking the next stage in this journey. Israel's journey is characterized by stages of liminality – moving from one land to another through different stages of the formation process. Similarly, as people living in the diaspora, we are always on the move, continually in transition, and constantly moving from one stage of liminality to the next.

The wilderness proves to be fertile ground for Israel's theological education. God's pedagogy or teaching approach includes both direct instructions to Moses and testing (15:25; 16:4).[11] Just as a teacher uses tests to assess students' knowledge and understanding, God, as a divine teacher, tests Israel for their knowledge of God. For these former slaves who have just come out of Egypt, this theological "boot camp" in the wilderness is difficult and demanding, but it is a necessary part of their journey of formation as the people of God. In this transitional phase, Israel enters a liminal in-between space, which is a time of confusion. This experience deconstructs their former identity as slaves in Egypt with the aim of reconstructing their new identity that is grounded in God's rescuing power. As shown in the diagram below, Israel's in-between space parallels Moses's own in-between time in Midian:

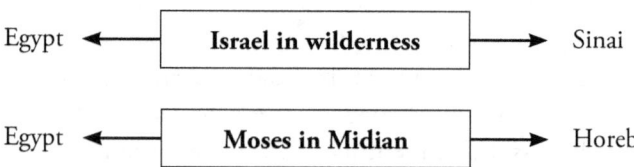

Figure 1: The In-Between Space of Israel and Moses

---

11. Bills, *A Theology of Justice in Exodus*, 173. Testing occurs in Exodus 15:25; 16:4; 17:2, 7; 20:20; Numbers 14:22. Hamilton rightly entitles Exodus 15:22–18:27 "Testing Time in the Wilderness." Hamilton, *Exodus*, 237. The motif of testing involves two aspects: God tests Israel (15:25; 16:4) and Israel tests God (17:2, 7). The goal of God testing Israel is to know whether Israel would obey God or not. God often disapproves of Israel testing him because it shows their disbelief and lack of trust.

Exodus 15:22–18:27

Just as Moses's identity was deconstructed in Midian, so Israel's identity was forged through this deconstructing wilderness experience. Just as Moses spent 40 years in Midian, Israel spent 40 years in the wilderness. During this in-between space of the wilderness, Israel faced five lessons that were characterized by the lack of resources, external threats from enemies, and the need for leadership restructuring.[12] Through these challenges, God tested Israel while teaching them about who he is and who they are. Below are the five lessons Israel learned through their wilderness journey:

Lesson 1: Lack of water (15:22–27)
Lesson 2: Lack of meat and bread (16:1–36)
Lesson 3: Lack of water again (17:1–7)
Lesson 4: The threat of the Amalekites (17:8–15)
Lesson 5: Leadership and governance (18:1–27)

When Israel experiences a lack, their typical response is to complain against Moses and Aaron. This complaining can also be described as whining, grumbling, or murmuring – repeatedly uttering words of complaint in a low voice. Here is the general pattern of Israel's wilderness journey: they experience a lack, they grumble, God tests them, and then God provides. The internal and external threats Israel faces reflect the challenges and struggles of their identity during this in-between stage. Through each incident, God demonstrates both mercy and judgment. The wilderness journey is a journey from knowing God's transcendent power to knowing God's providential care for his people. In this wilderness journey, Moses becomes the mediator between Israel and God through various tests (15:24; 16:2–7; 17:2–7; 8–16), and Israel moves a step closer toward becoming the people of God, a kingdom of priests, and a holy nation.

---

12. Bills summarizes Israel's lessons about God and his rulership in the wilderness: God is Israel's new king (15:18), God provides (15:22–17:7), God protects (17:8–16), and God establishes polity (18:1–27). Bills, *A Theology of Justice in Exodus*, 172. Meyers sees four crises in Israel's wilderness experience: water, food, military, and organizational crisis. Meyers, *Exodus*, 128–140.

THE WILDERNESS TRADITION IN CHINESE SPIRITUALITY

Chinese Christians are familiar with the stories of Israel's experience in the wilderness. In the Chinese context, the wilderness symbolizes a place of nothingness, a lack of resources, the loss of a sense of direction, spiritual dryness, and even darkness, as well as the place where one faces temptations. At the same time, the wilderness also represents a time for quiet reflection and an opportunity to be with God and hear from God. Therefore, the wilderness connotes both space and time, both a place of danger as well as a place of hope, both the experience of loneliness and the opportunity for renewal. In this sense, the wilderness is not just a transitional phase between realms but a crucial period for receiving fresh insights for the future.

Closely associated with the image of the wilderness is manna. If the wilderness represents one's present state of life, then manna represents the spiritual nourishment God provides during this time. Someone who finds themselves in a wilderness time needs "manna" to sustain and guide them forward. Another significant symbol of the wilderness is its association with the presence of God, often referred to as "walking with God in the wilderness" – a concept reflected in the traditional title of the book of Numbers.[1]

The popularity of wilderness symbolism in the Chinese Christian context is evident in its frequent appearance in book titles, particularly devotional or meditative books that address spirituality and a person's relationship with God. Here are a few examples: "Manna in the Wilderness: Walking with God,"[2] "A Table in the Wilderness,"[3] "Out of the Wilderness, Into Freedom,"[4] "A Pastor's Voice in the Wilderness,"[5] "Blessings in the Wilderness,"[6] and "The Trial of the Wilderness: Victory over Temptations."[7]

The wilderness tradition is not limited to the experience of the Israelites but also encompasses the experience of Jesus in the wilderness, facing Satan's temptations (Matt 4:1–11; Mark 1:12–13; Luke 4:1–13). In summary, the image of the wilderness and its associations offer a wealth of spiritual insights for our reflection, particularly within the Chinese Christian spiritual tradition.

---

1. For example, Ka-Leung Wong, *Zai Kuang Ye Zhong Yu Shang Di Tong Xing: Min Shu Ji Xi Du* (Hong Kong: Logos Publishing, 2008). Chen Zuan De, *Zai Kuang Ye Zhong: Min Shu Ji Xin Xi* (Taiwan: Olive Publishing, 2002). A DVD teaching series on the book of Numbers has also been entitled "Interpretations

of Numbers: Who will Lead me to Walk in the Wilderness." Stephen Lee, Min Shu Ji Shi Yi: Shui Ling Wo Jing Kuang Ye Lu (Hong Kong: Han Yu Sheng Jing Xie Hui, 2012).
2. Sun Da Zhong, *Kuang Ye Ma Na* (New Tai Pei: Olive Publishing Ltd, 2019). This devotional series has three volumes.
3. Watchman Nee, *Kuang Ye De Yan Xi* (Hong Kong: Ji Du Tu Publishing House, 2007).
4. Bai He, *Kuang Ye De Zhu Fu* (Taiwan: Hua Xuan, 1997).
5. Yang Mu Gu, *Kuang Ye Lian Li: Sheng Guo Shi Tan De Cao Lian* (Hong Kong: Zhuo Yue Shu Lou, 1992).
6. Bai He, *Kuang Ye De Zhu Fu* (Taiwan: Hua Xuan, 1997).
7. Yang Mu Gu, *Kuang Ye Lian Li: Sheng Guo Shi Tan De Cao Lian* (Hong Kong: Zhuo Yue Shu Lou, 1992).

15:22–27 LACK OF WATER

After the Israelites crossed the Red Sea, Moses led them into the wilderness of Shur. The Hebrew word "Shur," meaning "wall," symbolized an obstacle in this context. The Chinese idiom "to hit the wall" refers to encountering an obstacle or setback. From the people's perspective, "Shur" was an obstacle, but from a divine perspective, it was a test.

15:22–24 Bitter Water

When the Israelites arrive at a place called Marah, which means "bitter," they find that the water there is bitter and undrinkable.[13] It is unclear whether the place was named before or after the Israelites got there. After three days without water, the sight of water must have been a relief to the Israelites; to their dismay, however, the water is bitter, making it undrinkable. The Chinese saying *ku kou liang yao* means "bitter mouth, good medicine," which suggests that bitter-tasting medicines may have greater healing power. Although many traditional Chinese remedies are known for their bitter taste, the bitter water at Marah had no medicinal benefits. This bitter water is "bad news" for the Israelites.

The bitter and undrinkable water at Marah is the final straw for the Israelites. Their frustration has reached boiling point, and they direct their anger toward Moses, demanding, "What are we to drink?" (15:24). The tone of their question was likely accusatory, with an emphasis on the word "what."

---

13. Marah may connect with the meaning of the name Miriam. If so, it associates the episode of Marah with the presence of Miriam in Exodus 15:20–21 in an ominous way.

The Israelites are anxious about the possibility of dying of thirst and blame Moses and his leadership for their predicament. This question might also have been a sarcastic challenge to Moses's authority. The Israelites are confused about their identity[14] – if God had rescued and made them his people, why are they facing this life-threatening situation? They are also confused about Moses – if Moses had truly been sent by God, why was he not able to provide them with water to drink? Finally, they are confused about God – if God was all-powerful and good, why was he allowing them to face such a hardship? Similarly, for many African Americans, their first taste of freedom was a bitter one. Their newfound freedom in new lands was not as they had imagined, and the promised land seemed elusive. They found themselves moving from one crisis to the next.[15]

No one denies that water is crucial for survival. Without water, people become agitated, desperate, and angry. When the Israelites ask, "What are we to drink?" Moses does not turn on them in anger but, instead, cries out to God. The exact content of Moses's plea to God is not recorded, unlike the people's complaints, which are reported in direct speech. This direct speech allows readers to see the situation from the people's perspective and empathize with their feelings.

15:25–26 God's Show and Tell

God then shows Moses how to make the water drinkable. The word "show" is not used in its usual sense but in the sense of "to shoot" – like shooting an arrow – or "to teach" (*yarah*) – which is also the root of "Torah," which means law or instruction. God uses this incident as a teaching moment to instruct the Israelites about who he is. When Moses follows God's instructions and throws a piece of wood into the water, the water becomes sweet – a reversal of the first plague where the waters of the Nile had turned into blood. This demonstrates God's sovereignty over water – he is able to turn water into blood or make bitter waters sweet. The motif of water also recalls the Red Sea crossing, where God divided the sea so that Israel could walk on dry ground, which also echoes God's separation of the waters on the third day of creation. God is a creator par excellence. Turning this bitter, undrinkable, or "sick" water

---

14. Fretheim aptly names Israel at the time of the wilderness journey as "life as an adolescent." Fretheim, *Exodus*, 171. In the wilderness journey, Israel is not a child, but neither is Israel an adult. Israel's behavior is reminiscent of a teenager who tends to be self-centered, attempts to exert autonomy apart from the parents, and at times difficult to control his or her temper.
15. Fentress-Williams, "Exodus," 85.

into sweet water symbolizes a new creation and demonstrates God's power to bring order from chaos and healing from sickness.

God's command to Moses to throw something into the water stands in direct contrast to Pharaoh's command to throw the Hebrew boys into the Nile (Exod 1:22). Water holds the polarity of life and death. While God's command brings life, Pharaoh's command brings death. God also uses this incident as a teaching moment by issuing a ruling and thus testing the Israelites. What was the purpose of God's test? In Deuteronomy, as Moses looked back and reflected on this wilderness journey, he told the Israelites, "Remember how the Lord your God led you all the way in the wilderness these forty years, to humble and test you in order to know what was in your heart, whether or not you would keep his commands" (Deut 8:2). The purpose of the test was to see whether Israel would obey God and keep his commands. Each complaint from the Israelites reflects a lack of trust in God's providential care. The harsh realities of the wilderness weaken their previously professed faith (Exod 14:31). Meanwhile, every scarcity and every challenge they face becomes a test of their memory – would they choose to remember how God had led and provided for them in their wilderness journey? The process of identity formation involves reconciling past memories with the new reality of the present and navigating between the old identity and the new one. Crucial questions arise: Will Israel rely on their past memories of God's powerful deeds, or will they question God's power to provide for them in the wilderness? Will they trust in God's power in light of his past deeds, or will they question God's power each time they face an obstacle?

God speaks directly to the Israelites, using a conditional statement followed by a warning: "If you obey me, I will let you be free from the diseases which I have put on the Egyptians."[16] These "diseases" might refer to the sixth plague, which involved a skin disease (9:8–11), or it could be a metaphor referring to all the negative things that Egypt represented. This disease might refer to a "deathly system of scarcity-anxiety-accumulation-monopoly-violence sanctioned by Pharaoh."[17]

God concludes this divine oracle with an authoritative statement: "For I am the Lord, who heals you" (15:26).[18] God has the power to inflict diseases

---

16. My paraphrase.
17. Walter Brueggemann, "The Doctor Will See You Now," *Word & World Supplement Series* 7 2017): 8.
18. Literally, "because I am the Lord, your healer." God's healing power is indicated by purifying the bitter water and making it sweet.

on whomever he wishes, but God can also heal. God's power is manifested both in inflicting diseases and in healing people. God is a divine healer par excellence, able to turn bitter into sweet.[19] In the events narrated in Exodus 16–18, readers can discern God's "health agenda," in contrast to the diseases and afflictions of Egypt:

- —in place of anxiety, the "fear not" of restful Sabbath;
- —in place of scarcity, the administration of enough;
- —in place of accumulation, a daily gift;
- —in place of monopoly, enough for all; and
- —in place of violence, a capacity to share, with no one lacking.[20]

15:27 Elim

In this first lesson in the wilderness, God reveals his new identity as their healer, offering new reasons for Israel to place their trust in God. This episode concludes with the Israelites arriving at a place called Elim – meaning "oaks" or "terebinths" – where they find 12 springs of water and 70 date palms. The people camp beside the water – a scene of tranquility and contentment reminiscent of the imagery in Psalm 23. Here, the image of God is not just that of a divine healer but also a provider and a shepherd who leads his people to a place of sustenance and rest, evoking the image of God as a shepherd-leader in Exodus 15:13. This first wilderness lesson sets the pattern for the wilderness stories that follow, where obeying God's commands is essential for Israel to become the people God wants them to be.

---

19. God's ability to turn bitter into sweet is demonstrated in the story of Naomi (Ruth 1:20). The name "Naomi" means sweet or pleasant, and "mara" means bitter. In Ezekiel's temple vision, when the water comes down from the threshold of the temple and then goes east, it is healed and enlivens every living creature (Ezek 47:8).
20. Brueggemann, "The Doctor Will See You Now," 7. It is appropriate to call God "Dr. YHWH," and Moses the Physician's Assistant in this story as proposed by Brueggemann.

ELIM AND ITS RECEPTION: WEST AND EAST

In the history of interpretation, the association of Elim with 12 springs and 70 date palms has led to fascinating interpretations. For example, during the medieval period, Ramban (1194–1270) pondered the significance of the number of springs and palm trees in Elim, citing Rabbi Eliezer haModai, who explained that at the time of creation, God had created Elim with 12 springs that corresponded to the 12 tribes of Israel and 70 palm trees that corresponded to the 70 elders of the Sanhedrin. Later, Rabbi Joseph Solomon Delmedigo (1591–1655) wrote a book titled *Elim* (Heb. *Sefer Elim*) – structured around Numbers 33:9 – addressing 12 general and 70 specific religious and scientific questions asked by a Karaite Jew.[1]

In *Against Marcion* (Book IV 24:3–5), Tertullian (160–225) addresses the question of why Christ chose 70 missionaries besides the Twelve. He asks, "If the twelve followed the number of the twelve fountains of Elim, should not the seventy correspond to the like number of the palms of that place?" Origen (185–254) gave a series of sermons on the book of Numbers, in which he interpreted "Elim" allegorically as the "rams and thus leaders of Christ's flock." Therefore, the 12 springs and 70 palm trees represent the Twelve and other apostles of Jesus.[2]

In the Chinese context, the name "Elim" has become a prominent Christian symbol. Elim Bookstore, a well-known Christian bookstore and publisher in Taiwan and Hong Kong, is one notable example. Many Chinese churches, Christian organizations, and Christian schools also use the name "Elim." For instance, a Chinese church in Auckland, New Zealand, has designed a logo that features a spring and a palm tree alongside a cross and named the church "Elim Bread of Life Christian Church."[3] Elim often symbolizes water as a life source. Since water represents the word of God in the Christian tradition, many church fellowships use the name "Elim." In Chinese contexts, "Elim" is also a popular name for women.

---

1. J. Haberman, "Delmedigo, Joseph Solomon," *Encyclopaedia Judaica*, vol. 5, 544.
2. Depending on the location of Sinai, Elim was either situated in Wadi Gharandel (55 mi. SE of Suez) or 'Ayun Musa (9 mi. SE of Suez). Chloe Sun, "Elim," *EBR* 7:721–722.
3. http://www.elimbolcc.com.

God leads the Israelites from a place in the wilderness that had bitter water to a place with abundant water, teaching them a valuable lesson about his provision and human obedience. With memories of Egypt still fresh in their minds, Israel begins their journey of theological education in the wilderness – a liminal stage in their journey toward Sinai. Even the fruitless wilderness becomes fertile ground of learning in Israel's journey of identity formation, serving as a paradigm for Israel's later history during the period of the exile and beyond.[21]

16:1–36 LACK OF MEAT AND BREAD

This lengthy episode in the wilderness stirs up Israel's memory of their captivity in Egypt. The Israelites long for the past with a nostalgic or melancholic yearning. People are most likely to become nostalgic when encountering tough times in new lands, especially when the old place seems better than the present one. Those living in the in-between space may find themselves yearning for home, their cultural and ethnic roots, or what is familiar, especially when facing racism, discrimination, hate crimes, isolation, tragedy, or the death of a loved one in a new country. For example, when my long-time college friend in the United States died of COVID-19 during the pandemic, his wife returned to her home country in Asia to be reunited with relatives and friends and receive their comfort and support to cope with her loss. In such instances, the memory of home becomes a sanctuary of comfort and healing.

In the United States, migrants in areas that have fewer Chinese people often miss authentic Chinese food, the convenience of public transportation, and being around people of the same ethnicity who speak the same language. One purpose of establishing Chinatowns in highly Chinese-populated areas is to alleviate this yearning for a home.

Encountering tough times in new places not only evokes memories of the past but may also create a tendency to romanticize the past. As migrants or former migrants, people living in the diaspora face many challenges as minorities in a dominant culture. Studies show that reflecting on the past may provide social support, which helps ease difficulties during the transitional phase of relocation.[22] Many diasporans seek comfort in their own "Egypt" – wherever that may be.

---

21. For example, Ezekiel recounts how Israel rebelled against God in the wilderness as a parallel memory for Israel in exile (Ezek 20:33–39).
22. Chan, *Chinese Identities*, 84.

Food is a significant aspect of life, as expressed by the traditional Chinese saying, "Food is like heaven for people." Many second-generation children of migrant parents living in the diaspora may not always retain their parents' ethnic language and cultural customs, but their love for Chinese or other ethnic foods endures. For those originally from Hong Kong, going for *dim sum* and enjoying a cup of hot black tea with condensed milk remains a favorite pastime, even while living in the diaspora, far from home.

16:1–3 Missing "Home"

Six weeks after the exodus (16:1), the Israelites leave Elim and arrive at the wilderness of Sin, which lies between Elim and Sinai.[23] This location highlights, once again, the in-between state of the Israelites, who find themselves in the middle of the wilderness between two "desirable places" – the oasis of oaks in Elim and Mount Sinai, the abode of God.[24] Little do they realize that they are about to face their next test. This time, the test will involve the lack of food.

The people complain against Moses and Aaron because they have no food – specially, "meat" (16:2–3). They seem to quickly forget that God had recently provided them with sweet water. Now "the whole community grumbled" (16:2). This was an escalation of the number of people involved when compared to the previous scene in Exodus 15:24, where it says "the people" without the adjective "whole" or "all." The people's complaint is exaggerated: "If only we had died by the LORD's hand in Egypt! There we sat around pots of meat and ate all the food we wanted, but you have brought us out into this desert to starve this entire assembly to death" (16:3).[25] The memory of pots of meat and all-you-can-eat food in Egypt is juxtaposed with the present threat of starvation, as if they are saying, "It would have been better to die in slavery than be struck by hunger."

When faced with the lack of food, the Israelites' memory of Egypt becomes distorted. At this moment, they feel a strong "pull" toward Egypt and resent being "pushed" into a new reality in the wilderness. Their immediate need for food overpowers their desire for freedom or to become Yahweh-worshipers. The survival instinct drowns out everything else and becomes the primary drive for living. Their physical needs takes precedence over their mental and

---

23. Sin and Sinai share two consonants (s, n). We are not sure if they have any correlations between them.
24. R. W. L. Moberly, *Old Testament Theology: Reading the Hebrew Bible as Christian Scripture* (Grand Rapids: Baker Academic, 2013), 76.
25. Compare Numbers 11:4b–6.

spiritual needs. "Ate all the food we wanted" is literally "when we ate bread to our satisfaction." Now, as Israel faces the threat of starvation in the wilderness, they perceive their former life in Egypt as a more satisfying way of living.

In a parallel passage in Numbers, the food that the Israelites yearn for includes fish, cucumbers, melons, leeks, onions, and garlic (Num 11:4b–5). Leeks, onions, and garlic are essential ingredients in Chinese cooking, used both as vegetables and as condiments that enhance tastes and add savory flavors to a dish. Fresh fish, either roasted or steamed, together with leeks, onions, and garlic, make a delicious meal. Cucumber, with its crisp and refreshing taste, is a great complement to a fish dish, adding nutritional value, texture, color, and flavor. In many Asian countries, particularly those near coastal areas or along the Pacific Ocean, fresh fish and seafood are an integral part of the food culture.

In contrast, for those living in the diaspora, fresh fish is a rare treat, and people usually consume frozen fish. In many places in Asia, fresh chicken and fish are usually slaughtered at the time of purchase; in the diaspora, however, frozen chicken and fish are the norm. Therefore, those in the diaspora can readily identify with the Israelites who yearned for the food they had once enjoyed, especially fresh meat, seafood, and other savory foods back in Egypt. For many migrants, the idea of home is far more than food and includes people and places. Indeed, migration involves both visible and invisible losses.[26]

Israel's romanticizing of their life in Egypt suggests that they are caught between Canaan and Egypt, God and Pharaoh, a new identity as God's redeemed people and an old identity as slaves of Pharaoh. In their eyes, being slaves in Egypt seems, on the surface, to be a safer option. At least there is no need to worry about food. At least it is a stable life compared to the unpredictability of their present condition in the wilderness. For Israel, missing Egypt involves longing for its stability, familiarity, and, paradoxically, its "homelike" feeling. During this transitional time, Israel must "forsake both Egyptian imprisonment and nourishment if they are to be the people of Yahweh."[27]

---

26. These losses vary depending on one's circumstances and the story of migration. In light of Exodus 16, the visible loss may include the loss of consuming fresh seafood in certain places in the United States, the loss of family members who choose to reside in the countries of origin, and the loss of social and financial status in one's former home country. The invisible loss may include one's past heritage and the connection with the parental and grand-parental heritage. Lee, *Doing Asian American Theology*, 114–121.

27. J. H. Hunt, "Murmuring," in *DOTP*, 579.

16:4–12 God Tests His People

After hearing the complaints of the people, God responds by telling Moses that he will rain bread from the sky and that the people are to gather a portion each day. The motif of testing reappears here. Through this act, God will test them to see if they will obey his law. God goes on to instruct Israel to gather twice the amount on the sixth day. The motif of "daily bread" also surfaces in this scene since God's provision occurs daily. This is intended to teach Israel to trust God for each new day since God's mercies are new every morning (Lam 3:22–23).

Moses and Aaron convey God's words and instructions to the Israelites, interpreting their complaint against them as a complaint against God himself (16:7–8, 12). It is worth noting that God promises to provide meat and bread to their satisfaction – "all the bread you want" (16:8). The same idea of "satisfaction" appears earlier in Exodus 16:3 – "ate our fill" – suggesting that while Israel laments and yearns for the satisfaction of their appetites as in Egypt, God is able to satisfy this same yearning in the wilderness. God's answer to their lack of meat and bread is not a return to Egypt but, rather, trust in God's daily provision in the barren wilderness, a principle reflected in Jesus's teaching to his disciples to pray, "Give us today our daily bread" (Matt 6:11).

The meat and bread will be provided in the form of quail and manna (16:1–3). The phrase "the glory of the LORD" appears for the first time in the Bible here in verse 7. In this context, it means that through God's provision of manna in the morning, the presence of God will be manifested. The statement "Then you will know that I am the LORD your God" (16:12) explains God's motive behind the provision of food. Even more significantly, this statement serves as another teaching moment for Israel about what it means to know and trust God's provision. God intends not only for the Egyptians to know him but for all people to know him through his ongoing intervention in human history.

16:13–21 God Provides Meat and Manna

Exodus 16:13–21 presents a detailed account of how the meat and bread were provided.[28] First, migratory quails arrived in the evening and covered

---

28. Another version appears in Numbers 11:31–32. "Bread" (*lehem*) in Exodus 16 refers to manna, but it can also mean "food" more generally. In biblical poetry, meat and bread can be taken as a word pair (Exod 16:3, 8, 12) that symbolizes a complete meal (Gen 18:6–7; 1 Sam 28:24) or a merism pointing to two different kinds of food – animal-based and plant-based. Ephraim Landau, "Meat/Bread as a parallel Word-Pair in Biblical Poetry: A Key to Understanding Exodus 16:1–15," *JBQ* 47, no. 1 (2019): 3–20.

the camp. The next morning, a layer of dew surrounded the camp; when it disappeared, a fine, flaky substance remained. These quails, though small in size, migrate in large numbers from central Europe to Africa during the spring and are easily captured by hunters when, exhausted by their travels, they land on the ground to rest.[29]

Quail meat, which has a lean, chicken-like taste, an earthy texture, and an exotic flavor, is considered a delicacy in Chinese and other Asian cultures. The dew and flaky substance that appeared in the morning became known as "manna" (meaning, "what is it?") because the Israelites did not recognize it and asked one another, "What is it?" (*man hu*), as the narrator later explains (16:31). The manna is described as being like coriander seed, white, tasting like wafers made with honey, and resembling resin (Exod 16:31; Num 11:7). In modern terms, manna resembled a dessert, although we do not know how sweet it was. Perhaps manna might have tasted like sweet rice cakes or crispy rice cereal. The honey-like taste of manna suggests a connection with the land of Canaan, which is described as a land flowing with milk and honey (Exod 3:8, 17; 13:5). Thus, God's provision of manna during the wilderness journey might have been a foretaste of the sweetness of the land of Canaan for Israel. Moses describes the manna as "the bread the LORD has given you to eat" (16:15).

Along with the meat and bread (the dessert), divine instructions are given on how to gather and consume this food:

1. Each person is to gather the meat and manna according to their needs, an omer per person (16:16).[30]
2. No one is allowed to leave any meat and manna until the morning (16:19).

After laying out the rules for eating, Exodus 16 records the people's responses. This entire episode serves as a test from God. First, God gives instructions and observes whether the people follow them. Those who follow the instructions pass the test, while those who do not fail. As it turns out, everyone gathers just enough food for each day – no one has an excess or a shortfall, demonstrating the sufficiency of God's provision. As Moberly aptly

---

29. Sarna, *Exodus*, 88. Tigay, "Exodus," 131. Hoffmeier, *Ancient Israel in Sinai*, 173.
30. An omer is a tenth of an ephah (Exod 16:36). An ephah is about 35 liters. The word omer only occurs in Exodus 16:36. Some suggest that when this verse was written, the measurement "omer" was no longer used often. The word "ephah" occurs in Leviticus and Numbers and throughout the historical books. Hamilton, *Exodus*, 259.

points out, "The heavenly bread is resistant to one of the most basic of human urges: 'to save up and to hoard.'"[31] This episode teaches Israel that in God's economy, everyone has enough and there is no need to hoard. Those with larger appetites who gathered more manna did not have an excess, while those with smaller appetites who gathered less were not in need. This experience was nothing short of a miracle. God's daily provision of bread taught Israel to live in the present, to entrust each day to God's care, and to orient their lives according to God's instructions.

Some people disobey Moses and keep the leftovers until morning, which then breeds worms, becoming smelly and inedible (16:20).[32] In addition, when the sun grows hot in the morning, the manna melts. In this extended episode of meat and manna, the people's obedience is tested every day, just as God had told Moses (16:4). Unfortunately, not everyone passes the test (16:20). This lesson about manna teaches Israel that "man does not live on bread alone but on every word that comes from the mouth of the LORD" (Deut 8:3).

The story of manna has profound implications for the Christian life. When the people asked Jesus for a sign to believe in him, he replied, "Very truly I tell you, it is not Moses who has given you the bread from heaven, but it is my Father who gives you the true bread from heaven. For the bread of God is the bread that comes down from heaven and gives life to the world" (John 6:32–33). Jesus then declared, "I am the bread of life. Whoever comes to me will never go hungry, and whoever believes in me will never be thirsty" (6:35). Just as the story of manna emphasizes the importance of obeying the word of God as the source of life, Jesus invites believers to come to him as the ultimate source of life.

---

31. Moberly, *Old Testament Theology*, 82. Also, Fristchel, "Exodus 16 as an Alternative Social Paradigm," 37–38.
32. Stinky (*ba'ash*), the same word is used in Exodus 5:21; 7:21; 8:14. Stinky describes the sense of smell. In Exodus, the word first appears in 5:21 after Pharaoh demands that the Israelite slaves maintain the same quota of bricks – but now without straw being given to them. Then the foremen of the Israelites complain to Moses and Aaron that they have made the Israelites "stinky" in Pharaoh's sight. The second recorded appearance of the word is in 7:21 after the first plague. The Nile becomes "stinky" so that the Egyptians could not drink from it. The next recorded appearance of the word appears in 8:14, describing the corpse of the frogs piling up and the land becoming stinky. In all three references, the word "stinky" has something to do with the Egyptians and thus it appears in the context of estranged relations, whether it is Israelite-Egyptian or God-Pharaoh. Here, in Exodus 16, the leftover manna breeds worms and becomes stinky, suggesting the estrangement between the disobedient Israelites and God.

16:22–30 Teachings about Sabbath Observance

With the provision of meat and manna comes God's teaching on Sabbath observance (16:22–30).[33] In the wilderness journey, law and narrative are intertwined, with law emerging from the narrative context and the narrative context providing the rationale for the law. Verse 21 serves as both an introduction to the instruction on Sabbath observance and a brief conclusion to the previous section about the provision of meat and bread. The Sabbath instruction teaches Israel to reorder their work-rest schedule according to God's created order, as opposed to following Pharaoh's work schedule that demanded ceaseless labor for his building projects (5:13).

On the sixth day, the people gather twice as much manna as usual. Moses then instructs them to keep the leftover manna until the next day, which will be "a holy Sabbath to the Lord" (16:22–23). The people follow Moses's instructions. Astonishingly, the food does not spoil or breed worms as it had done previously. This remarkable condition of the food – its preservation and freshness if kept overnight on the sixth day but its spoiling if kept overnight on other days of the week – demonstrates that this is a miracle only made possible through divine intervention. This time, the people listen to Moses. For six days, they gather food; but on the seventh day – the Sabbath – there is nothing to gather. Since the essence of the Sabbath is "to cease," people are expected to stop working – and this includes gathering food, which is a physical activity and a form of work.

Moses further explains to the people that God has established the ordinance of the Sabbath and provided twice the amount of bread on the sixth day so that no one needs to gather food on the seventh day. The people rest on the seventh day, in imitation of God resting on the seventh day of creation (Gen 2:2). This pattern of six days of work followed by a day of rest mirrors the creation account in Genesis, where God set apart the seventh day and made it holy (2:3). While in Egypt, the Israelites worked to survive, but God now teaches them to balance work and rest, thus introducing a new way of living. By linking food provision and Sabbath observance, God teaches the people to rely on his provision rather than on their own abilities. Regular Sabbath

---

33. Geller discerns two theological strands in Exodus 16 – covenantal and priestly. The former strand focuses on the theme of testing, while the latter's concern is the cultic institution of the bread. Sabbath functions as the connector between the two. These two strands are different but complementary and they help to explain the complex composition of this chapter. Stephen A. Geller, "Manna and Sabbath: A Literary-Theological Reading of Exodus 16," *Int*, Jan (2005): 5–16.

observance would serve as a constant reminder to Israel of God's identity and their own identity as God's redeemed people.

The importance of the Sabbath rest is seen by its repetition in the book of Exodus.[34] Since the Sabbath observance in Exodus 16:22–30 predates the giving of the Sabbath law at Sinai, it is clear that the purpose of this Sabbath observance is to follow God's created order in Genesis 2:1–3 rather than simply fulfilling a legalistic requirement. The NT adopts a more flexible approach to the observance of the Sabbath, as demonstrated by Jesus's healings on the Sabbath and his assertion that "the Sabbath was made for man, not man for the Sabbath. So the Son of Man is Lord even of the Sabbath" (Mark 2:27).

In contemporary times, Christians generally regard Sunday as a day of worship. However, since Sunday often involves service and work for clergy, many churches encourage their pastors to take Monday off as a day of rest. While some people choose Saturday as their Sabbath day, many still consider Sunday the Christian Sabbath. Regardless of the specific day that is chosen, the work-rest cycle is a design ordained by God for humanity, reflecting a divine mandate to align with the created order for our own well-being. The subject of the Sabbath will be elaborated further in the discussion on the Ten Commandments.

For Israel, observing the Sabbath is crucial in establishing their new identity as God's people who adhere to this work-rest cycle, as opposed to being Pharaoh's slaves who work unceasingly on a daily basis. The meticulous instructions regarding the Sabbath observance in relation to gathering food provide a critical lesson for Israel in the wilderness: resting in God and entering God's rest takes precedence over their concerns about food. By observing the Sabbath, even in times of scarcity, Israel will learn to trust God's provision and reorder their priorities. Similarly, today, Christians – including clergy – must also practice a healthy work-rest rhythm to ensure sustainable living and service.

16:31–36 More on Manna

Exodus 16:31–36 continues the story of manna that began in Exodus 16:21, with the Sabbath instructions seemingly interrupting or being inserted into the manna narrative. While this passage might be interpreted as an afterthought or postscript to the manna story, it can also be viewed as the central focus that is framed by the preceding narrative. The reference to 40 years suggests that this passage was inserted later, as an editorial comment, to remind future

---

34. Exodus 20:8–11; 31:12–17; 35:2–3.

generations of Israelites about God's provision of bread during Israel's wilderness journey.

This passage – with its account of the command to keep an omer of manna as a reminder of God's provision of bread in the wilderness (16:31–32) – echoes the earlier identification of the bread as "manna" and the command to "take an omer of manna" (16:15–16). In obedience to this command, Aaron places an omer of manna in a jar, which is then kept with "the tablets of the covenant law" – that is, the ark of the testimony or the ark of the covenant. Chapter 16 concludes by stating that Israel ate manna for 40 years until they reached the border of Canaan.[35]

The mention of the "ark" (Exod 25 and 37) and "forty years" in this passage suggests that the construction of the ark had already been completed and that 40 years had elapsed by the time this manna-Sabbath story was written.[36]

17:1–7 LACK OF WATER AGAIN

The Israelites journeyed in obedience to God's command (17:1) and were led by God in their journey through the wilderness. They did not wander aimlessly but as directed by their divine leader and guide. As believers, although our journeys sometimes seem aimless, directionless, long, and arduous, knowing that God leads the way, goes before us, and holds the map for our journey in his hand gives us hope and a sense of purpose in our journey of becoming.

As the Israelites journey on in stages from the wilderness of Sin[37] and camp at a place called Rephidim,[38] they find that there is no water to drink. It is not clear whether this lack of water was because the Amalekites – whose attack is described immediately after this episode – controlled this region. For the second time, scarcity of water becomes an issue in Israel's wilderness journey. Although the Israelites should have remembered the earlier incident at Marah – where God turned bitter water into sweet water (15:22–25) – and

---

35. When the Israelites entered Canaan and started eating some of the produce of the land, the manna ceased on that very day (Josh 5:12–13).
36. The forty-year refers to a long period of time idiomatically. This would include the construction of the tabernacle, the installation of the priesthood, the law giving at Sinai, the incident of the golden calf, and the settlement in Canaan. This is another piece of evidence showing that the book of Exodus is not recorded in strictly chronological order and that there are layers of editorial work. The explanation of the omer in verse 36 also shows that later readers may not have been familiar with this measurement, so the narrator had to explain.
37. "In stages" in Hebrew is "in their journeyings." The Israelites were not aimlessly moving around in the wilderness but were orderly in their progression.
38. Rephidim is the last station on the journey from the Red Sea to Sinai (Exod 19:2; Num 33:15–15), but its exact location is uncertain. Sarna, *Exodus*, 93.

trusted in God's ability to provide water again, they do not do so. Instead, they quarrel (*rib*) with Moses and urgently demand water, saying, "Give us water to drink" (17:2), which is an escalation of their previous complaint, "What are we to drink?" (15:24).

Moses replies, "Why do you quarrel [*rib*] with me? Why do you put the LORD to the test [*nasah*]?" (17:2). "Quarrel" and "test" became two markers of the people's ingratitude and forgetfulness during the in-between space of the wilderness. "Quarrel" is a legal term, as if this were a dispute in a court of law, with the people seeing themselves as being in the right and Moses as being in the wrong. "Test" is a recurring theme in the wilderness journey. Although Moses sees this situation as one where the people are testing God, in fact, God is also testing the people's obedience (15:25; 16:4). The motif of testing works in both directions.[39]

The people then grumble against Moses, making an even more serious accusation: "Why did you bring us up out of Egypt to make us and our children and livestock die of thirst?" (17:3).[40] Earlier, they had complained about dying of hunger; now they grumble about dying of thirst. At this point, living as slaves in Egypt seems preferable to the possiblity of dying in the wilderness. Once again, Israel feels the "pull" back to Egypt and resents being "pushed" into the new reality of the wilderness. The threat of dying of thirst turns the people into a hostile mob who even threaten Moses's life. Moses cries out to God for help, asking, "What am I to do with this people? They are almost ready to stone me" (17:4).

As in earlier instances, God comes to the rescue. He instructs Moses to go before the people, along with some of the elders, and take his staff. God promises to stand before Moses by the rock at Horeb while Moses strikes the rock with his staff, causing water to flow from it for the people to drink. The staff of Moses – which he had used to strike the Nile (7:20) and which had been transformed into God's weapon – is now to be used to strike the rock and bring forth water by God's command.[41]

Verse 7 summarizes the outcome of this episode. Moses follows God's instructions in the presence of the elders of Israel. He also names the place Massah and Meribah – dual names that capture and memorialize the dual behavior of the people's quarreling and testing God in the wilderness by asking,

---

39. See also Deuteronomy 8:2, 16.
40. Compare Exodus 16:3.
41. Compare Numbers 20:2–13.

"Is the LORD among us or not?"[42] The entire episode is portrayed through verbal exchanges between the people and Moses, as well as between Moses and God. The use of dialogue to drive the plot makes the quarrel scene come alive for readers – we can almost hear the different parties arguing with each other.

This incident had a profound impact on the collective memory of Israel and serves as a negative archetype for rebellion against God. When recounting Israel's history, Moses cites this incident as a prime example of the people's disobedience (Deut 6:16; 9:22). The psalmists also invoke this memory as a painful reminder of Israel's wilderness experience with God (Pss 81:7; 95:8–9). Previously, God had tested Israel through the lack of water and food. This time, the test does not originate from God but, rather, from the people's questioning or testing whether God is truly with them.

17:8–16 THE THREAT OF THE AMALEKITES

The wilderness, like in-between spaces in life, is a vulnerable and perilous place. Israel's journey through the wilderness is marked by scarcity of food and water, as well as enemy attacks. Both the lack and the attack directly threaten their survival. Only with God on their side will they be able to endure this arduous journey. At the same time, they must reevaluate their relationship with outsiders and restructure themselves internally to ensure long-term sustainability. Exodus 17:8–18:27 could well be titled "Israel's foe and friend," with the Amalekites representing their foes or adversaries and Jethro symbolizing a friend or ally. Both parties stand outside Israel's ethnic and religious community, and they illustrate contrasting attitudes toward Israel.

Despite their seemingly distinct content, the stories of the lack of water (17:1–7) and the attack of the Amalekites (17:8–16) share similar themes, such as the staff of Moses, the similar Hebrew consonants and sound in "test" (*nasah*) and "banner" (*nissi*), and the role of Moses as a mediator between divine power and human ability. The motif of wiping out the remembrance of the Amalekites also contrasts with the memorialized places – Massah and Meribah – in the preceding story. In this way, the battle against the Amalekites becomes a paradigmatic story for understanding Israel's relationships with its enemies in the future – for example, Saul's war against the Amalekites (1 Sam 15) and Mordecai's refusal to bow to Haman in the book of Esther (Esth 3:1–2). Over time, the Amalekites became Israel's archenemy. In the NT context, the equivalents of the Amalekites include the spiritual forces of

---

42. Massah means "test." Meribah means "quarrel."

darkness described in Ephesians 6:12 and "Babylon," which epitomizes evil in Revelation 17–18.

17:8-9 The Amalekites Came

While the Israelites are encamped at Rephidim, the Amalekites come and fight against them. The reason for the attack is not disclosed in the text, but perhaps they were camping on the territory of the Amalekites or the Amalekites perceived Israel as a threat to their national security. Deuteronomy 25:17–19 speaks of the Amalekites attacking Israel from behind, targeting the stragglers who had grown faint and weary. This text also notes that the Amalekites did not fear God (Deut 25:18). The name Amalek is non-Semitic and appears in the genealogy of Esau (36:12). Amalek's mother, Timna, was the concubine of Eliphaz, Esau's firstborn son. In the book of Esther, Haman is described as a descendant of the Amalekite king Agag (Esth 3:1).

Confronted with the Amalekite attack, Moses instructs Joshua to choose men to fight against the Amalekites and stations himself on top of a hill with the staff of God in his hand.[43] Joshua obeys, and Moses, along with Aaron and Hur, climb to the top of the hill. This marks a departure from the typical pattern of earlier stories where God instructs Moses on what to do (15:25–26; 16:4–5, 11–12, 16, 23, 32; 17:5–6). In this case, Moses instructs others in the absence of a direct command from God. While the text does not explain the reason for this shift, this shift suggests that the role of the Amalekite attack is different from the previous tests in the wilderness journey. While the precise nature of this role is subject to debate, one possibility is that Israel is now more experienced and mature in their relationship with God and, therefore, God allows them to make their own decision. Another possibility is that God is using this incident as another test to see how Israel responds without a direct command from God, similar to the way parents observe their children's reactions to danger to see if they are ready for more responsibility.

17:10–13 Moses against the Amalekites

Sandwiched between the descriptions of Joshua's military prowess (17:10, 13) is an interesting episode that focuses on the hand or hands of Moses. As the story unfolds, Israel's victory in battle depends on the position of Moses's hands. In the Bible, "hand" often symbolizes strength and power.

---

43. This is the first occurrence of Joshua in the Pentateuch. The fact that the author did not elaborate about him suggests that Joshua was a well-known figure to the original audience.

When Moses's hand is raised, Israel prevails in the battle; when his hand falls, the Amalekites prevail. Since the "hand" in verse 11 is singular in Hebrew,[44] Moses might have been raising his right hand or alternating between his right and left hand. However, the use of the plural "hands" in verse 12 could also imply that he raised both hands at some point. The ambiguity surrounding the question whether Moses raised one hand, both hands, or alternated between hands has sparked much discussion. However, what is clear from the narrative is that when Moses's hands grow heavy, Aaron and Hur get a stone for Moses to sit on and support him on either side so that his hands remain steady until sunset (17:12), highlighting the crucial role played by the hands of Moses in determining the outcome of the battle.

There are different theories about the meaning of Moses's hand being "raised" or "held up." Some suggest that it represents a magical gesture used to perform a miracle, while others propose that when Moses raised his hands, he also raised the staff of God as a divine weapon. Intertextual studies by both Michael Widmer and Charlie Trimm confirm that in the OT, raising one's hands is a common gesture of prayer,[45] signifying human limitation and dependence on God to win battles. The content of Moses's prayer might not have been a specific request to God to defeat the enemy but, rather, a plea for God's mercy toward Israel.[46] This intercessory role is a key aspect of Moses's ministry during the wilderness journey.

The Amalek episode is the first occasion since the plagues and the sea-crossing where we encounter another war. Given the recurring theme of testing in Exodus 15:22–17:7, it seems reasonable to interpret this lack of direct instructions by God as a test, whereby God sought to determine whether Israel would rely on God through prayer or depend on their own abilities.

---

44. The Samaritan Pentateuch indicates "his hands," in plural, so do the NIV editors.
45. Michael Widmer, *Standing in the Breach: An Old Testament Theology and Spirituality of Intercessory Prayer*, SIPHRUT 13 (Winona Lake: Eisenbrauns, 2015), 58–82. His research includes discovering the parallel themes between Exodus 17:8–16 and Moses's intercessory prayer in the golden calf incident in Exodus 32–34. He argues that the role of Moses in Exodus 17 anticipates his role in Exodus 32–34. Charlie Trimm, "God's staff and Moses' hand(s): The battle against the Amalekites as a turning point in the role of the divine warrior," *JSOT* 44 (2019): 198–214. Still, the understanding of Moses's raised hands as prayer is contested. Childs, for example, disagrees with this interpretation and thinks that nothing in the story suggests it. Childs, *The Book of Exodus*, 313–314.
46. This implication comes from an intertextual reading of Moses's intercessory role in Exodus 32–34. Another parallel text is Numbers 14. See Widmer, *Standing in the Breach*, 81–91.

Exodus 15:22–18:27

Between Divine Control and Human Responsibility

Between the polarity of the power and frailty of Moses's hands, there exists a tension that emphasizes the dynamic interaction between God's power and human agency. The heaviness (*kabed*) of Moses's hands during the battle with the Amalekites sets the stage for Jethro's advice to Moses in the next chapter, where Jethro witnesses the heaviness (*kabed*) of Moses's administrative duties. Just as Moses required the support of other leaders in the battle against the Amalekites, he also needed the support of others in the task of governing the people and administering justice.

In the broader context of Exodus, the divine-human partnership in battle (17:8–16) forms a literary bridge between God's earlier demonstrations of military might and the subsequent establishment of human leadership structures in Exodus 18.[47] Moses would not have been able to hold up his hands in prayer without the help of Aaron and Hur. This incident, along with Moses's frailty, sets the stage for Jethro's advice to Moses to appoint 70 elders to assist him. Throughout the wilderness journey, unexpected events occur, and it is vital that people adjust and adapt to new challenges as they arise.

The narrative highlights a collaboration between prayer, divine intervention, and human effort, with Moses raising his hands in prayer while Joshua, the commander-in-chief, leads the army in battle. Moses acts as a mediator between God's divine power and the human army. The narrator concludes the battle story by stating that "Joshua overcame the Amalekite army with the sword" (17:13). "Overcame" (*khalash*) is literally "to prostrate" or to weaken an enemy to the point of making them prostrate themselves. Some scholars argue that this was not a total victory but an attack that resulted in heavy casualties for the enemy.[48] But regardless of which interpretation is chosen, this marks the first instance where Israel fights for their survival in the wilderness. They must confront their enemies to survive and to become adept in military strategy in preparation for future battles. This battle theme is also consistent with the fact that Israel left Egypt in military formation (Exod 12:51), illustrating that God's intention for Israel was that they become not only a kingdom of priests and a holy nation but also a nation prepared for military engagement.

---

47. "Literary bridge" or "Janus parallelism." Janus is named after the two-headed Roman God Janus. Janus parallelism is often used in Ancient Near Eastern poetry to refer to a middle literary unit that connects the preceding and subsequent literary units. Trimm, "God's staff and Moses' hand(s)," 209.
48. Sarna, *Exodus*, 96.

This fight against the Amalekites was the first of many battles that Israel would face, setting the stage for Israel's eventual conquest of Canaan.

17:14–16 To Remember Not to Remember

The remainder of Exodus 17 focuses on preserving the memory of God's actions and erasing the memory of the Amalekites. God instructs Moses to record this battle in a book. The purpose of documenting this memory is to memorialize the event: God would completely destroy the Amalekites (17:14). To remember not to remember is the point of this writing. The command to "make sure that Joshua hears it" is significant because Joshua will succeed Moses as Israel's leader and lead Israel into battle against the Canaanites. Significantly, God commands Moses to "make sure that Joshua hears it" (17:14), rather than simply telling Moses to inform Joshua. This phrasing stresses that Joshua was to be the direct recipient of the report. Thus, the battle event (17:8–13) is memorialized through both writing and hearing, providing a dual testimony to its validity and certainty. Moses then builds an altar and names it "The Lord is my Banner [*nissi*]" (17:15).

We can imagine Moses raising his hands or staff as he stands on a hill as a visible sign of God's banner.[49] Since "test" (*nasah*) and "banner" (*nissi*) have the first two consonants (*ns*) in common,[50] they link these two stories, which might be the author's way of subtly suggesting that God is indeed present with Israel in response to their earlier accusatory question in Exodus 17:7.

The act of building an altar and naming it serves to preserve the memory of what God did for Israel in the battle against the Amalekites.[51] The final verse of the chapter anticipates a future where God will continue to wage war against the Amalekites from generation to generation.[52] In Deuteronomy, Moses urges the second generation of Israelites to remember to blot out the memory of Amalek, emphasizing, "Do not forget!" (Deut 25:19). When it comes to memory, there are things to remember, things to forget, and things

---

49. Fretheim puts it vividly, saying that "Moses's hand and God's hand are elided." Fretheim, *Exodus*, 195.
50. If "test" is understood to be a military term, then it is possible that "banner" or "sign" is connected to the idea of testing. Helfmeyer, "נָסָה nissâ," *TDOT* IX, 443.
51. Other incidents of building an altar include Genesis 12:8; 33:20; 35:7; Judges 6:24.
52. The first few words of this verse in Hebrew are obscure. The verse begins: And he said, "because the hand upon the throne of Yah." This could mean that God has sworn (NASB). NIV takes it as "Because hands were lifted up against the throne of the Lord." It could also mean "I swear by the Lord's throne." See Tigay, "Exodus," 134.

to remember to forget. What we choose to remember and forget helps define and shape our identity.

In the broader narrative, the story of the Amalekites parallels the story of Israel's former enemy – Pharaoh. Scholars note that the pattern of storytelling in the Amalekite episode mirrors the earlier account of the ten plagues through, for example, the use of "tomorrow" (17:9), the heaviness (17:12), and the staff of God (17:9).[53] Although Israel prevailed over Pharaoh at the sea-crossing and Pharaoh receded to the background, a new "Pharaoh" now rises up to fight against Israel at Rephidim. While this suggests that hostile forces will continue to oppose Israel, God vows to be at war with these forces (17:16). Haman in the book of Esther and Hitler in the twentieth century could be viewed as embodiments of Amalek, reflecting the persistent presence of anti-Semitism in some parts of the contemporary world.

In later accounts, the memory of Israel's wilderness journey and its challenges has been depicted in various ways, depending on each author's perspective and interests at the time of writing. For example, Psalm 105 looks back on that journey and emphasizes God's provision of quail and manna (referred to as "bread of heaven") and how he brought forth water from a rock (105:40–41). In contrast, Psalm 106 focuses on Israel's forgetfulness and their repeated testing of God (106:13–14). In Psalm 78, the psalmist recounts both God's provision of water (78:15–16) and the people's rebellion and disbelief (78:17–20), while also recording that God rained down manna and meat despite the people's waywardness (78:21–29).[54] Indeed, what people choose to remember and how they remember it plays an important role in identity formation.

18:1–27 LEADERSHIP AND GOVERNANCE

In Chinese and Asian cultures, the father-in-law usually holds a special position in the family. If a man wants to marry a woman, he requires the permission and blessings of her father – a gesture that demonstrates respect and submission to the father-in-law's authority. Therefore, it is not surprising that Moses showed respect toward his father-in-law, Jethro, who plays a prominent role in Exodus 18.

---

53. Fretheim, *Exodus*, 194. Bills, *A Theology of Justice in Exodus*, 183.
54. For other examples of how later biblical writers recount the wilderness tradition, see Fretheim, *Exodus*, 173.

Exodus

This chapter shifts from the earlier theme of tests to the theme of leadership restructuring, which forms a fitting conclusion to the first phase of Israel's wilderness journey and sets the stage for the law-giving at Sinai. The second phase of the journey begins in Numbers 11–21. As God teaches Israel who he is through this wilderness journey, Israel gradually begins to understand their new identity as God's people and what this identity entails in everyday life, particularly in their relationship with God and with others. While Moses is clearly their leader, the episode where Moses's hands grow weary demonstrates that he is still human and needs help and support from others (17:8–13). Exodus 18 reinforces this idea and describes how a structured system of leadership is established to administer justice more effectively. This theme of administering justice then paves the way for God's law-giving in Exodus 19–24. The essence of God's law is to ensure that Israel administers justice to needy and vulnerable groups in society. This focus on justice is integral to Israel's call to be a kingdom of priests and a holy nation (19:6) – not just in name but in their treatment of others.

This chapter contains two scenes. The first scene narrates the visit of Jethro, Moses's father-in-law (18:1–12), while the second scene deals with Jethro's proposal for a structured judicial system (18:13–27).[55] In the first scene, Jethro acknowledges and praises what God has done for Israel. The second scene deals with Jethro's wise counsel to Moses regarding a structured system of leadership to rule God's people. The key word that connects this chapter with the previous pericope in Exodus 17:8–16 is "heavy" (*kaved*). Just as Moses's "heavy" hands (17:12) – "grew tired" in NIV – needed the support of Aaron and Hur, his "heavy" (*kaved*) responsibilities in the wilderness require the support of others – "The work is too heavy for you" (18:18). This chapter also contrasts the hostility of the Amalekites with the friendliness of Jethro, the priest of Midian, toward Moses and the Israelites, emphasizing that not all nations are enemies of Israel and that it is only those who actively oppose Israel would become the objects of God's wrath.

---

55. Fretheim thinks that the theme of chapter 18 is faith and family. The author intends to integrate Jethro, the father-in-law of Moses, into Israel's faith and Israel's new identity as a community of faith. Fretheim, *Exodus*, 195. Hamilton notes that the word "father-in-law" appears twelve times in chapter 18 (18:1, 2, 5, 6, 7, 8, 12 [2x], 14, 17, 24, 27). Hamilton, *Exodus*, 277. Many scholars have realized from this chapter's timeline in the Pentateuch that its events may come after the Sinai narrative. The order of the stories in the Pentateuch may not be arranged chronologically but thematically to meet the author's purpose. In this case, it would be the contrast between the Amalekites in chapter 17 and the Midianite (i.e., Jethro) in chapter 18 that this chapter is placed here.

18:1–12 Jethro's Visit

Exodus 18 introduces Moses's father-in-law as Jethro, which differs from the earlier mention of his name as Reuel (2:16–22).[56] Hearing what God had done for Israel, particularly his rescue of Israel from Egypt, Jethro comes to visit Moses, along with Moses's wife Zipporah and their two sons.

Reading between the lines, we might assume that Moses had sent Zipporah and their two sons back to Midian when he went to Egypt to confront Pharaoh and bring Israel out of Egypt.[57] Verse 3 functions as a parenthesis that reiterates the meanings of the names of Moses's sons. These names symbolize two major themes in Moses's journey. The first son, Gershom (2:22), represents Moses's in-between or liminal existence in Midian, while the second son, Eliezer, represents Moses's transformational identity through experiencing God's deliverance from Pharaoh (2:15). The name Eliezer, which means "My God is help," signifies Moses's recognition of God's help: "My father's God was my helper; he saved me from the sword of Pharaoh" (18:4). Being or feeling like a sojourner does not prevent a person from experiencing the power of God. Many times, it is precisely in a vulnerable situation or context that we are likely to experience God's power. Both negative and positive encounters with God play an important role in our journey of identity formation.

When Jethro arrives with Zipporah and Moses's two sons, Moses has already set up camp at the mountain of God.[58] Moses goes out to meet them. He then bows down, and kisses and greets his father-in-law. As they enter the tent, Moses tells Jethro everything God has done for Israel, summarizing God's deeds in two broad strokes: God's rescue of the Israelites from Pharaoh and the Egyptians, and God's rescue of the Israelites from all the hardships of their wilderness journey. Here, the narrator summarizes in one sentence the contents of Exodus 7–17 (18:8). Jethro responds by praising God (18:9–11) and offering sacrifices to God (18:12). The narrator's detailed description of Jethro's words and actions contrasts sharply with his more detached description of the Amalekites, which does not include any mention of their thoughts, emotions, or motives.

---

56. The different names may indicate different sources. Many scholars consider the Pentateuch to have four different sources (JEDP). For more, see Alexander, *From Paradise to the Promised Land*, 3–61. Exodus 2 would be a J source, whereas Exodus 18 would be an E source.
57. Earlier, we see that Moses's wife and sons accompanied him to Egypt (4:20); now, we find Moses has sent away his wife and sons to be with Jethro (18:2). Something must have happened between 4:20 and 18:2 without an explicit explanation from the narrator.
58. The repetitive uses of Elohim rather than Yahweh in this chapter demonstrates that it is an E source. The Mountain of God is Horeb (Exod 3:1).

Jethro's response consists of the following:

1. He rejoices over all the goodness that God had shown to Israel by delivering and rescuing them from the hand of the Egyptians (18:9).
2. He blesses God for rescuing Israel from the hand of Pharaoh and the Egyptians (18:10).
3. He acknowledges that God is greater than all other gods (18:11).[59]

Jethro's statement "now I know" reflects his understanding of God's supremacy over all other gods, including the gods of Egypt. This realization echoes the song of Moses – "Who among the gods is like you, LORD?" (15:11) – and aligns with God's intention for Israel to "know that I am the LORD your God, who brought you out from under the yoke of the Egyptians" (6:7) and his desire to be known among the Egyptians and the whole world.[60] God's ultimate goal has always been to be known not only by Israel but by all nations. Jethro then offers a burnt offering and sacrifices to God and partakes in a sacrificial meal before God along with Aaron and all the elders of Israel.[61] Upon hearing about God's mighty deeds on behalf of Israel, Jethro responds by worshiping the God of Israel, giving thanks, and acknowledging what God has done for his people.

This scene serves as a model for Israel to share their faith with outsiders. Just as Moses recounts the story of God's deliverance of Israel from the Egyptians and his interventions in their hardships in the wilderness to Jethro – an outsider and a Midianite priest – Israel is also called to share their faith with other nations so that all people might acknowledge God's supremacy and give thanks to him. God's deliverance of the Israelites from Egypt is on display so that all can see God's power over history and politics.[62]

18:13–27 Jethro's Proposal

The previous scene (18:1–12) portrays the positive response of a non-Israelite to what God had done for Israel, with Jethro symbolizing the Gentile nations. In contrast, this scene (18:13–27) focuses on Jethro's proposal for the establishment of a structured system of leadership within Israel. This demonstrates

---

59. It is remarkable for a Midianite priest to acknowledge the LORD (the personal name of God).
60. Compare Exodus 7:5; 8:22; 9:14, 16; 10:2; 16:2; Leviticus 26:45.
61. Sarna, *Exodus*, 99.
62. Fretheim, *Exodus*, 196–197.

that an outsider can be a blessing to Israel and that not all Gentiles are like Pharaoh or the Amalekites. While people living in the diaspora may encounter discrimination and opposition from those who are against migrants or foreigners, there are also individuals and groups who support and advocate for migrants and foreigners.

The day after Jethro's confession, "Now I know that the LORD is greater than all the gods," he observes an ordinary day in the life of Moses. Seeing that people were coming to Moses from morning till evening to seek his judicial decisions, Jethro inquires about the reason for this situation.[63] Moses explains that the people came to him to inquire of God and that his role is to judge each case according to God's instructions (18:15–16). The mention of God emphasizes that the ultimate source of judicial authority is God, with Moses functioning as just a mediator between God and the people of Israel.

Jethro then counsels Moses, expressing disapproval of Moses's leadership style: "What you are doing is not good" (18:17).[64] In many Asian cultures, elders such as parents, uncles, and in-laws are generally perceived as having authority over the younger generation. Jethro's disapproval must have carried considerable weight with Moses. Jethro explains that the workload is too much for one person and warns that Moses would soon be worn out if he continued in this way (18:18). Just as Moses's hands grew heavy on the hill at Rephidim (17:12), this task is too heavy for him to bear alone. Just as Moses needed help and support from Aaron and Hur on that hill at Rephidim, Jethro sees that Moses needs help with the heavy task before him. Jethro speaks authoritatively to Moses: "Listen now to me and I will give you some advice" (18:19).[65]

Jethro's counsel is that Moses should act as the people's representative before God, bringing their disputes to God and also teaching them God's laws and ways (18:19–20).[66] Since the beginning of the wilderness journey, God has been on a mission to teach Israel his ways and his laws (15:25–26). God's instructions frame the wilderness narrative (15:22–18:27). Each lesson

---

63. In the legal context, the judge is sitting, and the people are standing (1 Sam 22:6; 1 Kgs 3:16; Prov 20:8). Hamilton, *Exodus*, 285.
64. The expression "not good" first appears in the creation story when God saw that it is not good for the man to be alone (Gen 2:18). Here, Jethro functions as a higher authority, evaluating what is good and what is not good with Moses's leadership.
65. "Listen" is imperative, without a polite marker. "Advise" (*ya'ats*) can be translated as "counsel" (Num 24:14; 1 Kgs 12:8; Isa 7:5).
66. The mention of "law" (*torah*) harkens back to Exodus 15:25 (the word "show" is derived from the same root as *torah*) and paves the way for chapters 19–24, where Moses functions as a teacher of God's law.

in the wilderness journey reveals a new aspect of God's character to Israel and prepares them for the next stage in their journey.

Jethro advises Moses to choose capable and trustworthy men who fear God[67] and hate dishonest gain to be leaders over thousands, hundreds, fifties, and tens and serve as judges in their disputes. These leaders would handle minor disputes and only bring difficult matters to Moses. Jethro concludes that if Moses follows his advice, he will be able to "stand the strain" and all the people will go home in peace (18:23). Earlier, the people stood (*'amad*) before Moses, awaiting his judicial decisions. Now, if Moses follows Jethro's advice, Moses will be able to stand (*'amad*) in the sense of enduring and sustaining his ministry over the long term. Jethro's proposal is a win-win solution, and Moses recognizes this and follows his father-in-law's advice (18:24).

Jethro demonstrates both authority and humility in acknowledging God's role in the proposed leadership restructuring (18:23). Jethro's proposal is presented on his own initiative, with no mention in Scripture that it comes from God. However, by repeatedly acknowledging God in his advice to Moses (18:19–23), Jethro serves as a mediator or spokesperson for God, demonstrating that an outsider can not only be friendly toward the Israelites but can also contribute to the insiders. Jethro's wise counsel prepared Israel to administer justice and be a kingdom of priests under God's law. The chapter concludes with Moses accepting Jethro's recommendations and implementing these by reorganizing Israel's leadership structures (18:24–26). The establishment of a new leadership structure to administer justice to the people seems a fitting ending to the wilderness narrative, providing Israel with a sustainable internal system for the administration of justice. Moses then sends his father-in-law back to his own land, Midian. The act of "sending" forms a neat *inclusio* with Exodus 18:2, where Moses sent Zipporah away.

The Wilderness Journey as a Journey of Becoming

The wilderness journey serves as a bridge and transition between two major literary units: Israel's departure from Egypt and the giving of the law at Sinai. In the wilderness, Israel experiences a transitional phase that is similar to Moses's time in Midian, where he felt ambivalent about his identity – neither fully Egyptian, nor fully Hebrew, nor fully Midianite, as reflected in the naming of his son, Gershom. Similarly, Israel's sentiments toward Egypt and

---

67. The requirement of choosing leaders who fear God echoes the character of the Hebrew midwives in chapter 1 (Exod 1:17, 21).

the wilderness are ambivalent. On the one hand, they long for the stability of Egypt; on the other hand, they resist the adventure of a field education of knowing God and obeying him during their arduous journey in the wilderness. This in-between condition in the wilderness is a major theme in the Pentateuch.

Just as Moses gradually learns who God is, Israel also slowly begins to understand their relationship with God. Through the crises in the wilderness, Israel learns that God is a healer, guide, teacher, provider, and protector. Their complaints, challenges to Moses's authority, longing for Egypt, frustrations in the wilderness, diet of quail and manna, battles against the Amalekites and other enemies, and leadership restructuring do not prevent them from experiencing God's power and protection.

In Exodus 15–18, Israel's testing in the wilderness results in a largely positive outcome as they learn more about who God is. However, in Numbers 11–21, as Israel continues their journey in the wilderness, their murmuring reflects a lack of faith in God's provision and guidance, leading to almost the entire generation perishing in the wilderness. Later, as Moses reflects on Israel's journey – from God's rescue to their wilderness wandering – he poses this rhetorical question to them: "Has any god ever tried to take for himself one nation out of another nation, by testings, by signs and wonders, by war, by a mighty hand and an outstretched arm, or by great and awesome deeds, like all the things the LORD your God did for you in Egypt before your very eyes?" (Deut 4:34). The answer is a resounding "no." This question echoes the lyrics of Moses's earlier song: "Who among the gods is like you, LORD? Who is like you, majestic in holiness, awesome in glory, working wonders?" (Exod 15:11).

God uses the liminal space and experience of the wilderness journey to teach Israel about who he is and about their identity as his people. God does not merely want Israel's obedience but Israel's heart.[68] Israel's wilderness journey resonates with our own journeys with God, which also include both positive and negative aspects – both the "pull" of the familiar life in Egypt (the home country) and the "push" toward a new adventure with God in new places. As Israel passes through one liminal space in the wilderness, another awaits them in Exodus 19–24. The process of identity formation involves moving through various stages of liminality until, finally, we reach a permanent state of being at home with God. In this sense, we are always on a journey of becoming.

---

68. Fentress-Williams, "Exodus," 87.

LEADERSHIP IN CHINESE CHURCHES AND THE SILENT EXODUS

In various church cultures, the establishment of leadership structures depends on denominational traditions and theological positions. The relational dynamics between the pastor, the elders, and the chairperson of the board are often delicate and fraught with tension. In some churches, the lead pastor is the sole authority; in other churches, power resides with the elders; and there are also churches where the chairperson of the board is intentionally given greater power. Sometimes, conflicts and power struggles between these groups even lead to church splits.

Confusion about roles is a recipe for disaster. Exodus 18 offers a model for establishing a clear leadership structure, with clearly defined roles for leaders in every tier. Jethro's counsel to Moses also emphasizes the importance of good character – people who are competent, God-fearing, trustworthy, and honest (18:21). While no structure or person is perfect, one thing is clear – no pastor can do it all. Delegation and division of labor are necessary, and there must be proper checks and balances to ensure accountability. Ultimately, everyone is accountable to God. Pastors and elders are shepherds of the flock entrusted to them by God (1 Pet 5:2), and the chairperson of the board should not lord it over people like a boss but, instead, should be accountable to the leadership structure.

In most immigrant churches in North America, there are usually two to three congregations – one for the first generation, who speak and worship in their native tongue, and another for their second-generation children, who speak and worship in English or the language of the host country. Unfortunately, the second-generation ministry is often considered "secondary" or seen as merely a "babysitting" service for the benefit of the first generation. As a result, when the second generation reaches maturity, they tend to leave the church in large numbers, with some even abandoning the Christian faith altogether. This phenomenon – widely known as the "silent exodus" – reflects the disconnection experienced by church-raised young people who feel that their immigrant churches are insensitive to their culture and out of touch with broader American society.[1] Although, over time, English-speaking Asian American Christians have established their own churches and may seem "silent no more," the voice of Asians in America is still a minority voice,[2] and the "silent exodus" remains a persistent issue.

Many factors have contributed to the "silent exodus," including the lack of a peer community, intergenerational conflicts, leadership issues, disagreements about the church's vision, differences in worship styles, not having a "voice," and the lack of biblically sound and relevant sermons.[3]

---

1. Helen Lee coined the term "Silent Exodus" in 1996 to describe the exiting of second-generation Korean Christians from their immigrant churches. Later, other ethnic groups also adopted this term, including Chinese Christians. Helen Lee, "Silent Exodus," *Christianity Today*, August (1996): 50–53.
2. Helen Lee, "Silent No More," *Christianity Today*, October (2014): 39–47.
3. Andrew Y. Lee, "The Future of English Ministry in Diaspora Chinese and Asian Churches," in *Reflections of Asian Diaspora: Mapping Theologies and Ministries*, ed. Sam George (Minneapolis: Fortress, 2022), 181–203.

EXODUS 19–24
IDENTITY CONSTRUCTION AT SINAI

When living in the diaspora, people become aware of varying attitudes toward laws. For instance, in some parts of Asia, jaywalking is a common practice and is not considered a violation of the law.[1] When no vehicles are in sight, people may cross the street regardless of the presence of a stop sign, the color of the traffic light, or other traffic rules. Pedestrians may not always wait for the traffic light to turn green before crossing the street. However, this is not always the case in other countries, where disobeying traffic rules is considered breaking the law and can result in penalties such as fines.

On a more serious note, immigration legislation in new countries can impact the trajectory of a person's life and even affect the rest of the extended family. For instance, the Chinese Exclusion Act, which was enacted by the United States Congress in 1882, suspended Chinese immigration for up to 10 years. As a result, families were separated, and those who remained in the host country suffered from overt and covert discrimination. In contrast, the Immigration and Nationality Act of 1965 (also known as the Hart-Celler Act) encouraged the migration of those with advanced professional skills, permitting them to work legally in the United States.[2]

In contemporary culture, people are well aware of the significance of law in any society. The law functions as a guide to regulate social behavior, providing order and structure to protect human rights and uphold justice, which is the backbone of a healthy society. Technically, the law can be understood as a constitution or the judicial system; more generally, it can also be viewed as instructions or guidelines for ethical living. The ancient Israelites viewed the law as God's gift. This law was not meant to restrict Israel but, rather, to guide them in flourishing as the people of God. In Deuteronomy, Moses urges Israel to keep God's law, emphasizing that their obedience would demonstrate their wisdom and distinguish them from their neighbors: "Observe them carefully, for this will show your wisdom and understanding to the nations, who will

---

1. That is, crossing or walking in the street or road without regard for traffic lights or approaching traffic.
2. For more on the discrimination against the Chinese in both the United States and other countries, see Kuhn, *Chinese Among Others*, 263–307.

hear about all these decrees and say, 'Surely this great nation is a wise and understanding people'" (Deut 4:6).

At the same time, although the law is clear, there is some ambiguity in how these laws are to be applied, particularly in the repeated "you shall not" commands and the prohibition against idolatry (Exod 20:2–5; 22:20; 23:13, 24–33) – are these commands to do or prohibitions to avoid? On the one hand, God uses the law to form Israel into the people of God. On the other hand, God's law curtails what the people can do in the future. Therefore, there is a tension between what they must do (ethical ideals) and what they must avoid (prohibition) because of their inability to keep the law.

OVERVIEW

In the biblical context, the term "law" generally refers to God's instructions for how the Israelites are to live. The "law" (*torah*) acts as God's finger, pointing to the path along which God expects and desires Israel to walk. These instructions reveal God's expectations for the people, which made obedience to the law a crucial aspect of their identity formation. When God led Israel out of Egypt, they were just emerging from their experience of enslavement, which was the only identity they had known. They had worked for different pharaohs for four generations, but now they needed a shift in identity – from serving Pharaoh to serving God, with all the ramifications accompanying such a shift. This identity shift was a process that required time and adjustments, and the people often relapsed, falling back into their former identity or swinging back and forth between their old and new identities.

The ten plagues, along with God's protection and provision during the wilderness journey, helped Israel to understand the character of God and their own identity in relation to him. This knowledge of God became a vital part of Israel's transition from being a nation of slaves to becoming a holy nation. In particular, the laws concerning slaves resonated with Israel's former identity as slaves in Egypt and taught Israel how they should treat slaves now that they had been rescued and redeemed by God. How Israel treated others demonstrated their new identity as the people of God and reflected God's ideals of compassion and justice, which were to guide their behavior.

In Exodus 19–24, God used the law to shape Israel into his image-bearers, forming them into a kingdom of priests and a holy nation (19:6). This new identity would be realized through God's revelation of the law and Israel's obedience to it. Although Israel's neighbors also had laws to govern their lives, the law revealed at Sinai demonstrates God's special care for vulnerable and marginalized groups in society. God's concern for these vulnerable groups reflects God's view of justice and what it meant for Israel to live as a holy nation.

In ancient contexts, laws were often more practical, reflecting the social and economic contexts of the time rather than being purely legislative. For example, Hammurabi's law codes present a vision for an ideal society rather than providing a set of laws that people must obey. The laws in the Pentateuch share both similarities and differences with their ancient Near Eastern neighbors. While reflecting the legal norms of ancient societies, they also reflect Yahweh's unique requirements that distinguished them from the surrounding nations.[3] We can think of these ancient laws as a form of wisdom or guidance for wise living.[4]

In the OT, "holiness" usually signifies being "set apart" rather than merely behaving in a holy manner.[5] As a holy nation set apart for God, Israel was called to showcase their identity as God's people to their neighbors by how they treated others. This emphasis on human rights distinguished Israel from the surrounding nations. While Exodus 1–18 deals with Israel's conversion out of Egypt and identity confusion in the wilderness, Exodus 19–24 focuses on Israel's identity construction through God's law. Both conversion and confusion are integral to Israel's identity formation. Identity conversion and confusion are learned through experience, whereas identity construction is achieved through practice.

Exodus 19–24 presents an enclosed structure (*inclusio*), with the Mount Sinai incidents on both ends framing the Ten Commandments and the Book of the Covenant within. This structure is shown below:

---

3. According to Wells, those who dismiss the Pentateuchal laws as if they had nothing to do with the actual practice are misguided. For more on the nature of biblical law and its affinity with Ancient Near Eastern law codes and practices, see Bruce Wells, "What is Biblical Law? A Look at Pentateuchal Rules and Near Eastern Practice," *CBQ* 70, no. 2 (Apr 2008): 223–243. For the connection between biblical law with the narratives in Genesis and Exodus and the origin of the law, see Calum M. Carmichael, *The Origins of Biblical Law: The Decalogue and the Book of the Covenant* (Ithaca: Cornell University Press, 1992). For a helpful chart on the other ancient Near Eastern law codes, see Raymond Westbrook and Bruce Wells, *Everyday Law in Biblical Israel: An Introduction* (Louisville: Westminster John Knox, 2009), ix. The cuneiform law codes include Hittite laws, Laws of Eshnunna, Laws of Hammurabi, Laws of Lipit-Ishtar, Laws of Ur-Namma, Middle Assyrian Laws, and Neo-Babylonian Laws.
4. Imes, *Bearing God's Name*, 37.
5. A study of the root holiness (*qdsh*) refers not only to moral purity or divine transcendence, but that it is also relational – in the sense of people being "consecrated" and "devoted" to God in a covenantal relationship. Peter J. Gentry, "The Meaning of 'Holy' in the Old Testament," *BSac* 170 (October–December 2013): 400–417.

Table 4: The Structure of Exodus 19–24

Mount Sinai (19:1–25)
Ten Commandments (20:1–17) People's Response (20:18–21) Book of the Covenant (20:22–23:33)
Mount Sinai (24:1–18)

19:1–25 THEOPHANY ON MOUNT SINAI

Exodus 19 serves as a prelude to God's giving of the law in Exodus 20–23 – that is, the Ten Commandments and the Book of the Covenant. This is followed in Exodus 24 by a covenant ritual that "seals the deal." The significance of Mount Sinai as the location of God's revelation cannot be overstated. Mount Sinai, which plays a crucial role in both biblical theology and Jewish cultural and religious memory, is known as "the cosmic mountain"[6] or the "mountain of the covenant" and serves as an "entry to Jewish tradition."[7] As Imes states, "At Sinai, everything changes. The Hebrews discover who they are and, more importantly, whose they are."[8]

19:1–6 Called to Be a Holy Nation

The significance of the exodus event is so great that the narrator uses it as a reference point to date subsequent events.[9] Exodus 19:1 notes that three months have passed since the Israelites left Egypt and arrived at the wilderness of Sinai – the wilderness described in Exodus 15:22–18:27, including the time the Israelites camped at Rephidim (17:1, 8). Exodus 19:2 records the continuation of their journey from Rephidim to the wilderness of Sinai. Israel

---

6. Morales, *The Tabernacle Pre-Figured*, 17. In the ancient Near East, the cosmic mountain was seen as a sacred space, the dwelling of the gods, the intersection between heaven and earth, the highest point of the earth, and the foundation and navel of creation. Morales, *The Tabernacle Pre-Figured*, 2.
7. Jon D. Levenson, *Sinai and Zion: An Entry into the Jewish Bible* (New York: Harper One, 1985), 13.
8. Imes, *Bearing God's Name*, 28.
9. Using the event of Exodus as a means to date or point to other events is called "event sequencing." LeFebvre argues that the Pentateuch uses event sequencing to indicate chronology rather than dates (Exod 19:1; 40:17; Num 9:1–3). LeFebvre, *The Liturgy of Creation*, 57, 61.

camped in front of the mountain, which, though unnamed, is understood to be the mountain of God (compare 18:5).[10]

Sinai as a Cosmic Mountain

As we read Exodus 19, it is important to bear in mind the different areas of the mountain and their respective boundaries regarding eligibility to ascend to these different areas. Mount Sinai is divided into three parts: the top of the mountain, the middle of the mountain, and the foot of the mountain. Only Moses is permitted to ascend to the top of the mountain, where God descends.[11] The priests are allowed to ascend to the middle section of the mountain. The foot of the mountain is where the Israelites reside. This three-part division of Mount Sinai prefigures the three-part structure of the tabernacle: the Holy of Holies, the place of God's presence; the Holy Place, where the priests conduct their ministry; and the Outer Court, where the Israelites offer sacrifices to God.[12] The degree of holiness increases as one moves from the foot of the mountain toward the top, with the higher areas being holier than the lower ones. The following diagram illustrates these parallel structures between Mount Sinai and the tabernacle:

---

10. In Exodus 3:1, Moses accidentally comes across the mountain of God, which is named "Horeb." Here in Exodus 19, the mountain of God is traditionally understood as Mount Sinai. Perhaps the mountain has two different traditions attached to it or the narrator of Exodus uses different sources to compose the book of Exodus.
11. Aaron's access to the summit of Mount Sinai is by invitation only (Exod 19:24). Morales introduces the gate liturgy in the Ancient Near Eastern Text and the Old Testament, where Adam (due to his transgression) must descend the mount of God (=Eden). Now Moses, functioning as the "New Adam," is called to ascend to the mount of God (Sinai). Morales, *The Tabernacle Pre-Figured*, 214.
12. Sarna, *Exodus*, 105. For the symbolism of the tabernacle in relation to the temple, creation, and the cosmic realm, see G. K. Beale, *The Temple and the Church's Mission: A Biblical Theology of the Dwelling Place of God*, NSBT 17 (Downers Grove: InterVarsity Press, 2004), 29–50. J. Scott Duvall and J. Daniel Hays, *God's Relational Presence: The Cohesive Center of Biblical Theology* (Grand Rapids: Baker Academic, 2019), 31.

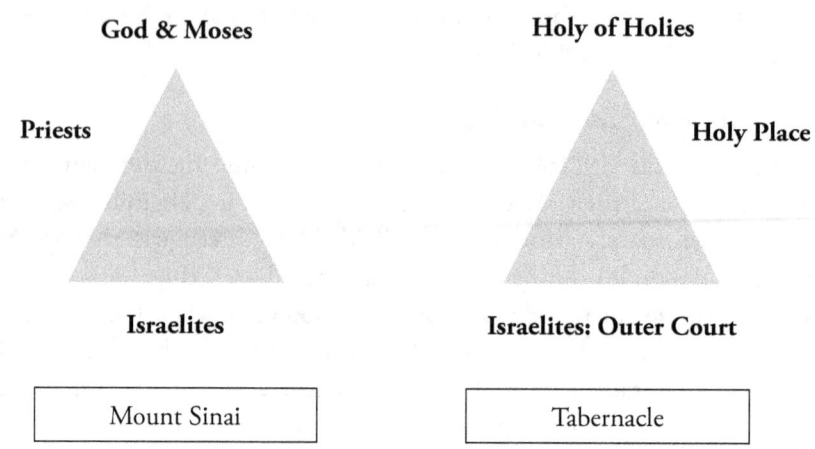

Figure 2: The Threefold Structures of Mount Sinai and the Tabernacle

Although verse 3 does not identify the specific location of the mountain where God calls Moses, the narrator later identifies this as the top or summit of the mountain (19:20). God's message to Moses contains the following elements: a) You have seen what I did to the Egyptians and how I bore you on eagles' wings to bring you to myself (19:4); b) If you truly obey me and my covenant,[13] then you shall be my treasure (*segulah*)[14] among all the peoples because all the earth is mine (19:5); and c) You shall be to me a kingdom of priests and a holy nation (19:6).

On Eagles' Wings

If I were to choose memory verses for my students from the book of Exodus, I would definitely include Exodus 19:4–6. In this brief passage, God describes the lengths to which he went – "you yourselves have seen what I did to Egypt" – to bring about his plans for Israel. He uses a zoological metaphor to explain what he did for them – "I carried you on eagles' wings." In ancient Near Eastern iconography, eagles' wings symbolize protection, and in Egyptian iconography, deities and angelic beings are often depicted as having wings.[15]

---

13. Sarna indicates that the word "covenant" appears first in Exodus here. Sarna, *Exodus*, 103. It marks a brand-new page in the God-Israel relationship.
14. Other translations include "my own possession" (NASB), "treasured possession" (NIV, ESV, NRSV), "special treasure" (NKJV), and "my own little flock" (TLB).
15. See Othmar Keel and Christopher Uelinger, *Gods, Goddesses, and the Images of God in Ancient Israel*, trans. Thomas H. Trapp (Minneapolis: Fortress, 1998), 250–256. The imagery of the

By using this imagery, God reveals himself as the protector of his people.[16] The image of eagles also represents purposeful rather than aimless flying, with a clear destination in mind – reflecting God bringing Israel to himself. All of God's actions in bringing the Israelites out of Egypt were for the purpose of bringing them to himself and enabling them to know "whose they are." Envision God as an eagle, soaring across the wilderness, carrying Israel on his wings and bringing them to himself. Picture God as an eagle parent training its young to fly and catching them when they stumble.[17] The Israelites no longer belong to Pharaoh or Egypt but to God alone. Belonging to God marks Israel's new identity.

Knowing "whose we are" is crucial for identity formation. In the diaspora, people are scattered and often distanced from their countries of origin and their ethnic and cultural roots. The question arises: Are we to identify ourselves ethnically, geographically, culturally, or religiously? Diasporans may have multiple identities and multiple consciousnesses, and sometimes, they may favor one identity over the other. At times, having multiple identities results in people shifting identities according to their context.[18] Seeing God's heart for the Israelites reminds people in the diaspora that regardless of their ethnic, geographical, and cultural identities and struggles, everyone belongs to God. This spiritual identity is not meant to flatten each person's particularities but to add a new layer of meaning – identity formation is an ongoing quest in new lands. Integral to the image of a flying eagle is the eagle's ability to carry weight, in this case, symbolizing Israel's transformation from being weighed down by slavery to being a people lifted up and carried by God. While the Israelites felt the weight of enslavement in Egypt, God swept down and scooped them up, as if they were as light as feathers, and carried them off. Zornberg beautifully

---

wings of God may also reflect a borrowing from Egyptian iconography of winged deities. See Keel, *The Symbolism of the Biblical World*, 190–192. For example, William P. Brown, *Seeing the Psalms: A Theology of Metaphor* (Louisville: Westminster John Knox, 2002), 20–23. See Bills' research on the meaning of the eagles' wings, Bills, *A Theology of Justice in Exodus*, 187–188, note 73, 75.

16. Zornberg added that the image of the eagle's wings also conveys intimacy, love, speed, and power. Zornberg, *The Particulars of Rupture*, 258.

17. Tigay, "Exodus," 137. Compare Deuteronomy 32:11.

18. Debbie Hearn Gin has written about Ruth in the Old Testament and about her own experience as an Asian American. She often finds herself shifting identities depending on the different contexts in which she finds herself. She calls this "multivocality" – an ability which at times may seem frustrating but can also be liberating. Debbie Hearn Gin, "Ruth: Identity and Leadership from Multivocal Spaces," in *Mirrored Reflections: Reframing Biblical Characters*, eds. Young Lee Hertig and Chloe Sun (Eugene: Wipf & Stock, 2010), 57–71.

portrays Israel's new identity by saying that Israel's "past identities are swept up in a rush of God's wings."[19]

Israel as God's Treasure

God uses three identity markers for Israel: a treasured possession, a kingdom of priests, and a holy nation (19:5–6). God sees Israel as his crown jewel, but this special status is conditional upon Israel's obedience to God and his covenant (19:5). The image of Israel as treasure or a treasured possession envisions God having a treasure box filled with all kinds of sparkling stones and gems, among which Israel is his most precious and cherished jewel. This special designation conveys the idea of royal status and exclusive possession of royalty.[20] Later, Deuteronomy reveals that God's choice of Israel was not because of their number but simply because of God's love for them (Deut 7:7–8). "For me" (*li*)[21] appears three times in Exodus 19:5–6. "For me as a treasure" is parallel to "for me is all the earth." Here, "earth" refers to all other nations and people groups. All people on earth belong to God, but Israel belongs to God in a special way. Compared to other nations, Israel is not morally or spiritually special (quantitatively), but they are special because of God's election (qualitatively) – and he would also bless the nations through them.[22] God's affection for Israel defines their identity. Identity is not about how Israel sees themselves but how Israel sees themselves through God's eyes. Belonging to God and being God's treasure define who Israel is.

Israel's Mission

God extends the imagery of "treasure" to Israel's mission to be a kingdom of priests and a holy nation. At this stage, Israel had no official priestly system. However, the concept of a priest was common in the ancient Near East. In the pre-Sinaitic period, for example, we have Melchizedek, who was a priest of God Most High (Gen 14:19), and Jethro, who was a priest of Midian (Exod 2:16). To be a priest is to be a bridge or mediator between God and human communities, officiating over rituals that facilitate proper communication and relationships between the two parties. Priests are distinct from commoners

---

19. Zornberg, *The Particulars of Rupture*, 258.
20. Tigay, "Exodus," 137.
21. "*My* treasured possession," "earth is *mine*," and "for *me* a kingdom" in the NIV.
22. Bills, *A Theology of Justice in Exodus*, 190.

and are chosen to shoulder the sacred responsibility of administering justice and ethics within the human realm.

Israel's former identity as slaves in Egypt will be transformed as they become a kingdom of priests, with God reigning as king. Just as Moses functions as a priest between God and Israel, Israel is to function as a priest between God and all other nations, bringing the knowledge of God to the rest of the world so that everyone may come to know the God of Israel. Israel is set apart for God as a holy nation among all the nations of the earth. This designation of Israel as a kingdom of priests and a holy nation offers a hopeful vision for their future. However, this emphasis on Israel's identity and mission as a kingdom of priests is inseparable from their special place as God's treasure. Before being chosen to carry out God's mission to the nations, Israel is cherished as God's treasured possession. Israel's being, belonging, and doing are held together by their special relationship with God. The apostle Peter alludes to Exodus 19:6 when he exhorts his readers to "declare the praises of him who called you out of darkness into his wonderful light" (1 Pet 2:9).

19:7–17 Preparing to Meet God

In this scene, although Moses is not specifically called a priest, he performs a priestly function by mediating between God and Israel. He communicates to Israel what God reveals to him on Mount Sinai and conveys the people's responses to God. This back-and-forth communication occurs several times at Sinai. In this way, Moses acts as a new Adam, entering the presence of God and bridging the gap between sinful people and the most holy God.[23] Having visited Mount Sinai, I know that the journey from the foot of the mountain to the summit is about an hour's walk and involves a steep climb. This climb is difficult and not suitable for those who have health issues such as knee problems and cardiovascular conditions. In his role as mediator, Moses must have gone up and down the mountain numerous times, which would have required him to be in excellent physical condition.

When the people hear what God says through Moses, they respond with a pledge of obedience: "We will do everything the LORD has said" (19:8). God then announces his coming and instructs Moses on how to prepare the people

---

23. Morales, *The Tabernacle Pre-Figured*, 214. The context of this new Adam is grounded in the notion of gate liturgy in the ancient Near East. Due to rebellion against God, Adam must descend from the Garden of Eden, and now Moses is called to ascend to the abode of God, into God's presence. For more on the gate liturgy, see Morales, *The Tabernacle Pre-Figured*, 100–105.

to meet him (19:9–13).[24] The key prerequisite for meeting God is holiness – both the people and their surroundings must be set apart for a holy God. The preparations include washing clothes, setting boundaries to prevent the people from approaching or touching the mountain, and waiting for the sound of the ram's horn before approaching the foot of the mountain.[25] For both humans and animals, the penalty for touching the mountain is death by stoning or shooting with arrows (19:13). This severe punishment emphasizes the holiness of the mountain where God descends and underscores the importance of obedience to God's commands to avoid the dire consequence of death. Since touching the holy mountain would violate God's holiness, violators are warned of severe consequences as a deterrent to disobedience. The severity of God's warning matches the severe penalty for offenders.

The Sinai area is characterized by a mountainous range with several peaks. God chose a particular mountain within this range as his temporary dwelling place to meet with Moses and Israel.[26] Therefore, this specific mountain became a "holy mountain" or holy ground, where everyone was expected to abide by the host's rules.[27] This scene parallels Moses's encounter with God at Horeb, where he saw the burning bush and was instructed by God to remove his sandals because he stood on holy ground (3:5–6). God's precise and detailed instructions reflect both his transcendent holiness and his desire for Israel to approach him with utmost care and caution.

When Moses relays God's message to Israel, he includes the additional instruction to "abstain from sexual relations" (19:15).[28] It is unclear whether God told Moses to include this command or whether Moses added it to provide practical guidance for Israel. The instruction to wait for three days recalls the symbolic significance of the "third day" in the OT – for example, at creation, when God separated the water and dry land (Gen 1:9–10) and when Abraham looked up and saw Mount Moriah on the third day of his journey

---

24. It is uncertain how many times Moses went up to the summit of Mount Sinai to receive instructions from God.
25. Although the exact location of the mountain that people are allowed to ascend is not specified, it can be inferred from 19:17 that it refers to the foot of a mountain.
26. "The mountain" in Exodus 19 always carries a definite article, which means that it is a specific mountain in the midst of the Sinai mountain range (19:12, 13, 14, 16, 17).
27. Levenson rightly says of this home "YHWH's home in no man's land." Levenson, *Sinai & Zion*, 19.
28. Sexual relations in some situations were considered ritually unclean. Compare 2 Samuel 11:11.

(Gen 22:4). The "third day" also foreshadows Jesus's resurrection on the third day. In the biblical tradition, the third day represents a day of transformation.[29]

On the morning of the third day, as God descends upon the summit of Mount Sinai, he is accompanied by dramatic meteorological phenomena – thunder, lightning, and a thick cloud upon the mountain, accompanied by a loud trumpet blast. As a result, the people tremble (19:16). Later, Moses recalls this moment, saying, "At that time I stood between the Lord and you to declare to you the word of the Lord, because you were afraid of the fire and did not go up the mountain" (Deut 5:5). The writer of Hebrews contrasts this theophany on Mount Sinai and the people's fear of that fearsome presence with the joyful experience of the heavenly Jerusalem (Heb 12:18–24). This section concludes by stating that Moses brought the Israelites out of the camp to meet God and "they stood at the foot of the mountain" (19:17). Here, "stood" (*yatsab*) suggests that they "stationed themselves," and "the foot of the mountain" was the location where the people could remain without offending God's transcendent holiness, an act that would result in death. This verse emphasizes, yet again, Moses's role as mediator between God and Israel.

19:18–25 Theophany on Mount Sinai

Verse 18 focuses on God's descent on Mount Sinai. The narrator vividly describes the dramatic theophany accompanied by smoke and fire. Mount Sinai is covered in smoke as if it were ascending from a furnace. The presence of fire accompanying God's descent recalls Moses's burning bush encounter. In later biblical accounts, God's presence is often accompanied by fire and smoke as manifestations of God's presence.[30] The writer of Hebrews asserts that God is "a consuming fire" (Heb 12:29). The mountain trembles violently, mirroring the people's reaction of trembling as they witness the theophany described in Exodus 19:16. No one who encounters God can remain unchanged. God's presence – which caused even the apparently immovable mountain to shake – disrupts even his own creation.

The visible manifestation of divine presence is compounded by sound – the very sound of God's voice. In meteorology, thunder and lightning are connected – lightning rapidly heats the air, causing it to expand, which in turn produces thunder as the lightning passes through the atmosphere. Not

---
29. See Lunn, "'Raised on the Third Day According to the Scriptures,'" 523–555.
30. For example, Deuteronomy 4:24; Isaiah 6:4; Ezekiel 1:27; Hebrew 12:29.

surprisingly, in ancient times, thunder was used to describe the voice of God.[31] Seeing with their own eyes God's transcendent presence on Mount Sinai – accompanied by fire, lightning, smoke, thunder, and a shaking mountain – must have been an awe-inspiring sight for the Israelites. Verse 20 twice mentions that God descended upon the top (literally, "head") of Mount Sinai, indicating that the precise location of his descent was the summit rather than any other part of the mountain. God then calls Moses to ascend to the top of the mountain. The repetition of "top" further emphasizes that this area is the holiest part of the mountain. This is the only site on the mountain where God meets Moses, and thus, the top of Mount Sinai prefigures the "Holy of Holies."[32]

God's first words to Moses are a stern warning for the people and the priests regarding how they should approach God. Since God had made this special mountain his temporary abode, anyone who approached this holy abode had to abide by the owner's house rules. God warns the Israelites against forcing their way through to see God lest they fall from the mountain – the phrase "many of them perish" (19:21) is literally "lest many fell from it." God then warns the priests to consecrate themselves or risk being punished by God. Both warnings reflect God's "house rule" of holiness, previously given to Moses (19:12–13). Violating these rules could have dire consequences, including death.

The implication that God allowed the priests to approach him (19:22) suggests that they were permitted to ascend the mountain but not to its top, which was reserved exclusively for God and Moses. This arrangement mirrors the structure of the tabernacle, where only the priests were permitted to enter the Holy Place and only the high priest was allowed to enter the Holy of Holies – once a year on the Day of Atonement (Lev 16). Moses thus prefigures the role of the high priest of Israel.

In verse 23, Moses responds by reminding God of the previous instructions to set boundaries around the mountain and consecrate it (19:12). God then tells Moses to descend and then ascend the mountain again, this time bringing Aaron with him. However, God warns that the priests and the people must not approach him and that if they did, he would punish them. Moses obeys these instructions and brings Aaron up to the summit of Mount Sinai, which serves as God's temporary home. While Moses and Aaron are permitted to come to God at the summit, the priests and the people remain at the places

---

31. For example, Psalms 18:13; 29:3–9; Job 37:4–5.
32. See Figure 2 on page 188.

designated for them: the middle of the mountain for the priests and the foot of the mountain for the people. Aaron shares a privileged position with Moses, but his access to the summit is by invitation only.[33]

The threefold division of Mount Sinai into top, middle, and foot mirrors the tripartite structure of the tabernacle: the Holy of Holies, the Holy Place, and the Outer Court. Similarly, the three groups of people – Moses, the priests, and the Israelites – also parallel this threefold division. The higher the location on the mountain, the greater the holiness. Although God chooses Mount Sinai as his temporary home, his ultimate desire is not to remain on a high mountain away from the people but to dwell among his people. For this reason, God would later instruct Moses to build the tabernacle so that God might dwell among the Israelites (Exod 25:8). God's transcendent holiness and God's immanence – reflected in his desire to be present among his people – reflect the human struggle to reconcile these two seemingly opposite qualities.

20:1–17 THE TEN COMMANDMENTS

The Decalogue (the Ten Commandments) and the Book of the Covenant (20:22–23:33) constitute the core of the Sinaitic covenant, which is the foundation for Israel's perception of their identity as God's people and their fellowship with him. The Ten Commandments are not an isolated law code but are integrated into the larger narrative of God's rescue of the Israelites. This close connection between narrative and law emphasizes that God's law is intertwined with his rescue and redemption of his people. As Christopher Wright remarks, "The Ten Commandments can be seen as given in order to preserve the rights and freedoms gained by the exodus, by translating them into responsibilities."[34]

---

33. Cao Jian mentions an interesting interpretation of Mount Sinai by Liu Ting Fang, who views the history of religion as an evolutionary process of replacing old ideas with new ones. In this case, Liu contrasted Moses with Aaron, in that Moses ascended Mount Sinai to receive new ideas from God, whereas Aaron remained with the old ideas and conveyed them to the masses at the foot of the mountain. As a result, the new idea of God prevailed and became the force that moved history forward. See Cao Jian, *Chinese Biblical Anthropology: Persons and Ideas in the Old Testament and in Modern Chinese Literature; Contrapuntal Readings of the Bible in World Christianity* (Eugene: Pickwick, 2019), 114.
34. Christopher J. H. Wright, *Old Testament Ethics for the People of God* (Downers Grove: InterVarsity Press, 2004), 262.

THE CONFUCIAN VIRTUES OF KINDNESS AND RIGHTEOUSNESS

If someone were to ask, "What is the moral code that guides human ethics?" I would point to Confucius's virtues of kindness or benevolence (Chinese: *rén*).[1] *Rén* or *rén ài* (kindness + love) denotes the qualities of empathy, altruism, and selfless love toward others. In contemporary Western terms, someone who has *rén* could be described as a philanthropist or a humanitarian who seeks the good of other people and is driven by a vision of kindness. The Chinese character (logogram) for *rén* has two components: a person on the left and the number two on the right (仁). This simple logogram conveys the idea of a person who is seeking harmony between two people or suggests how two people should treat each other with kindness. This idea of *rén* represents a benevolent attitude and behavior that bears a striking similarity to the biblical commandment to "love your neighbor as yourself" (Lev 19:18). *Rén* captures the essence of the fifth through tenth commandments and embodies the ideal for how we are to treat one another.

Alongside *rén*, we have the concept of *yì* (義), which combines the principles of righteousness, justice, and faithfulness.[2] To say that someone embodies *yì* means that the person strives to do what is right, does not engage in stealing, lying, or using unethical means to achieve goals, and is loyal and faithful to others. The Ten Commandments and the Book of the Covenant place great emphasis on the right treatment of marginalized groups and the responsibility of those in positions of power to act with both *rén* and *yì*. The eighth and ninth commandments, along with laws dealing with slavery, personal injuries, and many other issues, reflect this broad concept of *yì*. The dual pillars of *rén* and *yì* (仁義) – benevolence and justice – summarize the essence of the OT law.

---

1. See the top five virtues of Confucius. Keith N. Knapp, "Three Fundamental Bonds and Five Constant Virtues," *Sāngāng Wǔcháng*, 2252. Compare: In James Legge's translation of Confucius's *Analects*, he translates kindness (*ren*) as "virtue" – "The virtuous rest in virtue; the wise desire virtue"; "If the will be set on virtue, there will be no practice of wickedness." See the chapter on benevolent unity in Confucius, *The Analects of Confucius*, trans. James Legge, Bilingual Study edition (Las Vegas: Dragon Reader, 2016), 28–29.
2. See Knapp, "Three Fundamental Bonds and Five Constant Virtues," 2252. Compare: "The master said, 'The mind of the superior man is conversant with righteousness; the mind of the mean man is conversant with gain.'" See Confucius, *The Analects*, 32.

The law serves as a rule of thumb and a moral compass for Israel, setting them apart from other nations.[35] Moses urges Israel to obey God's law as a way of distinguishing themselves from other nations. He asks, "And what other nation is so great as to have such righteous decrees and laws as this body of laws I am setting before you today?" (Deut 4:8). The psalmist also distinguishes Israel from other nations, stating, "He has revealed his word to Jacob, his laws and decrees to Israel. He has done this for no other nation; they do not know his laws" (Ps 147:19–20). In addition, Psalm 1 emphasizes the importance of meditating on God's law (*torah*), which yields a fruitful life. Psalm 119, the longest psalm in the Psalter, is a Torah Psalm that uses an eightfold repetition of the Hebrew alphabet to emphasize the completeness of God's law.[36]

The Ten Commandments use the language of "you shall not," while the Book of the Covenant frequently uses "if, then" statements, although it also includes "you shall not" statements. The former is known as apodictic law, while the latter is called case law or casuistic law.[37] It is worth noting that the "you" in the apodictic law is in the masculine singular, suggesting that the law is addressed to the male head of the household, who is then responsible for teaching God's law to his wife and children. However, this does mean that the law did not apply to females in Israel.[38]

The "you shall not" statements suggest prohibitions, but the underlying sentiment is God's anxiety (or foreknowledge) that Israel could not keep the law and would violate the law. The law's ambivalent nature is expressed through its ethical vision and anxiety that Israel may not live up to it. Nanette Stahl notes that an important function of biblical law is its liminality. She contends that biblical law often exists in Israel's transitional moments and is rife with ambiguities and instabilities, especially regarding the divine-human relationship. While the law provides stability and order in a chaotic world, it also contains

---

35. For the significance of intertwining law and narrative, see Fretheim, *Exodus*, 201–207. For a detailed study of biblical law and its application to the Christian life, see Roy E. Gane, *Old Testament Law for Christians: Original Context and Enduring Application* (Grand Rapids: Baker Academic, 2017). Richard E. Averbeck, *The Old Testament Law of the Life of the Church: Reading the Torah in the Light of Christ* (Downers Grove: IVP Academic, 2022).
36. Psalm 119 is an acrostic psalm with 176 verses, arranged alphabetically by 22 Hebrew letters, with 22 stanzas. Each of the eight verses of each stanza begins with the same Hebrew letter.
37. For more on the differences between the two kinds of laws, see Gane, *Old Testament Law for Christians*, 86–93.
38. See Gane, *Old Testament Law for Christians*, 83. For whose interest is the Ten Commandments? See Clines's insightful article. David J. A. Clines, "The Ten Commandments, Reading from Left to Right," in *Interested Parties: The Ideology of Writers and Readers of the Hebrew Bible*, JSOTSup 205 (Sheffield: Sheffield Academic Press, 1995), 26–45.

themes of destabilization that resonate with the surrounding narratives. In this situation, law and narrative form a dialogism and are polyphonic in nature.[39]

The Ten Commandments hold profound significance for Israel, as well as for Jewish, Christian, and Catholic believers. Their impact on moral and ethical perspectives across different denominations is evident in their enduring reputation and familiarity throughout church history. Even many non-Christians have heard of the Ten Commandments. Although the Ten Commandments were originally intended for Israel, these commandments are often perceived and received across cultures as embodying natural and universal law that applies to all humanity.[40] While the contents of the Ten Commandments share similarities with other ancient Near Eastern laws, three of these commandments are uniquely Israelite: the worship of one God, the prohibition of idolatry in all its forms, and the observance of the Sabbath.[41] In other words, the first four commandments set Israel apart from the surrounding nations as God's people. It is significant that these commandments directly oppose the Egyptian context, where multiple gods were worshiped, graven images were made, there was no Sabbath observance, and slaves were mistreated.

Scholars note that the structure of the law narrative in Exodus mirrors the general structure of covenant treaties in the ancient Near Eastern world, specifically treaties between a suzerain and a vassal, as shown in the table below:[42]

---

39. Nanette Stahl, *Law and Liminality in the Bible*, JSOTSup 202 (Sheffield: Sheffield Academic Press, 1995), 12–17. Though Stahl acknowledges both the positive and negative features of biblical law, her view tends to be more negative than positive.

40. For the significance of the Ten Commandments in western culture and its distinct nature, see Patrick D. Miller, *The Ten Commandments*, Interpretation: Resources for the Use of Scripture in the Church (Louisville: Westminster John Knox, 2009), 1–3.

41. Sarna, *Exploring Exodus*, 144. The sabbath command includes slaves and sojourners (20:10). So, we may add one more to Sarna's list: the treatment of vulnerable groups as a distinction of the law given to Israel. In the Book of the Covenant, how Israel should treat vulnerable groups becomes more pronounced.

42. Levenson applies the six elements in the treaty to Exodus 19, and observes three of the six elements are present there. Levenson, *Sinai & Zion*, 27–32. See the treaty in Victor H. Matthews and Don C. Benjamin, *Old Testament Parallels: Laws and Stories from the Ancient Near East*, 2nd ed. (New York: Paulist, 2001), 87–90. Block divides the covenant stipulation at Sinai in Exodus 19–24 into seven stages. Stage 1: The vassal's preparation for the coming of the divine Suzerain (Exod 19:7–15). Stage 2: The arrival (Parousia) of the divine suzerain (Exod 19:16–25). Stage 3: The suzerain's declaration of the foundations of the covenant (Exod 20:1–21). Stage 4: The first expansion of the covenant stipulations (Exod 21:1–23:19). Stage 5: The suzerain's appeal for exclusive and undivided loyalty (Exod 23:20–33). Stage 6: The covenant-ratification procedure (Exod 24:1–11). Stage 7: The suzerain's provision of the foundational covenant document (Exod 24:12–18; 31:18). Daniel I. Block, *Covenant: The Framework of God's Grand Plan of Redemption* (Grand Rapids: Baker Academic, 2021), 152–170.

Table 5: Suzerain-Vassal Treaties in the Ancient Near East

	Steps	Contents	Exodus
1	Preamble	The suzerain identifies himself.	20:1–2a
2	Historical Prologue	The suzerain states his relationship with the vassal.	20:2b
3	Stipulations	The suzerain lays out the general stipulations, followed by the specific stipulations.	20:3–17; 20:22–23:33
4	Deposition of the Text	The legal document is to be placed in a designated location, often the temple.	25:16; 40:20
5	List of Witnesses	The witnesses are often the gods of the ancient Near East or nature – for example mountains, rivers, heaven, and earth.	
6	Curses and Blessings	The treaty ends by stating the consequences of violating the stipulations and promises of blessing if the stipulations are obeyed.	23:25–33

The absence of treaty witnesses in the Ten Commandments and the Book of the Covenant highlights God's exclusive authority in this covenant. Invoking other gods as witnesses would undermine God's supremacy over them. In Deuteronomy, Moses invokes heaven and earth as witnesses to the covenant between God and Israel (Deut 4:26; 32:1). Although heaven and earth are not divine beings, they are God's creations (Gen 1:1).

The suzerain-vassal treaties were often deposited in the temples of the gods, which points to the inseparable relationship between law and temple.[43] This explains why, within the structure of Exodus, the construction of the tabernacle (Exod 25) comes immediately after the covenant-making ceremony between God and Israel (Exod 24). In addition, the tablets of the Ten Commandments are deposited inside the ark of the covenant (25:16; 40:20).

Exodus 20 begins with the conjunction "and," indicating that the Ten Commandments continue from the previous narrative of God's descent on Mount Sinai, Moses's ascent to meet with God, and God's speech. God begins with a preface: "I am the LORD your God, who brought you out of Egypt, out

---

43. For example, a Hittite treaty ends with a colophon saying that the treaty was made into seven tablets. One of them was placed before the sun goddess of Arinna, one before the Hittite storm god, and one before the storm god of lightning while others were placed in the kings' houses. "The Treaty of Tudhaliya IV with Kurunta of Tarhuntašša on the Bronze Tablet Found in Hattuša," trans. Harry A. Hoffner, Jr. (*COS* 2.18: 106).

of the land of slavery" (20:2). In this introduction, God uses his personal name "the Lord," which is represented by the tetragrammaton YHWH. "Your God" reflects the covenantal relationship between God and Israel. The phrase "who brought you out of Egypt" refers to God's act of rescuing the Israelites from Egypt, a land that symbolized death for Israel. "Out of the land of slavery" further reinforces Israel's former predicament and identity as slaves of Pharaoh. This self-introduction not only establishes a prologue for the covenantal stipulations that follow but also serves as the foundation for what comes next.

First Commandment: No Other Gods

Many Asian people are familiar with the practice of polytheistic religions – worshiping multiple deities and ancestors. Similarly, the Egyptians also practiced polytheism, and Pharaoh regarded himself as a god incarnate. When God used the ten plagues to strike down the gods of Egypt (Exod 12:12), this demonstrated the pervasive presence of multiple gods in the Egyptian worldview. Living as Hebrew slaves in Egypt, the Israelites would have become accustomed to this polytheistic environment. Later, during the golden calf incident, it seems likely that the Israelites drew inspiration for the golden calf from Egyptian iconography and architecture – which often featured images of calves – or from Pharaoh's building projects, where again they might have encountered images of calves.[44]

When God pronounces that "you shall have no other gods before me," he is calling Israel to make the shift from their former allegiance and identity as Hebrew slaves under Pharaoh to a new identity as God's people, with God as their new sovereign. The mention of "no other gods" presumes the presence of these "other gods." Therefore, the idea behind the first commandment is monolatry rather than monotheism. Monolatry presupposes the existence of other gods but asserts that there is one supreme God, whereas monotheism is

---

44. The images of calves have been prominent in the ancient Near East, in glyptic art, sculpture, and reliefs. Several Egyptian deities bear the image of a calf or bull and appear in iconography and theology. See N. Wyatt, "Calf," in *DDD*: 180–182. For example, in the Egyptian pantheon, Hathor is pictured as a woman with bovine ears and as a cow who sustains life and gives birth to the sun. Van Voss, "Hathor," 385. Apis is the most sacred bull of the Egyptians and has been the object of worship since the early history of Egyptian civilization. Apis is linked with fertility and regeneration and thus is associated with the gods of rebirth and resurrection. Apis represents another Egyptian deity Ptah, who is perceived as the creator god of Memphis and holds the epithet "Bull of the Earth." See R. L. Vos, "Apis," in *DDD*: 68–72. Images, frescoes, and paintings about calves appear in mortuary temples and tombs in the Valley of the Kings in Thebes, Egypt, and in the Egyptian Museum in Cairo.

the belief that there is only one true God, thus denying the existence of other gods.[45] The Song of Moses reflects this idea of monolatry: "Who among the gods is like you, Lord?" (Exod 15:11). Since God is the one who rescued Israel from Egyptian slavery, he now invites Israel to enter into this special relationship and bear a new identity as his people.

Whenever someone turns from their former religious identity – whether from an atheistic worldview or a polytheistic context – and chooses to embrace Christ, that person becomes a new creation (2 Cor 5:17). The phenomenon of the diaspora facilitates the spread of people across the globe, creating opportunities for them to come to know God in new lands, not least through the Chinese churches in these places. Displacement or relocation has a way of changing people's worldviews and opening their minds to new things. It is often far more challenging to adopt a new faith and engage with a new culture while remaining in just one place that is surrounded by polytheistic influences.

---

45. Mark S. Smith, *The Early History of God: Yahweh and the Other Deities in Ancient Israel*, 2nd ed. (Grand Rapids: Eerdmans, 2002), 2–3. For a study on the development of monotheism in ancient Israel as well as the points of contact between the idea of monotheism and Asian myths in fighting evil forces, see Koowon Kim, "Yahweh and Other Gods," in *Exploring the Old Testament in Asia: Evangelical Perspectives*, eds. Jerry Hwang and Angukali Rotokha (Carlisle: Langham Global Library, 2022), 25–40.

IDOL WORSHIP IN THE ASIAN CONTEXT

In countries where atheism is prevalent, it may be challenging to accept the existence of a spiritual realm that is beyond the physical world and sensory perception. Those who hold such beliefs may view the concept of "gods" as something that motivates them, such as success, wealth, or fame. In the context of the relationship between house churches and the state, some pastors may consider the state as a "false god" or "idol" that is opposed to the church. For example, Pastor Wang Yi, who has been imprisoned for refusing to comply with state regulations, argues that just as a bride has only one husband, the church should have only one head – that is, Christ alone. In support of his position, he cites the first commandment: "You shall have no other gods before me" (Exod 20:3). He writes: "Once the church falls into the trap of being ruled by emotions, depending on power, or yielding to politics on matters of doctrine, priesthood, or sacraments, they have worshiped a false god."[1] Anything that replaces the priority of God in a person's life can become an idol – for example, anything that replaces the priority of God in a person's life – even things like filial piety, honoring cultural and family traditions, or conforming to certain social norms – can become an idol.[2]

Apart from atheistic regimes, in many Asian countries, people worship visible deities such as Buddha, Guān Yīn, or Má Zǔ. Some even venerate their ancestors although it is not always clear whether these worshipers venerate these ancestors as deities or are simply showing respect to these deceased people.[3] Others practice various forms of local or folk religions. In Chinese restaurants around the world, it is common to find a small red shrine at the entrance, where offerings of fruit and incense are made to deities or ancestors.

In countries like Taiwan and Thailand, temples and shrines are widespread. In Hong Kong, for example, one subway station is named "The Queen of Heaven," pointing to the veneration of this goddess in that region. Similarly, the name "Huáng Dà Xīan" reflects the worship of that deity in that city. The presence of numerous shrines, both large and small, reflects the polytheistic and pluralistic nature of East Asian and South Asian spirituality.[4] With the diaspora spreading across the globe, the tradition of worshiping the deities in people's countries of origin is now being taken to different parts of the world, just as Christianity is spreading in the global village.

---

1. Nation and Tseng, eds, *Faithful Disobedience*, 27, 108.

2. Athena E. Gorospe with Charles Ringma, *Judges: A Pastoral and Contextual Commentary*, ABCS (Carlisle: Langham Global Library, 2016), 143.
3. The Western missionaries to China from the seventeenth century have condemned Chinese ancestral worship as incompatible with Christianity which worships one God alone. Yet they often confuse the difference between a religious practice and a cultural rite. The key is to define and understand what ancestral worship really means and whether it falls under the category of idolatry. For the historical context of the issue with ancestral worship, see Lung-Kwong Lo, "The Nature of the Issue of Ancestral Worship among Chinese Christians," *Studies in World Christianity* 9, no. 1 (2003): 30–42.
4. South Asia is surrounded by multiple religions and deities such as Hinduism, Islam, and tribal religions. George and Swarup, "Exodus," 77.

Second Commandment: No Representations of God

In the ancient Near East, it was common to find representations of gods and goddesses in temples, palace structures, and people's houses.[46] Similarly, in Asian religious practices, images of deities such as Buddha, Guān Yīn, and Guān Gōng are found in shrines. These images typically take the form of human statues, and people engage in their folk religions by worshiping these statues as representations of their objects of veneration. This iconic worship of sculptured images contrasts sharply with the second commandment, which forbids Israel to engage in such practices. Instead, Israel's worship is to be aniconic – that is, worshiping God without representing him through any images. This commandment serves as the backdrop for the Israelites' later rebellion in the golden calf incident (Exod 32).

Aside from the Sabbath commandment, the second commandment is also noteworthy for being the second longest among the Ten Commandments (20:4–6).[47] It prohibits the Israelites from making any sculptured image or likeness of anything in the heavens above, on the earth beneath, or in the waters below the earth. By mentioning these three realms, this commandment effectively prohibits the creation of any image whatsoever.[48] God commands the Israelites not only to refrain from making any representation of God or other

---

46. E.g. Rachel stole her father's household gods (Gen 31:19). For the practice of family religion, see Karel van der Toorn, *Family Religion in Babylonia, Syria and Israel: Continuity and Change in the Forms of Religious Life* (Atlanta: Society of Biblical Literature, 2017).
47. Compare Deuteronomy 4:12–24.
48. "In heaven above" includes the sun, moon, and stars. "On the earth beneath" includes animals and cultic trees for worship. "In the water below" includes the river and what is in it. See Tigay, "Exodus," 140.

deities but also to avoid worshiping such images.[49] The term "an image" or "graven image" (20:4 KJV) refers specifically to an image intended to represent God or other deities.[50] As the creator of all things, God refuses to be reduced to a graven image in any form, even if such an image is made from God's own creation. Moses provides the best commentary on the second commandment in his exhortation to the Israelites:

> You saw no form of any kind the day the LORD spoke to you at Horeb out of the fire. Therefore watch yourselves very carefully, so that you do not become corrupt and make for yourselves an idol, an image of any shape, whether formed like a man or a woman, or like any animal on earth or any bird that flies in the air, or like any creature that moves along the ground or any fish in the waters below. (Deut 4:15–18)

The prohibition against worshiping sculptured images is accompanied by both a rationale and a consequence:

> I, the LORD your God, am a jealous God, punishing the children for the sin of the parents to the third and fourth generation of those who hate me, but showing love to a thousand generations of those who love me and keep my commandments. (Exod 20:5–6)

In three successive self-descriptive terms – "I," "the LORD," and "a jealous God" – God emphasizes his very essence as Yahweh and stresses that he, as Israel's God, is a jealous God. When the word "jealousy" is used of God, it often carries an intense emotion and force, sometimes translated as "zeal."[51] In Hebrew, the word picture to describe jealousy is "to turn red or black,"[52] which can be visualized as God's face changing color when seeing Israel worship anything other than God. This holy jealousy forbids Israel to make or worship any sculptured image. The prophetic literature frequently uses the marriage metaphor to describe God's relationship with Israel, portraying God as Israel's

---

49. It may include the prohibition of worshiping other gods in their sculptured images. Miller, *The Ten Commandments*, 48. It seems that only sculptured images that are made for the purpose of worship are prohibited. Images such as the cherubim over the ark of the covenant are allowed (Exod 25:18–20).
50. The same word *pesel* appears in Micah's idolatry (Judg 17:3–4, 18), the image of Asherah set up by King Manasseh (1 Kgs 21:7), a graven image in Isaiah 40:20.
51. For example, Isaiah 37:32; 59:17; Nahum 1:2; Zechariah 1:14.
52. *BDB*, 888. *HALOT*, 1109.

husband. In this context, Israel's worship of other gods is depicted as adultery. Thus, idolatry is viewed as spiritual adultery in the context of the God-Israel relationship.[53] While the first commandment prohibits any replacement of God, the second commandment prohibits any representation of God.

The consequences of obeying or violating the second commandment involve receiving either divine mercy or divine wrath. The phrase "third and fourth generation" contrasts with "a thousand generations," with the latter referring to a long time rather than a literal one thousand generations since the word "generation" is absent in the Hebrew text. Likewise, the mention of "third and fourth generation" implies a limited time frame.

Chinese culture is largely communal rather than individualistic. The concern about generations and how to preserve the family legacy for future generations runs deep in Chinese blood. Therefore, the punishment extending to the third and fourth generation of those who violate God's commandments poses a significant threat to one's security and instills fear of the God of the OT. God's true nature and a writer's portrayal of God in literature are often different. In this passage, we should not expect these numbers – "a thousand generations" and "third and fourth generation" – to be literal.[54]

In the Bible, the concepts of love and hate often connote the idea of making choices. For example, God's love for Jacob and his hate for Esau (Mal 1:2–3) signifies God's choice of Jacob over Esau. God does not truly hate Esau since he blessed Esau with descendants (Gen 36). Those who hate God are those who reject God, disobey his laws, and are unfaithful to his covenant. This understanding aligns with the description "those who love me and keep my commandments" (Exod 20:6). While God's wrath against the disobedient is short-lived, his mercy or loyal love (*khesed*) endures for a very long time. Therefore, the benefits of obeying God's commandments far outweigh the consequences of disobedience.

---

53. For example, God asks Hosea to marry Gomer as a way of showing his love for Israel. Other texts include Isaiah 54:5–6; 62:4–5; Jeremiah 2:1–3; 3:1; Ezekiel 16, 23. For more on God as Israel's husband, see Nelly Stienstra, *YHWH is the Husband of His People: An Analysis of a Biblical Metaphor with Special Reference to Translation* (Kampen: Kok Pharos Publishing House, 1993). Gerlinde Baumann, *Love and Violence: Marriage as Metaphor for the Relationship between YHWH and Israel in the Prophetic Books*, trans. Linda M. Malony (Collegeville: Liturgical Press, 2003).
54. Eric A. Seibert, *Disturbing Divine Behavior: Troubling Old Testament Images of God* (Minneapolis: Fortress, 2009), 172–173. One way that Seibert suggests to achieve such differentiation is to adopt a Christocentric hermeneutic, evaluating Gods' behavior through Jesus Christ. Seibert, *Disturbing Divine Behavior*, 185–187.

Third Commandment: No Misuse of God's Name

In Chinese, the term *tian ah* is used to express feelings of surprise or frustration, an idiom similar to saying "Oh, my God."[55] Traditionally, the phrase "taking the name of God in vain" has been understood as a prohibition against using the name of God or Jesus to swear or curse as often depicted in movies or on television. In the OT and the ancient Near East, however, people swear *by* the names of their gods.[56] While swearing is also one way of taking the name of God in vain, this phrase has more far-reaching implications. The expression "take the name" (*nasa'*) literally means "bear the name" or "lift up the name." In Hebrew culture, a name represents a person's character, being, and attributes. Therefore, the name of God signifies who God is.[57]

The phrase "bear the names" or "carry the names" also appears in Exodus 28:29–30, where Aaron carries the names of the Israelites on the "breastpiece of decision" over his heart when he enters the Holy Place.[58] Bearing someone's name over one's heart is a way of rightly remembering that person. Aaron, as the high priest, bears or carries the names of the Israelites in his heart before God, thereby serving as their mediator – representing them before God and interceding for them. Therefore, the third commandment prohibits misrepresenting God in both words and behavior.[59] This commandment reinforces the first two commandments by emphasizing that worshiping God above all other gods involves not only avoiding reducing God to an image but also representing God rightly. Like the second commandment, the third commandment is followed by a motive clause that warns of the consequence for violating the commandment – God will not leave the guilty unpunished.[60]

To this day, some Jewish people hold the third commandment in such high regard that they refrain from pronouncing the name of God (YHWH). Instead, they use terms like "Adonai" (meaning "the Lord") or "HaShem" (meaning "the name") when addressing or referring to God. Some even choose to use "G-d" instead of "God" in their writings to avoid spelling out the full name of God.

In ancient times, swearing by the names of their gods reflected a person's loyalty and devotion to these deities. In the ancient Near Eastern culture, the

---

55. Literally, "Oh Heaven!"
56. Compare Deuteronomy 6:13.
57. Compare Exodus 3:13–15; 6:2–3; 15:3; 34:6–7.
58. See Imes, *Bearing God's Name*, 50.
59. Miller provides examples of misusing the name of God in Exodus 22:28 and Leviticus 24:10–16. Miller, *The Ten Commandments*, 103.
60. The motives are often provided by God, which include the reason for justice, the promise of divine blessings or issuing of warnings. See Gane, *Old Testament Law for Christians*, 100–104.

phrase "You shall not misuse the name" referred to calling on a god's name when swearing an oath. In this command, Moses instructs Israel to swear oaths using God's name but warns them not to make false statements that would discredit God's name. Similarly, they must not invoke the names of other gods in making such oaths. For instance, Leviticus 19:12 states, "Do not swear falsely by my name and so profane the name of your God. I am the Lord." Similarly, Leviticus 24:16 declares that anyone who blasphemes the name of God shall be put to death. These laws uphold the absolute sanctity of God's name.

The Fourth Commandment: Observe the Sabbath Day

The Chinese saying "time is money" reflects how the pursuit of wealth often becomes the motivating factor that drives people to work endlessly, often without taking a day of rest. The Sabbath commandment directly addresses this attitude and reminds people of the significance of creating a "palace in time" within their weekly schedule.[61] It reminds us that the God of the Sabbath will provide for our needs, just as God provided the Israelites with manna on the Sabbath day when they ceased their work (Exod 16:22–30).

The fourth commandment is unique because no Sabbath mandate exists in any other ancient Near Eastern laws.[62] There is also no Sabbath in Egypt. The significance of the Sabbath commandment is reflected in its placement at the center of the Ten Commandments and by its length, which spans four verses (20:8–11). Moreover, the Sabbath command serves as a hinge that links the first three commandments that focus on humanity's relationship with God with the rest of the commandments. It includes both a mandate and a prohibition, and it is not limited to human relationships but extends to the welfare of animals that were used in farming. When humans observe the Sabbath, their animals – such as cattle – can also enjoy rest. This demonstrates that the God of Israel, unlike Pharaoh, is a compassionate and considerate God.

---

61. Abraham Joshua Heschel, *The Sabbath: Its Meaning for Modern Man* (New York: Farrar, Straus and Giroux, 1951), 12.
62. Sarna, *Exodus*, 111.

Table 6: The Division of the Ten Commandments

Commandments 1–3	Commandments regarding God	Exodus 20:2–7
Commandment 4	The commandment regarding God and all God's creation	Exodus 20:8–11
Commandments 5–9	Commandments regarding human beings	Exodus 20:12–16
Commandment 10	Commandment regarding one's own heart	Exodus 20:17

In the Bible, the word "remember" always implies a call to action.[63] Israel was to set apart the seventh day from the rest of the days, with the word "holy" – which is repeated twice – forming an *inclusio* with the Sabbath command (20:8, 11). This commandment is rooted in God's week of creation and serves to restore order to Israel's way of life.[64] God worked for six days and then rested on the seventh day and blessed it, and Israel is to follow this divine design for their good.

The Sabbath commandment names seven categories of people: you, your son, your daughter, your male servant, your female servant, your animals, and any foreigner. This emphasizes that rest on the Sabbath was a collective responsibility for all, regardless of social status or gender. These seven categories symbolize the totality of creation, who are all called to rest as God did on the seventh day. The inclusion of animals reflects their function in working in the fields. The mention of "the foreigner [*ger*] residing in your towns" once again reveals God's concern for the vulnerable who live on the margins of society. The mention of all people, including foreigners, as well as animals in this command points to God's care for all creation; furthermore, it reflects God's own figurative rest after creation (Exod 31:12–17). Everyone – God, people, and God's creation – cease from work on this sacred day and participate in the divine rest.

---

63. For example, God remembered Rachel and opened her womb (Gen 30:22). God remembered his covenant with Abraham, Isaac, and Jacob, and he therefore took notice of them and rescued the Israelites (Exod 2:24–25). Moses urged people to remember the day of Exodus, and they shall therefore not eat anything leavened (Exod 13:3).
64. A similar sabbath command in Deuteronomy focuses on God's rescue as the motivation for observing the sabbath (Deut 5:12–15).

For pastors, setting aside one day a week as a Sabbath for refreshment, renewal, and reorienting themselves with God is wise since Sunday is often a working day for them. Observing the Sabbath as the climax of the week helps to foster a rhythm of work and rest that will help us anticipate the ultimate Sabbath of an eternity with God.

In Abraham Heschel's classic study on the Sabbath, he coins the term "a palace in time," which views the Sabbath as a cathedral in time and a sanctification of time. On this day, the sacredness of time comes first, followed by Israel as the people called to be a holy nation and then by the tabernacle, which reflects the sacredness in space.[65] In light of Israel's former status as Pharaoh's slaves, who built the storage cities of Pithom and Rameses and endured endless physical labor, the Sabbath command comes as a welcome surprise.[66] It teaches Israel that the God who rescued them from Egypt is nothing like Pharaoh. The Sabbath commandment makes God more "human-like" and invites humans to participate in God's rest.[67]

God rests, and God desires that Israel also rest. In God's economy, he does not need Israel's endless production to show off his glory or assert his reign. God created humans so that they might enter his divine rest. Israel's new identity as the people of God requires them to adapt to these new rules for their own good. In the NT, even though the Sabbath commandment is no longer a mandate, there still remains a Sabbath rest for the people of God.[68] The writer of Hebrews urges believers to enter and embrace this ultimate rest (Heb 4:8–11). This rest is not reserved only for the original chosen people but now includes sojourners, outcasts, and others who are outside the original covenant. As Asians and other non-Jewish ethnic groups, we, too, are sojourners on this earth. We, too, are included and invited to enter God's rest in God's eternal home – which is our true and permanent home.

In the NT, Jesus invites those who are weary and heavy-laden to come to him and find rest in him, taking his yoke and learning from his gentleness and humility and finding rest for their souls (Matt 11:28–30). The Sabbath commandment reminds all Christians to set aside a day to rest from their

---

65. Heschel, *The Sabbath: Its Meaning for Modern Man*, 9–10, 15.
66. See Brueggemann's list of verses on Israel's labor in Exodus 5. Walter Brueggemann, *Sabbath as Resistance: Saying No to the Culture of Now* (Louisville: Westminster John Knox, 2017), 3–4.
67. This is not to reduce God to a human level but to refer to God as showing compassion and grace.
68. For example, Jesus heals people on the Sabbath because he is the Lord of the Sabbath (Matt 12:1–8; Mark 2:23–28; Luke 6:1–5).

work, to cease their endless striving, and to trust in God's daily provision and sustenance. Observing the Sabbath is, therefore, good news for the Israelites, who have transitioned from being slaves in Egypt to their new identity as the people of God – a process of identity construction.

The first, second, and fourth commandments stand in contrast to the Egyptian cultural-religious milieu: Israel is to worship only one God, in contrast to the polytheism of Egypt; they are not to make or worship graven images, in contrast to the Egyptians' idolatry; and they are to observe the Sabbath rest, a practice that was unknown in Egyptian society. God introduces a new paradigm, whereby Israel shifts from being slaves of Pharaoh to their new identity as the people of God.

The Fifth Commandment: Honoring Parents

The fifth to the ninth commandments deal with how to relate to and treat other human beings. Beginning with the duty to honor one's parents, this section then gives instructions about respecting the sanctity of life, honoring marriage, protecting property rights, and upholding truth. The tenth commandment deals with the problem of covetousness, which is often the underlying cause for mistreating others.

In Confucius's *Analects*, the three fundamental social relationships are those between father and son, lord and subordinate, and husband and wife, with the father-son relationship being viewed as the most important.[69] In Chinese, the word for "honor" in this context is the compound word *xiào* + *jìng*. *Xiào* has two parts: the upper part is the word for "old" (老) or "elderly," while the lower part is the word for "son" (子). Together, they form a logogram depicting a son carrying an aging parent, reflecting the sense of honoring one's parents in the Chinese context. The term *jìng* simply means respect. Thus, *xiào jìng* reflects a son caring for and respecting his elderly parents. Since *xiào* is considered one of the highest virtues in Chinese culture, many Chinese Christians resonate deeply with the fifth commandment.[70]

---

69. Knapp, "Three Fundamental Bonds and Five Constant Virtues," 2252.
70. Trimm's study on the fifth commandment confirms the view that the commandment is not about children obeying their parents but adult children caring for their aging parents. Charlie Trimm, "Honor Your Parents: A Command for Adults," *JETS* 60, no. 2 (2017): 243–263. Myers's study shows that in ancient Israel the relationship between parents and children was often interdependent. While young children relied on their parents to shoulder most of the labor, when those children became older, they were expected to care for their aging parents. Carol Myers, "The Family in Early Israel," in *Families in Ancient Israel*, ed. Leo G. Perdue et al. (Louisville: Westminster John Knox, 1997), 32–33.

Exodus 19–24

The Hebrew word for "honor" is *kabed*, which means "heavy" or "weight." This word is used in Exodus in various contexts to describe "heavy" things: Pharaoh's heavy heart (7:14), Moses's heavy tongue (4:10), the heavy pestilence (9:3), and the heavy cloud (19:16). The essence of the fifth commandment is showing significant respect and care for one's parents. In Chinese culture, elderly parents often live with their adult children rather than in nursing homes. As a result, the responsibility of caring for both their children and their elderly parents often falls on the shoulders of the adult children, creating what some call the "sandwich generation."

Unlike the other commandments, this one carries a promise that those who honor their parents will enjoy long life in the land God gives them. The consequences of violating this commandment are mentioned in the next chapter (Exod 21:15, 17).[71] Paul cites this commandment to encourage the Ephesian Christians to obey their parents, emphasizing that it is "the first commandment with a promise" (Eph 6:1–3).

Filial piety is a virtue that is greatly valued in both ancient Near Eastern and Chinese cultures, as well as in many others cultures. In the Ugaritic epic *Aqhat*, a poem on filial piety outlines the responsibilities of a son, which include both familial and religious duties to his ancestors.[72] Similarly, in Confucius's *Analects*, filial piety is regarded as a significant expression of one's virtue, encompassing parental obedience, proper burial for one's parents, offering sacrifices on behalf of their deceased parents and ancestors, supporting one's parents, and treating them with reverence.[73] Both cultures emphasize the importance of caring for parents while they are alive and honoring them

---

71. Compare Deuteronomy 21:18–21; Proverbs 23:19–22; 30:17.
72. The poem goes like this:
   To set up his Ancestor's stela, the sign of his Sib in the sanctuary;
   To rescue his smoke from the Underworld,
   To protect his steps from the Dust;
   To stop his abusers' spite,
   To drive his troublers away;
   To grasp his arm when he's drunk,
   To support him when sated with wine;
   To eat his portion in Baal's house,
   His share in the house of El;
   To daub his roof when there is mud,
   To wash his stuff when there's dirt."
See Simon B. Parker, "Aqhat" (CAT 1.17 column I: 26–33) in *Ugaritic Narrative Poetry*, ed. Simon B. Parker, Writings from the Ancient World Series (Atlanta: Scholars Press, 1997), 53.
73. The concrete ideas of filial piety can be gleaned from these sayings: "The Master said, 'While his parents are alive, the son may not go abroad to a distance. If he does go abroad, he

after they have passed away. Thus, in many Asian folk and family religions, veneration of the dead is a crucial part of honoring one's parents. In contrast, the biblical view focuses on honoring parents while they are alive, with no mention made of honoring them after their death. This focus on the present emphasizes the urgency of showing care and respect for one's parents while they are still alive.

Given that the Ten Commandments focus on general ethical principles rather than specific instructions for every scenario, discretion is required when applying these commandments to specific situations such as living with abusive parents, experiencing incest, relating to parents who are struggling with substance or alcohol abuse or mental challenges, or when parents' political views are extreme and result in them becoming verbally abusive.[74] While the NT affirms the command to honor one's parents (Matt 19:19; Eph 6:1–3; 1 Tim 5:8), this may sometimes appear to conflict with Jesus's teachings on discipleship (Matt 10:37–39). As Christians read their priorities to follow Christ, the challenge is to continue honoring their parents while giving first place to Christ. In Asian cultures, where atheism and religious pluralism are prevalent, tensions arise when parents do not share the same faith as their children. Children must take a stand for their faith and continue to show respect to their parents without compromising their faith.[75]

The Sixth Commandment: You Shall Not Murder

This commandment expresses a universal belief in the sanctity of human life that transcends cultures and time. This is a natural law or a general revelation of God that is ingrained in human consciousness, irrespective of religious beliefs. When God spoke to Noah, he established the moral, ethical, and theological foundation for the sixth commandment by saying, "Whoever sheds human

---

must have a fixed place to which he goes.'" ("Fixed place" in Chinese is *fang*, which may refer to direction or method.) "The Master said, 'If the son for three years does not deviate from the way of his father, he may be called filial.'" Confucius, *The Analects of Confucius*, 12–13.

74. For example, Marshall L. S. Scott, "Honor Thy Father and Mother: Scriptural Resources for Victims of Incest and Parental Abuse," *Journal of Pastoral Care*, XLII, no. 2 (Summer 1988): 139–148.

75. For more on honoring parents and the tensions in the Asian culture, see Jeanette Yep, Peter Cha, Paul Togunaga, Greg Jao, Susan Cho Van Riesen, *Following Jesus without Dishonoring Your Parents* (Downers Grove: InterVarsity Press 1998). Chen helpfully states the challenge of radical discipleship in Jesus's command to follow him and takes that as the priority over parental expectations. Diane G. Chen, "Filial Piety and Radical Discipleship in Matthew" in *T&T Clark Handbook of Asian American Biblical Hermeneutics*, eds. Uriah Y. Kim and Sang Ai Yang (London: T&T Clark, 2019), 340–350.

blood, by humans shall their blood be shed; for in the image of God has God made mankind" (Gen 9:6). This statement emphasizes that despite creating the animal kingdom, God places a high value on human life because human beings are created in his image.[76]

The word "murder" refers to taking another person's life with malicious intent, and this often involves premeditation.[77] This act violates the sanctity of God's creation, undermines social structure, and destroys human relationships. Although the penalty for murder is not specified in the Ten Commandments, the Book of the Covenant says that the one who willfully kills another person will be put to death (Exod 21:14).[78] The law also distinguishes between intentional murder and accidental killing. Those who killed accidentally, without criminal intent, were able to seek protection in one of the "cities of refuge" that were established throughout the land of Israel (21:13).[79]

In the NT, Jesus expanded the understanding of this commandment, moving from the prohibition of the outward act of murder to address the inner attitude of anger: "Anyone who is angry with a brother or sister will be subject to judgment" (Matt 5:22). Both the OT and the NT show that God sees and cares about a person's intentions and what goes on in their heart.[80] The issue of suicide, however, is not explicitly addressed in this commandment, and one must look elsewhere in Scripture for answers.[81]

The Seventh Commandment: You Shall Not Commit Adultery

The term "adultery" (*na'p*) is used in the context of marriage, usually referring to a man engaging in sexual relations with another man's wife.[82] This commandment is concerned with the sanctity of the marriage covenant. The covenant of marriage binds a man and a woman together in a bond that God ordained at creation: "A man leaves his father and mother and is united to

---

76. Compare Leviticus 24:21.
77. For example, Deuteronomy 5:17; Hosea 4:2; Jeremiah 7:9; 1 Kings 21:19. When the word is a participle, it is used in the context of a manslayer who kills without intent, as in Deuteronomy 4:42; 19:3–6. See *BDB*, 953.
78. Though Exodus 21:14 uses the word "killing" instead of "murdering," the meanings are similar. See Miller, *The Ten Commandments*, 228.
79. See Numbers 35:9–34; Joshua 20:1–9.
80. Compare Genesis 6:5–6; Jeremiah 17:9–10.
81. For how suicide is related to the sixth commandment, see Smedes' discussion in Lewis B. Smedes, *Mere Morality: What God Expects from Ordinary People* (Grand Rapids: Eerdmans, 1983, reprinted in 1996), 111–117.
82. *BDB*, 610. It may be used in the betrothal stage. *HALOT*, 658.

his wife, and they become one flesh" (Gen 2:24). Therefore, any illegitimate sexual relationship – that is, a sexual relationship outside the marriage bond – breaks this covenant.

In the prophetic books, the prophets often employ the marriage metaphor to depict the relationship between God and Israel. When Israel followed and worshiped other gods, this was viewed as both idolatry and adultery. Committing adultery is seen as akin to violating the covenant with God, as in the first commandment. Since God views marriage as a sacred covenant, he hates divorce (Mal 2:10). Adultery not only destroys the individual's marriage but also the other party's marriage. Its damaging effects also extend to the families of the man and woman who commit adultery.[83] Deuteronomy 22:13–30 elaborates on the seventh commandment in various contexts, and the severity of the death penalty reflects the seriousness with which God regards marital fidelity.

In cultures where family units form the backbone of social structures, committing adultery can have even more far-reaching and devastating consequences. Proverbs often use the adulterous woman as a symbol of foolishness or folly that leads to death and warns young people to avoid her (Prov 5:3–9; 7:6–27). Instead, they are urged to be faithful to their own wives and to drink from their own cisterns (Prov 5:15–19). The seventh commandment upholds the sanctity of marriage and situates the sexual relationship in the context of this sacred bond. This commandment is closely linked to the eighth commandment because, in ancient times, a wife was considered a man's property and, therefore, adultery was viewed as stealing what belonged to someone else.

People living in the diaspora must often travel between multiple worlds and sometimes reside in multiple homes transnationally. The emergence of such "astronaut families" sometimes leads to marital infidelity. The term "astronaut family" (*tai kōng rén*) carries at least three levels of meaning: a) a family in flight, commuting, traveling, and crossing borders; b) a family straddling two places simultaneously; and c) a married couple separated by physical and geographical distance.[84] The command against adultery is particularly relevant to married couples living apart from one another.

In the Chinese context, committing adultery is referred to as *wai yü* – which means "outside encounter" or "foreign encounter" – which signifies a

---

83. In the Ten Commandments, the addressee is "you" in the masculine singular form. Therefore, God is addressing the man in the Israelite community.
84. Chan, *Chinese Identities*, 123.

married person "meeting" someone outside the bond of marriage and engaging in an illicit relationship with them. A person who commits adultery is also described as "derailing" (*chū guǐ*), evoking the image of a train veering off its tracks, causing harm to both oneself and others.

In the NT, Jesus broadens the scope of the seventh commandment from the outward act of adultery to a person's inner desires: "Anyone who looks at a woman lustfully has already committed adultery with her in his heart" (Matt 5:28). By focusing on the condition of the heart, Jesus offers a deeper understanding of this commandment, emphasizing that while the commandment addresses outward behavior, it ultimately reflects the condition of one's heart.

The Eighth Commandment: You Shall Not Steal

This commandment concerns the protection of other people's property. The word "steal" (*ganab*) in cognate languages conveys the meaning of "hurting the side,"[85] signifying that stealing from someone causes harm to that person's side. Although such harm may not be fatal, it results in both material loss and emotional suffering for the victim. Christians may not often steal another's property or goods; however, in today's context, plagiarism is also a form of stealing. Failing to credit the rightful owner of intellectual property or quoting someone without a proper acknowledgment is considered plagiarism. In addition, even actions such as taking more napkins or straws than we need from a restaurant violate the eighth commandment.

The Book of the Covenant refers to kidnapping as a form of stealing (Exod 21:16). Kidnapping someone is akin to stealing that person's life. The law also spells out the consequences for stealing an ox or a sheep (22:1–4). The commandment against stealing includes other unethical behaviors such as breaking pledges, withholding deposits entrusted to a neighbor, and withholding wages. Therefore, this commandment is closely related to the previous commandment against adultery and the next commandment to "not give false testimony."[86]

In the NT, thieves are grouped together with adulterers and idolaters as people who will not inherit the kingdom of God: "Neither the sexually immoral nor idolaters nor adulterers nor men who have sex with men nor thieves nor the greedy nor drunkards nor slanderers nor swindlers will inherit

---

85. *BDB*, 170. The word is used when Laban accuses Rachel of stealing his family gods (Gen 31:30, 32).
86. Leviticus 6:2–5 and 19:11–14 provide a more detailed account of stealing and lying. See Miller, *The Ten Commandments*, 363–365.

the kingdom of God" (1 Cor 6:9–10). This verse encompasses transgressors of the sixth through the tenth commandments.

The Ninth Commandment: You Shall Not Give False Testimony

The context of this commandment is understood to be a court of law or a legal context, where providing honest and truthful testimony is of utmost importance. The court is where people expect justice to be served, and bearing false testimony or lying in court undermines the very essence of justice. In South Asia, it is common for rich people to pay large sums of money and get people to lie for them in court.[87] This practice perverts justice and violates the ninth commandment.

The book of Proverbs frequently emphasizes the significance of speaking the truth and warns against a lying tongue:

> An honest witness tells the truth, but a false witness tells lies (Prov 12:17).

> Truthful lips endure forever, but a lying tongue lasts only a moment (Prov 12:19).

> An honest witness does not deceive, but a false witness pours out lies (Prov 14:5).

> A truthful witness saves lives, but a false witness is deceitful (Prov 14:25).

While the book of Proverbs offers general principles for ethical and wise living, it does not address the complexities of real-life situations. For example, in Exodus, the Hebrew midwives lie to Pharaoh (or at least do not tell the whole truth) to save the Hebrew boys, and yet Scripture does not condemn their behavior. Instead, God rewards them with households of their own because they feared God (Exod 1:17, 21), demonstrating that God sometimes allows humans to act according to their own convictions or natural inclination to move history toward his own purposes. Proverbs and the ninth commandment provide a general moral and ethical standard of truthfulness, particularly in the legal context. However, in evaluating other instances of deception in Scripture or elsewhere, discretion must be used in applying these standards and the specific circumstances and context must be taken into consideration.

---

87. George and Swarup, "Exodus," 106.

In the NT, the command "you shall not give false testimony" has been broadened to include a prohibition against swearing an oath. Jesus said, "Do not swear by your head, for you cannot make even one hair white or black. All you need to say is simply 'Yes' or 'No'; anything beyond this comes from the evil one" (Matt 5:36–37). This emphasizes that speaking truthfully is integral to character and conduct. Like the eighth commandment, this commandment establishes a general ethical guideline but does not address specific ethical ambiguities such as whether white lies are acceptable or whether exaggerating constitutes a lie.[88]

The Tenth Commandment: You Shall Not Covet

While the first nine commandments focus on a person's outward behavior in relation to God and others, the tenth and final commandment is the only one that addresses a person's inner being – their desire. Just as the Sabbath commandment names seven groups, including people and animals, the tenth commandment also names seven categories of a neighbor's possessions: house, wife (viewed as the husband's property at the time), male servant, female servant, ox, donkey, and anything else belonging to the neighbor (20:17). The number seven symbolizes completeness or totality.[89] The Hebrew word for "covet" (*khamad*) can be translated as desire, longing, or taking pleasure and delight. It has a range of meanings, from positive feelings of "delight" to the negative implications of "covet" or envy that may lead to causing damage to others' possessions. In Genesis 3:6, the word *khamad* describes how the woman saw that the fruit of the tree was "desirable," which led to her taking and eating it. Her desire to be wise caused her to disobey God's command, resulting in catastrophic, cosmic consequences. This term is also used in other contexts, such as the Israelites' desire for Saul to be their king (1 Sam 9:20).[90]

Covetousness, which is the intense desire to possess something that is not one's own, lies deep within a person and is the result of humanity's sinful nature.[91] This covetousness often leads to actions such as taking what does not belong to us, as Eve did when she took the forbidden fruit – which she

---

88. For various social contexts that involve lying, see Smedes, *Mere Morality*, 224–238.
89. Deuteronomy places house before wife (Deut 5:21).
90. Other examples include Deuteronomy 7:25; Joshua 7:21; Isaiah 53:2; Micah 2:2.
91. The Bible presents a spectrum of coveting, ranging from the merely thought or attitude in one's mind to the actual act of taking and seizing caused by one's covetousness. While it may be difficult to prosecute someone based on one's inner covetousness in a court of law, God does look into people's hearts and weigh them (Prov 21:2). Aurelian Botica, "The Tenth

saw was good to eat and desirable for gaining wisdom – despite God's prohibition. Why does the tenth commandment, which focuses on covetousness, serve as the culmination of the Ten Commandments, which largely focus on behavioral imperatives? This is because covetousness is interconnected with the rest of the commandments, nearly all of which deal with transgressions that stem from the desire to covet.

Covetousness lies at the root of issues that affect our relationship with both God and others. For example, some people deem worshiping one God to be insufficient and desire to worship multiple gods – "the more, the merrier," as in many Asian contexts. Worshiping multiple gods reflects a lack of trust in the one true God, who alone provides and sustains life. With regard to the second commandment, people desire to worship God through visible images and icons, despite the command to worship an aniconic God. The Sabbath commandment commands rest, but people desire to work endlessly to produce, achieve, and become self-sustainable, rather than relying on God as their provider. Adultery is born out of a covetous desire for another's wife. Stealing arises from the desire to possess another's property. Ultimately, covetousness fuels other unethical behaviors that harm relationships with one's neighbors and, by extension, the broader community.

The tenth commandment, which addresses desire, is particularly challenging because desires reside deep within a person's innermost being. Unlike outward behavior, which is easier to observe, inner motives and inclinations are difficult to detect. Therefore, while most of the other commandments stipulate penalties for violators, the tenth commandment does not do so.

In the NT, the greedy are listed among those who will not inherit the kingdom of God (1 Cor 6:10; Eph 5:5), and greed is even equated with idolatry (Col 3:5).[92] This emphasizes that the tenth commandment is concerned with the "original sin" of covetousness and anticipates the NT teachings on character formation, which seek to eliminate the vice of greed.[93] Overall, the Ten Commandments are concerned with the Israelites' relationships with God, their families, their neighbors, and their own hearts.[94]

Commandment and the Concept of Inward Liability," in *Windows to the Ancient World of the Hebrew Bible: Essays in Honor of Samuel Greengus*, eds. Bill T. Arnold, Nancy L. Erickson, John H. Walton (Winona Lake: Eisenbrauns, 2014), 51–66.
92. The love of money is a form of covetousness (1 Tim 6:9–10).
93. Ben Leslie, "Ethical Perspectives on the Tenth Commandments," *RevExp* 113, no. 4 (2016): 538–545.
94. See the table in Block, *Covenant*, 191.

Exodus 19–24

The Ten Commandments simply state the commands, but most of the consequences for their violations appear later in the book of Exodus and in Deuteronomy, as shown in the table below:

Table 7: The Ten Commandments and the Consequences of Their Violation

	The Ten Commandments	The Consequences of Violation
1	No other gods (Exod 20:3).	Stoned to death (Deut 17:2–7).
2	No representations of God (Exod 20:4–5).	God will punish the violators and their children to the third and fourth generations (Exod 20:4–5). Death penalty (Exod 32:27–28).[95]
3	No misuse of God's name (Exod 20:7).	God will find them guilty (Exod 20:7).
4	Keep the Sabbath day (Exod 20:8–11).	Put to death and cut off from among the people (Exod 31:14–15).
5	Honor parents (Exod 20:12).	Put to death (Exod 21:15, 17).[96]
6	Do not murder (Exod 20:13).	Put to death (Exod 21:12, 14).[97]
7	Do not commit adultery (Exod 20:14).	Both the man and the woman shall be put to death (Deut 22:22).[98]
8	Do not steal (Exod 20:15).	Different rules apply to different cases of stealing. Every case involves compensation for lost goods (Exod 22:1–8).
9	Do not bear false witness (Exod 20:16).	The judge will investigate and will use the "measure for measure" rule to dispense justice (Deut 19:18–19).[99]
10	Do not covet (Exod 20:17).	The violator will not inherit the kingdom of God (1 Cor 6:10; Eph 5:5).

---

95. Compare Deuteronomy 27:15: "Cursed is anyone who makes an idol – a thing detestable to the Lord, the work of skilled hands – and sets it up in secret."
96. Compare Deuteronomy 27:16, "Cursed is anyone who dishonors their father or mother."
97. Compare Deuteronomy 27:24, "Cursed is anyone who kills their neighbor secretly."
98. Compare Deuteronomy 27:20, 22–23.
99. Compare Proverbs 19:5.

Six of the Ten Commandments carry the death penalty for violators.[100] The NT teaches that "the wages of sin is death" (Rom 6:23). God's moral and ethical standards reflect God's absolute holiness and unwavering commitment to justice.

When the Pharisees asked Jesus, "Teacher, which is the greatest commandment in the Law?" Jesus replied by quoting Deuteronomy 6:5 and Leviticus 19:18: "Love the Lord your God with all your heart and with all your soul and with all your mind" and "Love your neighbor as yourself." He also affirmed that these two commandments encapsulate the essence of "all the Law and the Prophets" (Matt 22:34–40). Similarly, Paul summarizes all the commandments in a single command: "Love your neighbor as yourself" (Rom 13:9–10). The Israelites' treatment of their neighbors reflects their identity as the people of God.

The ethical ideals expressed in the Ten Commandments are set in a context where it was assumed that people would worship other deities, make graven images, take God's name in vain, fail to observe the Sabbath, dishonor their parents, commit murder, adultery, and theft, bear false witness, and covet. Therefore, there is tension between the ideal vision of the Ten Commandments and the harsh reality of the world that Israel inhabits. Nevertheless, the Ten Commandments establish the fundamental moral and ethical principles that God's people must follow to establish a society that reflects God's holiness and justice.

The Book of the Covenant (Exod 20:22–23:33) provides further details and practical applications of each commandment, primarily in the form of case law.

20:18–21: THE PEOPLE'S RESPONSE

The scene described in this passage follows directly from Exodus 19. When God delivers the Ten Commandments to Moses on the top of Mount Sinai, the people are gathered at the foot of the mountain (19:17, 24). They witness thunder, lightning, the sound of trumpets, and smoke, which accompanied God's theophany. Their response, however, is not joy and excitement but fear and trembling (*nuʿa*). Although this term differs from the word used in Exodus

---

100. Based on the teachings in Deuteronomy, the death penalty is a means to safeguard the image of God (Deut 19:4–13), purge evil from the land (Deut 19:13; 21:1–9), and serve as warning to potential offenders (Deut 21:21). See Mona P. Bias, "Old Testament Law and Ethics," in *Exploring the Old Testament in Asia: Evangelical Perspectives*, eds. Jerry Hwang and Angukali Rotokha (Carlisle: Langham Global Library, 2022), 109.

19:16 (*harad*), both terms convey a similar sense of fear. The people are shaking – inside and out. God's transcendent presence evokes a conflicting fear within them: Do they want God to draw near to them or to stay far away? The people "stayed at a distance" and asked Moses to speak to them on God's behalf because they were afraid that they would die if God spoke to them directly.

When we fear something – such as a wildfire – our natural reaction is to stay away from it. The comment that the people stayed or remained "at a distance" is repeated twice for emphasis (20:18, 21). After Jacob wrestled with the angel of God, he realized that even though he had seen God face to face, his life had been spared (Gen 32:30), which implies that it was generally believed that a person could not see God and remain alive. God repeatedly warns the Israelites not to approach or touch the mountain of God, lest they die (Exod 19:12, 21, 24). Later, when Moses asks to see God's glory, God responds, "You cannot see my face, for no one may see me and live" (Exod 33:20). There is a tension between the God who wants to be known and the fear that God's presence evokes in his people.

Moses then comforts the people, urging them not to fear and assuring them that God has come to test them. This motif of testing, which featured prominently in Israel's wilderness journey, recurs here. The purpose of this test is to see whether or not the people truly fear God, with this fear serving as a safeguard against sinning against God. In the book of Job, fearing God and shunning evil are frequently paired to depict a righteous person since it is fear of God that motivates a person to refrain from doing anything that would displease God.[101] Deuteronomy expands on this account through the first-person perspective of Moses, who describes God's appearance in fire, cloud, and deep darkness (Deut 5:22). The leaders of the tribes and the elders then approach Moses, asking him to speak to God directly because they fear that hearing God's voice might prove fatal. Their words to Moses – recorded in direct speech – convey their fear of being in the presence of God (5:24–27). God hears them and grants their request that Moses should act as an intermediary (5:28–33).

As the people stand at a distance, Moses approaches the thick cloud where God is. Once again, the narrator highlights Moses's special status compared to the rest of the Israelites and his role as a mediator between God and Israel.

---

101. Job 1:1, 8; 28:28.

20:22–23:33 THE BOOK OF THE COVENANT

There is a joke among Chinese Christians that when people read the book of Exodus, they cannot come out from Egypt because the meticulous laws and regulations given after the exodus event, along with the painstaking details about the construction of the tabernacle, make this difficult reading. The Ten Commandments are relatively easy to understand, but the numerous laws that follow often seem strange to modern readers and do not seem immediately relevant to contemporary contexts, as a result of which readers often lose interest. This frustration is not limited to Chinese people but is a common experience among many readers of the Bible. People are generally drawn to narratives, but reading legal texts is more challenging.

One way to address this challenge is to approach the legal texts in the Bible as mini-stories or hypothetical scenarios drawn from modern life. Each law can be viewed as arising from a real-life context that sheds light on different aspects of daily life in ancient Israel and illustrates how people resolved issues by applying God's law.[102] This approach is supported by the fact that the Ten Commandments arise out of a narrative context. For example, in 2019, the contested extradition bill in Hong Kong emerged from a murder case: a young man killed his pregnant girlfriend in Taiwan and returned to Hong Kong, but the police could not charge him with murder or extradite him because there was no extradition agreement between Taiwan and Hong Kong.[103] Similarly, immigration laws in the United States often originate from real-life situations that involve an influx of undocumented migrants who cross the border every day. Gun control laws are a response to frequent gun violence across the country. Similarly, abortion laws have been shaped by the increasing number of women seeking abortion, not to mention the personal stories and situations surrounding each of these cases.

When reading the case laws in the Book of the Covenant, we should view these as hypothetical "reality shows" in ancient Israel. These case laws often describe a situation or state of affairs that could arise and then offer a possible solution.[104] These laws thus offer "windows" into Israel's daily life,

---

102. Bartor's study offers a fresh perspective to reading law as narrative. She sees the laws as "embedded stories" within a "frame story." The narrative elements include concrete situations, phenomena, characters, and events. Assnat Barton, *Reading Law as Narrative: A Study in the Casuistic Laws of the Pentateuch* (Atlanta: Society of Biblical Literature, 2010), 7, 14.
103. "2019 Hong Kong extradition bill." https://en.wikipedia.org/wiki/2019_Hong_Kong_extradition_bill.
104. Barton, *Reading Law as Narrative*, 9.

giving readers a glimpse of situations that might have arisen and illustrating how these could have been handled. These laws aim to uphold human rights and protect life and property, while serving as a deterrent against violations. Just as with the Ten Commandments, they reflect God's ethical ideals while also acknowledging the grim reality of human sinfulness, which meant that these offenses could have taken place in ancient Israel.

While the Ten Commandments outline general principles relating to a person's relationship with God and others, the Book of the Covenant addresses specific scenarios that were likely to arise in the lives of the ancient Israelites. These case laws are cultural, situational, and time-sensitive, and not all of them are relevant to contemporary audiences. However, the underlying principles of these case laws – embodying the two pillars of benevolence (*rén*) and justice or righteousness (*yì*) toward other human beings – remain applicable today. These laws are both an extension and the concrete applications of the Ten Commandments, and our interpretive task is to discern these underlying principles. Below are some helpful guidelines for this discernment process:[105]

1. The principle should be reflected in the text.
2. The principle should be timeless.
3. The principle should correspond to the teaching of the rest of Scripture.
4. The principle should not be culturally tied.
5. The principle should be relevant to both biblical and contemporary audiences.

The table below shows how the Book of the Covenant reflects and expands upon the specific principles of the Ten Commandments.

---

[105]. Taken from J. Scott Duvall and J. Daniel Hays, *Grasping God's Word: A Hands-On Approach to Reading, Interpreting, and Applying the Bible*, 3rd ed. (Grand Rapids: Zondervan, 2012), 365.

Table 8: The Book of the Covenant and the Ten Commandments

Ten Commandments (Exodus 20:3–17)	The Book of the Covenant (Exodus 20:22–23:19)
1st Commandment: No other gods	Laws concerning sacrificing to other gods (22:20) and mentioning the names of other gods (23:13).
2nd Commandment: No representations of God	Laws concerning making other gods (20:23).
3rd Commandment: Name command	Laws concerning blaspheming God (22:28).
4th Commandment: Sabbath command	Laws concerning slaves on the seventh year (21:2–6), rest for the land on the seventh year (23:10–11), and rest for people and cattle on the seventh day (23:12).
5th Commandment: Honoring parents	Laws concerning striking parents and cursing parents (21:15, 17).
6th Commandment: Do not murder	Personal injuries, premeditated murder, manslaughter, miscarriage, and goring oxen (21:12–14; 18–36; 22:2; 23:7b).
7th Commandment: Do not commit adultery	There is no specific law dealing with adultery, but there is a related incident of a man seducing a virgin (22:16–17).[106]
8th Commandment: Do not steal	Laws concerning kidnapping (21:16) and stealing an ox or a sheep (22:1–4; 7–13).
9th Commandment: Do not give false testimony	Laws concerning false reports, including false testimony in the court of law (23:1–3; 6–8).
10th Commandment: Do not covet	There are many cases that arise because of covetous desires, including stealing (22:1–4; 7–13), seducing a virgin (22:16–17), taking interest from the poor (22:25), taking someone's cloak as a pledge (22:26–27), and taking a bribe (23:8).

The case laws in the Book of the Covenant are organized according to themes and do not follow the sequence of the Ten Commandments. These case laws cover a range of contexts.

---

106. More specific laws concerning adultery appear in Deuteronomy 22:13–30.

A noteworthy feature of these case laws is that each law is "highly selective in its contents and exceedingly limited in its scope."[107] These laws were not intended to solve every problem that emerged in ancient Israel. Rather, people were expected to be guided by common sense, cultural norms, and traditional teachings in their decision-making. Similarly, in today's context, Christians cannot expect the Bible to provide explicit answers to every situation; instead, they must use their discernment to apply biblical principles in different contexts and situations. The general rule of thumb for interpreting and applying these laws requires deriving the basic principles from the Ten Commandments. Christians may use the *Shema* – which emphasizes loving God with all one's being (Deut 6:5) – and the principle of loving one's neighbor as oneself (Lev 19:18) as foundational moral and ethical guidelines for their daily living and decision-making.[108]

There are striking resemblances between case laws found in the Book of the Covenant and the Code of Hammurabi – which dates back to 1750 BCE – suggesting that there were shared ethical codes across the ancient Near Eastern world. Studying the similarities and differences between the biblical laws and these ancient law codes can enhance our understanding of both the shared and distinctive aspects of Israel's ethics, which in turn can deepen our understanding of who God is as revealed through these case laws.[109] David P. Wright argues that the Covenant Code – that is, the Book of the Covenant – has been influenced by the Code of Hammurabi and suggests that this borrowing took place during the Neo-Assyrian period (740–640 BCE) when Assyria had strong control over Judah and Israel. The similarities of form and content between the two law codes, especially at the point in the law collection where its genre changes – for instance, from casuistic law to dyadic list form – invite curiosity. Wright suggests that this shift from the Babylonian law-giver Hammurabi to Israel's one, true God Yahweh, may indicate that the writer of the Covenant Code had an ideological agenda and was symbolically asserting

---

107. Sarna, *Exploring Exodus*, 170.
108. Bias, "Old Testament Law and Ethics," 119.
109. For more on the comparative study of Israelite law and Hammurabi's law, see Hays, *Hidden Riches*, 121–145. *COS* 3:335–353. Martha T. Roth, *Law Collections from Mesopotamia and Asia Minor*, 2nd ed., Writings from the Ancient World 6 (Atlanta: Society of Biblical Literature, 1997), 71–142. For a detailed study of the interconnections between Hammurabi's law code and the Book of the Covenant in Exodus, see David P. Wright, *Inventing God's Law: How the Covenant Code of the Bible Used and Revised the Laws of Hammurabi* (Oxford: Oxford University Press, 2009).

God's superiority over this powerful nation.[110] In contrast, Cynthia Edenburg maintains a more open view regarding the relationship between the Book of the Covenant and the Code of Hammurabi because the former has distinctive literary features that are not found in the Code of Hammurabi.[111]

One important area of comparison between the two law collections is the treatment of disadvantaged groups in society. While the Code of Hammurabi safeguards the interests of the elite class, the Book of the Covenant protects the rights of vulnerable and marginalized groups in society.[112]

Exodus 20:22–23:19 – commonly referred to as the Book of the Covenant or the Covenant Code – deals primarily with specific cases within Israelite society but also includes apodictic laws.[113] Many of the concrete incidents are presented hypothetically, using "if" or "when" (*ki*) statements to depict possible scenarios that may arise in the future.[114]

20:22–26 The Altar Law

This section begins with the phrase "Then the Lord said to Moses," which indicates a shift from the previous text. The first set of laws pertains to the worship of God. Israel has just witnessed God speaking to them from heaven – that is, the theophany at the top of Mount Sinai – and God now reiterates the second commandment that forbids Israel to make gods of silver or gold – literally, "You shall not make with me gods of silver and gods of gold, you shall not make them" (20:23, translation mine). The particle "with me" (*'iti*)

---

110. Wright, *Inventing God's Law*, 3–7, 15–16. While Wright's argument for the date of the Book of the Covenant seems convincing, it is also possible that Hammurabi's Law carries God's general revelation, as all truth is God's truth.
111. For example, the laws in Exodus 22:20–23:9 form a discrete section framed by the inclusion of not oppressing the sojourners because Israel was once a sojourner in Egypt (22:20; 23:9). The laws in 23:10–19 are also a distinct section marked off by two regulations concerning the fruit of the land (23:10, 19). Cynthia Edenburg, "The Book of the Covenant," in *The Oxford Handbook of Biblical Law*, ed. Pamela Barmash (Oxford: Oxford University Press, 2019), 158.
112. Sarna, *Exploring Exodus*, 177.
113. The name "the Book of the Covenant" is based on Exodus 24:7. There are three law codes in the Pentateuch: Book of the Covenant (Exodus 21–23), the Holiness Code (Leviticus 17–27), and the Deuteronomic Collection (Deuteronomy 12–26). These three law codes have similarities as well as differences. Their differences suggest the gradual development of the law in the forty years from Sinai to Moab in Deuteronomy. See Averbeck, *The Old Testament Law for the Life of the Church*, 105.
114. Glenville divides the laws in the Book of the Covenant into three types: 1. Statutory law (Exod 21:1–22:16), addressing various legal laws. 2. Cultic law (Exod 20:24–26; 22:17–19), concerning the worship of Yahweh. 3. Social law (Exod 22:20–23:9), concerning the vulnerable group. Mark R. Glanville, *Freed to Be God's Family: The Book of Exodus* (Bellingham: Lexham Press, 2021), 15.

may seem confusing.[115] Does God mean "you shall not make images of other gods while I am present"? Or does he mean "you shall not make images of other gods together with me," which seems to imply that Israel could make these images alone. The latter interpretation seems unlikely and contradicts God's commands elsewhere. In light of the first commandment – "you shall not have other gods before my face" (in Hebrew) – this should be understood as "in my presence" or "before me."

Instead, God commands Israel to make an altar of earth for him and offer sacrifices on it. Since the altar is associated with worship, the first law in the Book of the Covenant is associated with worship.[116] God then promises, "Wherever I cause my name to be honored, I will come to you and bless you" (Exod 20:24). The laws concerning proper worship conclude with two additional instructions, along with reasons. First, the stones used to build the altar must remain uncut since cutting the stones would defile the altar. Second, the Israelites were not to approach the altar using the steps, lest their nakedness be exposed. In other contexts, exposing one's nakedness is considered unclean, disgraceful, inappropriate, and profane.[117]

The laws pertaining to the altar set the stage for the covenant ratification described in Exodus 24 – where Moses builds an altar where the people can offer sacrifices (24:4) – and the altar in the courtyard of the tabernacle (27:1–8). The blending of laws on worship and ethical stipulations in the Book of the Covenant underscores the interconnectedness of worship and ethics.[118] Our relationship with God affects our relationships with other people, and vice versa. The Israelites are called to live ethically as a reflection of their new identity as God's people. They are also required to worship God properly in order to live ethically. The close connection between worship and ethics plays a key role in Israel's identity formation.

21:1–11 Laws about Slaves

The chapter opens with the statement, "These are the laws you are to set before them," with "laws" (*mishpatim*) referring to ordinances. The root meaning of the word is "justice" (*mishpat*), suggesting that the laws God is about to

---
115. NIV translates it as "alongside me," while NASB translates it as "beside me."
116. Before God's giving of the law, the altars were the "occasional testimonies to sacred space" (Gen 8:20; 12:7). Tremper Longman III, *Immanuel in Our Place: Seeing Christ in Israel's Worship* (Phillipsburg: P&R, 2001), 15.
117. For example, Genesis 3:7; 9:21; Leviticus 18:6–23; Isaiah 47:3; Habakkuk 2:16.
118. Block, *Covenant*, 195.

give Moses are concerned with justice. The various laws in the Book of the Covenant primarily reflect a concern for justice within the community. At the same time, these laws are also future-oriented, akin to prophecies, anticipating possible scenarios that are likely to arise within the community that would require resolution, protection, and safeguarding.[119]

Laws concerning slaves may seem irrelevant in contemporary contexts; in ancient Israel, however, slaves were viewed as a distinct class of people who worked in, with, and for the family. These laws are specific to the context and culture of the time.[120] The focus here is not the legitimacy of slavery, as some argue, but to demonstrate God's great compassion for people who are at the lowest tier of society and are, therefore, vulnerable to oppression. By instituting these laws, God demonstrates that his concern goes beyond simply feeling sorry; instead, he takes their rights seriously and acts to ensure justice by actively righting wrongs and preventing exploitation. During the crossing of the Red Sea, God intervened militarily on behalf of Israel; in giving these laws, God's intervention takes the form of legal advocacy for disadvantaged groups within Israelites society. Through this approach toward the question of slaves, God was setting out concrete ways in which Israel could live out their call to be a kingdom of priests and a holy nation.

The laws concerning slaves are interwoven with the Sabbath command and presented within the category of family laws that address the concerns of marginalized members of the household. This approach to slave legislation is unprecedented in the ancient Near East.[121] However, the rights granted to slaves under these laws have profound implications both for the faith of the ancient Israelites and for Christians today, demonstrating that the God we serve cares for all people who are created in his image, including slaves. It is not true that there are no slaves in today's world – child slavery, sex slavery,

---

119. Carmichael, *The Origins of Biblical Law*, 23.
120. Richard E. Averbeck, "Slavery in the World of the Bible," in *Behind the Scenes of the Old Testament: Cultural, Social, and Historical Contexts*, eds. Jonathan S. Greer, John W. Hilber, and John H. Walton (Grand Rapids: Baker Academic, 2018), 424.
121. Slaves are included in Israel's religious life. They too observe the Passover and the Sabbath. Wright, *Old Testament Ethics*, 334. Carmichael reads the slave laws in light of the experiences of Jacob in Laban's house and Joseph in Potiphar's house. Carmichael, *The Origins of Biblical Law*, 80–87.

and domestic slavery are prevalent in many countries, including Africa.[122] The next section describes some specific laws concerning slaves.[123]

21:2–6 Regulations Pertaining to Male Slaves

After having served for six years, a Hebrew slave must be set free in the seventh year without any conditions. This law sets a limit on the duration of slavery, emphasizing that slavery was never meant to be a lifetime condition.[124] This law is part of a series of hypothetical scenarios, introduced with "if" (*'im*) clauses, with each subsequent scenario building upon the previous one. This progression of laws suggests that a logical and reasoned argument is being advanced.

A. If he comes as a single man, he shall leave as a single man.
B. If he comes as a married man, then his wife shall leave with him.
C. If his wife was given by his master, then the wife and any children they bore belong to his master, and he shall leave by himself.
D. If he chooses to stay with his master, then his master shall bring him before the judges and pierce his ear with an awl at the door or the doorpost,[125] symbolizing that he shall serve his master for life.

In this scenario, the narrator includes the direct speech of the slave who intends to stay with his master: "I love my master and my wife and children and do not want to go free" (21:5). This insertion offers a glimpse into the personality, emotions, and inner world of the nameless slave, presenting his point of view rather than just the narrator's view.[126] Despite being faceless, this slave is given a voice and personhood and is presented as someone who has desires and wishes just like any other human being and knows what he wants and does not want. This voice of the slave provides a window into an otherwise dry legal text, allowing readers to catch a glimpse of the slave's inner

---

122. Prostitution often involves slavery. Some parents sell their children to become maids or "house boys" who are often abused by their oppressors. Rubin Poho, "Slavery," in *Africa Bible Commentary*, ed. Tokunboh Adeyemo (Grand Rapids: Zondervan, 2006), 89.
123. Compare Deuteronomy 15:12–18.
124. Lifelong slavery is limited to foreign slaves, not Hebrew slaves (Lev 25:39–55).
125. Ear piercing may symbolically point to listening to the master's orders. See Tigay, "Exodus," 144.
126. Bartor's study shows that the point of view is one of the literary techniques of the narrator who through disclosing the point of view of the characters further teaches the spirit of the law. The lexical markers often include sensory or cognitive perceptions, such as sight, hearing, knowing, and understanding. See Barton, *Reading Law as Narrative*, 164–165. Deuteronomy 15:12–15 further reveals the inner psyche of this slave through his direct speech. In that account, it includes a motive clause and a divine promise.

world – he loves his master, his wife, and his children, and despite having the option to leave his master, he chooses to remain with his master permanently as part of the master's extended family. Remarkably, in ancient Israel, a slave could be integrated into the family, reflecting God's concern and care for the welfare of this marginalized group in society.

In Israel, there were two distinct categories of slavery: temporary debt slavery and permanent chattel slavery. In some instances, a person could choose to become a permanent chattel slave instead of a debt slave (21:5–6).[127]

21:7–11 Regulations Pertaining to Female Slaves

Female slaves still exist in the contemporary world. In South Asia and other parts of the majority world, girls are sold for both slavery and the sex trade.[128] This grim reality prompts us to rethink the relevance of these ancient laws as we consider how to address these forms of modern slavery and protect the vulnerable among us. The laws on female slaves differ from those for male slaves, and no reasons are provided for these differences. While some argue that this differential treatment reflects the gender inequality of the time, God specifically addresses the conjugal rights of female slaves (21:11), which reflects a concern that goes beyond mere survival. Therefore, when evaluating the issue of gender equality in this context, it is important to consider both the cultural context of the time and the scriptural context. Below are the specific hypothetical scenarios, introduced with "if" clauses:

A. If a man sells his daughter as a female slave, she is not to be set free in the way a male slave is set free.
B. If she is displeasing in the eyes of her master who choses her for himself,[129] then he must let her be redeemed. However, the master does not have the authority to sell her to foreign people because to do so would be to act faithlessly toward her.[130]

---

127. Averbeck, "Slavery in the World of the Bible," 424. Chattel slaves can be acquired from Israel's neighbors, from the sojourners who lived with them, and from prisoners of war or warfare refugees. Averbeck, "Slavery in the World of the Bible," 428.
128. George and Swarup, "Exodus," 107.
129. Or does not choose her. The Hebrew here can be understood as "to him" (*lo*) or "no" (*lo*).
130. Because of the ambiguity involved in this law, the circumstances under which the female slaves displease the master are unclear. Who would redeem her? What are the acts of the master's faithlessness to which the text refers?

C. If he chooses her for his son, then he shall grant her the rights of a daughter, meaning that she should receive the same treatment as his own daughters.

D. If he marries another woman after purchasing the female slave, he must not deprive the female slave of three things: food, clothing, and marital rights. If he fails to provide these things, then she shall go free without any payment. "Marital rights" (*'onah*) means cohabitation – a euphemism for sexual relations – and this word occurs only here in the OT.[131] While food and clothing are basic human needs for survival, marital rights do not seem to belong to the same category and demonstrate God's concern for female slaves that goes beyond basic human rights.

21:12–36 Laws about Personal Injuries

In many parts of the United States, advertisements for personal injury attorneys can be seen on billboards, television, and social media. Personal injuries may occur in various contexts – for example, physical bullying in schools due to lack of supervision, trips and falls due to uneven pavements or inadequate lighting on streets, and accidents in restaurants where a waiter might spill a boiling beverage on someone and cause harm. These incidents can happen to anyone, regardless of ethnicity or race. Similarly, even though the cultural context of ancient Israel was different from contemporary culture, personal injuries were part of daily life.

The lengthy section devoted to laws concerning personal injuries (21:12–36) reveals their prevalence in ancient Israel. These laws address various forms of harm, including the physical and verbal abuse of one's parents and slaves, as well as injuries caused by animals. Since personal injuries sometimes result in death, some of these laws are directly linked to the sixth commandment: "You shall not murder." Each of the incidents described in these laws can be viewed as a mini-narrative of the "dark side" of life in ancient Israel. These laws aim to regulate human behavior and ensure that the punishment fits the crime. In addition, the laws concerning goring oxen serve as a reminder that since both humans and animals share the same physical space, disorder, and

---

131. *BDB*, 773. The word is associated with time and may refer to a period of conjugal time. See *HALOT*, 855.

chaos would ensue if there were no proper regulations governing the control of animals.

Exodus 21:12–17 departs from the previous "if" clauses and adopts a simpler "anyone who" format,[132] but Exodus 21:18–36 reverts to "if" (*weki*) clauses. In these laws concerning personal injuries, the key to determining the punishment depends on whether or not the intention was to kill. The OT laws are concerned not only with behavior but also with the person's heart – that is, their inner motive. This is consistent with the NT teaching that sin begins in the mind; a person who harbors sinful thoughts has already sinned.[133]

A key verb in these personal injury laws is "strikes" (*nakah*), which could cause bodily harm or death (21:12).[134] This term *nakah* is also translated "attacks" (21:15), "hits" (21:18), and "beats" (21:20). The laws concerning personal injuries are closely tied to the concept of holiness. Anthropologist Mary Douglas, in her study on ritual and purity in Leviticus, defines holiness as completeness and wholeness since most laws on cleanliness are linked with the concept of God's holiness.[135] This suggests that any behavior that violates the law of wholeness – such as causing physical or emotional harm to someone – falls short of God's ideal for his people. This law of holiness also applies to other moral behaviors, including stealing, lying, bearing false witness, using dishonest weights and measures, and harboring hatred toward someone in one's heart.[136]

21:12 Killing Intentionally

This law stipulates that anyone who strikes another person shall be put to death. The word "strike" (*nakah*) frequently appears in the book of Exodus, often denoting an act of striking that has fatal consequences – for example, Moses strikes an Egyptian and causes his death (2:12), and God strikes the firstborn in Egypt (12:12). The term often carries the connotation of an intent to kill. The twofold repetition of the word "death"[137] emphasizes the certainty of the punishment.[138]

---

132. In Hebrew, "he who," presuming the original audience was Israelite male.
133. The heart in the Bible refers mostly to one's mind. For example, Matthew 5:21–22; 27–30.
134. These laws place less emphasis on the emotional and mental damage to the victims.
135. Douglas, *Purity and Danger*, 63.
136. Douglas, *Purity and Danger*, 67.
137. Hebrew infinitive absolute + Hophal imperfect.
138. When God warned Adam not to eat from the tree of the knowledge of good and evil, God repeated the word "die" twice for emphasis: "but you must not eat from the tree of the knowledge of good and evil, for when you eat from it you will certainly die" (Gen 2:17). Although

21:13 Killing Unintentionally

This law states that if someone kills another person without premeditation but "God lets it happen," then God will designate a place to which the killer may flee. Although not defined here, this place is later identified as a city of refuge.[139] The meaning of "God lets it happen" is unclear and is literally translated as "but God cause to meet by or through his hand."[140] The idea seems to be that while the person did not intend to kill, death occurred and that, somehow, God was involved in this outcome. It is not clear how much responsibility lies with God in such an instance. However, the fact that God prepares a place of refuge suggests that God does not hold the killer accountable for the action. The city of refuge serves as protection from further bloodguilt rather than as a punishment for killing without prior intent.[141]

21:14 Killing Someone Deliberately

This law stipulates that anyone who deliberately kills their neighbor will be taken from God's altar and put to death. The word "deliberately" (*zid*) literally means "to act proudly," indicating a premeditated killing. "My altar" refers to the altar described in Exodus 20:24–26. While Exodus 21:12–14 expands on the sixth commandment, "You shall not murder," verses 15 and 17 address the fifth commandment which deals with honoring parents and the penalties for violation. In addition, one of the two cases regarding dishonoring parents is closely connected to the commandment "You shall not murder."

21:15 Killing Parents

This law stipulates that anyone who strikes their parents shall be put to death. This law parallels verse 12, which has the same verb "strike" and imposes the same penalty of capital punishment. Since it is difficult to imagine a scenario where someone would intentionally strike their father and mother in such a manner that would potentially lead to their death, the inclusion of this law raises questions about the reasons someone might commit such a heinous crime. No specific scenarios are provided in the text and no mention is made

---

Adam did not die instantly, he did later. The vocabulary used in the law "you shall certainly die" recalls the original sin that Adam incurred. It also reflects the New Testament teaching that the wages of sin are death (Rom 6:23).
139. Numbers 35:6, 11–14; Deuteronomy 4:41; 19:1–3; Joshua 20:1–2.
140. The NASB translates it as "God let him fall into his hand."
141. In Numbers 35:10–34, God's instruction to Moses is that the killer will not die before standing trial before the congregation. In cases of manslaughter without the prior intent to kill, the congregation will judge between the killer and the avenger.

of the mental state of the person who committed the crime, the condition of the parents, or the intent behind the act. In the modern context, mental instability or abuse by parents may lead to such crimes being committed. The simplicity of the law highlights its severity and strictness, allowing no excuse or justification for such behavior. Since specific circumstances are not spelled out, this law serves as a general principle.

21:16 Kidnapping

This law stipulates that anyone who kidnaps another person shall be put to death, regardless of whether they "actively" kidnap and sell the individual or merely "passively" possess the kidnapped individual. As the word for "kidnapping" (*ganab*) is the same as the term for "stealing," this law is an extension of the eighth commandment, "You shall not steal." The punishment for kidnapping is the same as for intentionally striking someone or striking one's parents – namely, capital punishment – which indicates that, in the eyes of the law, striking and stealing are considered equally serious offenses.[142]

Human trafficking is a form of kidnapping that is prohibited under this law. An example of this offense is Joseph's kidnapping and sale into slavery by his brothers, and no theological or allegorical interpretation can change the fact that the brothers effectively "stole" Joseph's life from him.

21:17 Cursing Parents

This law stipulates that anyone who curses their parents shall be put to death. The word "curse" (*qalal*) means "make light of," "belittle," or "despise." The Book of Proverbs also contains teachings about cursing parents and notes the dire consequences of such an act: "If someone curses their father or mother, their lamp will be snuffed out in pitch darkness" (20:20); "There are those who curse their fathers and do not bless their mothers" (30:11); and "The eye that mocks a father, that scorns an aged mother, will be pecked out by the ravens of the valley, will be eaten by the vultures" (30:17). Disrespecting parents, whether through words or actions, incurs the same penalty as striking them.[143]

Proverbs emphasizes the importance of honoring elderly parents, with many of its teachings focusing on how adult children should treat their aging

---

142. Deuteronomy further clarifies this law by stating that the object of kidnapping is "a brother from the sons of Israel" (Deut 24:7).
143. Proverbs includes a couple of incidents of stealing from parents: "Whoever robs their father and drives out their mother is a child who brings shame and disgrace" (19:26) and "Whoever robs their father or mother and says, "It's not wrong," is partner to one who destroys" (28:24).

parents. For instance, Proverbs 23:22 says, "Listen to your father, who gave you life, and do not despise your mother when she is old." Particularly in Asian contexts, elderly parents often belong to a less fortunate and disadvantaged group, relying on their children for care and support. While we may find it difficult to understand why the law is so severe, this reflects the importance placed on respecting and honoring parents, especially in their old age.

21:18–19 Injuries Resulting from a Quarrel

Beginning in verse 18, the rest of this chapter uses "if" clauses to present a range of hypothetical situations describing personal injuries that might occur, along with their corresponding penalties. These laws provide detailed descriptions and can be read as "mini-narratives" of plausible real-life scenarios.[144]

Verse 18 describes a situation where a quarrel could escalate into violent actions, such as one person striking another with a stone or fist in the heat of the moment. The verdict is determined by the severity of the injury. If the injured person does not die and can still walk with the aid of a staff, the offender will not face capital punishment. However, the offender must compensate the victim for lost time and provide for the victim's care until recovery is complete.[145] Although the rationale for leniency is not stated, we can infer that it is based on the assumption that the offender did not intend to cause harm.

While this case is more detailed than the previous ones (Exod 21:15–16), it still leaves several questions unanswered. For instance, how would compensation be determined if the victim suffers permanent damage to the lower back or is left with a permanent disfigurement? How is the offender held accountable if the victim does not recover fully? How is the cost of pain and suffering calculated in such circumstances? The lack of such details implies that these case laws are intended to be principle-based guidelines rather than strict legal codes that can be directly implemented in all situations.

21:20–21 Striking Slaves

This law addresses the treatment of slaves. If an owner strikes their male or female slave with a rod, resulting in the death of the slave, the owner will be punished but the exact penalty is not specified. If the victim "recovers" (literally, can "stand") in a day or two, no punishment is imposed because the slave is

---

144. Barter names it "reality-mimicking texts." Barter, *Reading Law as Narrative*, 85.
145. The "lost time" is comparable to the contemporary context in the United States that the offender will pay for the injured person's loss of salary during the time of sick leave.

considered the owner's "property" (literally, "silver"). This "mini-narrative" illustrates a scenario where an owner might be abusing a slave, perhaps by repeated beating with a rod until the slave dies. Imagine the kind of force and the number of blows required to cause such an outcome. This law raises questions about the unjust system of slavery, the discriminatory social structure, and the economic inequality between the haves and the have-nots. Chung Man Anna Lo observes that "no cuneiform law collection deals with physical assault against one's own slave, whether chattel or debt slaves, not to mention that there is no cuneiform law imposing capital vengeance against slave owners because of their fatal assault against their own slave, as Exod 21:20 requires."[146]

As twenty-first-century readers, we must remember that the OT originates from a different cultural and historical context and that these laws were meant for ancient Israel. We should interpret these laws based on their underlying principles and refrain from applying them rigidly or indiscriminately to our contemporary contexts.[147]

21:22–25 Striking a Pregnant Woman

This law, which is one of the most detailed statutes dealing with personal injuries, deals with situations involving pregnant women. Its inclusion suggests that such cases were likely to occur in biblical times. This law begins with an "if" statement: if people (plural) are fighting and then hit a pregnant woman, causing her to give birth "prematurely" (21:22). The multiple levels of ambiguity inherent in this law spark curiosity.

First, the "why" question – the cause of these people's struggle is not specified. Second, the "how" question – the nature of their struggle is not described. Third, the "how many" question – it is not stated how many men (NIV has "people") are involved, and both the plural "men" and the singular "he" appear in this law (21:22).[148] Fourth, another "how" question – precisely how does their fight cause a pregnant woman to lose her fetus? Fifth, the "what

---

146. Chung Man Anna Lo, *The Laws of the Imperialized: Understanding Exodus 19–24 as a Response to Imperial Legal Traditions* (Carlisle: Langham Academic, 2024), 130.
147. For a helpful discussion on reading biblical laws, see Matthew Richard Schlimm, *This Strange and Sacred Scripture: Wrestling with the Old Testament and Its Oddities* (Grand Rapids: Baker Academic, 2015), 104–120.
148. For the ambiguity in the number of men involved in this law Mukujina suggests using Exodus 2:13–14 as a parallel text, in which one of the key indicators of the offending party is to identify who is the initiator or instigator of the fight. John Mukujina, "Literary Solutions to Legal Problems: The Contribution of Exodus 2.13–14 to Exodus 21.22–23," *JSOT* 37, no. 2 (2012): 151–165.

happened" question – the exact circumstances of the woman's premature birth are unknown. It is also unclear why she is present during this fight and what her relationship is to these people.[149] Sixth, another "what" question (which is, perhaps, the most relevant to most readers) – the meaning of "premature" is unclear. In the Hebrew text, it is literally "her boys came out," and the word "boy" (*yeled*) is plural here and can refer to a fetus or a young boy.

Is this a case of premature birth (NIV, NASB, NKJV) or a miscarriage (NRSV, MSG)?[150] What is meant by "come out"?[151] Are the babies born alive, indicating a case of premature birth, or are they dead, pointing to a miscarriage? These ambiguities make it difficult to determine whether this law relates to miscarriage – that is, an involuntary abortion. In addition, this case is grouped under personal injury, but it is not clear who is regarded as the injured party: the pregnant woman or her unborn babies? This further complicates the implications of the law.

Since the penalty for causing a woman to lose her unborn "boys" is monetary, this law seems to deal with a fetus that is not yet regarded as a fully developed human being. Therefore, the loss of an unborn fetus is not treated with the same severity as taking the life of a fully developed human being, where the penalty is capital punishment (21:12, 14–15).[152] Although laws relating to pregnant women, miscarriage, and abortion are complex and highly controversial, the famous principle of "life for life, eye for eye" (21:23–25) arises from this law.[153] This principle emphasizes that the punishment should fit the crime.

On 24 June 2022, the United States Supreme Court overturned the historic *Roe v. Wade* ruling of 1973 that guaranteed a woman's right to abortion.

---

149. For possible scenarios of this woman's role in this law based on parallel texts in the Old Testament, see Mukujina, "Literary Solutions to Legal Problems," 157–159.
150. ESV seems to have the most literal translation, "her children come out." The CUV translates it "abortion," whereas the CNV renders it "miscarriage."
151. The verb "come out" usually describes a natural birth of children (Gen 25:25–26; 38:27–30), but in Numbers 12:12, it describes a stillbirth. Elsewhere the Pentateuch refers to miscarriage using the word, *sakal* (Gen 31:38; Exod 23:26). Therefore, "come out" in Exodus 21:22 points to a premature expulsion of the unborn and underdeveloped fetus or child. See D. P. O'Mathuna, "Bodily Injuries, Murder, Manslaughter," in *DOTP*, 93–94.
152. For more on the identity of the fetus and whether the fetus is considered a person, see Russell Fuller, "Exodus 21:22–23: The Miscarriage Interpretation and the Personhood of the Fetus," *JETS* 37, no. 2 (June 1994): 169–184. Fuller surveyed the related ancient Near Eastern Text and the interpretive history of this law and concluded that the evidence points to the miscarriage view rather than premature birth.
153. Traditionally understood as "lex talionis." Hammurabi is the first one who introduced this principle. See Sarna, *Exodus*, 125–127.

Exodus 21:22 is sometimes used in the ongoing debate on pro-life and pro-choice. However, due to the ambiguity of this law, it is problematic to use this verse either to support or oppose contemporary arguments about abortion.

In the diaspora, migrants are subject to the changing laws of their host countries. For example, the overturning of *Roe v. Wade* affects everyone living in the United States. Both Scripture and the law of the United States remain ambiguous regarding what constitutes a human person and at what stage of development a fetus is regarded as a person. Although Exodus 21:22 seems to suggest that a fetus is not a full human being, other passages in Scripture teach otherwise.[154] The one-child policy in China, which was implemented from 1980 to 2015 to address overpopulation, resulted in a very large number of abortions. In Asia, although abortions are performed, these do not typically generate the same level of controversy as in the United States.

21:26–27 Injury of Slaves

This law addresses the injury of a specific body part of a slave, irrespective of gender. While upholding the principle of the punishment fitting the crime, the law also extends the law of retaliation (Latin: *lex talionis*). If a man strikes his slave in the eye, causing permanent damage to it, such a slave – regardless of their gender – must be set free. The same principle applies to other body parts, such as a tooth. In this case, it is not a rigid application of the "eye for eye" principle between two equal parties; instead of equal retribution, the slave receives freedom.

Similar law codes appear in the Laws of Hammurabi (LH):

> LH 116, 196, 197, 198, 199
>
> [116] If the distrainee should die from the effects of a beating or other physical abuse while in the house of her or his distrainer, the owner of the distrainee shall charge and convict his merchant and if (the distrainee is) the man's son, they shall kill his (the distrainer's) son; if the man's slave, he shall weigh and deliver 20 shekels of silver; moreover, he shall forfeit whatever he originally gave as the loan.[155]

---

154. For example, Psalms 51:5; 139:13–18; Jeremiah 1:5. For a helpful discussion on abortion and Exodus 21:22, see Tremper Longman III, *The Bible and the Ballot: Using Scripture in Political Decisions* (Grand Rapids: Eerdmans, 2020), 135–154.

155. A distrainer is one who is forced to satisfy an obligation using distress. A distrainee is one whose property has been seized by way of distraint.

¹⁹⁶ If an *awīlu* should blind the eye of another *awīlu*, they shall blind his eye.¹⁵⁶

¹⁹⁷ If he should break the bone of another *awīlu*, they shall break his bone.

¹⁹⁸ If he should blind the eye of a commoner or break the bone of a commoner, he shall weigh and deliver 60 shekels of silver.

¹⁹⁹ If he should blind the eye of an *awīlu*'s slave or break the bone of an *awīlu*'s slave, he shall weigh and deliver one-half of his value (in silver).¹⁵⁷

Though Hammurabi's law code and the Exodus law code share similarities in their arrangement of the laws, the treatment of affected persons, the conditions in which the physical assault took place, the impact on slaves, and the penalty for fatal cases, the law of retribution in Exodus 21:26–27 reflects a higher ethical standard compared to the "eye for eye" principle.¹⁵⁸

God's concern for the welfare of slaves is strikingly evident in these laws. Given the Israelites' former status as slaves in Egypt, these laws must have resonated deeply with them, emphasizing that God is on the side of the slaves and cares for their well-being. God's intention in establishing these laws was that Israel would emulate God's compassion and justice and demonstrate what it meant to be God's treasure, a kingdom of priests, and a holy nation (Exod 19:6). The inclusion of female slaves (21:20, 26) further reinforces God's concern for the marginalized in society. God's benevolence and justice are reflected in these laws.

21:28–36 Injuries Caused by Goring Oxen

The extensive laws regarding goring oxen indicate that people and oxen shared the same physical space in ancient Israel. These laws bear striking similarities to ancient Near Eastern laws such as the Laws of Eshnunna and the Laws of

---

156. *Awīlu* refers to man or gentleman, and often follows after the word "if." M. E. J. Richardson, *Hammurabi's Laws: Text, Translation and Glossary* (London: T&T Clark, 2004), 156.
157. "The Laws of Hammurabi (2.131)," trans. Martha Roth (*COS*: 343, 348).
158. The ethical principle of "an eye for an eye" aims to achieve a kind of commensurability in dealing with cases of personal injury, yet it is difficult to find the exact compensation that matches the injury. Negotiation between the parties involved becomes a necessary component of ensuring just compensation for the injured party. Herbert B. Huffmon, "'An Eye for An Eye' and Capital Punishment," in *The Oxford Handbook of Biblical Law*, ed. Pamela Barmash (Oxford: Oxford University Press, 2019), 119–123.

Hammurabi with regard to compensation for the harm or loss due to the activities of the ox and the owner's responsibility to ensure the safety of others.[159] Lo's comparative study of the Book of the Covenant in relation to other ancient Near Eastern laws suggests that the narrator's particular interest was cases where oxen gored people, including slaves. While the Laws of Eshnunna (LE 42–47A) and the Code of Hammurabi (LH 253–270) treat the goring ox cases as business and negligence issues, the goring ox laws in Exodus regard them as a physical assault on people, thus reflecting a special concern for protecting human life, including the lives of slaves.[160]

In this section, God outlines several possible scenarios in which the ox and its owner might violate the law and specifies the penalties in each instance. These scenarios consider instances where an ox kills a human, a human kills an ox, and an ox kills another ox. The victims can include men or women, sons or daughters, or slaves. The laws also focus on determining liability.[161] The scenarios considered in these laws are described below:

A. If an ox gores a person and causes their death, the ox will be stoned to death, but the owner will not be punished (21:28).[162]
B. If the owner was aware that the ox had been in the habit of goring but did nothing about it, and the ox then kills another person, both the ox and the owner will face the death penalty.[163] The ox will be stoned, but the owner's method of execution is not specified. However, the owner may redeem his life by paying whatever sum is demanded (21:29–30).
C. The same rule applies in cases where the ox gores a child and the child dies. The owner of the ox will be put to death (21:31), illustrating the "life for life" principle.

---

159. "The Laws of Eshnunna (2.130)," trans. Martha Roth (*COS* 2:335, 349–350).
160. Lo, *The Laws of the Imperialized*, 136–140.
161. Westbrook and Wells, *Everyday Law in Biblical Israel*, 28.
162. This scenario presumes that the owner is unaware or not suspicious that his ox might commit such an act.
163. While the laws of the goring ox bear resemblance to other Ancient Near Eastern laws in considering the awareness of the owner regarding the condition of his ox, ancient Israel's willingness to impose capital punishment on the owner of the ox while allowing compensation is a novelty and a stricter punishment. Herbert B. Huffmon, "'An Eye for An Eye' and Capital Punishment," 125. Laws of Eshnunna (LE 54) and Laws of Hammurabi (LH 251) indicate that if an ox had a habit of goring people, and caused a person's death, then the penalty for the owner was only monetary instead of stoning the ox and putting its owner to death as in Exodus 21:29. Lo, *The Laws of the Imperialized*, 139–140.

D. If the ox gores a slave, whether male or female, the owner must give the master of the slave 30 shekels of silver, which was the cost of a slave at that time. But the ox will be stoned, which indicates that this law regards the life of the slave as equal to that of any other human being (21:32).
E. If anyone opens or digs a pit but leaves it uncovered and an ox or donkey falls into it, that person must make monetary restitution to the owner of the animal, and the dead animal becomes the property of the one who dug the pit (21:33–34).
F. If anyone's ox strikes another person's ox and it dies, both parties must sell the live ox and share the proceeds equally and also divide the dead ox among themselves (21:35).
G. In the above scenario, if the ox had been in the habit of goring and its owner did nothing about it, then the owner must compensate "animal for animal" and take the dead animal in exchange (21:36).

In the twenty-first century, although we may not share our physical space with oxen, many of us have pets, such as cats or dogs. Owners of aggressive dogs are responsible to ensure that their dogs do not hurt other people and are liable if their dogs harm another human being. If a dog has a history of attacking people, the owner must take precautions such as using a strong leash or building a more secure fence to prevent the dog from escaping and harming people.

The laws on personal injuries reflect God's concern for all people, regardless of gender or social status. This is evident in the frequent reference to both genders (21:28, 29, 31, 32) and in God's treatment of slaves as human beings, with both male and female slaves receiving equal treatment (21:26–27, 32). For example, an ox that gored a slave, whether male or female, would be stoned to death (21:32). God's concern for the lives of all human beings, free or slave, is remarkable.

These laws concerning personal injuries emphasize the fact that humans are embodied beings and that harm to any part of the body affects a person's sense of self and well-being. These laws emphasize God's care for human bodies. God created human beings with a body, which is an integral part of our sense of self.[164] Moreover, one's body exists in relation to others' bodies.[165] Thus, bodies distinguish one person from another. This bodily boundary is created by God (Gen 1:26–28) and must be respected by all human beings. Bodies are naturally vulnerable to injury or violation by both internal and external forces – for example, disease or physical assault. Since humans are made in the image of God, intentional injury to another person's body is seen as a direct assault on God's creation.

22:1–15 Laws about Property

These laws are an extension and application of the eighth commandment, "You shall not steal." They safeguard the property of individuals and recognize that property is an extension of a person. Any violation of property rights, whether by theft or damage, threatens personal rights, possessions, and social stability. These laws also recognize that since stealing another's property violates their personal boundaries, protecting a person's property is equivalent to protecting their boundaries. In ancient Israel, a person's property included their animals, servants, and wives. These laws are also linked with the laws concerning personal injuries. Below are various scenarios, including the prescribed restitution and penalties.

A. If anyone steals an ox or a sheep and then slaughters or sells it, they must compensate the owner by giving five oxen for a stolen ox and four sheep for a stolen sheep (22:1).

B. If a thief (22:1) is caught breaking in at night and is struck by the owner of the house and dies, the owner is not guilty of bloodshed. If the incident occurs during the daytime, however, the owner is held responsible for such a death. The underlying rationale for this distinction seems to be that at night, a person, fearing for their own life and that of their family, may strike the thief to death. But in the daytime, the owner would be in a much better position to assess whether the thief really poses a threat. If the owner kills a thief in broad daylight when the thief has no intention of killing anyone, the bloodguilt falls on the owner.

---

164. Stephanie Paulsell, *Honoring the Body: Meditations on a Christian Practice* (San Francisco: Jossey-Bass, 2002), 16.
165. Paulsell, *Honoring the Body*, 22.

C. If someone allows their animal to graze in another person's field, they must compensate the owner from the best of their own field or vineyard (22:5).
D. If a fire breaks out and spreads to thornbushes and destroys the grain or the field, the person who started the fire must make restitution, though there is no mention of the form this restitution is to take (22:6).
E. If someone entrusts their goods to another for safekeeping and the goods are stolen, the thief, if caught, must pay back double. If the thief is not caught, the owner of the house must appear before the judges to settle the matter (22:7–8).[166] The general ruling in verse 9 states that in all cases of illegal possession of another's property, both parties shall appear before the judges[167] to settle the matter.[168] Whoever is found guilty by the judges must pay back double to the other party (22:9). The Hebrew word for "pay back" is derived from the word *shalam* (which means "complete"), from which is derived the word *shalom* (meaning "peace"). Thus, by making restitution, the offender makes peace with the offended and restores their relationship.
F. If someone entrusts their animal or goods to a neighbor for safekeeping and these are subsequently damaged or destroyed, the neighbor must swear an oath before God affirming his innocence and no restitution is made to the owner. However, if the property is stolen, the neighbor must make restitution to the owner. If the animal was torn to pieces by a wild animal, the neighbor must bring the remains as evidence, in which case no restitution is needed (22:10–13).
G. If someone borrows an animal from a neighbor[169] and it is injured or dies in the owner's absence, the borrower must make full restitution. If the owner is present with the animal at the time of the injury

---

166. In Hebrew, "before God." But most translations render "before judges" (NIV, NASB, NKJV). ESV renders "God." The parallel texts about "before judges" appear in Deuteronomy 17:9; 19:17.
167. In Hebrew, "before God."
168. For the discussion on the direct speech declaration "This is it" involved in this judicial scene, see Bartor, *Reading Law as Narrative*, 95–98.
169. "An animal" is not in the text; it is inferred from the context "if it is injured or dies."

or death, then the borrower is not required to make restitution. If the animal was hired, then money paid for the hire covers any loss (22:14–15). This law is about determining whether the borrower's negligence contributed to the animal's injury or death.

While losses involving livestock or property can usually be compensated through material or monetary means, reparation for the loss or harm caused to human lives is a much more complex issue. How does one make reparation for political imprisonment, torture, or genocide?[170]

22:16–23:9 Miscellaneous Laws

This set of laws deal with a variety of areas, including social responsibility and laws concerning one's relationship with God (22:20, 28) and other people, particularly vulnerable and marginalized groups such as virgins, sojourners, and the poor. While not as detailed as the previous section on personal injury laws, this corpus of laws mixes both "if" statements and "do not" statements. Consistent with previous laws, these laws also reflect the two pillars of Confucius's benevolence and justice.

22:16–17 Seducing a Virgin

If a man seduces a virgin who is not yet engaged and has sexual relations with her, he must pay a dowry and marry her.[171] Unlike rape (Deut 22:22–29), seduction involves persuasion or deception rather than coercion.[172] If the woman's father absolutely refuses to accept this arrangement, the man must pay the dowry or "bride-price" for virgins.[173] Since a woman's virginity was highly valued in the ancient Near East, premarital sexual relations diminished her marriage prospects. Since a dowry was usually part of the engagement

---

170. This is a question raised regarding the families of those who receive financial support from the government of the Philippines. These families have members who suffered through President Marcos's dictatorship. Gorospe with Ringma, *Judges: A Pastoral and Contextual Commentary*, 298.
171. A dowry was a gift normally given by a father to his daughter upon her marriage. Its contents often consisted of clothing, jewelry, furniture, kitchen utensils, and personal servants. Though the term for dowry appears only twice in the Old Testament (1 Kgs 9:16; Mic 1:14), many other accounts assume its place. An obvious story is Shechem seducing Dinah and then deciding to marry her (Gen 34). Another example is Caleb's daughter Achsah asked for a field as well as a spring of water from her father upon her marriage to Othniel (Judg 1:14–15). See Chloe Sun, "Dowry and Bride Price," *EBR* 6:1132–1133.
172. Sarna, *Exodus*, 135.
173. The plural use of virgins may refer to the law's application to all virgins.

(Gen 34:12), this law aims to safeguard both the social and economic standing of women.[174]

22:18 Sorceress

"Do not allow a sorceress to live" (22:18). A sorceress is someone who practices magic, and the use of the feminine form of this word presupposes that those who practiced sorcery were mostly women. However, there were also male sorcerers – for example, Pharaoh's sorcerers (7:11) – as well as wise men and magicians.[175] The severity of the punishment underscores God's abhorrence of manipulating the spiritual realm for human gain. The link between this law and the previous one about seducing a virgin may lie in the common method of persuasion through deception.

In many parts of Asia, people practice fortune-telling or other forms of magic in an attempt to predict someone's fate by examining palm prints or analyzing a person's genealogy. There are even calendars that contain auspicious and inauspicious days for the year. God strongly condemns any form of sorcery because it contradicts trusting in God for one's future.

22:19 Bestiality

"Anyone who has sexual relations with an animal is to be put to death" (22:19). It is considered unnatural for people to engage in sexual relations with animals, as also emphasized in Leviticus: "Do not have sexual relations with an animal and defile yourself with it. A woman must not present herself to an animal to have sexual relations with it; that is a perversion" (Lev 18:23).[176] God created human beings in God's image and animals according to their own kinds. Going against God's created order is a direct challenge to God's sovereignty and his intention for his creation. In Scripture, going against God's design often leads to alienation from God.

---

174. Tigay, "Exodus," 148.
175. These sorcerers are male in Exodus 7:11.
176. Compare Deuteronomy 27:19, "Cursed is anyone who has sexual relations with any animal."

22:20 Idolatry

"Whoever sacrifices to any god other than the LORD must be destroyed" (22:20) – or "put under the ban."[177] This law echoes the first commandment and stipulates a penalty for those who violate it.

22:21–24 Vulnerable Groups

God's concern for vulnerable groups in society is a unique feature of the Book of the Covenant, setting it apart from other ancient Near Eastern laws. This divine concern invites our thoughtful reflection.[178]

This law is aimed at protecting vulnerable members of society, including sojourners, widows, and orphans. A sojourner (*ger*) is understood as a "foreigner" (NIV) or "stranger" (NASB). Moses describes himself as a *ger* in Midian and names his firstborn son Gershom, reflecting his status as a sojourner in Egypt.[179] The same word "oppress" that was used to describe the Egyptians' oppression of the Israelites (Exod 3:9) is repeated in God's command to Israel, "Do not mistreat or oppress a foreigner" (22:21). God warns Israel not to repeat the injustice that was done to them and then gives them a reason, traditionally known as a motive clause, for this command: "for you were foreigners [in Hebrew, *gerim*, plural of *ger*] in Egypt" (22:21). This appeal to their shared experience of being foreigners adds an empathetic dimension that encourages Israel to obey this law.[180]

Not only does Moses experience the plight of being a *ger*, but the Israelites as a collective body also experience this identity. Their former identity as an

---

[177]. The word "put under a ban" (*kharam*) applies to things that are devoted to God, whether for good or for destruction. It is used in the context of Israel's warfare (1 Sam 15:3) and ritual sacrifice of animals (Lev 27:28–29). It appears first here in the Old Testament. The *kharem* texts are troublesome for readers due to their close association with the act of genocide. We need to bear in mind that these texts appear in the earlier phase of Israel's history, and we need to bring these texts into conversation with God's ultimate goal for creation – a shalom vision. See Schlimm, *This Strange and Sacred Scripture*, 79–81.

[178]. From a postcolonial lens, two primary responses to domination are rejection and subversion – the outright rejection of the dominant party or a subtle resistance through subversion in the form of rewriting or reinterpreting law. If the Book of the Covenant is dependent on Hammurabi's Law, then the writer of the Exodus may use the concern for the sojourner as a way to subvert Israel's identity as one who used to be a sojourner in Egypt but now becomes a hybrid reality – one who shares both similarities with the dominant host and retains differences from it. Drawing from William Morrow's study, Wright, *Inventing God's Law*, 350–352. William S. Morrow, "Resistance and Hybridity in Late Bronze Age Canaan," *RB* 115 (2008): 321–339.

[179]. See my commentary on the social status of *ger* in Exodus 2.

[180]. Thomas Kazen, *Emotions in Biblical Law: A Cognitive Science Approach*, HBM 36 (Sheffield: Sheffield Phoenix, 2011), 99.

oppressed people should motivate them to treat vulnerable people with kindness (*rēn*). Therefore, God exhorts his people not to be like the Egyptians, who treated the Israelites – the foreigners in their midst – harshly. God reminds the Israelites of their former oppressed state and calls them to live in accordance with their new identity by treating vulnerable groups in their midst with kindness. The Israelites are specifically instructed not to take advantage of [*ʿnh*] or "afflict" (RSV) any widow or orphan (22:22).[181] The word "afflict" [*ʿnh*] is also used to describe the Egyptians' affliction of the Israelites (Exod 1:11). God also warns that if they do afflict these vulnerable groups, God will hear the cry of the afflicted and respond with anger against the oppressors, killing them with the sword and leaving their wives widowed and their children fatherless. God applies the "measure for measure" principle, executing poetic justice.

The NT portrays Jesus as identifying with the vulnerable in society. He taught that giving even a cup of cold water to the least in society is like welcoming Jesus himself and declared that such a person will not lose their divine reward (Matt 10:42).

---

181. Widows are vulnerable in many societies across cultures. For example, in India, the attitude toward widows is generally negative. A widow is expected to spend the rest of her life in mourning for her deceased husband and is forbidden from wearing jewelry. Some widows are blamed for the death of their husbands while others are stripped of having an identity by being perceived as an "it." Havilah Dharamraj, *Ruth: A Pastoral and Contextual Commentary*, ABCS (Carlisle: Langham Global Library, 2019), 47–48.

LAW AND IMMIGRATION IN THE UNITED STATES

The inclusion of sojourners in biblical laws reflects God's deep concern for this marginalized group. These people hold a special place in God's heart. Despite being deprived of a kinship network and land ownership, these laws include them alongside the Israelites to enjoy the Sabbath (Exod 20:10), the Passover (Exod 12:48–49), and other festivals (Deut 16:11, 14; 26:11). God intends that Israel should treat sojourners as part of God's family, thereby reflecting God's heart for the vulnerable and the underprivileged. The absence of similar provisions relating to sojourners in other ancient Near Eastern law codes further highlights the distinction between God and other deities.

The patriarchs of Israel were themselves sojourners (Gen 12:10; 20:1; 21:23; 23:4; 26:3), and the Israelites lived as sojourners in Egypt (Gen 15:13). Moses himself experienced life as a sojourner while in Midian (Exod 2:22). When God commands Israel to show kindness and mercy to the sojourners in their midst, he expects them to remember their own identity as sojourners. This identity shapes who they are as God's people (Exod 22:21; 23:9) and influences their treatment of others. Similarly, as Christians, we recognize that this world is not our permanent home. In this sense, we are all sojourners, anticipating our eternal home with God in heaven.

Terms like migration, immigration, and illegal immigrants are commonly used to refer to the diasporans. In the United States, for example, immigration is a contentious issue. Some people support immigration and advocate for allowing those who cross the border to stay in the country, while others strongly oppose letting outsiders become part of the United States.[1] Both groups have their reasons, but the biblical mandate for Christians leans toward welcoming strangers. Several questions arise: Can we allow everyone who wants to come to the United States to do so? Do governmental agencies have the necessary resources, and does the country have the capacity to accommodate all migrants? On what basis should we grant immigrant status or offer asylum? Is poverty a valid reason for granting asylum? How should we handle cases where people lie about their reasons for crossing the border? What about those who patiently wait to enter the United States through the proper channels? Will the time and effort expended on dealing with border crossings delay the process for those who follow the proper procedures to obtain immigrant status?

> The immigration issue is not as black and white as it may appear and requires ongoing reflection, legislation, and engagement.[2] The Relational-Theological Model – which considers how God treats sojourners in the Bible and commands Israel to treat sojourners in their midst with kindness because they themselves were once sojourners – addresses both relational and theological aspects and sheds light on how Christians should respond to the immigration issue.

---

1. For legislation related to immigration in the United States, see Tan, *Introducing Asian American Theologies*, 177–178.
2. For more on the teaching of hospitality and welcoming strangers in the Bible and its implications for contemporary immigration and legislation, see Carroll, *Christians at the Border*, 103–135. For the expanded version of biblical teachings related to immigration, see M. Daniel Carroll R. *The Bible and Borders: Hearing God's Word on Immigration* (Grand Rapids: Brazos, 2020). For reflection and assessment of three major models of migration (the Hospitality Model, the Legal Model, and the Relational Model) and his "vocational" approach to migration, see Leopoldo A. Sánchez M., "Theological Approaches to Migration: Their Impact on Missional Thinking and Action," in *Migration, Transnationalism, and Faith in Missiological Perspective: Los Angeles as a Global Crossroads*, eds. Kirsteen Kim and Alexia Salvatierra (Lanham: Lexington, 2022), 177–194.

22:25–27 The Poor

The poor and needy are those who are economically deprived and lack the resources to survive. This includes former slaves who were sold into poverty, those who had incurred debt, and those born into dire circumstances. When such poor people need help, the Israelites must help them because these people are also "his people" (22:25). In Hebrew, the word for poor is *'oni*, which means "the afflicted." The laws concerning the poor reflect God's "soft spot" for these people and his expectation that those who have the means – the "haves" – would help these "have-nots." In God's economy, the disparity between the rich and poor can be reduced if the "haves" show sensitivity and compassion to the "have-nots" by acting to meet their needs.

Concrete actions that demonstrate compassion include lending money without charging interest (22:25). God commands the Israelites not to become creditors of the poor.[182] The emphasis on the cloak as the "only" covering, along with the rhetorical question "What else can they sleep in?" (22:27a), further encourages the "haves" to see reality from the point of view of the poor and act with compassion toward the "have-nots."[183] God also warns that if the poor cry out to him, he will hear them because, as he says, "I am compassionate" (22:27b). God's compassion (*khanun*) is ingrained in his nature. This same compassion will later be revealed, after the golden calf incident, when God proclaims his name: "The LORD, the LORD, the compassionate and gracious [*khanun*] God" (Exod 34:6).

22:28 Cursing God or Rulers

In the command not to curse God – with the NIV rendering this "Do not blaspheme God" (22:28) – the same word *qalal* (meaning "curse") is used to describe cursing one's parents (21:17). The word itself means to make light of or to despise. This law serves as an extension and application of the third commandment, "You shall not misuse the name of the LORD your God" (20:7), which exhorts Israel to represent God rightly by not making light of God. In the second part of the verse, which forbids the Israelites to "curse the ruler of your people," a different word Hebrew for "curse" is used – '*rar*, which contrasts with the idea of blessing. A ruler (*nasi*) is someone who has authority over the people. This title is derived from a root word meaning "lifting up" or "carrying," indicating that leaders should be respected because they bear greater responsibility. In the OT, Abraham is recognized as a ruler by outsiders (Gen 23:6). In the wilderness account, there are rulers among the Israelites (Exod 16:22).

22:29a Do Not Hold Back Offerings

This law simply states that one should not delay in offering one's produce to God. No further explanation is given. Perhaps the emphasis on not delaying is because postponing the offering might lead to the temptation not to make an offering at all.

---

182. The law in Deuteronomy distinguishes foreigners from the Israelites. It commands Israel not to charge interest to their brothers, but it says they can do so to foreigners (Deut 23:19–20). Various laws are legislated to protect the rights of the poor, including lending graciously (Deut 15:7–8; Prov 14:21).
183. A parallel text of Exodus 22:26–27 is found in Deuteronomy 24:10–13, where Moses adds a motive clause for Israel to obey this law: "And it will be regarded as a righteous act in the sight of the LORD your God" (Deut 24:13).

Exodus 19–24

22:29b–30 Offer the Firstborn

This law serves as a reminder of what God had previously commanded Israel, echoing the statement "The first offspring of every womb among the Israelites belongs to me" (Exod 13:2). The term "firstborn" includes not only sons but also oxen and sheep. God also adds a new requirement, specifying that the animal must remain with its mother for seven days and then be offered to God on the eighth day. This command is new in Exodus but will appear again in Leviticus (Lev 22:27) and applies similarly to the circumcision of newborn babies (Lev 12:3). God's compassion extends to the animal world, reflecting his concern for all of creation.

22:31 Dietary Law

The basis of this law is holiness. Since God has set Israel apart as a holy nation, this holiness must also be demonstrated in what they eat. The law prohibits eating meat that has been torn to pieces in the field and instructs the people to throw such meat at the dogs. Leviticus makes it clear that animals "torn by wild beasts" are considered unclean (Lev 22:8). Jewish dietary laws distinguish between kosher (meaning "fit" or "proper") meat and non-kosher meat, with kosher meat referring to meat that is cut properly.[184] In the OT, dogs often symbolize lowly, unclean, wild, and potentially dangerous animals.[185]

Food is associated with the body. Since what a person eats enters the body, their dietary choices reflect their care for the body. Mary Douglas's understanding of clean and unclean food is helpful. She proposes that Israel's dietary laws follow the pattern of creation, in which there are three divisions – earth, water, and air. According to this view, an unclean animal does not fit completely into any of these categories, symbolizing falling short of being complete or holy.[186] Ko Ming Him reminds us that unclean food should not be viewed as morally unclean. The dietary laws are only intended to protect the body from ritual impurities and have nothing to do with people's moral

---

184. Tigay, "Exodus," 149.
185. See for example, 1 Samuel 17:43; 24:14; 2 Samuel 9:8; 16:9; 1 Kings 14:11; 16:4; 2 Kings 8:13; Psalms 22:16, 20; 59:6, 14; Proverbs 26:11; Ecclesiastes 9:4; Job 30:1; and Tobit 6.2 and 11:4, which reflect that dogs were regarded as sheepdogs, travel companions, and guardians. See Geoffrey David Miller, "Attitudes toward Dogs in Ancient Israel: A Reassessment," *JSOT* 32, no. 4 (2008): 487–500. Dogs are attested in Akkadian, Phoenician, Ugaritic, Arabic, Aramaic, Syriac, and Ethiopian texts. For more on the origin and lexical meanings of the dogs in the Old Testament and the ancient Near East, see D. Winton Thomas, "Keleb Dog: Its Origin and Some Usages of It in the Old Testament," *VT* 10, no. 4 (Oct 1960): 410–427.
186. Douglas, *Purity and Danger*, 67.

condition. By refraining from eating unclean food, people demonstrate their commitment to God's holiness and their covenantal relationship with him.[187]

23:1–3 Justice in Court[188]

Exodus 23:1–3 and 6–8 are situated in the context of the court of law and align with the ninth commandment, "Do not bear false witness" (Exod 20:16). These laws elaborate on what it means to bear false witness – for example, spreading false reports, conspiring with wicked individuals to provide false testimony, following the crowd[189] in doing evil, perverting justice by siding with the majority, and showing favoritism toward the poor. This law warns that while the crowd represents the majority, the majority is not always right. The law commands Israel to speak truthfully and remain impartial in a court of law, especially when dealing with the poor in a lawsuit.[190] Though the penalty for perverting justice is not stated, Proverbs teaches us that "a false witness will not go unpunished, and whoever pours out lies will not go free" (19:5).

23:4–5 Animals Belonging to Enemies

"Love your enemies" is not merely an NT teaching. In this law, God instructs Israel on how to treat their enemies by showing care for the enemy's animals, especially those used for transportation and carrying goods. This law presents two hypothetical scenarios. First, "If you come across your enemy's ox or donkey wandering off, be sure to return it" (23:4),[191] with the emphatic "return" stressing what Israel must do. Second, "If you see the donkey of someone who hates you fallen down under its load, do not leave it there; be sure to help them with it" (23:5). This portrays two people working together to lift the heavy load off the donkey to release it from its suffering.[192] These laws call on the Israelites to relieve the distress of animals belonging to an enemy.[193] Here, God acts as an animal advocate, guarding animal rights through the compassion

---

187. Ko Ming Him, *Leviticus: A Pastoral and Contextual Commentary*, ABCS (Carlisle: Langham Global Library, 2018), 106. For more on the dietary laws, see Him, *Leviticus*, 107–114.
188. The parallel text of Exodus 23:1–9 is found in Deuteronomy 10:17–18.
189. Literally, "many men."
190. The word "poor" (*dal*) in 23:3 is a different word from 22:25. It refers to people who are low, weak, and poor. It often appears in wisdom books and poetry. *BDB*, 195.
191. In Deuteronomy 4:1–4, the same law applies not to one's enemy, but to one's brother.
192. Compare Deuteronomy 22:4.
193. Bartor, *Reading Law as Narrative*, 166.

shown by his people and demonstrating that enmity between human beings should not affect the well-being of innocent animals.[194]

23:6–7 Social Justice

Exodus 23:3 commands Israel not to show partiality to the poor in legal disputes. However, since the poor and the needy are easily exploited in court, the law in Exodus 23:6–7 emphasizes the importance of upholding justice and protecting the rights of the needy by prohibiting the perversion of justice in legal disputes. Verse 7 reiterates this principle by forbidding the killing of the innocent and emphasizing that God will not acquit the guilty, thereby reinforcing the sixth commandment, "You shall not murder."

23:8 Do Not Take Bribes

This law prohibits Israel from accepting bribes because "a bribe blinds those who see and twists the words of the innocent" (23:8).[195] A bribe, by definition, involves offering money or favors to influence the judgment or conduct of a person in a position of trust.[196] The Book of Proverbs contains many teachings about the destructive consequences of accepting bribes (15:27; 17:8, 23). Although this law does not describe the specific forms that bribes can take, bribes may include money, gifts, favors, or promises to advance personal interests or careers. In some Asian cultures, bribery is a common practice in both the marketplace and social networks. Sometimes, it is difficult to distinguish between bribes and gifts, and the context and motivation of both the giver and the receiver should be carefully considered in each case.[197]

23:9 Do Not Oppress Sojourners

This law echoes Exodus 22:21 with minor variations. Here, the motive clause focuses not only on the identity of the "foreigner" or sojourner but also on the feelings associated with being a sojourner (*ger*). The reason Israel is to follow this law is emphasized by the affective dimension, expressed in the clause "you yourselves know how it feels to be a foreigner." The phrase "how

---

194. Compare Exodus 23:19b.
195. Compare Deuteronomy 10:17; 16:19.
196. "Bribe," in Merriam Webster's Dictionary. https://www.merriam-webster.com/dictionary/bribe.
197. For a detailed study on bribes, see Peter H. W. Lau, "Kinship, Patronage, and Corruption," in *Exploring the Old Testament in Asia: Evangelical Perspectives*, eds. Jerry Hwang and Angukali Rotokha (Carlisle: Langham Global Library, 2022), 216–223.

it feels" is literally "the soul (*nephesh*) of the foreigner," which involves one's inner core, the whole being and emotions. In the Chinese Union Version, this clause is translated as "because you know the heart of being a sojourner." The emphatic use of "you" further adds to the performative force of God's plea. This law reinforces the Israelites' identity as former sojourners in Egypt and now as God's chosen people.

23:10–13 Additional Sabbath Regulations

These laws are an extension of the fourth commandment regarding the Sabbath, with specific applications related to the land. While the fourth commandment mentions "animals," these laws refer specifically to "your ox and your donkey," which were commonly used for carrying loads and transportation in ancient times. Once again, the six-seven formula applies to these laws on Sabbath observance.

23:10–11 Land

Israel is instructed to cultivate their land for six years, but in the seventh year, they must let it lie unplowed and unused. This command not only serves to give the land a period of rest but also provides for the poor among the Israelites.[198] Whatever remains after the poor have gathered may be left for the wild animals in the field. This principle also applies to their vineyards and olive groves.

God's concern for the poor demonstrates that this group of people is always on his mind.[199] The land, being the shared space occupied by both people and animals, affects human livelihood and ecology. The pattern of work and rest is deeply ingrained in the fabric of life on this planet. In contemporary pastoral contexts, while some churches have established sabbatical systems for their pastors, other churches oppose this idea because it is not specifically mandated by biblical law. The application of Sabbath laws varies widely across cultures and countries. While the letter of the biblical law applies only to ancient Israel, the spirit of the law is timeless. We must thoughtfully discern the spirit of the law and apply it wisely in contexts that differ from ancient Israel. Since there

---

198. A different word for poor (*'ebeyon*) is used here. It can be translated as needy, someone in want. The three different words for the poor (Exod 22:25; 23:6, 11) reflect the persistence of their existence in the Israelite community and God's concern for them.
199. God reminds Israel that the poor will always be present in their land (Deut 15:7–11; Matt 26:11).

is both continuity and discontinuity in biblical laws, discretion and wisdom are required in applying these laws.[200]

23:12 People and Animals

In the fourth commandment, the rationale for observing the Sabbath is based on God's creational pattern. Since God made the heavens and the earth in six days and rested on the seventh day, consecrating it as holy, Israel is commanded to follow this pattern. In the Book of the Covenant, the reason for ceasing from work on the seventh day centers on rest and refreshment.[201] Three words are used to describe this state of renewal: Sabbath, rest, and refreshment. The idea of the Sabbath (*shabbat*) is to cease work, rest (*nuakh*) often connotes physical rest from labor, and refreshment (*napash*) comes from the word "soul" and "life," pointing to a renewed life. In the Chinese New Version, the word "refresh" is translated as "to take a little break" (*chuān xī yí xià*), which aptly captures the essence of the word.

What is notable about this Sabbath command is that it expands the Sabbath command found in the Ten Commandments. While Exodus 20:10 includes animals or livestock (*behemah*), Exodus 23:12 refers specifically to "ox" and "donkey" and adds the concept of "refreshment." This highlights the emphasis God places on the act of rest, which includes both people and animals, reflecting a divinely ordained "creation-inclusive theology."[202]

23:13 Additional Laws about Misusing God's Name

In Exodus 23:13, God urges Israel to be vigilant and forbids them to invoke the names of other gods. This echoes the first and third commandments, forming a fitting conclusion to this section of the law. By reminding Israel that he alone is their God, God expects Israel to follow his instructions as a way of reflecting their new identity as the people of God.

---

200. For more on the application of Old Testament law, see Gane, *Old Testament Law for Christians*, 137–218.
201. The motivation for the sabbath command in Deuteronomy is grounded in God's deliverance. See Deuteronomy 5:12–15.
202. A. Rahel Schafer, "Rest for the Animals? Nonhuman Sabbath Repose in Pentateuchal Law," *BBR* 23, no. 2 (2013): 185. Schafer surveyed four texts concerning the sabbath for animals (Exod 20:8–11; Exod 23:10–12; Deut 5:12–15; Lev 25:2–7) and discovered a progressive expansion of these texts. The table on page 171 of her article summarizes these expansions helpfully. Shafer states: "Exod 20 defines animal Sabbath rest; Deut 5 expands the motivation for Sabbath rest; Lev 25 expands the scope of Sabbath rest; and Exod 23 expands the definition, scope, and motivation." Schafer, "Rest for the Animals?" 170.

23:14–19 Laws about Festivals

This section of the law focuses on the significance of three national festivals (Festival of Unleavened Bread, Festival of Harvest, and Festival of Ingathering). Celebrating and observing these festivals is a way to reinforce group identity, whether ethnic, national, or religious identity. By participating in these celebrations, Israel preserves a sense of common heritage and strengthens the interconnectedness among households and social obligations.[203] Similarly, as already noted in relation to the Passover text, observing ethnic festivals in foreign lands is a way for people in the diaspora to forge common ethnic bonds. Practicing the same observances in different geographical locations fosters a sense of togetherness and helps individuals to cope with the stress and alienation of living in the diaspora. Often, those living in diasporic conditions observe both the festivals of the host country and those of their country of origin. Those who have lived in different countries for several years may celebrate the festivals of all the places where they have resided.

God commands Israel to celebrate three national festivals with a specific purpose: "to me" (23:14). These festivals are pilgrim festivals, which were later to be celebrated in Jerusalem. Their observance is intended not only to strengthen the pilgrims' ethnic and national identity but also to remind Israel of who they are and whose they are. Celebrating these festivals to God would strengthen their relationship with God. In addition, these festivals revolve around Israel's harvests and are characterized by feasting to celebrate God's goodness.[204] These three festivals are described in the sections below.

23:15 The Festival of Unleavened Bread

The origin of this festival dates back to the Passover event (Exod 12:14–20). When the Israelites left Egypt in haste, they ate unleavened bread, symbolizing that fateful night when God rescued them from Egypt. God commanded Israel to eat unleavened bread for seven days,[205] and the month of Abib (March–April) became the first month in Israel's calendar (12:1–2).[206] Abib means barley. The month marks the beginning of the barley harvest.[207] By rearranging the calendar, God established a new identity for Israel, emphasizing that

---

203. Meyers, "The Family in Early Israel," in *Families in Ancient Israel*, 40.
204. LeFebvre, *The Liturgy of Creation*, 52.
205. In the month of Abib 14, the Israelites celebrated the Passover. In the month of Abib 15–21, the Israelites observed the Feast of Unleavened Bread. See Leviticus 23:4–6.
206. After the Babylonian exile, this month is named Nisan. Compare Esther 3:7.
207. LeFebvre, *The Liturgy of Creation*, 40.

they were God's redeemed people. The command not to appear before God empty-handed resonates with Asian culture, where it is customary to bring a gift as a sign of respect and friendship. In Israel's context, this custom reflects respect for God.

23:16a The Festival of Harvest

This feast is also referred to as the "festival of weeks" (Exod 34:22).[208] It is celebrated on the fifteenth day of the seventh month (Lev 23:39), corresponding to September–October in our contemporary calendar. The feast marks the beginning of the wheat harvest and is celebrated for seven days, during which no regular work is permitted (Num 28:26). Among the Jewish people, this feast is called *Shavuot*, meaning "weeks" – which refers to the seven-week period leading up to the festival that culminates in Pentecost (Deut 16:9–12). Traditionally, this period – usually from late April to early June – is understood as the time it took for the Israelites to journey from Egypt to Sinai.[209]

23:16b–17 The Festival of Ingathering

This feast takes place at the end of the agricultural year when Israel gathers the fruit of their labors, typically in May–June of our contemporary calendar. It is also known as the Feast of Booths or Sukkot in the Jewish tradition, with Sukkot meaning "tents" or "booths." During the seven days of the feast, people would live in booths to remember how God had brought Israel out of Egypt (Lev 23:42–43). This festival is considered the most joyous time of the agricultural year; people would take leafy branches from palm trees and willow trees and rejoice before God (Lev 23:40).

These three festivals are spread throughout the calendar year for the males of Israel to observe (23:17).

Table 9: Israel's Festivals and When They Were Celebrated

Festival	Time of the year
The Festival of Unleavened Bread	March–April
The Festival of Ingathering	May–June
The Festival of Harvest	September–October

---

208. The festival is named the "Festival of Weeks" because it begins seven weeks after the firstfruit of barley is offered (Lev 23:15–16). LeFebvre, *The Liturgy of Creation*, 43.
209. Dharamraj, *Ruth: A Pastoral and Contextual Commentary*, 6, 73.

Israelite males are required to present themselves before God as a regular reminder of who they are and whose they are. The exclusion of women and children from these festival observances was probably due to the difficulties of travel in ancient times.

23:18–19 Purity of the Sacrifices

The laws in Exodus 23:18–19 may appear random at first glance, but they are related to the festival observances discussed in the previous section (23:14–17), and they emphasize how sacrifices should be offered. These two sections are linked by several factors, including the prohibition of leavened bread, the instructions regarding festival offerings, the offering of choice fruits, and the humane treatment of animals. The prohibition against eating leavened bread also being mentioned in Exodus 12:8. In addition, the fat from the animal sacrifice must be burned and not eaten (Lev 3:17; 7:23). The law on offering the best of the firstfruits is rooted in the belief that the firstborn belongs to God (Exod 34:19).[210] The command not to "cook a young goat in its mother's milk" (23:19) reflects God's concern for humane treatment in relation to animal sacrifices, as also seen in the law requiring the firstborn oxen and sheep to remain with their mother for seven days before being offered to God (22:30).[211] This humanitarian concern emphasizes God's desire that his people uphold the created order and design.

Although the Book of the Covenant shares similarities with ancient Near Eastern law codes, it is distinguished by several factors: the exclusive worship of one God, the prohibition of idolatry, the observance of the Sabbath, and the treatment of vulnerable groups in society. These distinctions are consistently present throughout the Book of the Covenant, as shown in the following table:

---

210. As early as Exodus 13:2, God commands Israel to offer their firstborn, whether sons or animals. The offering of first fruits is an extension of the law.
211. Compare Exodus 34:26; Deuteronomy 14:21. This law appears three times in the Pentateuch.

Table 10: The Distinctive Laws in the Book of the Covenant

Exodus 20:23	No idolatry
Exodus 21:1–11	Slavery laws
Exodus 21:12–36	Personal injury laws
Exodus 22:20	No idolatry
Exodus 22:21–27; 23:9	Vulnerable groups
Exodus 23:10–12	Sabbath mandate
Exodus 21:22, 26, 28; 22:16	Women's rights

The emphasis on the worship of one God and the prohibition of idolatry distinguishes Israel's faith from the polytheistic and pluralistic worldviews of its neighbors. This exclusive worship of one God is rooted in the narrative of God's rescue of Israel from Egypt to make them his own treasure (Exod 20:2). The Sabbath observance, which encompasses both human beings – including slaves and other vulnerable groups – and animals, distinguishes God's ideal from the practices of the Egyptian regime. The safeguarding of the rights and interests of vulnerable groups highlights God's compassion and justice, and God commands Israel to emulate God's concerns for these groups. The laws protecting the rights of women – including slave women, pregnant women, and virgins – further illustrate God's heart (*rén* and *yi*) for the vulnerable in society.

23:20–33 Closing of the Book of the Covenant

Exodus 23:20–33 functions as the concluding narrative for the Book of the Covenant, following the pattern of traditional covenant treaties that often end with a section on blessings and curses. While this closing section includes both warnings and promises, the greater space devoted to warnings reflects God's concern about whether or not Israel would obey God's words. However, the inclusion of specific blessings demonstrates God's benevolence and his desire to bless rather than to curse. The focus of the narrative is on the land that Israel is about to enter and on the worship of God rather than the gods of the land. In this sense, the Book of the Covenant echoes the first commandment, "You shall have no other gods before me," recognizing it as the driving force behind every other law.

The conclusion begins with the word "behold" or "look," directing the audience's attention to what follows. God promises to send an angel to go before Israel on their journey and bring them to the place God had prepared for them – the land of Canaan, the promised land. This angel first appears in the burning bush (Exod 3:2) and later accompanies Israel on their wilderness journey (14:19). Some view this angel as the pre-incarnate Christ, while others see him as a messenger or the Messenger of God (see Gen 32:24–32).[212] God's statement "My Name is in him" (23:21) suggests that God identifies with this angel; yet God maintains his own distinct identity – almost as if this angel is God's doppelganger. Since seeing this angel is akin to seeing God.[213] God exhorts Israel to obey the voice of the angel. If Israel obeys, God promises to do the following,

1. God will be an enemy to Israel's enemies (23:22).
2. God's angel will bring Israel to the land of the Amorites, Hittites, Perizzites, Canaanites, Hivites, and Jebusites, and God will wipe out these nations (23:23).[214]
3. God will bless their food and water and remove sickness from their midst (23:24–25).
4. God will ensure that no one will miscarry or be barren (23:26a).
5. God will grant the Israelites a full life span (23:26b).
6. God will defeat Israel's enemies (23:27).
7. God will send hornets to drive out the Hivites, Canaanites, and Hittites (23:28). Further details on how God will do this are also given (23:29–30), demonstrating that God has a plan of action in place.
8. God will define Israel's boundaries and deliver the inhabitants of the land into their hands, enabling Israel to drive them out. Divine and human initiatives will work together to accomplish God's promise of the land.

This narrative of conquest – with the violence described in Exodus 23:23–24, 27–28 – can be misinterpreted and misapplied in different cultural

---

212. See, for example, Walter Kaiser, Jr., *The Messiah in the Old Testament; Studies in Old Testament Biblical Theology* (Grand Rapids: Zondervan, 1995), 228. Dozeman uses an upper case "m" to designate this Messenger, understanding him as associated with the divine. Dozeman, *Exodus*, 555.
213. Compare Genesis 32:24–32.
214. "Wipe them out" (NIV) is literally "efface them," to erase them and to make them disappear from the face of the earth. This is the first mention of the Israelites' treatment of the Canaanites. As the story unfolds, the extermination of the Canaanites will be a gradual process. See Table 1 in Trimm, *The Destruction of the Canaanites*, 43.

contexts. For example, Naga nationalists in India identified themselves as the people of God – just as the Israelites were God's chosen people in the Bible – and alluded to the biblical conquest narratives to assert their distinct identity and political independence from the Hindu-majority India and justify their claim to land with the use of military force.[215] Therefore, readers must critically examine the appropriation of a biblical text, asking this question: What did it mean for the people of the time, and what does it mean for us today in different cultural and political contexts?

The Book of the Covenant concludes by reiterating the prohibition of idolatry, echoing the first commandment. It then provides a theological rationale for worshiping God alone and argues that making a covenant with the inhabitants of the land would cause Israel to sin against God and serving other gods would become a trap for them (23:32–33). The repeated use of the imperative "do not" in the last two verses emphasizes how urgent and important it is that Israel remain faithful to God. The warning against idolatry reflects God's concern about Israel's future. The promise of blessings and the warning of curses operate based on Israel's response of obedience or disobedience – if they obey, they will be blessed; if they disobey, they will experience the curses.

This in-between space has Egypt on one end and Canaan on the other. Israel must not call these places home or emulate the practices of the inhabitants of these places. Instead, the LORD God is to be Israel's chosen portion since it is he who rescued them from Egypt and gave them a new identity and laws to follow. As God says to Moses in Leviticus:

> Speak to the Israelites and say to them: "I am the LORD your God. You must not do as they do in Egypt, where you used to live, and you must not do as they do in the land of Canaan, where I am bringing you. Do not follow their practices. You must obey my laws and be careful to follow my decrees. I am the LORD your God." (Lev 18:2–4)

"I am the LORD your God" defines the God-Israel relationship. The laws, as given in both the Ten Commandments and the Book of the Covenant, reflect God's holiness and ethical ideals for Israel. By obeying these laws, Israel

---

215. Angukali Rotokha, "Exodus and Liberation: Naga Nationalism and the People of God," in *Exploring the Old Testament in Asia: Evangelical Perspectives*, eds. Jerry Hwang and Angukali Rotokha (Carlisle: Langham Global Library, 2022), 197–198.

learned how to become a holy nation and a kingdom of priests. Therefore, the practice or neglect of these laws contributes to Israel's identity construction.

While the laws and their remedies address the symptoms of sin, they cannot eradicate the inherent sinful nature of human beings. Understanding law-giving in a liminal context allows us to interpret these laws realistically. On the one hand, they express God's ethical ideals for his people. On the other hand, every named offense points to the fallen nature of Israel and the fallen world in which they lived. The law was given because of people's transgressions (Gal 3:19). Therefore, the law is transitional; the ultimate solution is Christ alone. As the apostle Paul explains, the law functions as a guardian (*paidagogos* – literally, "babysitter") to lead people to Christ (Gal 3:24). Jesus came not to abolish the law but to fulfill it (Matt 5:17). Only by believing in Christ can we become a new creation (2 Cor 5:17). The journey of identity formation continues – for Israel, in the past, and for us, in the present. This journey of knowing oneself is always a journey of becoming.

24:1–18 COVENANT-MAKING AT SINAI

How do we make a document or contract official? Many cultures would put the agreement in writing and have both parties sign the document to formalize the terms of the agreement. By signing the contract, the parties symbolically put into effect the agreement. The Sinai Covenant follows the pattern of ancient treaties between a suzerain and a vassal, which typically concluded with the vassal's acceptance of the agreement. In Exodus 19:8, the Israelites respond to God's covenant with a verbal agreement: "We will do everything the LORD has said." In chapter 24, they respond in a similar manner (24:3, 7), with Moses facilitating the official covenant ceremony. Exodus 19 and Exodus 24 – which function as bookends – contain seven occurrences of three key verbs: "speak" (*dabar*), "go down" (*yarad*), and "go up" (*'alah*).[216]

Table 11: The Relationship between Covenant Initiation and Covenant

Chapter 19	Chapters 20–23	Chapter 24
Covenant Initiation	The Ten Commandments and The Book of the Covenant	Covenant Ratification

---

216. Sarna, *Exodus*, 150.

Exodus 19–24

RATIFICATION

In both chapters 19 and 24, the setting is Mount Sinai, where God speaks to Moses on the summit, the elders gather in the middle, and the people of Israel congregate at the foot of the mountain. Moses once again acts as the mediator between God and Israel, receiving God's word and communicating it to the people. His repeated ascents and descents from Mount Sinai demonstrate his intermediary role. Exodus 24 comprises two major sections: the covenant ratification ceremony at the foot of the mountain (24:1–11) and the account of Moses receiving the two tablets from God on the mountaintop (24:12–18). This chapter serves as both a conclusion to Exodus 19–23 and an introduction to Exodus 25–40. At Sinai, the covenant between God and Israel is sealed, and Moses spends 40 days and 40 nights on the mountain, receiving instructions about how to construct the tabernacle. Therefore, the structure of Exodus from legal texts (19–24) to the tabernacle text (25–40) demonstrates Israel's identity construction, which leads to their identity conformation to God's ideal. Understanding and practicing God's law leads to Israel becoming Yahweh-worshipers.

24:1–11 Covenant Ceremony

God summons Moses to ascend Mount Sinai to meet him, along with Aaron, Nadab, Abihu, and 70 elders of Israel.[217] The command to "come up to God" means "go up to Mount Sinai and see God." The individuals who are to accompany Moses are the priests and elders, who are the leaders of the people. God instructs them to worship him from a distance, which implies that they were to come up the mountain but remain below the summit. God then singles out Moses from among this group of leaders and instructs him alone to approach God. The statement "Moses alone is to approach the Lord" (24:2) stresses Moses's privileged position among the leaders. God's repeated warnings forbidding the other leaders and the people to ascend the mountain further emphasizes the hierarchy of leadership within Israel: Moses, priests and elders, and people. This three-tiered structure foreshadows the threefold structure of the tabernacle.[218]

Positive responses from the people (24:3, 7) frame the covenant ceremony. When Moses relays God's words and laws to the people, they respond with

---

217. Nadab and Abihu are sons of Aaron (Exod 6:23) who later offer strange fire to God and then died before God (Lev 10:1–3).
218. See figure 2 on page 188.

one voice: "Everything the Lord has said we will do." The word "laws" here refers to "ordinances" or "judgments," which is the same word used in Exodus 21:1 to refer to the laws in the Book of the Covenant. Subsequent to this unanimous response, Moses records God's words, which presumably included the Ten Commandments and the Book of the Covenant. Moses then builds an altar at the foot of the mountain.[219] As part of the ceremony, Moses sets up 12 pillars to symbolize the 12 tribes of Israel. The people then sacrifice burnt offerings and peace offerings to God, and Moses sprinkles blood on the altar.[220] Moses then reads the Book of the Covenant to the people, who reaffirm their vow of obedience: "We will do everything the Lord has said; we will obey."

The ceremony concludes with Moses sprinkling blood on the people to ratify the covenant[221] and declaring, "Behold the blood of the covenant that the Lord has made with you in accordance with all these words" (24:8 ESV). The word "behold" – which is missing in the NIV translation – emphasizes the significance of this declaration. Both in the ancient Near East and in the OT, blood was often used to confirm a covenant. "These words" refer to the stipulations in the covenant – that is, the contents of both the Ten Commandments and the Book of the Covenant.

Exodus 24:9–11 describe how Moses, Aaron, Nadab, Abihu, and 70 of the elders of Israel follow God's command and come up to meet God. From the perspective of Moses and the leaders who ascend the mountain with him, they gaze upward and see the God of Israel from below the summit of the mountain. They observe what appears to be God's feet on "a pavement made of lapis lazuli, as bright blue as the sky" (24:10).[222] God, as he looks down from the summit of Mount Sinai, does not raise his hand against this group who were coming up the mountain even though his holiness warranted such a response. Earlier, God had warned that anyone who touched the mountain

---

219. The area at the foot or base of the mountain would correspond to the Outer Court in the tripartite design of the tabernacle.
220. This altar design follows the instructions concerning altar laws in Exodus 20:24–26. See T. D. Alexander, "Book of the Covenant," in *DOTP*, 99.
221. It is unthinkable Moses would sprinkle blood on the people. Sarna thinks that Moses sprinkled blood on the twelve pillars, which represent the people in twelve tribes. Sarna, *Exodus*, 151.
222. Compare Ezekiel 1:26; 10:1. Lapis lazuli is a rock consisting of dark blue color, mixed with golden and white patches. This appearance resembles the blue sky with sparkling stars and the white patches look like clouds. James E. Harrell, James K. Hoffmeier, and Kenton F. Williams, "Hebrew Gemstones in the Old Testament: A Lexical, Geological, and Archaeological Analysis," *BBR* 27, no. 1 (2017): 19.

would die and that God could break out against those who approached the mountain to see him or came up without being consecrated (19:12, 21–22).

Verse 11 may puzzle modern readers: "They saw God, and they ate and drank." Why would they eat and drink after seeing God? The word "saw" in this context conveys something more intense than to simply "gaze" (*hazah*). The priests and 70 elders gazed upon God and lived. Eating and drinking in this context becomes part of the ritual for peace offerings and covenant meals (compare Exod 18:12).[223] However, this act of fellowshiping with God through eating and drinking foreshadows the golden calf incident, where the people eat and drink at the foot of Mount Sinai in the absence of Moses (32:6).

24:12–18 Forty Days on Mount Sinai

The narrative focus now shifts from those who accompany Moses up the mountain to Moses himself. God summons Moses to come up to him and remain there, while the others remain somewhere between the foot and the summit of Mount Sinai. This time, Moses is accompanied by his aide, Joshua, who is portrayed as a military leader in Exodus 17 but now serves as Moses's assistant. It is uncertain whether Joshua came all the way up to the summit with Moses or remained with the priests and the elders as suggested by verse 2. Moses's instructions to the elders suggest that he had come down from the mountain at some point and was now ascending it once more.

Verses 15–18 take the reader to the summit of Mount Sinai. First, "the cloud" covers the mountain, the definite article "the" indicating a particular cloud that embodies the presence of God (13:21). Then, God's glorious and magnificent presence settles on Mount Sinai. "Dwell" (*shakan*, "settled" in NIV) foreshadows God's desire to dwell with his people through the tabernacle (25:8), which will represent God's earthly home. The cloud covers the mountain for six days; and on the seventh day, God calls Moses from the cloud. This mirrors the six-seven formula of both the creation story and the Sabbath command. This parallel between the tabernacle and the creation order, with the Sabbath playing a significant role, is a theme we will explore further in Exodus 25–40.

The narrator provides the reader with the perspective of the Israelites gathered at the foot of the mountain, who see the glory of God appearing like a consuming fire at the top of the mountain.[224] God's appearance in the form

---

223. For eating meals in the ritual context, see Leviticus 7:15–16.
224. Compare Exodus 20:18–21.

of fire recalls Moses's burning bush encounter (Exod 3:2) and the experience of God leading his people through the wilderness in a pillar of fire at night (13:21). Both the cloud and the fire represent God's presence.

The chapter concludes with Moses entering the cloud and remaining on the mountain for 40 days and 40 nights. This scene prepares the reader for the divine instructions to Moses regarding the construction of the tabernacle (Exod 25–31). Therefore, Exodus 19–24 serves as another liminal phase in Israel's journey of identity formation, illustrating the tension between the excitement of the divine law-giving and the anxiety surrounding the people's response.

The concept of this in-between space is not unique to Israel's wilderness journey but recurs at every stage in their journey until they reach their permanent home with God. If the wilderness journey out of Egypt represents the first stage of Israel's liminality (15:22–18:27), the revelation of God's law is the second stage of this liminality as they face the challenge of keeping the law (19:1–24:18), which culminates in the third stage of the liminality, exemplified by the golden calf incident, which takes place in Moses's absence and is one of Israel's greatest offenses against God (Exod 32–34).

FAMILY AND KINSHIP RELATIONS

Chinese culture places a high value on family and kinship relations. The family is considered the foundation for many areas of life – including children, homes, property, education, economy, food, and future prospects – and provides a framework within which to view everything in perspective. The adage "blood is thicker than water" is applicable to most Asian societies. Similarly, family is a significant social institution in the theology of the OT, and the character and activities of God can be understood through family and household roles.[1] For instance, the relationship between God and Israel is likened to that of a husband and wife (Isa 54:5; Jer 3:1; Ezekiel 16; Hosea 1–3), father and child (Isa 1:2), and even to a mother (Deut 32:18; Isa 49:14–16). In Exodus, Israel, formerly a house of slaves (13:3; 20:2), is described as God's firstborn son (4:22). Lau identifies three major significances of family in ancient Israel: a) honor and shame, which relate to a person's social standing within the community, b) traditions such as honoring parents, and c) land.[2] Wright also places family at the center of a triangle that involves God, Israel, and the land.³ Glenville titles Exodus, "Freed to be God's Family," and shows both God and their relationships as family members.⁴

In Chinese culture, the significance of family roles is reflected in the various names that designate relatives from both the mother's and father's side of the family, with different terms used to distinguish between their male and female siblings as well as male and female cousins. These terms, which include different honorifics, reflect the complex and intricate web of kinship relations.

The Ten Commandments and the Book of the Covenant were designed with families and households in mind, reflecting the centrality of family in the culture of that time, just as in Chinese culture today. The Sabbath, for example, extends to family members, including "you . . . your son or daughter . . . your male or female servant . . . your animals . . . any foreigner residing in your towns" (20:10–11). The fifth commandment emphasizes respect for one's parents, while the seventh commandment stresses marital fidelity. Similarly, the laws regarding slavery in the Book of the Covenant pertain to the treatment of slaves within one's household, and the prohibitions against striking and cursing parents emphasize proper treatment of one's parents. The practice of one's faith must start within one's own family, and this is seen particularly clearly in the Chinese and Asian contexts.

---

1. Leo G. Perdue, "The Household, Old Testament Theology, and Contemporary Hermeneutics," in *Families in Ancient Israel*, eds. Leo G. Perdue, Joseph Blenkinsopp, John J. Collins, Carol Meyers (Louisville: Westminster John Knox, 1997), 225, 248.
2. Lau, "Kinship, Patronage, and Corruption," 207–208. Lau considers Scripture from all over the Old Testament and is not limited to the Exodus.
3. Wright, *Old Testament Ethics for the People of God*, 339.
4. Glenville, *Freed to be God's Family*, 22. In the New Testament, Jesus redefines and expands the idea of family to include whoever does the will of God (Matt 12:46–50).

EXODUS 25–40
IDENTITY CONFORMATION
TO WORSHIP

In July 2022, I had the privilege of speaking at a joint church summer retreat in Amsterdam, the Netherlands. This four-day event brought together people from multiple Chinese churches in the area. They worshiped, fellowshiped, and ate together, which strengthened their inter-church relationships and facilitated spiritual renewal. I was struck by the fact that hundreds of attendees were of Chinese descent, having immigrated to the Netherlands from China, Hong Kong, Taiwan, and Southeast Asian countries such as Singapore, Malaysia, and Indonesia. While the first-generation immigrants spoke Mandarin, Cantonese, and Wenzhou dialects, their children were fluent in Dutch and their own native language, which was either Mandarin or Cantonese. The majority of adults and second-generation children spoke two or more languages, including English, which is part of the school curriculum in the Netherlands. During worship, translations were made available from Dutch to Mandarin or vice versa, but Dutch, English, Mandarin, and Cantonese were all used during times of socializing. In diasporic communities, people often speak their native languages even when they are living in a new community. They exist in a new hybrid condition, embracing both their home culture and language as well as the host country's culture and language. All these people were Protestant Christians, worshiping the same Lord – Jesus Christ. There was spiritual oneness but also plurality of ethnicity, culture, and race.

In the diaspora, local Chinese immigrant churches often serve as a religious and spiritual home for those who are far away from their country of origin. These churches play an important missional role in gathering scattered diasporans to worship God. The Chinese churches in Amsterdam are just one example of how people forge their religious identity in new lands. Many Chinese people in New Zealand, Australia, Africa, South America, the United States, Canada, the United Kingdom, and Europe attend Chinese churches, with first-generation migrants typically worshiping in their native languages and second- or third-generation migrants worshiping in the language of their host countries. For example, in the city of Los Angeles alone, there are over three hundred Chinese churches. The significant communities of Chinese migrants in the Bay Area (California), Houston (Texas), New York, Vancouver (Canada), and the greater Toronto area also attract worshipers to these Chinese immigrant churches. Therefore, Chinese immigrant churches become the embodied presence of God in the diaspora, shaping not only the religious identity of attendees but also their ethnic and cultural identities in new lands.[1]

As the psalmist notes, those who make idols and images will become like them (Ps 115:8). Indeed, we are whom we worship. The Chinese Christian identity is forged when these people turn from atheism or religious pluralism and become worshipers of God. Meanwhile, God uses these Chinese churches worldwide as missional stations that reach out to people in the diaspora. Through these local churches, the blessings of the Abrahamic covenant – promised to Abraham and, through him, to the nations – are partially realized.[2] The diaspora thus serves as a crucial link in the "from everywhere to everywhere missiology"[3] and "polycentric missiology," enabling diasporic people to gather together to worship the same God.[4]

The presence of global Chinese churches bears witness to God's presence and work among the nations. Through these churches, the scattered are once again gathered as one for worship. In the OT, the term "scatter" often connotes the idea of punishment, as in the case of those who built the tower of Babel being scattered (Gen 11:8–9) and the dispersion of the Israelites among the nations due to their covenant unfaithfulness (Deut 30:3; Ps 44:11). In contrast, "gathering" conveys a sense of hope (Pss 106:47; 107:3; Isa 11:12; Mic 4:6; Zeph 3:9–20). As diasporans travel, settle, and move again, the presence of Chinese churches on the global landscape provides a common space, enabling transformation from a state of scattering into a gathering in the presence of God. The current diasporic condition thus represents a new exodus – from everywhere to everywhere – for the worship of God.

---

1. From a cultural perspective, the spread of Christianity in the Chinese diaspora also contribute to the widening of the Chinese culture around the globe. Kuhn, *Chinese Among Others*, 483.
2. One example is the church planting effort of the Evangelical Formosan Churches in the Chinese diaspora. Sun, *Attempt Great Things for God*, 13–20.
3. George, "Diaspora: A Hidden Link," 52–53.
4. A phrase borrowed from Allen Yeh, *Polycentric Missiology: 21st-Century Mission From Everyone to Everywhere* (Downers Grove: IVP Academic, 2016).

THE PLACE OF CHINESE IMMIGRANT CHURCHES IN LOS ANGELES

For several decades, I have resided in Los Angeles – a place of diverse migrants, both documented and undocumented – and have come to see it as a "global crossroads," a "city of dreams," and a mission hub.[1] Los Angeles boasts the largest Asian population of any city in the United States.[2] It is a center of cultural creativity and innovation, a place offering people many new opportunities. Its strategic location on the Pacific Rim, bordering Mexico, coupled with its mild climate, attracts migrants from all around the world. In addition, the city's racial, religious, and political diversity makes it tolerant of various groups and a variety of beliefs.[3]

As a result of globalization, millions of people, including Chinese migrants, have migrated to Los Angeles. The history of Chinese migration to America spans from the early Chinese migrants of the 1840s–1860s, through the Chinese Exclusion Act in 1882, to the many subsequent waves of migration, with each wave or legislative act introducing its own unique dynamics.[4] Issues related to migration – such as immigration policies, legislation, acculturation, discrimination, diaspora, transnationalism, politics, religion, and mission – are intertwined, and form an intricate web.

Los Angeles, which has been named an "Asian Place," is home to 1.5 million Asians and Asian Americans.[5] The greater Los Angeles area is home to over 350 Chinese immigrant churches, representing multiple denominations. Most of these churches have two or three congregations, with first-generation immigrants worshiping in their native tongues (Mandarin, Cantonese, and Taiwanese) and their second-generation children worshiping in English. Despite challenges such as frequent church splits, conflicts between the generations over cultural differences, and debates regarding the role of women in ministry, these immigrant churches play an important missional role by gathering scattered diasporans from all over the world to worship God and participate in the propagation of the gospel to the Chinese diaspora. This is a sign of hope in the third millennium.

---

1. Kirsteen Kim, "Los Angeles as an Intersection," in *Migration, Transnationalism, and Faith in Missiological Perspective: Los Angeles as a Global Crossroads*, eds. Kirsteen Kim and Alexia Salvatierra (Lanham: Lexington, 2022), 5. Richard Flory, "City of Dreams: Los Angeles as a Cradle for Religious Activism, Innovation, and Diversity," in *Migration, Transnationalism, and Faith in Missiological Perspective*, 19.

2. Kirsteen Kim, "Los Angeles as an Intersection," 5.
3. For more on how to define Los Angeles and its culture, see Flory, "City of Dreams," 21–29.
4. For a history of Asian immigrants to California, see Rebecca Kim, "Making Their Mark," 94–99. For the effects of legislation against Chinese migrants in the United States, see Kuhn, *Chinese among Others*, 284–288.
5. Jason S. Sexton, "Borders and Barriers: Citizenship in California," in *Migration, Transnationalism, and Faith in Missiological Perspective*, 133.

OVERVIEW

Exodus 25–40 vividly portrays God's desire to dwell among his people through the construction of the tabernacle. God's embodied presence teaches Israel that God's presence is not meant to be confined to the summit of Mount Sinai and that he desires to descend and be near his people continuously (25:8).[5] However, the narrative also records that the people commit a great sin against God by worshiping the golden calf. The true worship of Yahweh or the false worship of Yahweh and his image becomes the crux of contention in Israel's identity formation in Exodus 25–40. The notion of "conformation" involves both formation of an identity and the ongoing process of conforming to God's way of worship, but Israel often fails to live up to this ideal. Throughout Israel's history, divine initiative and human unfaithfulness become a paradigmatic pattern that characterizes the relationship between God and Israel.

The Exodus story presents Israel's journey through multiple stages of liminality. In the first stage, they transition out of Egypt and begin their wilderness journey. In the second stage, God's theophany on Mount Sinai, along with the laws and promises, marks their entry into a new phase of liminality, where they tremble at the sight of the law-giving God. The third stage of liminality occurs during Moses's absence, leading to the making of the golden calf. Here, Israel's identity wavers as they are caught between Egyptian influences of the past and their new status as God's people. Through this ongoing process of formation and becoming, God helps Israel to understand their new identity by worshiping God alone and conforming to his way of worship as prescribed by God. If transformation is the goal of identity formation, then it can be defined

---

5. This descent culminates in the incarnation of Jesus, who, being equal with God, does not consider himself as such but chooses to descend and dwell (tabernacle) with human beings (John 1:14). One day, in the second advent of Jesus, he will dwell among his people for eternity (Rev 21:3).

as converting from the old identity to the new identity of belonging to God. By the end of Exodus, Israel's identity is still in the process of becoming.[6] While they are God's redeemed people, Israel is not yet conforming to God's ideals.

In Exodus 25–40, Israel will become worshipers of Yahweh through the proper construction of the tabernacle, which serves as the home of God on earth.[7] Sklar calls this a "palace-tent."[8] Constructing the tabernacle reflects God's mission to build a home for himself and his chosen people, including outsiders and sojourners. Thus, the building of the tabernacle – and later, the temple – carries an important missional impetus.[9] Since liminality is a human condition, the proper worship of God becomes a way forward in Israel's journey of becoming as they anticipate their final home with God.

In the ancient Near East, gods were linked with specific sacred sites where worship took place. However, the construction of the tabernacle in the wilderness teaches Israel that sacred space occurs wherever God reveals himself. In this sense, the God of Israel chooses to connect with his people through his presence in the tabernacle.[10]

In Exodus 14 and 15, God is depicted as a divine warrior. This martial image portrays the tabernacle as a military tent. In the Egyptian context, there were military tents in the Middle Kingdom and the New Kingdom. For example, tents are frequently mentioned in the records of Thutmose III (reigned 1479–1425 BCE). Thutmose III lived in a guarded tent throughout his military campaigns against his enemies, and the capture of the son of the King of Kadesh took place in his tent. Painted reliefs of military tents can be found on monuments and temple walls – particularly in the Luxor temple and the Ramesseum. The military tent of Ramses II at Kadesh, which is described as being rectangular in shape and oriented eastward, parallels the design of the tabernacle. Just as the golden throne of Ramses II is flanked by falcon wings,

---

6. Hanciles, *Migration and the Making of Global Christianity*, 46.
7. Volf and McAnnally-Linz, *The Home of God*, 5–6.
8. Jay Sklar, *Exodus*, ESV Expository Commentary (Wheaton: Crossway, 2025), forthcoming.
9. Wright, *The Mission of God*, 340. In the context of the diaspora, most evangelism and mission work is done within the Chinese diaspora context rather than reaching out to other ethnic groups, let alone white Americans. For the racial, cultural, political, and structural challenges facing Asians in California, see Rebecca Kim, "Making Their Mark," 95–97.
10. Fentress-Williams, "Exodus," 87. Divine presence is associated with God's body. Sommer argues that God's body is a fluid concept and appears in different locations: in heaven, in the burning bush, the standing stones, the ark, and in God's glory. Sommer, *The Bodies of God and the World of Ancient Israel*, 47–49, 60–61.

the ark of the covenant is flanked by two cherubim.[11] These parallels suggest that the tabernacle also has a military dimension – it is God's portable tent from where he will engage in future battles, as well as a sacred place for his people to worship him.

This mobile dwelling manifests God's ongoing desire to be with his people and fight for them on their journey toward a permanent home.

Here is a broad overview of the Exodus 25–40 narrative:

> Exodus 25–31: Instructions for the tabernacle: Right worship
> Exodus 32–34: The making of the golden calf: False worship
> Exodus 35–40: Construction of the tabernacle: Right worship

This structure has the incident of the golden calf sandwiched between the instructions for building the tabernacle and its actual construction.[12] While constructing the tabernacle symbolizes proper worship, the worship of the golden calf represents false worship. In Exodus 25–40, God's orderly design for the tabernacle is contrasted with the chaotic process of the people's creation and worship of the golden calf. The careful and meticulous instructions on how to construct the tabernacle form a direct contrast to the careless creation of the golden calf. The heavenly blueprint for the tabernacle is juxtaposed with the earthly counterfeiting of the divine image. As the narrative unfolds, the golden calf incident proves detrimental to the relationship between God and Israel, in particular, to the manifestation of God's presence. Later, Moses painstakingly recounts this history to the second-generation Israelites, warning them never to repeat the same mistake (Deut 9:12–21). Moses describes this mistake as a "great sin" (Exod 32:21). The psalmist also refers to this incident that kindled God's wrath (Ps 106:19–23). Therefore, Exodus 25–40 introduces the themes of order and chaos, right worship and wrong worship, and creation, de-creation, and re-creation.

The instructions concerning the Sabbath command (Exod 31:12–17; 35:1–3) form bookends to both the instructions for building the tabernacle and the golden calf incident, creating a framing device that connects the tabernacle to God's creational design for Israel. Even during the work of constructing the

---

11. Michael M. Homan, *To Your Tents, O Israel! The Terminology, Function, Form, and Symbolism of Tents in the Hebrew Bible and the Ancient Near East*, Culture & History of the Ancient Near East (Leiden: Brill, 2002), 63–67; 111–116. See plates 47 and 48.

12. Some scholars regard Exodus 24–40 as a literary unit in a chiastic structure with the story of the golden calf occupying the center. C. H. Park, "From Mount Sinai to the Tabernacle: A Reading of Exodus 24:12–40:38 as a Case of Intercalated Double Plot" (PhD diss., University of Gloucestershire, 2002), 183.

tabernacle, God expects his people to take a Sabbath rest, thus establishing a new paradigm of "building justly."[13] Promises and anxieties coexist, and their intensity escalates in this final section of Exodus, contributing to Israel's identity (trans)formation, becoming, and the ongoing journey with God.

To some readers, the meticulous details in the instructions for building the tabernacle may seem irrelevant or tedious, and some may skip this portion of Scripture altogether. However, the fact that over one-third of the book of Exodus is dedicated to these instructions about proper worship highlights their theological significance. It is in this section of Exodus that God's ultimate purpose in rescuing Israel is revealed – it is so that they may worship God alone and do so in a fitting manner, as already indicated in Exodus 3:12, which states that the goal of God's rescue is worship. The completion of the tabernacle is the pinnacle of the Exodus narrative.

25:1–40 INTERNAL CONSTRUCTION: THE INTERIOR OF THE TABERNACLE

Furniture is an essential component of any house. People choose furniture based on different criteria and priorities. Some prioritize functional value, disregarding the matching of colors and styles, while others pay special attention to whether the furniture reflects their social status. Still others regard budget and practicality as the most important considerations.

Many Chinese churches prioritize the practical functionality of their church buildings, considering factors such as capacity to accommodate the congregation, the availability of rooms for Sunday school, safety standards of children's facilities, and cost-effective furniture and equipment. However, few Chinese churches consider whether the design and decor of the building reflect the glory and beauty of God. In contrast, many Roman Catholic churches place great emphasis on the design of the church building as a reflection of divine beauty and glory. Numerous old churches in Europe have elaborately designed, with construction taking decades or even centuries to complete. As one beholds the decorated ceilings, pillars, and walls of these churches, their aesthetic beauty evokes awe.

The design of the tabernacle is not based solely on functionality or even theological symbolism; rather, its most significant feature is that it reflects the beauty and glory of God, as in the case of the priestly garments (Exod 28:2). The underemphasis on physical beauty in many Chinese churches may reflect

---

13. Bills, *A Theology of Justice in Exodus*, 216.

a deliberate deviation from Catholic or Eastern Orthodox churches, where icons, images, and visible artwork are perceived as expressions of faith. This de-emphasis, however, is not in line with the biblical principles underlying the artistic design of the tabernacle. Cornell argues that the tabernacle's mission involves beautiful art that reflects the beauty of God's creation as described in Genesis 1.[14] Therefore, there is biblical support for constructing God's house with artistic beauty.

As the narrative unfolds, readers will discover that the design of the tabernacle also carries theological significance for it prefigures the temple, the church, and the role of believers as priests.

25:1–9 Prelude to Building the Tabernacle

As we read through Exodus 25–31, we must remember that these instructions come directly from God to Moses during his 40-day stay on Mount Sinai (24:18). These lengthy and detailed instructions underscore the importance and significance of proper worship. However, Moses's prolonged absence creates a leadership vacuum, which ultimately leads to Israel's fall into idolatry with the golden calf (Exod 32–34).

First, God instructs Moses to ask the Israelites to "bring me an offering" (25:1). God then lays out the conditions for the offeror and their offerings. The condition for offerors relates to the heart – "from everyone whose heart prompts them to give" (25:2). "Prompts" (*nadab*) can be translated as incite, impel, be ready, or be willing, indicating the willing desire that comes from one's heart.[15] God does not wish people to bring their offerings out of coercion or peer pressure but, rather, willingly and freely, which contrasts sharply with Pharaoh's forced labor (1:11; 5:11). God then provides a list of the offerings that are required for building the tabernacle and making the priestly garments.[16] The following table lists the materials required to construct the tabernacle.[17]

---

14. Collin Cornell, "Art on Mission with the Tabernacle Builders," *Transformation* (2024): 1–16. The aura of divine presence attached to the tabernacle furniture is one way to explain their tedious and meticulous descriptions. Another way is to see these detailed descriptions as a genre of *ekphrasis*, bringing the things shown vividly before one's eyes. Gary A. Anderson, *That I May Dwell among Them: Incarnation and Atonement in the Tabernacle Narrative* (Grand Rapids: Eerdmans, 2023), 60–61, 72–73.
15. *BDB*, 621. *HALOT*, 671.
16. Sarna groups these materials into seven categories: metals, dyed yarns, fabrics (including fine linen, goat's hair, ram's skin dyed red, and goat's skin), timber (acacia wood), oil, spices, and gems. Sarna, *Exodus*, 156.
17. The text does not make any groupings. So there are different ways to group these materials.

Exodus 25–40

Table 12: Materials for Constructing the Tabernacle

	Materials (Exodus 25:3–7)	Tabernacle (Exodus 25:10–27:21; 30:1–38)	Priestly Garments (Exodus 28)
1	Metals: gold, silver, and bronze	Gold is all over the tabernacle, both inside and out.[18] Sockets are made of silver (26:19; 27:17), clasps are made of bronze (26:11; 27:17), the altar is made of bronze (27:1–6), the court of the tabernacle has sockets of bronze (27:9–19), the basin is made of bronze (30:17).	Gold appears in the ephod, breastpiece, and robe (28:5–8, 11, 14–15, 20–27, 33–35).
2	Blue, purple, and scarlet yarn[19]	The curtain for the tabernacle (26:1), the veil (26:31), the curtain for the entrance (26:36), the gate (27:16)	Breastpiece, ephod, robe (28:5–6, 15–16, 31–33)
3	Fine linen	The curtain (26:1), the veil (26:31), the curtain for the entrance (26:36), the court (27:9)	Breastpiece, ephod, robe (28:5–6, 15–16, 39)
4	Goat hair[20]	The covering of the tabernacle (26:7)	
5	Ram skins dyed red	The covering of the tabernacle (26:14)	
6	A durable skin[21]	The covering of the tabernacle (26:14)	

---

18. The ark (26:11–13), the cover of the tabernacle (25:17), Kerubim (25:18), table (25:24–26), utensils (25:29), lampstand (25:31), clasps (26:6).

19. Blue, purple, and scarlet are bright, vivid colors. They are the most expensive dye colors in antiquity. Their high value reflects the value of the tabernacle, which was constructed with the most precious materials. Blue and purple are often paired together, indicating royalty (Esth 8:15). Both blue and purple are derived from marine snails in rabbinic sources. The snail exudes a yellow fluid, but if it is exposed to sunlight it turns red-purple. The blue color is closer to violet, whereas the purple color is closer to red-purple. Marine snails were found on the Phoenician coast dating to the fifteenth century BCE at Ugarit. Together, these colorful yarns symbolize wealth, nobility, and royalty. See Sarna, *Exodus*, 157. The scarlet color or crimson, comes from the eggs and bodies of the worm *coccus ilicis*, which attaches itself to the leaves of the holly plant from which maggots are produced and their powder turns into a bright red color. Walter C. Kaiser, Jr, "Exodus," in *EBC* 2:452.

20. The NIV translates this as "another type of durable leather."

21. Or, "badger skin." The NASB translates it as "porpoise skin." The NIV renders it as "another type of durable leather," which is quite ambiguous. Its exact meaning is unclear. The rabbinic

	Materials (Exodus 25:3–7)	Tabernacle (Exodus 25:10–27:21; 30:1–38)	Priestly Garments (Exodus 28)
7	Acacia wood[22]	Ark (25:10), table (25:23), boards (26:15), bars (26:26–27), pillars (26:32, 37), altar (27:1)	
8	Olive oil	Lampstand (27:20)	
9	Spices	Anointing oil and fragrant incense (30:23–25, 34–35)	
10	Onyx stones[23]		Ephod (28:9–15), Breastpiece (28:20)
11	Gems		Breastpiece (28:17–20)

When God instructed Moses to gather offerings for the construction of the tabernacle, he had already envisioned its shape, texture, and appearance, but he required the Israelites to follow his instructions to bring that vision to fruition. It is important to note that the materials for building the tabernacle do not come from the Israelites but were provided by the Egyptians. God had granted the Israelites favor in the eyes of the Egyptians, who then supplied them with articles of gold and silver, as well as clothing, when they left Egypt (Exod 12:35–36), demonstrating that when God commanded the construction of a sanctuary, he also provided the necessary materials. The people's responsibility was to follow God's instructions. This has significant implications for contemporary church planting. Funding is always a concern when constructing a new church building. The provision of financial and material means may serve as a sign from God to proceed with establishing the new church.

---

sources associate this animal with the unicorn. Some identify it as a dolphin, and others identify it as a dugong found in the Red Sea area. See Sarna, *Exodus*, 158. The Book of Numbers has a more detailed description of the use of this skin as a covering (Num 4:6–14).

22. The word "Acacia" originates from Egypt, and acacia trees were prominent in the Sinai area. See Hoffmeier, *Ancient Israel in Sinai*, 209. Acacia wood is more durable, hard, and sustainable than most woods. Therefore, it is an excellent material for building furniture and flooring, and more. https://acaciawoodusa.com/pages/what-is-acacia-wood/. Acacia trees are found in the desert. Due to their slow growth, they are hard and dense and thus are resistant to decay. Almost all the structural features of the tabernacle are constructed with acacia wood. "Acacia," https://ww2.odu.edu/~lmusselm/plant/bible/acacia.php?todo=plantindex#:~:text=It%20is%20interesting%20to%20note,of%20the%20work%20brought%20it.

23. The JPS translates it as "lapis lazuli," a precious gem of uncertain identity. It appears in the Garden of Eden (Gen 2:12; Ezek 28:13), the ephod of the priest (Exod 28:9), and the breastpiece of the priest (Exod 39:13), the material in building the temple (1 Chr 29:2).

Exodus 25–40

Exodus 25:8 states the purpose of constructing the tabernacle: "Make a sanctuary for me, and I will dwell among them." In the exodus event, God had struck Egypt with plagues, battled on behalf of Israel in the Red Sea, and given the Ten Commandments from the summit of Mount Sinai. But God's greatest desire was to dwell with his people, to be present in their midst rather than appearing from high above, beyond their reach. The word "sanctuary" (*miqedash*) means "a holy place," a place set apart for God. The phrase "for me" emphasizes that the sanctuary is designated as God's residence – God's tent and home on earth. Since God does not need a physical space for his dwelling (Isa 66:1), the idea of God's home is symbolic rather than literal. The sanctuary thus becomes a tangible representation to help people to conceive of a sacred place that embodies God's presence.[24]

The word "dwell" (*shakan*) also means "sit" or "remain." In Chinese culture, when inviting someone to your home for fellowship, you would usually say, "Come to sit at my house." "Sit" in this sense means "come to my house and let's have some fellowship together." The purpose of constructing the tabernacle is so that God's presence may dwell, live, sit, and remain with Israel. God's desire to be intimately connected with his people shows that he is a relational God who wants to be accessible to people and enjoys their company. As the instructions for the tabernacle unfold, it becomes clear that this sanctuary is designed as a divine portable home that invites people into fellowship with God. Therefore, the tabernacle not only serves as a home for the Ten Commandments but, most important, is God's earthly home. The tabernacle becomes a concrete and tangible symbol of God's covenantal commitment to his people.[25]

Here, God is depicted as a master architect who proudly showcases the artistic design of his portable house to an apprentice. Moses is given the task of following the pattern or blueprint of the tabernacle and its furnishings according to God's precise instructions (25:9).[26] Each directive has theological and spiritual implications and symbolism beyond the merely physical aspects

---

24. It has been a common notion in the ancient Near East that deities dwell in heaven and earth. Since God is not limited by space and time, he can dwell in both heaven and earth simultaneously. Pekka Pitkänen, "Temple Building and Exodus 25–40," in *From the Foundations to the Crenellations: Essays on Temple Building in the Ancient Near East and Hebrew Bible*, eds. Mark J. Boda and Jamie Novotny, AOAT 366 (Münster: Ugarit-Verlag, 2010), 260.
25. Block, *Covenant*, 170. Block distinguishes "house" from "home." "House" refers more to the structure, while "home" involves not only a physical place but also the feelings of home that come with it.
26. Though the meaning of "pattern" or "blueprint" is unclear.

of the construction. Therefore, making sure that every detail is correct is critical in the grand scheme of things.

God first tells Moses how to construct the ark and then gives instructions about the table of showbread and the golden lampstand. The ark is to be placed in the Holy of Holies, while the table of showbread and the golden lampstand are to be located in the Holy Place. The tripartite division reflects a descending order of holiness, with the Holy of Holies being the holiest place; the materials used in each place are also in descending order of value, from gold to silver to bronze. The diagram below (not to scale) illustrates the tripartite division of the tabernacle and its furnishings.

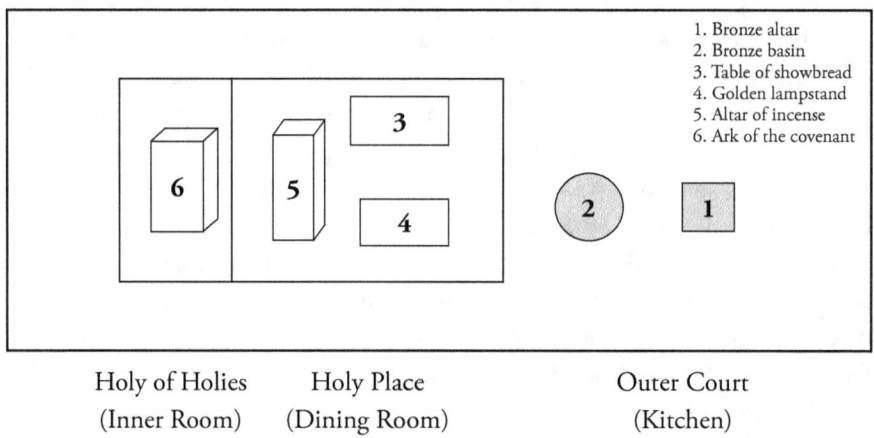

Figure 3: The Design of the Tabernacle as God's Home[27]

The design of the tabernacle reveals a tripartite layout with three distinct rooms that, in terms of a typical household, might be called the kitchen, the dining room, and the inner room. The bronze altar serves as the site for the animal sacrifices while the bronze basin is designated as the place for those who prepare the meat to wash and clean themselves. The table of showbread resembles a dining table with utensils (25:29), while the golden lampstand provides light to the dining room. The altar of incense is where the priest intercedes for the people. Finally, the ark of the covenant in the inner room is

---

27. For a more detailed figure of the tabernacle, see Averbeck, *The Old Testament Law for the Life of the Church*, 134. R. E. Averbeck, "Tabernacle," *DOTP*, 808.

where the high priest goes to meet with God on the Day of Atonement (Lev 16). In ancient times, temples were considered the earthly dwelling place of the gods. Similarly, the tabernacle serves as "heaven on earth."[28] The design of God's portable house or "mobile home" reflects his desire to dwell with Israel and enjoy their company.

In Exodus 25–27, God begins with instructions about the most sacred and interior section of the tabernacle and then moves outward. He gives instructions about the ark in the Holy of Holies, then progresses to the furnishings in the Holy Place and the bronze altar in the Outer Court. After introducing the priestly garments and the consecration of the priests (Exod 28–29), God instructs Moses on how to construct the altar of incense in the Holy Place and the basin in the Outer Court (Exod 30) before introducing the builders (Exod 31). Although the reason for placing the instructions for the altar of incense after the priestly garments is unclear, perhaps this was due to its immediate connection to the priestly work of offering incense on behalf of the people.

25:10–22 The Ark

Among all the furnishings in the tabernacle, the instructions for constructing the ark come first, highlighting its preeminent position. The tablets of the law are to be placed inside this ark. The "ark" (*'aron*) is literally a chest with a lid, which could also be used as a coffin (Gen 50:26) or as a container or a box to collect money for the temple workers' salaries (2 Kgs 12:9–12). However, this ark is different from any other chest since it was chosen and designed by God to serve as the dwelling place for his presence and to house a jar of manna (16:34), the tablets of the Ten Commandments (25:16; 31:18), and Aaron's staff (Num 17:10; Heb 9:4), with each of these items bearing witness to God's faithfulness and Israel's unfaithfulness.

God instructs that the ark be made from acacia wood and covered with gold. It is to be rectangular in shape, measuring 2.5 cubits in length and 1.5 cubits in width and height. Since one cubit is about 18 inches, the ark would have been approximately 45 inches long and 27 inches wide. Both the inside and outside of the ark are to be overlaid with gold (25:11). Since the ark is designed to be portable, to facilitate carrying, it features four golden rings and two wooden poles overlaid with gold (25:12–15). "The tablets of the covenant law" (25:16) refers to the two tablets containing the Ten Commandments (31:18).

---

28. Longman, *How to Read Exodus*, 136. Beale, *The Temple and the Church's Mission*, 31–38.

God then instructs Moses on how to construct the lid of the ark (25:17–21). This lid is no ordinary cover. Referred to as the "atonement cover" in the NIV and the "mercy seat" in the NASB,[29] in Chinese, it is translated as *shī ēn zuò*, meaning "a seat that gives mercy." The word "cover" (*kaporet*) means "propitiation," referring to the act of appeasing the anger or wrath of a deity or higher authority. In biblical tradition, this word is often translated as "atonement." However, the text does not state how atonement will be accomplished through this cover. This suggests that God's revelation is a progressive and ongoing process. The width and length of the cover are exactly the same as the dimensions of the ark (25:10, 17). God also instructs Moses to make two cherubim of gold and place them at either end of the mercy seat. The cherubim are to face each other, with their outstretched wings covering the mercy seat and their faces turned toward it (25:18–20).[30]

Cherubim first appear in the garden of Eden, where God stations them to guard its eastern entrance (Gen 3:24). In the tabernacle, cherubim are woven into the fabric of the curtains (Exod 26:1; 36:8) and the veil that separates the Holy of Holies from the Holy Place (26:31; 36:35), symbolically serving as guardians of the sacred spaces of the tabernacle. Cherubim are also featured in the design of the temple. For instance, images of cherubim are carved into the cedar planks that form the inner walls of the temple and the olive wood doors (1 Kgs 6:29–35; 2 Chr 3:7), as well as on the bases of the bronze lavers, alongside images of lions and oxen (1 Kgs 7:29–36).[31] Traditionally, cherubim were regarded as angelic beings with wings – as in Ezekiel's vision (Ezek 1:5–28; 10:1–20)[32] – and as guardians of God's property, as in the garden of Eden. Symbolically, the cherubim function as guards of the ark and the mercy seat. Some interpretations view the cherubim as forming a throne for the manifestation of the glory of God.[33]

The construction of the ark and the mercy seat is mentioned first because it is the site where God's presence is most frequently manifested. It is from

---

29. Same with the ESV, NKJV, and RSV.
30. The Hebrew expression is interesting here. It is literally, "And their faces, each to his brother."
31. *BDB*, 500–501.
32. In Ezekiel's vision, the cherubim have four faces, including faces of a man, a lion, a bull, and an eagle (Ezek 1:10). In another vision, the cherubim appear to have faces of a cherub, a man, a lion, and an eagle (Ezek 10:14).
33. *BDB*, 500.

"there above the cover between the two cherubim that are over the ark of the covenant law" (25:22) that God will "meet with" and speak with Moses.[34]

In the OT, the ark is perceived as the footstool of God's throne (1 Chr 28:2; Pss 99:5; 132:7–8; Isa 66:1; Lam 2:1), and thus the Holy of Holies can be envisioned as the throne room where God is enthroned.[35] If the ark is God's footstool, it follows that God's presence extends from heaven to earth and from earth to heaven. As Fretheim remarks, "God is present and active wherever there is a world."[36] In addition, the ark is perceived as a symbol of divine presence so that the Israelites would carry the ark into battle (Num 10:35–36; 1 Sam 4:1–4; Ps 24:7–10). In the NT, the believer's body becomes the temple of the Holy Spirit, pointing to the indwelling presence of God. Therefore, the symbolism of the ark in the Holy of Holies carries over from the OT to the NT.

25:23–30 The Table

The narrative now shifts from the Holy of Holies to the Holy Place, where the first item of furniture is the table of showbread. Like the ark, this table is crafted from acacia wood but is slightly smaller in size, measuring 2 cubits in length, 1 cubit in width, and 1.5 cubits in height (25:23). The height of the table matches that of the ark, and it is overlaid with gold and has a gold border. This table is also portable and has four golden rings on the corners of its feet and acacia wood poles overlaid with gold for ease of transportation (25:24–28).

The most remarkable aspect of the table is the items to be placed on it. God instructs Moses, "And make its plates and dishes of pure gold, as well as its pitchers and bowls for the pouring out of offerings. Put the bread of the Presence on this table to be before me at all times" (25:29–30). In a typical household, the dining table holds eating utensils such as plates, dishes, pitchers, and bowls. God's instruction to use pure gold to make these utensils suggests that their purpose is not functional but symbolic. These golden utensils serve a metaphorical purpose: as the host, God invites his people to partake in a meal in his home and enjoy fellowship with him. In this sense, the dining table

---

34. Compare Exodus 30:6, 36; Leviticus 16:2; Numbers 17:4; 1 Samuel 4:4; 2 Samuel 6:2; 2 Kings 19:15; Psalm 80:1; Isaiah 37:16. Whether God is enthroned between or above the cherubim is debatable. In Exodus 25:22; 30:6; Leviticus16:2 it is "above," but in 1 Samuel 4:4; 2 Samuel 6:2; 2 Kings 19:15; Psalm 80:1; Isaiah 37:16, the preposition "above" (or "between") is absent. The ambiguity in the precise location of God's presence points to divine mystery.
35. Longman, *How to Read Exodus*, 135.
36. Terence E. Fretheim, *God and World in the Old Testament: A Relational Theology of Creation* (Nashville: Abingdon, 2005), 23.

and its utensils concretize what it means for God to dwell among his people (25:8) and for people to commune with God.

The requirement that the bread of the Presence[37] be on the table at all times points to God's continual presence with his people. That the bread is on display "before me" (25:30) indicates that it is not meant for consumption but serves a symbolic purpose. Although the precise symbolism is not made clear, it may point to God's provision of food or daily sustenance. Leviticus offers additional details about this bread of the Presence, specifying that 12 loaves made of fine flour are to be arranged in two rows, with incense placed on each row as a memorial portion and offering to God (Lev 24:5–7). Aaron and his sons are instructed to enter the Holy Place to eat this bread every week in the presence of God (Lev 24:9).

In many Asian cultures, people bring food and fruit to offer to their gods at shrines. One ancient Near Eastern creation story depicts the gods as flies hovering over the food brought to them by humans.[38] In contrast, God does not need food since the whole world and everything in it already belongs to him (Ps 50:8–13). Rather, the bread of the Presence serves as a reminder of God's covenant with Israel and provides food for Aaron and his sons (Lev 24:8–9). The priests are to receive God's provision of bread and eat it in the Holy Place while also presenting the 12 loaves as offerings from the 12 tribes to God.[39]

25:31–40 The Lampstand

The second piece of furniture in the Holy Place is the lampstand.[40] Detailed instructions are given for constructing this lampstand. First, the lampstand is to be made of pure gold. Second, the lampstand, including its base and shaft, is to be made of hammered work. Third, its cups, bulbs, and blossoms are to be made of a single piece of gold (25:31). Detailed instructions are also given about the design of the branches of the lampstand, the shape of the cups,

---

37. Literally, "bread of faces."
38. The reference is from Gilgamesh XI. "The gods smelt the fragrance, The gods smelt the pleasant fragrance, the Gods like flies gathered over the sacrifice." Stephanie Dalley, trans. *Myths from Mesopotamia: Creation, the Flood, Gilgamesh, and Others* (Oxford: Oxford University Press, 1989), 114. John H. Walton, *Chronological and Background Charts of the Old Testament*, revised (Grand Rapids: Zondervan, 1994), 81.
39. Ko, *Leviticus: A Pastoral and Contextual Commentary*, 217–218.
40. In Revelation, the apostle John speaks of another set of seven lampstands, symbolizing the seven churches he was addressing. Beale and Kim, *God Dwells Among Us*, 41.

the position of the bulbs, and the number of lamps.[41] Although no reason is given for the emphasis on the lampstand being made from one piece of gold (25:31, 36), this reflects the idea of unity. The shape of the lampstand, with its seven branches, resembles a tree, probably representing the tree of life, a well-known symbol in biblical tradition.[42] The floral images, with their cups and bulbs, suggest a blossoming and flourishing tree. This lampstand-tree image and symbolism evokes the creation narrative, recalling the tree of life in the garden of Eden, which represents a paradisial space.[43]

The text emphasizes that the lampstand and its accessories are made of pure gold (25:31, 36, 38, 39), which matches the material used for the interior and exterior of the ark, the mercy seat, the table of showbread, and the utensils placed on the table of showbread (25:11, 17, 24, 29). The lampstand serves the practical function of illuminating the Holy Place (25:37). As the lampstand shines, the golden hue of its light fills the interior of the Holy Place with a glorious radiance. The oil used for the lampstand burns continuously, symbolizing God's ongoing presence with his people (27:20–21).[44]

The significance of the lampstand is evident in its enduring presence in Jewish culture. Pictorial representations of the lampstand can be found in synagogues, tombs, catacombs, and amulets,[45] serving as a symbol of Judaism and an emblem of the State of Israel. In addition, many OT scholars, myself included, display replicas or images of the lampstand in their offices.

Verse 40 forms an *inclusio* with verse 9, bookending the divine instructions concerning the construction of the ark, the table of showbread, and the lampstand. All these elements are to be built in conformity with the pattern that God reveals to Moses on the mountain (25:9, 40).

---

41. Despite these details, the descriptions of the lampstand are ambiguous on multiple levels. The architectural design of the shaft and cups along with the botanical terms of the lampstand suggest Egyptian influence. See Sarna, *Exodus*, 164.
42. For example, Genesis 2:9; 3:22, 24; Proverbs 3:18; 11:30; 13:12; 15:4; Revelation 2:7; 22:2, 14, 19. Though not stated explicitly, the tree in Psalm 1 also suggests that it is a tree of life (Ps 1:3; Jer 17:8). The trees of life are also present in Ezekiel's temple vision (Ezek 47:7, 12). See also, Beale and Kim, *God Dwells Among Us*, 42.
43. Pitkänen, "Temple Building and Exodus 25–40," 278.
44. In South Asia, the practice of the light remaining lit in the temple is common in various religious traditions. George and Swarup, "Exodus," 115.
45. Tigay, "Exodus," 159. Sarna, *Exodus*, 165. There is a series of concise articles on the reception history of the lampstand (menorah) from the Hebrew Bible, Second Temple Judaism, Rabbinic Judaism, and Medieval Judaism to modern Judaism to Christianity in a variety of forms including textual and visual aspects in *EBR* 18: 645–661.

26:1–27:21 EXTERNAL CONSTRUCTION: THE EXTERIOR OF THE TABERNACLE

Our first impression of a building is often influenced by its exterior. While some churches prioritize the interior design, others place greater emphasis on the exterior appearance. In the United States, many Chinese churches use industrial warehouses as their worship space, as a result of which outsiders are often unaware that these buildings serve as churches. In such cases, practicality and functionality take precedence over other considerations. Cost is the main factor that contributes to the "low profile" appearance of these Chinese churches because decorating the exterior with precious gems or gold is costly and may even invite theft. In contrast, the exterior of the tabernacle is described in colorful, glorious, and eye-catching detail, indicating that God values both the interior and exterior of this structure. Everything about the tabernacle reflects divine beauty and glory.

26:1–14 Curtains

The instructions now shift from the interior furnishings in the Holy of Holies and the Holy Place to the exterior curtains that serve as the coverings or the roof of the tabernacle.[46] At first glance, the number of curtains required for the tabernacle can seem confusing since the text does not explicitly state their number. Based on the instructions provided in this section of Scripture, the tabernacle appears to have four layers of curtains, each made from materials of decreasing value, with the finest material used in the lowest layer and a durable skin[47] – the least valuable but most durable material – used in the uppermost layer. The table below describes the four layers and the materials used:

---

46. Anderson notices the word "curtain" appears 14 times in Exodus 26:1–14, suggesting its importance. Anderson, *That I May Dwell among Them*, 15.
47. The exact nature of this durable skin (*tahash*) is uncertain. It has been translated in various ways, including "the dolphin skin" (ISV), "the porpoise skin" (NASB), "a covering of the other durable leather" (NIV), "fine goatskin leather" (NLT), "badgers' skins" (KJV, NKJV), "sealskins" (ASV, JPS), and "fine skin" (NRSV). Noonan's research suggests this skin may indicate a type of leather. Benjamin J. Noonan, "Hide or Hue? Defining Hebrew *taḥaš*," *Biblica* 93 (4), (2012): 586–589.

Table 13: Materials Used for Different Layers of the Curtain

Layers of the Curtain	Materials Used
1. The lowest layer (26:1–6)	Finely twisted linen and blue, purple, and scarlet yarn, with cherubim (26:1); Clasps made of gold (26:6)
2. The second layer (26:7–13)	Goat hair (26:7); Clasps made of bronze (26:11)
3. The third and fourth layers (26:14)	Ram skins dyed red for the third layer and a durable skin for the fourth layer (26:14)

The lowest layer consists of "ten curtains of finely twisted linen and blue, purple and scarlet yarn, with cherubim woven into them by a skilled worker" (26:1). Each curtain measures 28 cubits in length and 4 cubits in width (equivalent to 12.8 x 8 meters) and is joined with four other curtains to create two sets of curtains. In addition, 50 blue loops are made and fastened along the edge of the end curtain of each set, and then 50 clasps of gold are made and inserted into these loops to form the tabernacle into a unified whole (26:2–6).

The second layer is made of goat hair – a coarser material than the finely twisted linen in the lowest layer – and is laid above the previous layer (26:7). This layer consists of 11 curtains, each measuring 30 cubits in length and 4 cubits in width (equivalent to 13.7 x 1.8 meters), which is larger than the previous layer. These curtains are grouped into two sets, one with five curtains and the other with six. The meaning of "fold the sixth curtain double at the front of the tent" (26:9) is unclear but may refer to "leaving an overhang of 10 cubits on the north and south sides so that the coverings of the goat hair just touch the ground."[48] To fasten the curtains and form them into one unit, 50 loops and 50 bronze clasps are made (26:8–11). Furthermore, the overhanging part is to hang down over the back of the tabernacle (26:12–13).

The instructions then briefly describe the third and fourth layers of curtains. The phrase "over that" (26:14) indicates that these layers are to be placed on top of the previous two layers. The third layer is made of ram skins dyed red, a material commonly used by shepherds, herdsmen, and travelers to construct tents due to its durability.[49] The fourth layer is made of a durable skin, provid-

---

48. Sarna, *Exodus*, 168.
49. L. Devries, "Sheepskin," *ISBE* IV: 466. Kaiser remarks that the ram skins have had all the wool removed and then have been dyed red, making them appear very much like "Moroccan leather." Kaiser Jr, "Exodus," 453.

ing the strongest protection for the roof of the tabernacle.[50] The reasons for choosing these materials are not explained in the text, which suggests that the original audience would have been familiar with their properties and functions.

26:15–30 Frames, Bases, Crossbars

After the instructions about the exterior curtains, we read detailed instructions for the construction of the tabernacle's frames. While the curtains represent the "soft" component of the exterior, the frames and bases form the hard, structural component (the "bones") that holds the entire tabernacle together. The tabernacle has three sides, with the east side open and the other three sides made of vertical frames crafted from acacia wood, with silver bases to stabilize them. Each frame has two parallel projections.[51] The south and north sides of the tabernacle have 20 frames each, supported by 40 silver bases. The west side – the rear of the tabernacle – has six frames, each 10 cubits high (4.6 meters) and 1.5 cubits wide (0.3 meters), though its thickness is not specified (26:15–22). For the rear corners of the tabernacle, God instructs Moses to make two frames that are "double from the bottom all the way to the top and fitted into a single ring" (26:24). Altogether, there are to be 8 frames and 16 silver bases – two under each frame (26:23–25). The instructions regarding the construction of these corner frames are somewhat ambiguous.

While gold is chosen as the metal with which to overlay the interior furniture of the tabernacle, silver is chosen as the material to construct the bases for the frames of the tabernacle, probably due to its durability and also because, being less valuable than gold, it symbolically reflected the intentional design of diminishing holiness in different parts of the tabernacle. The ark of the covenant, being the holiest piece of furniture in the tabernacle, is overlaid with pure gold. Therefore, the varying values of the metals used indicate a deliberate design that reflects varying degrees of holiness.

Crossbars made of acacia wood are to be used to secure the frames. Five crossbars are used for the frames on one side of the tabernacle, and another five crossbars are used on the other side of the tabernacle to the west. The central crossbar is to extend from end to end at the middle of the frames. The crossbars and the rings that hold them, as well as the boards, are to be overlaid with gold. God then instructs Moses to erect the tabernacle according to the plan shown to him on the mountain (26:26–30). Together with the curtains,

---

50. See note on Exodus 25:5.
51. Literally, "hands." Other translations include "tenons" (NASB, JPS).

the tabernacle will radiate with the colorful beauty of gold, blue, purple, and scarlet, manifesting the glory and beauty of divine presence.

26:31–37 Veil and Screen

The instructions now return to the interior of the tabernacle, focusing on the curtain that divides the Holy Place from the Holy of Holies. This curtain is the veil or curtain that was torn from top to bottom when Jesus died on the cross (Matt 27:51). It is to be made of blue, purple, and scarlet yarn and finely twisted linen that matches the tabernacle's outer curtains. The cherubim skillfully woven or embroidered into the veil enhance its aesthetic beauty and value. The presence of cherubim – who are often associated with God's presence – conveys the idea that this veil guards and protects the sacred space and prevents it from being profaned.

The veil is to be hung using gold hooks on four acacia wood posts overlaid with gold, which are supported by four silver bases. Its function serves as a partition between the Holy Place and the Holy of Holies. God instructs Moses to position the ark of the testimony and the mercy seat inside the veil – in the Holy of Holies – and the table of showbread outside the veil, facing north, in the Holy Place. The lampstand is to be placed opposite the table of showbread, toward the south (26:31–35).

To form the entrance to the tent, God instructs Moses to make a screen of blue, purple, and scarlet yarn and finely twisted linen, matching the color and materials used for the veil. The mention of "the work of an embroiderer" suggests that the screen, like the veil, is a work of art created by a skilled artist. God then instructs Moses to "make gold hooks for this curtain and five posts of acacia wood overlaid with gold. And cast five bronze bases for them" (26:37). While the veil is supported by silver bases, the screen has bronze bases. The shift from gold to silver and then to bronze as one moves from the interior to the exterior of the tabernacle symbolizes a transition from higher to lower levels of holiness but also reflects increasing durability.

27:1–8 The Bronze Altar

The instructions now shift from the entrance of the tabernacle to the Outer Court. The first object one sees upon entering the tabernacle is the altar,[52] where people and priests come together to offer sacrifices. The altar is to be

---

[52]. It is, then, not a surprise that the altar law is mentioned first in the Book of the Covenant (Exod 20:22–26). The altar also dominates the first seven chapters of Leviticus.

made of acacia wood and overlaid with bronze. It is square in shape and measures five cubits in length and width (7.5 feet or 2.3 meters) and three cubits in height (4.5 feet or 1.35 meters). This altar features four bronze horns at its corners, perhaps intended to hold the animal sacrifice in place.[53] Later narratives describe people seeking refuge by grasping the horns of the altar.[54] The horns and the altar are not made separately but formed as one piece, perhaps symbolizing unity.

All the utensils associated with the altar are to be made of bronze, including the pots for removing the ashes, shovels, sprinkling bowls, meat forks, and firepans. These utensils resemble those used in household kitchens. The altar is designed to be portable and is carried with poles. It is also hollow, and Rabbinic sources suggest that the empty space is filled with earth to prevent the fire from damaging the altar and burning the sacrifice.[55] Overall, the altar resembles a cooking stove where God receives people's sacrifices, after which he has fellowship with them by dining at the table in the Holy Place.[56] This image of dining together – similar to a meal shared by family members sitting around a dining table – connotes intimacy and fellowship, underscoring God's desire to be with his people.

27:9–21 The Outer Court

After giving instructions on how to build the altar in the Outer Court, God now directs Moses's attention to the structure of this Outer Court. This refers to the entire tabernacle enclosure, including its outer frame, curtains,[57] and the pillars that support the whole tabernacle structure. Referring to a diagram of the tabernacle will help readers to visualize its structural design and symmetry.

The tabernacle's courtyard is to measure 100 cubits long (45.7 meters or 150 feet), 50 cubits wide (22.9 meters or 75 feet), and 5 cubits high (2.3 meters or 7.5 feet) – which is exactly half the height of the tabernacle. On the south and north sides of the tabernacle, there are 20 pillars and 20 bronze bases, with silver hooks and bands on the pillars. The curtains that cover these pillars are made of finely twisted linen (27:9–11). At the west (rear) and east sides of the tabernacle, there are 10 pillars with 10 bases.

---

53. Compare Psalm 118:27.
54. For example, when the plan of usurpation of David's throne fails, Adonijah grasps the horns of the altar and asks Solomon to spare his life (1 Kgs 1:51).
55. Tigay, "Exodus," 161.
56. Longman, *How to Read Exodus*, 139.
57. Or, "hangings" (NASB).

The whole enclosure has three sides, with an entrance measuring 20 cubits on the east side. This entrance is shielded by a screen that also measures 20 cubits and is made from blue, purple, and scarlet yarn and finely twisted linen, crafted by an embroiderer (27:16). The quality and colors of the materials match those used to make the veil of the tabernacle (26:36), reflecting its artistic beauty and God's careful design. All the utensils of the courtyard, and also its tent pegs, are made of bronze rather than gold or silver, symbolizing that the tabernacle is designed to reflect increasing levels of holiness from the outside in, as reflected in the use of bronze in the Outer Court and silver and gold inside, with the ark of the covenant – the most holy object – being made of pure gold.

The last two verses of chapter 27 return to the subject of the lampstand. God tells Moses to instruct the Israelites to bring "clear oil of pressed olives for the light so that the lamps may be kept burning." The word used for "light" here is literally "luminary," the same word used in Genesis 1:14–16. Some may wonder why the author of Genesis chose not to name the sun and the moon but, instead, used the word "luminary" to designate them. However, reading Genesis 1 in light of Exodus, we see the close connection between the tabernacle and the creation narrative. Just as the lampstand functions as a luminary to give light to the Holy Place, the sun and the moon serve as luminaries that give light to the world. In a broader sense, the whole world is God's Holy Place, filled with his presence.

It is also worth noting that the word "luminary" is only used to designate the lights on the tabernacle lampstand, emphasizing the irrefutable connection between the creation narrative and the tabernacle.[58] The diagram below illustrates this connection:

---

58. Beale, *The Temple and the Church's Mission*, 34.

Exodus

Figure 4: The Luminaries and the Golden Lampstand

The tripartite division in the creation of the world parallels the tripartite structure of the tabernacle. In ancient cosmology, the temple is seen as the mini-cosmos where the gods reign. Therefore, the temple symbolizes "heaven on earth."[59] Since the tabernacle serves as a prototype of the temple, it reflects divine presence and design. We will revisit the theme of creation and temple later, after examining the account of the completion of the tabernacle construction.

The words "be kept burning" (27:20) literally mean "to ascend" or "to go up," evoking the image of the lights ascending to give light to the Holy Place. While the frame and furnishings of the tabernacle require one-time construction, if the lampstand is to give light without ceasing, this necessitates a constant supply of oil. "Clear oil of pressed olives" refers to the oil already described in Exodus 25:6. "Clear" denotes refined oil that is free from impurities. The production of clear oil involves pounding the olives in a mortar with a pestle rather than grinding them in a mill and then filtering through a strainer. This refined oil is reserved exclusively for use in the lampstand in the tabernacle.[60]

Some Chinese Christians offer a spiritualized interpretation of biblical texts, reading the text from a faith perspective and then applying it to their spiritual journey or relationship with God. In this regard, some may understand the "clear oil of pressed olives" as a metaphor for the believer's process of sanctification, where believers need to be hard-pressed by God through suffering or hardships to become instruments worthy of being used by God

---

59. Beale, *The Temple and the Church's Mission*, 36.
60. Sarna, *Exodus*, 176.

as "lights." Some Chinese pastors offer this approach to reading Scripture to encourage their congregations to persevere in their faith when faced with harsh realities or persecution. Though this form of interpretation can be taken as a spiritual application of the text, it may not be what the narrator intends to convey to the audience.

Initially, Aaron and his sons are charged with the responsibility of lighting the lampstand. However, in later texts, Aaron is solely responsible for this sacred task (Exod 30:7–8; Lev 24:3; Num 8:1–3). The mention of Aaron here also serves as a fitting transition into the next two chapters, which contain instructions about priestly garments and the consecration of priests.

28:1–29:46 RIGHT CLOTHING AND THE RITE OF PASSAGE

In various church traditions, special clothing is worn by pastors and priests to distinguish them from laypeople. For example, a detachable white collar – often referred to as a clerical collar – is buttoned onto a black clergy shirt, and this shirt is usually fastened by metal studs at the front and back to keep it in place.[61] In the Roman Catholic and Episcopal-Anglican traditions, clergy often wear elaborate and colorful robes with sashes when conducting services or performing other priestly functions. In most Chinese Christian traditions, although pastors do not wear special clothing in their day-to-day ministry, they often wear their ordination robes on special occasions such as when conducting baptism services or officiating at weddings or funerals. Putting on special garments signifies that the services being performed are sacred and affirms the legitimacy of those performing these services.

28:1–5 Priestly Garments

Following the mention of the priests who serve at the tabernacle – namely, Aaron and his sons (27:21) – the focus now shifts to the priestly garments. In the OT, as in many other cultures, clothing not only serves to cover and protect the body but, more importantly, functions as a symbol of identity and status. A change in clothing signifies a change in identity, position, and status. For example, a police uniform immediately identifies a person's role in law enforcement. A person's uniform identifies their role and function.

The tripartite design of the priestly garments, corresponding to the tripartite division of the tabernacle, consists of three pieces of clothing: the robe, the

---

61. Wayne, "History of the Clerical Collar," https://www.mycollarsandcuffs.com/2016/09/20/history-of-the-clerical-collar/.

ephod, and the breastpiece, which reflect increasing levels of holiness from the outside in. The colors of the garments – gold, blue, purple, and scarlet – match the colors used in the tabernacle. The gems and precious stones used for the ephod and the breastpiece are also mentioned in Exodus 25:7 and evoke the image of the glittering stars in the sky.[62] This elaborately adorned garment not only reflects the beauty and glory of God but also emphasizes the special role of Aaron, the high priest (28:2). When a priest puts on this attire, he is set apart and consecrated to serve as a mediator between two worlds – the human and the divine realms.[63]

God had called Israel to be a kingdom of priests, and the special identity and status of the priests serves as a vivid picture of Israel's role and a model for them to emulate as they carry out their priestly function among the nations. Israel is expected to mediate between two worlds – God and the nations – by teaching the nations who God is and bringing the nations into the family of God.

Aaron and his sons – Nadab, Abihu, Eleazar, and Ithamar – are chosen by God from among the Israelites to minister as priests who are set apart by God to serve him.[64] The priestly garments are described as holy, set apart from the profane, and designed for glory and beauty. The skilled workers who make these garments are endowed by God with "wisdom" (28:3). Since "skilled workers" literally means "wise of heart," in this context, "wisdom" refers to artistic skill. The priestly garments are to be made with both skill and a spirit of wisdom. Although skill can be developed through practice, a spirit of wisdom comes from God (Prov 9:10).

Another function of the priestly garments was to set apart the priests for service to God (28:3–4). When the priests wore these garments, they acted as mediator between God and Israel. The garments included six items: a

---

62. Beale, *The Temple and the Church's Mission*, 39.
63. Carmen Joy Imes, "Between Two Worlds: The Functional and Symbolic Significance of the High Priestly Regalia," in *Dress and Clothing in the Hebrew Bible: "For All Her Household Are Clothed in Crimson,"* LHBOTS, ed. Antonios Finites (London: T&T Clark, 2019), 29–62. Christine Palmer, "Israelite High Priestly Apparel: Embodying an Identity between Human and Divine," in *Fashioned Selves: Dress and Identity in Antiquity*, ed. Megan Cifarelli (Havertown: Oxbow Books, 2019), 117.
64. Nadab and Abihu are named among those who went up to Mount Sinai (Exod 24:1). They later offered strange fire to God and died before God (Lev 10:1–3). Eleazar and Ithamar served as priests when Aaron was alive (Num 3:4). Eleazar succeeds Aaron as the high priest (Num 20:25–28).

breastpiece, an ephod, a robe, a woven tunic, a turban, and a sash.[65] Instructions for the garment to be worn by the high priest, Aaron, are given first (28:6–39), followed by instructions pertaining to the garments of his sons (28:40–43). The descriptions of Aaron's priestly garments are far more elaborate than those of his sons, highlighting the higher and "holier" status of the high priest compared to regular priests. The high priestly garment symbolizes the highest order of holiness and "can only be worn by one man at one time in all of Israel."[66]

The distinctiveness of the priestly garments is similar to the way a modern graduation ceremony might have the graduates from different degree programs wearing different colored gowns and sashes or hoods to distinguish one program or school from another. Typically, the higher the level of the academic degree, the more colorful and costly the regalia.

28:6–14 Ephod

The ephod is a vest-like garment that is worn over the robe but beneath the breastpiece. It corresponds to the middle portion of the tabernacle – the Holy Place.[67] The ephod is made of the same finely twisted linen and uses the same colors as the curtain and the veil: gold, blue, purple, and scarlet. One can imagine the high priest wearing the golden ephod that reflects the light of the sun in the Outer Court as well as the light of the golden lampstand in the Holy Place. The ephod of the high priest radiates divine luminosity.[68]

Like the first layer of the curtain and the veil (26:1, 31), the ephod is also designed by skilled hands. Two shoulder straps of the same color and material are used to secure the ephod on Aaron's shoulders. Two onyx stones, each engraved with the names of six tribes of Israel according to their birth order, are mounted on the shoulder straps,[69] symbolizing Aaron bearing their names before God as a memorial. The twice repeated "memorial" in Exodus 28:12 emphasizes Aaron's role in remembering the Israelites and God's mindfulness of them.[70]

---

65. Exodus 28:4 mentions six items, but the plate and the undergarment (Exod 28:36, 42) are mentioned later.
66. Palmer, "Israelite High Priestly Apparel," 118.
67. The reason why the ephod is mentioned before the breastpiece could be because the breastpiece depends on the ephod to be put in place, as the two are one unit. See Imes, "Between Two Worlds," 31, note 6.
68. Palmer, "Israelite High Priestly Apparel," 123.
69. Genesis 29:32–30:24; 35:16–18.
70. Sarna, *Exodus*, 179.

28:15–30 Breastpiece

The breastpiece, a square pouch that is worn on the chest, is the most conspicuous part of the priestly garment. It measures about 24 centimeters (9.5 inches) and is adorned with precious gemstones.[71] The proportion of space devoted to instructions about the breastplate reflects its significance. It is also described as "the breastpiece of judgment" (NASB) or a "breastpiece for making decisions" (NIV). The NIV's translation is straightforward since it renders the word "judgment" as "making decisions." "Judgment" (*mishpat*) involves discerning God's will. The Urim and Thummim are kept inside the breastpiece and function as instruments for decision-making, but how exactly they work remains unclear (28:30). Urim comes from the word meaning "light," whereas "Thummim" comes from the word meaning "complete." Perhaps these instruments reflect God's light in illuminating the decision-making process and the complete will of God.

Similar to the ephod, the breastpiece is made of the same color and material – gold, blue, purple, and scarlet in fine twisted linen, crafted skillfully by hand. Mounted on the ephod are 12 stones, arranged in 4 rows, each representing the name of one of the sons of Israel. Of these 12 stones, only the identities of turquoise and lapis lazuli are confirmed. A study of these gemstones shows that turquoise is virtually absent in the archaeological record of Egypt and the ancient Near East after the twelfth century BCE, which suggests that the tradition of the breastpiece of the high priest belongs to a much earlier date than some scholars think. Also, 5 of the 12 stones have Egyptian etymology, being mentioned in the New Kingdom period (1550–1100 BCE).[72] These stones are engraved like a signet ring and their arrangement is shown in the following table.[73]

---

71. A span (Exod 28:16) is "the maximum distance between the top of the little finger and the thumb," so it is about 9 or 9.5 inches. The word is believed to be of Egyptian origin. See Sarna, *Exodus*, 180.
72. Harrell, Hoffmeier, and Williams, "Hebrew Gemstones in the Old Testament," 43–45.
73. Different translations render the names of the stones differently. This table follows the NIV's translation. It is worth noting that nine of twelve stones appear in Ezekiel 28:13 ("You were in Eden, the garden of God; every precious stone adorned you: carnelian, chrysolite and emerald, topaz, onyx and jasper, lapis lazuli, turquoise and beryl. Your settings and mountings were made of gold; on the day you were created they were prepared"), describing the gemstones found in the Garden of Eden, suggesting the close affinity between the high priest, the tabernacle, and the Garden of Eden. See Sarna, *Exodus*, 190.

Table 14: Stones on the Breastpiece[74]

Row	Stones
1	Carnelian, chrysolite, and beryl
2	Turquoise, lapis lazuli, and emerald
3	Jacinth, agate, and amethyst
4	Topaz, onyx, and jasper

God also instructs Moses to make braided chains of pure gold, resembling ropes, and gold rings to fasten the breastpiece to the ephod. The detailed description of how to fasten the breastpiece to the ephod "so that the breastpiece will not swing out from the ephod" (28:28) demonstrates its utmost importance. Whenever Aaron enters the Holy Place, he is to carry the names of the sons of Israel over his heart as a continuous memorial before God. With the Urim and Thummim inside the breastpiece, Aaron will always bear the means of decision-making for the Israelites over his heart before God. The repetition of "over his heart" (28:29–30) emphasizes the position of the breastpiece above the chest, symbolizing that Aaron carries and bears the Israelites in (or close to) his heart. Aaron is to remember the people of God as he enters the Holy Place before the presence of God and make decisions on their behalf or for their well-being.

28:31–35 Robe

The ankle-length robe known as the "robe of the ephod" is blue and is worn beneath the breastpiece, forming a unified garment with the ephod. This robe corresponds to the Outer Court of the tabernacle. Some scholars suggest that this was a sleeveless[75] and poncho-style robe,[76] opening at the top, with a binding to prevent tearing.[77] The hem is adorned with pomegranates of blue, purple, and scarlet that alternate with gold bells.

Pomegranates, which symbolized fertility in the ancient world, feature in the temple of Solomon[78] and are mentioned frequently in the Song of

---

74. The precise color and identity of each of these stones may be difficult to confirm but carnelian is most likely reddish, and beryl is green. Harrell, Hoffmeier, and Williams, "Hebrew Gemstones in the Old Testament," 10, 17.
75. For example, Tigay, "Exodus," 165.
76. Imes, "Between Two Worlds," 34.
77. The opening of the robe is called the "lip" (Exod 28:32).
78. 1 Kings 7:42; 2 Kings 25:17; Jeremiah 52:23; 2 Chronicles 3:16; 4:13.

Songs.[79] Whenever Aaron enters or leaves the Holy Place, the tinkling of the golden bells on the hem of his garment would signal his location and give an audio sense of his presence.[80] People would hear the high priest's footsteps in the Holy of Holies even though they could not see him. "So that he will not die" (28:35) emphasizes that violating God's instructions, particularly acting contrary to God's holiness, results in death.[81]

28:36–39 Turban and Gold Plate

A pure gold plate[82] with the inscription "HOLY TO THE LORD" is to be fastened to the front of Aaron's turban with a blue cord. This plate serves as a constant reminder that Aaron is set apart by God to perform priestly services. Since the word for plate (*sis*) means "blossom" or "flower," this may point to its artistic and beautiful design, like a blossoming flower. Aaron is to wear this turban on his forehead, symbolizing that Aaron would bear the guilt involved in the sacred gifts consecrated by the Israelites so that they might be accepted by God (28:38).

This section concludes with instructions to use fine linen for weaving Aaron's tunic and for making his turban. His sash is to be made by an embroiderer (28:39), just as with the screen for the entrance of the tabernacle (26:36) and the screen for the gate of the Outer Court (27:16).

28:40–43 Garments for Aaron and His Sons

The next set of instructions is about the priestly garments for Aaron's sons, which includes all priests. Moses is to make tunics, sashes, and caps for them for the purpose of bestowing dignity and honor upon them (28:40).[83] While Aaron's priestly garment includes an ephod, a breastpiece, and a robe, his sons wear only tunics, highlighting the superior status of Aaron's priesthood. While the materials used for Aaron's garment are also used in the interior of

---

79. For example, slices of pomegranate are used to describe the bride's temples (Song of Songs 4:3; 6:7), the metaphorical description of the bride's body (Song 4:13), the orchard (6:11), and the bride's "drink" (8:2). It seems that pomegranate is used exclusively for the female character in the Song of Songs. Unsurprisingly, this book is associated with the temple imagery. Sun, *Conspicuous in His Absence*, 140–147.
80. Palmer, "Israelite High Priestly Apparel," 121.
81. In South Asia, though worshipers may not wear bells when entering a temple or sanctuary, bells are rung. When the priests chant certain prayers or make offerings, bells are also rung. George and Swarup, "Exodus," 118.
82. Or, "the frontlet."
83. NASB renders it as "for glory and for beauty."

the tabernacle, the material used for his sons' garments matches the hangings of the Outer Court, reflecting their subordinate position.[84] God then instructs Moses to dress Aaron and his sons in these garments, anoint them, ordain them,[85] and consecrate them so that they may serve God as priests. The detailed instructions about the priestly garments emphasize the importance of preparing Aaron and his sons to serve as priests before God.[86]

The chapter concludes by describing the linen undergarments that Aaron and his sons must wear whenever they enter the tabernacle. These undergarments, which provide cover from the waist to the thigh, are designed to cover their nakedness and thus prevent them from incurring guilt and dying. Notably, there is no mention of footwear, implying that the priests enter the tabernacle barefoot. This practice is consistent with God's instructions to Moses and Joshua to remove their sandals in his presence because they stand on holy ground (Exod 3:5; Josh 5:15). When entering God's home, one must abide by the house rules of the host.

29:1–9 Consecration of the Priests

With the priestly garments now prepared, the priests must undergo a formal process of consecration before they are able to perform the services of the priesthood. This practice of consecration is similar to the contemporary ordination service for pastors. While the nature of the ordination service varies depending on denominational and church traditions, it typically takes place at the church where the pastoral candidate is ministering. After serving in congregational ministry for a specified time period, the pastoral candidate typically goes through an ordination process that involves examination by an ordination committee, which must assess and approve the candidate's conduct, faith, and theological and denominational knowledge. The climax of the ordination service usually includes "initiating" the candidate into pastoral ministry by laying on hands by the ordination committee. The candidate then faces the congregation and is given a robe as a symbol of their new role as an ordained pastor and receives the acceptance and blessing of the congregation.

---

84. Tigay, "Exodus," 166.
85. Literally, "fill their hands." Since hands symbolize power, "fill their hands" may refer to the idea of giving them the power to serve as priests.
86. Chapter 28 can be added to Gentry's texts in defining the meaning of holiness. He cites Exodus 3, 19, and Isaiah 6 to argue for the meaning of holiness as "consecrated" and "devoted" to the service of God rather than the meaning of separation in its strictest sense. Gentry, "The Meaning of 'Holy' in the Old Testament," 400–417.

After this service, the pastoral candidate becomes an officially ordained pastor with the new title "Reverend."

In the Chinese Christian context, those who have not yet been ordained are often referred to as "ministers" (*Chuán daò rén*, which means "a person who preaches the Word"), while those who have been ordained are called "pastors" (*Mù shī*, which means "the one who shepherds"). Despite many differences in detail, Exodus 29 may resonate with contemporary church practices.

Exodus 29 begins with God's instructions to Moses regarding the ritual of consecrating the priests to God. This ritual reflects the rite of passage to a new status, where the priests must enter from the "outer, profane world to the sanctity of the tabernacle precinct."[87] During the ordination process, Moses acts as the "Master of Ceremonies" and serves as a mediator between God and the priests. The consecration ritual lasts seven days and involves the following steps:[88]

A. Moses shall present the sacrifices (29:1–3).
B. Moses shall bring Aaron and his sons to the entrance of the tabernacle and cleanse them with water (29:4).
C. Moses shall dress Aaron in the priestly garments, including the turban and the sacred emblem that is attached to the turban (29:5–6).
D. Moses shall anoint Aaron's head with oil (29:7).
E. Moses shall put tunics on the sons of Aaron and gird them with sashes (29:8–9).

The instructions then shift back to the sacrifices mentioned at the beginning of the chapter.

29:10–28 The Sacrifices

The sacrifices consist of one bull and two rams. First, Aaron and his sons lay their hands on the bull and confess their sins. Moses then slaughters the bull at the entrance of the tabernacle, sprinkles some of its blood on the horns of the altar, and burns the fat and kidneys as a sin offering on the altar. Next, Aaron and his sons lay their hands on the first ram, slaughter it, sprinkle its blood on the altar, cut it into pieces, and offer it as a burnt offering on the altar. Then Aaron and his sons lay their hands on the second ram, slaughter it, and apply

---

87. Morales, *The Tabernacle Pre-Figured*, 263.
88. A parallel text appears in Leviticus 8–9.

some of its blood on the right earlobe, thumb, and big toe of Aaron and his sons, symbolizing the dedication of their entire bodies. Finally, Moses takes some of the blood and some of the anointing oil and sprinkles this on Aaron, his sons, and their garments to consecrate them and their priestly garments.

After the sacrifices of the bull and the two rams, Moses takes the fat of the ram, along with the unleavened bread and oil, and places these in the hands of Aaron and his sons. After they wave these as a wave offering before God, Moses takes these things from their hands and burns them on the altar as an offering to God. Moses then takes the breast of Aaron's ram and waves it as a wave offering, and this will be Moses's share. For Aaron and his sons, Moses consecrates the breast of the wave offering and the thigh presented (other translations call this the "heave offering") as their perpetual portion.

29:29–30 The Priestly Garments

These verses emphasize the importance of the priestly garments as essential attire for the priests to carry out their duties. During the seven days of consecration, Aaron's sons are required to wear these garments whenever they enter the Holy Place of the tabernacle.

29:31–42a The Food for the Priests

This passage gives instructions about what the priests were to eat during the seven-day ordination service.[89] God instructs Moses to take the ram of ordination and boil it in a sacred place. Aaron and his sons are to eat it, along with the bread from the basket (29:2–3). This meal serves as a sacrificial meal, as prescribed in Leviticus 7:13 and 7:15; laypeople are forbidden to eat it and any leftovers are to be burned.[90] The repetition of "because they are sacred" (29:33–34) emphasizes the sacred status of this bread reserved for the priests.

Verses 35–37 state that this entire ritual must be repeated every day during the seven-day ceremony. This seven-day ritual can be seen as a liminal phase in which the priests are not yet officially ordained but are in a transitional phase that is fraught with both danger and possibility.[91] Verses 38–42 then return

---

89. The parallel text of Exodus 29:31–37 appears in Leviticus 8:31–36, where the service is divided into seven units, concluding with an approbatory formula, though this formula varies in Leviticus 8:33. Anderson, *That I May Dwell among Them*, 79–80.
90. Lay people are literally "strangers" or "foreigners," highlighting their profane nature in comparison with the sacred status of the priests.
91. Imes, "Between Two Worlds," 52. Anderson notices the repetition of the word "altar" in verses 36–37, which marks a transition from focusing on Aaron to the altar where he will serve. Anderson, *That I May Dwell among Them*, 81.

to the subject of the animal sacrifices that Moses is to offer on the altar. The two rams are to be offered at twilight each day, along with fine flour mixed with oil and wine, at the entrance of the tabernacle, where God will meet with Moses and speak to him. The mention of "twilight" recalls the timing of the Passover (12:6), suggesting the keeping of the memory of God's rescue of the Israelites as they make the daily sacrifice of the rams.

29:42b–46 The Lord's Visitation

The detailed instructions about the ordination process conclude with God's reassuring promises, expressed in the first person, that he will meet with the Israelites at the entrance of the tabernacle. God sets apart the tabernacle and its altar, as well as Aaron and his sons as priests to God. God will dwell among the Israelites and be their God. That was why he wanted them to build the tabernacle according to his design. Exodus 29:46 expresses the book's theological purpose statement: "They will know that I am the LORD their God, who brought them out of Egypt so that I might dwell among them. I am the LORD their God" (29:46). All the lengthy and meticulous instructions given to Moses point to this grand mission of God to be known by this people whom God had rescued from Egypt and made his own special people. God longs to dwell among them and be in a covenantal relationship with them.

30:1–31:18 THE ALTAR OF INCENSE, THE OIL, AND THE BUILDERS

In many Asian cultures, the veneration of local deities and dead ancestors through folk religion has been prevalent since antiquity. Burning incense to honor these deities or ancestors is a common ritual used in worship and in seeking to appease these deities and seeking personal favors. Chinese Christians living with family members who follow such practices face a dilemma: Are they to participate in this religious tradition out of respect for their family's tradition, or, in obedience to the first commandment, "You shall have no other gods before me," should they refuse to do so? Although the cultic practices in God's tent of meeting resemble the practices in many ancient religions and cultures, this does not imply that all religions are the same. The worship of Yahweh is not the same as the worship in traditional Chinese folk religions.

Exodus 30 presents five scenes, which may be viewed as an appendix to the description of the tabernacle. Each scene, except the first, begins with a similar phrase: "Then the LORD said to Moses" (30:11, 17, 22, 34; see also 31:1, 12). This chapter provides detailed instructions about various elements in the Holy Place, including the altar of incense and the holy oil used to light the golden lampstand. In chapter 31, the focus shifts to the builders of the tabernacle. The instructions for the construction of the tabernacle conclude with the Sabbath command.

Together, these two chapters present seven scenes, six of which relate to the construction of the tabernacle while the seventh focuses on the Sabbath command. The following table illustrates the structure of these seven literary units.

Table 15: The Seven Literary Units in Exodus 30–31

Unit	Exodus 30–31
1	Altar of incense (30:1–10)
2	Atonement money (30:11–16)
3	Basin for washing (30:17–21)
4	The holy anointing oil (30:22–33)
5	The incense (30:34–38)
6	The builders of the tabernacle (31:1–11)
7	The Sabbath command (31:12–18)

The pattern of work and rest in the instructions for the tabernacle parallels the pattern of creation in Genesis. This parallel highlights the close connection between the construction of the tabernacle and the creation of the world, which suggests that the purpose of the tabernacle is to restore the divine order God established when he created the world.

30:1–10 Unit 1: The Altar of Incense

The reason the instructions for the altar of incense are placed here rather than after chapter 27 is probably because of their connection to the priests. Only the priests are permitted to enter the Holy Place to burn incense at the altar of incense, and they cannot do so unless they are properly dressed and consecrated. Therefore, it makes sense to include the instructions concerning the priestly garments and ordination before addressing the priestly duties in the Holy Place, which include burning incense and lighting the golden lampstand.

The altar of incense, like the ark and the table of showbread, is made of acacia wood. It is square in shape, with a length and width of one cubit each (1.5 feet or 0.45 meters), and stands two cubits high (3 feet or 0.9 meters), making it nine inches higher than the table of showbread. This altar has horns, overlaid with gold all around. It is also portable, with gold rings and poles for carrying. The precise location of the altar is specified: "in front of the curtain that shields the ark of the covenant law – before the atonement cover that is over the tablets of the covenant law – where I will meet with you" (30:6). This specific location is given to distinguish it from the altar in the Outer Court.

The next set of instructions pertains to Aaron. He is responsible for burning incense on the altar of incense every morning and tending to the golden lampstand, ensuring that the incense burns continuously before God. God then warns against offering unauthorized incense on this altar, foreshadowing the incident where Nadab and Abihu, Aaron's sons, offer "unauthorized fire" before God at this altar and die (Lev 10:1–3).[92] As high priest, Aaron is also responsible for making atonement on the horn of this altar once a year on the Day of Atonement, the holiest day of the year (Lev 16).[93]

30:11–16 Unit 2: Atonement Money

The connection between the census and the previous section about the construction of the altar of incense is twofold. First, the census tax serves as an atonement for the Israelites; second, it is to be used for the construction of the tabernacle (30:15–16). "Take a census" literally means "lifting up the heads," which refers to a head count. Those who are counted in the census must make atonement for themselves so that there will be no plague among them. Being counted in the census protects a person and prevents dire consequences. The amount of this tax is half a shekel, and the age of requirement for participation is 20, which is also the required age for entering military service (compare Num 1:2–3). This tax is not an annual payment but a one-time contribution toward the construction of the tabernacle.[94]

30:17–21 Unit 3: Basin for Washing

The focus now shifts to the Outer Court. Having completed the instructions for constructing the altar in the Outer Court (Exod 27) and making the priestly garments (Exod 28), there is one more detail concerning the priestly functions in the Outer Court: cleansing. God instructs Moses to build a basin

---

92. Anderson's study on Nadab and Abihu concludes that their sin is not clearly specified. The whole incident invites terror and human discernment of God's instruction. The cost of the slightest human error is deadly. Therefore, Anderson takes this incident as an illustration of an apophatic theology. Anderson, *That I May Dwell among Them*, 134–140.
93. The word "atonement" is literally "covering" (from the root *kpr*), which appears again in Exodus 30:12, 15–16.
94. Sarna, *Exodus*, 195.

for washing. Like the altar in the Outer Court, this basin is made of bronze, and Moses is to fill the basin with water and place it "between the tent of meeting and the altar" (30:18). Aaron and his sons must wash their hands and feet from this basin whenever they enter the tabernacle structure or approach the altar to offer incense. Failure to do so will result in death.

The repeated instruction to wash their hands and feet to avoid death reinforces the seriousness of this ritual and its consequences. Although no details are given about the design of the basin, since the priests had to wash both their hands and their feet, it is likely that the basin had two tiers, with the top tier used for washing hands and the lower tier for washing feet. The priestly garments do not include footwear, suggesting that the priests go barefoot – therefore, washing their feet makes sense in the context of cleansing.

30:22–33 Unit 4: The Holy Anointing Oil

This section gives instructions about preparing the holy anointing oil that is used to anoint various items: the tent of meeting, the ark of the covenant, the table of showbread and its articles, the golden lampstand and its accessories, the altar of incense, the altar of burnt offering and its utensils, and the basin with its stand. The anointing oil – first mentioned in Exodus 25:6 – is made by mixing specified amounts of spices, including liquid myrrh, fragrant cinnamon, fragrant calamus, cassia, and olive oil (30:23–24).[95] Liquid myrrh, considered the finest and choicest myrrh, is produced by careful pressing and mixing.[96] Fragrant cinnamon, also known as spiced cinnamon, comes from trees that are native to what is today Sri Lanka in South Asia.[97] Calamus, also known as cane, stalk, or reed, is another component of this oil. The identity of cassia, however, remains unclear. The anointing oil is also used to anoint Aaron and his sons, consecrating them to minister as priests to God (30:30). The precise formula for making the oil and its exclusive use for consecrating holy vessels and priests emphasizes its sacredness. Anyone who violates the rules pertaining to this oil – either by attempting to replicate the formula or by using the oil for any other purpose – is to be "cut off from their people" (30:33), highlighting the gravity of seriousness to keep this instruction.[98]

---

95. Sarna indicates that the list of orders is in decreasing order of value. Sarna, *Exodus*, 198. "Spices" occurs frequently in the Song of Songs (4:10, 14, 16; 5:13; 6:2; 8:14).
96. *BDB*, 600. Myrrh appears frequently in the Song of Songs (1:13; 3:6; 4:6, 14; 5:2, 5, 13).
97. Sarna, *Exodus*, 198. Cinnamon also appears in Song of Songs 4:14 and Proverbs 7:17.
98. "Cut off" may refer to immediate death, premature death, the death of one's descendants, or banishment from a community. See Hamilton, *Exodus*, 516.

30:34–38 Unit 5: The Incense

This section provides a more detailed account of the ingredients used in making the incense, which is first mentioned in Exodus 25:6 and is closely connected with the anointing oil. This incense is to be used exclusively by the priests as they minister at the altar of incense. The ingredients for the incense include equal amounts of fragrant spices – gum resin, onycha, and galbanum – and pure frankincense. Gum resin may refer to drops from balsam or persimmon trees. It is not clear what onycha refers to, but its name, which means "nail," suggests that it might be a nail-shaped mollusk.[99] Galbanum is a gum resin extracted from a plant that grows in Turkistan, Persia, and Crete. It emits an odor when burned, but its odor is diffused when mixed with other spices. Frankincense is literally "whiteness" because it emits white smoke when burned.[100] This incense mixture must be salted, pure, and sacred. God then instructs Moses to take some of the mixture and grind it into a very fine powder. Part of this powder is to be placed before "the ark of the covenant law in the tent of meeting, where I will meet with you" (30:36). God also warns that anyone who attempts to replicate this incense formula will be "cut off from their people." The exclusivity of both the anointing oil and the incense for use in the tabernacle accentuates their sacredness, emphasizing that these are reserved for the holy God. The distinctive fragrance and aroma of the anointing oil and the incense underscore their function, which is to offer God a pleasing aroma from the worshipers. In Scripture, incense is often associated with prayer (Ps 141:2; Luke 1:10; Rev 5:8; 8:3–4). For the priests, burning incense on behalf of God's people is an act of worship. Although burning incense has parallels in Chinese and other Asian folk religions, the object of worship in such cases is entirely different. God demands exclusive worship.

31:1–11 Unit 6: The Builders of the Tabernacle

Just as the priests are set apart by God to serve in the tabernacle, God chooses the builders for the special task of constructing the tabernacle. This emphasizes that whoever is involved in the construction and service of the sacred space must be set apart by God for that purpose. God cares not only about the beauty and glory of the physical building and the garments of the priests who serve in the tabernacle, but also about the quality and character of the builders.

---

99. Sarna, *Exodus*, 199.
100. Sarna, *Exodus*, 199. Frankincense also appears frequently in the Song of Songs (3:6; 4:6, 14).

God chooses Bezalel from the tribe of Judah to build the tabernacle. Bezalel's name means "in the shadow of God," which implies that he is under God's protection. His father's name is Uri, which means "light."[101] It is uncertain whether Bezalel's grandfather, Hur, is the same person mentioned in Exodus 17. God has filled Bezalel with "the Spirit of God, with wisdom, with understanding, with knowledge and with all kinds of skills" to do what God has instructed (31:3). This is the first appearance of the term "wisdom" (*hokmah*) in the OT. Here, it refers to the skill and craftsmanship required to make artistic designs for work in precious metals and for cutting wood and stones for the tabernacle. To partner with Bezalel, God chooses Oholiab and a "dream team" of skilled workers.[102] The word "skilled" here is literally "wise of heart," reflecting the wisdom given by God to Bezalel and his team. From the provision of materials for building the tabernacle to its design, and from the priests who minister in the tabernacle to the workers who construct it, the entire process is guided and enabled by God. This does not mean that God orchestrates everything and people act like robots. Rather, God uses the artistic training and gifts of Bezalel and his team to "shape raw materials into beautiful form."[103]

Exodus 31:7–11 specifies that these skilled workers chosen by God are responsible for making the furniture, utensils, priestly garments, anointing oil, and fragrant incense according to the instructions God has given Moses. This brief summary follows the order of instructions already given in Exodus 25:10–31:6 and brings to a close the lengthy instructions for building the tabernacle. However, the real climax of all these instructions is found in unit 7, which deals with the Sabbath command.

31:12–18 Unit 7: The Sabbath Command

Up to this point, the construction of the tabernacle – the sacred space – has been the central focus of the narrative. The detailed instructions for its construction conclude with the Sabbath command, elevating the narrative to a new level and adding another dimension to the sacred space – namely, sacred time. Moreover, the Sabbath command both echoes and reinforces the close connection between the tabernacle and the creation of the world. Therefore, scene seven serves as the climax for multiple parts of the narrative. First, it

---

101. Compare 1 Chronicles 2:20; 2 Chronicles 1:5.
102. Oholiab means "the tent of the father," implying he is the right person to build God's tent.
103. Cornell, "Art on Mission with the Tabernacle Builders," 10.

serves as a conclusion for the first six scenes in Exodus 30–31. Second, it brings to a close the narrative of Exodus 25:10–31:11. In addition, the Sabbath command echoes the Sabbath day in the creation narrative (Gen 1:1–2:3) and points forward to the Sabbath command in Exodus 35:1–3, which precedes the actual construction of the tabernacle.[104]

In the Ten Commandments, God had already given the Sabbath command (20:8), indicating that it builds on the pattern of creation (20:9–11). In this concluding section, God introduces a new dimension: the Sabbath command becomes a sign between God and Israel throughout their generations as a perpetual covenant (31:13, 16–17). The repeated use of "sign," "holy," and the six-seven-day pattern highlights the significance of the Sabbath and its connection with creation, while the repeated warning about the death penalty highlights the dire consequence of violating the Sabbath command (31:14–15).

The Sabbath, as a sign of the covenant, has profound significance because it connects with other covenantal signs, such as the rainbow and circumcision.[105] This sign serves as a tangible symbol and reminder of God's commitment to fulfill his promises to Israel. The fact that God is the one who sanctifies Israel (31:13) is in line with God's earlier declaration that Israel will be a holy nation to God (19:6). While Israel is responsible for obeying God's commands, the task of sanctification is carried out by God.

The six-seven-day work-rest pattern establishes a new identity marker for Israel. Even during the construction of the tabernacle, they are commanded to observe the Sabbath and rest on the seventh day. This work-rest pattern forms a striking contrast to Pharaoh's work-work pattern (5:13). Furthermore, this pattern also reminds contemporary clergy and all those who "build God's kingdom" to follow God's example and rest amid the unceasing demands of ministry. Exodus 31:17 anthropomorphizes God, describing how he worked for six days but rested and was refreshed on the seventh day. The word "refreshed" (*naphash*) is associated with the word "soul" (*nephesh*), indicating a restoration of the whole being, including one's energy, inner strength, and emotional and mental state. If even God rested after creating the world, how much more should Israel follow this new pattern of life? The Sabbath reorients a person toward God and his way of living. Building the tabernacle creates a sacred space for God in our lives, while observing the Sabbath command

---

104. Zornberg goes on to say that the "Shabbat sanctity overrides that of the Mishkan." Zornberg, *The Particulars of Rapture*, 463 (Mishkan in Hebrew means "sanctuary").
105. Block, *Covenant*, 165.

reminds us to set apart a sacred time to enter God's rest and worship him. Therefore, the work-rest pattern is also a work-worship way of life.

Both the creation narrative and Exodus 31:12–18 emphasize that observing the Sabbath involves cessation from work, blessing, and consecration.[106]

> ## ASIAN WORK ETHICS AND THE FALSE PERCEPTION OF REST
>
> Generally speaking, Asians are known for their strong work ethic, though there are always exceptions. Asians, including the Chinese, believe in hard work and often view working tirelessly as a reflection of their character and spirituality. This work ethic, which is evident across every area of work, is also found in Christian ministry, especially among first-generation Asians in the diaspora. Many believe that hard work will eventually pay off and consider laziness a vice. In this context, the idea of rest is sometimes equated with laziness or a lack of productivity. A Christian psychologist Siang-Yang Tan once criticized the Chinese concept of "attempting great things for God," arguing that the drive to attempt great things for God can push a person to take on too many tasks and depend on human initiative to make things happen. This may lead to a relentless drive to succeed at all costs, which is detrimental to mental health. Instead, he suggested that we should strive to "attempt things for a great God," a shift in perspective that emphasizes God rather than human effort.[1]
>
> For Asian pastors or first-generation Christian pastors in the diaspora, Sunday is usually a workday. In this cultural context, devotion, diligence, and sacrifice – rather than rest – are seen as indicators of spirituality. Sometimes, working unceasingly, even to the point of exhaustion, is considered "spiritual" and an act of self-denial. Some pastors and missionaries serve until death, while others refuse to retire for fear of being "unfaithful" to God.[2] Some churches do not have sabbatical policies for pastors, and pastors who request a sabbatical may

---

106. Daniel C. Timmer, "Creation, Tabernacle, and Sabbath: The Sabbath Frame of Exodus 31:12–17; 35:1–3," in *Exegetical and Theological Perspective*, Band 227 Forschungen zur Religion und Literatur des Alten und Neuen Testaments (Gottingen: Vandenhoeck & Ruprecht GmbH & Co., 2009), 67–74.

face scrutiny from church boards or church members. In this Chinese cultural context, suffering and persistence are often viewed as reflecting one's faithfulness, whereas seeking rest is considered a sign of idleness or laziness.[3] But a rest-less life is contrary to the teachings of Scripture, where God demands that Israel remember the Sabbath day and take seriously Sabbath observance even during the construction of the tabernacle. Although some Chinese Christians prioritize spiritual rest over bodily rest, God commends both spiritual and physical rest (Exod 20:8–11).[4] Physical rest is not an expression of a lack of spirituality; on the contrary, true spirituality includes honoring the Sabbath and resting.

In the NT, although the Sabbath does not necessarily fall on Sundays, the idea of rest remains prominent in its teachings. For example, Jesus invites those who are weary and burdened to come to him to find rest (Matt 11:28), and the author of Hebrews urges believers to enter God's rest (Heb 4:1). If we fail to establish a work-rest pattern, how can we yearn for eternal rest? The mandate to observe the Sabbath even while engaged in God's work – such as constructing the tabernacle – reminds us that rest is not a sign of laziness but a healthy way of life that prepares us for the eternal Sabbath.

---

1. A personal conversation with Siang-Yang Tan.
2. Chinese American administrator-scholar Maria Liu Wong writes about her missionary father, who is in his late seventies but still refuses to retire due to his call to full-time ministry, which is believed to be for life. Maria Liu Wong, *On Becoming Wise Together: Learning and Leading in the City* (Grand Rapids: Eerdmans, 2023), 32.
3. Wong, *On Becoming Wise Together*, 33.
4. Sometimes the word "rest" (*nuah*) and "sabbath" appear together and are used interchangeably (Exod 20:11). However, the former often denotes the idea of rest in general, including physical and bodily rest, whereas the latter carries a spiritual meaning as in entering God's rest. When "rest" is used for animals in Exodus 23:12, it clearly refers to physical rest.

The narrative spanning Exodus 25–31 concludes with the statement that God "finished speaking to Moses on Mount Sinai" (31:18). This serves as a reminder to the reader that Moses has now been on the mountain for 40 days and 40 nights (24:18) and that the Israelites have not seen him at all during this entire period. God then gives Moses the two stone tablets of the testimony that are "inscribed by the finger of God" (31:18). This section ends with the two tablets of the testimony, mirroring how the instruction for building the tabernacle began with the construction of the ark of the testimony and forming an *inclusio* between Exodus 25:10 and Exodus 31:18.[107]

Before moving on to the next section of the Exodus narrative, it is important to note the significant symbolic meaning of the tabernacle furniture in relation to Jesus. While this kind of symbolic interpretation is also present in the Western Protestant tradition, it is particularly well received in the Chinese Christian context.[108] The following table illustrates how each piece of furniture in the tabernacle structure is a symbolic counterpart to the work of Jesus in the NT:

Table 16: The Tabernacle and Its Symbolism in Jesus

	Tabernacle and Its Furniture	Symbolic Representation of the Work of Jesus
1	Tabernacle – the whole structure	The indwelling presence of Jesus (John 1:14)[109]
2	Mercy seat	The redemptive work of Jesus (Heb 9:5, 12)
3	The veil that separates the Holy of Holies from the Holy Place	The body of Jesus (Matt 27:51; Mark 15:38; Luke 23:45; Heb 10:20)
4	Golden lampstand	Jesus is the light of the world (John 8:12)
5	Table of showbread	Jesus is the bread of life (John 6:51)
6	Altar of incense	Jesus is the great high priest who intercedes for God's people (Heb 7:24–25)
7	The sacrifice on the altar in the Outer Court	Jesus is the sacrifice who died for the sins of humanity (Heb 10:12)
8	Brazen basin	The blood of Jesus cleanses people from sin (Heb 9:13–14)
9	Priesthood in the line of Aaron	Jesus is the high priest in the order of Melchizedek (Heb 5:10; 6:20)

---

107. For details on the meaning of the testimony, see Block, *Covenant*, 166–169.
108. For example, David M. Levy, *The Tabernacle: Shadows of the Messiah: Its Sacrifices, Services, and Priesthood* (Bellmawr: The Friends of Israel Gospel Ministry, Inc., 1993).
109. "Dwelling" (NIV) in this verse is literally "tabernacling."

32:1–34:35 FALSE WORSHIP AND COVENANT RENEWAL

Worshiping images or using images to represent deities was a common practice in the ancient Near East, and such practices continue to be prevalent in many Asian cultures, including the Chinese diaspora. In such traditions, people may use any object to represent their gods, including celestial beings such as the sun, moon, and stars, mythic animals such as dragons, statues of Buddha, or even pictures of pop stars who they may refer to as "idols."

The story of the golden calf is considered a "primal scene" of idolatry[110] and an "interruption" in God's plan to bring Israel into his presence.[111] The exact identity of the golden calf is a matter of endless debate. Some suggest that it represents a god in Egypt, though they do not explain how the Israelites got this idea.[112] Others argue that since Aaron tells the people, "These are your gods,[113] Israel, who brought you up out of Egypt" (Exod 32:4), the calf represents the God of Israel. Still others consider that the golden calf represents Moses, who has become a godlike figure in the minds of the Israelites.[114] There is also a belief – based on ancient Near Eastern iconography – that the golden calf represents the pedestal – that is, the base that supports a statue – of God's throne.[115] The ambiguities surrounding the plural term "gods" (*elohim*) and what these gods represent add to the difficulties of interpreting the golden calf incident.[116]

We generally interpret the golden calf as symbolizing the people's attempt to create a tangible representation of the divine presence in the absence of Moses, who had functioned in that role in the minds of the people. What is clear from this incident is that when the people worshiped the golden calf, they violated the covenant they had entered into with God and vowed to obey (Exod 24:3, 7). Therefore, Exodus 32 continues where Exodus 24 left off.

---

110. Jan Assmann, *Moses the Egyptian: The Memory of Egypt in Western Monotheism* (Cambridge: Harvard University Press, 1997), 211.
111. Duvall and Hays, *God's Relational Presence*, 35.
112. Assmann thinks that the calf is the Egyptian image of the god Apis. Assmann, *Moses the Egyptian*, 211.
113. NIV translates in plural, "These are your gods," based on the Hebrew text, though "gods" (*elohim*) can also be understood as a singular or collective noun referring to "god" or "God."
114. For example, Myung Soo Suh proposed this view and argued that the Israelites were asking Aaron to make god(s) to go before them because they did not know where Moses was. Myung Soo Suh, *The Tabernacle in the Narrative History of Israel from the Exodus to the Conquest*, Studies in Biblical Literature 50 (New York: Peter Lang, 2003), 85–87.
115. Sarna, *Exodus*, 203.
116. The story of the golden calf raises multiple questions and invites interlocution. For example, why does the people's transformation and laughter lead to their being portrayed as "stiff-necked" people? How can Moses, a great legislator, be threatened with being written out of the story? Ngwa, *Let My People Live*, 163.

Exodus 32–34 form a literary unit containing several scenes that move forward rapidly. Although the narration of the golden calf incident takes only six verses, its aftermath concerning divine presence and absence is described at length in Exodus 32:7–34:35. After the golden calf incident, God proclaims his name and attributes that become a credal formula in later biblical traditions, especially in the Book of the Twelve.[117] In addition, in the aftermath of this incident, God's presence is no longer manifested in the same way as in the period prior to it. Therefore, the golden calf incident is a watershed moment that leaves a serious and tainted mark on the national history and collective memory of Israel. In Psalm 106:19–23, the psalmist attributes this incident to Israel's failure to remember the God who had been their savior (Ps 106:19–23). Similarly, Nehemiah describes this event as an act of blasphemy against God (Neh 9:18).

As Moses remains with God on Mount Sinai for 40 days and 40 nights, the journey toward the promised land comes to a temporary halt, creating a leadership vacuum among the Israelites at the foot of the mountain. This transition period represents another stage of liminality in Israel's wilderness journey, one characterized by danger, uncertainty, and apprehension. The following is an outline of Exodus 32–34:

32:1–6	The golden calf
32:7–14	God's anger and Moses's intercession
32:15–35	The breaking of the covenant
33:1–11	God's presence diminished
33:12–23	God's presence negotiated
34:1–28	The renewal of the covenant
34:29–35	Moses's face shines

32:1–6 The Golden Calf

While Moses is on Mount Sinai, receiving divine instructions on how to build the tabernacle, the people at the base of the mountain grow impatient, perceiving that Moses is delaying to return to them.[118] The words "so long" (*bosh* in

---

117. For example, Psalm 86:5; Joel 2:13; Jonah 4:2; Nahum 1:3.
118. In some countries, when leaders fight for freedom or advocate for the rights of the oppressed, they may be arrested and detained without a proper trial. Some simply disappear. In such a context, and given Moses's absence, the people's anxiety is understandable. George and Swarup, "Exodus," 123.

Hebrew) has a double meaning: delay and shame. Taken together, this points to the ambiguity and anxiety surrounding the people's perception of Moses's absence.[119] The narrative reveals that "when the people saw" Moses's delay, they call upon Aaron, saying, "Come, make us gods who will go before us. As for this fellow Moses who brought us up out of Egypt, we don't know what has happened to him" (32:1). The expression "this fellow Moses" places emotional distance between the people and Moses. The absence of Moses creates a leadership vacuum that leads to a crisis. Therefore, the apparent motivation for Israel to make "gods" who will go before them seems to be their need for a visible substitute for Moses to act as their god or gods.[120]

The narrative shifts immediately to Aaron's response, without revealing his emotions or inner feelings. Aaron orders the people to take off the gold earrings worn by their wives and children and bring these to him. The narrator then notes that Aaron uses the gold to make "an idol cast in the shape of a calf, fashioning [*yatsar*] it with a tool" (32:4) but does not give details about this process or mention how long it took.[121] The brevity of this account of the creation of the golden calf contrasts sharply with God's meticulous and extensive instructions for building the tabernacle (Exod 25–31). The process of fashioning the image may reflect ancient Near Eastern ritual practices associated with image-making.[122] The nature of the engraving tool is unclear but could refer to a stylus used for writing or a rush pen,[123] leading to the theory that Aaron not only made the golden calf but designed it with this pen.[124]

In the ancient Near East – including Egypt, Canaan, and Mesopotamia – the calf was a common symbol representing strength, fertility, and prowess.[125]

---

119. The root of the word "delay" (*bosh*) means shame. Does it suggest that the absence of Moses implies some kind of shameful feelings from the point of view of the people? Holbert translates it as "shamefully late." John C. Holbert, "A New Literary Reading of Exodus 32: The Story of the Golden Calf," *QR* 10, no. 3 (Fall, 1990): 46–68, especially 46–47. Zornberg names the golden calf story as "the time factor" and understands *bosh* as referring to the sixth hour (i.e. before midday) since *sheh* in Hebrew means six. The absence of Moses is measured by time – his lateness. Zornberg, *The Particulars of Rapture*, 401.
120. For a detailed analysis and proposal of this view, see Stephen L. Herring, "Moses as Divine Substitute in Exodus," *CTR* 9, no. 2 (Spring 2012): 53–68.
121. If, as some scholars suggest, Aaron had made a molten image, this would have meant that he used materials with a high melting point that could be liquefied by heat.
122. For more, see Herring, "Moses as Divine Substitute in Exodus," 55–57.
123. For example, Isaiah 8:1.
124. Elizabeth Vandyke, "Designing the Golden Calf: Pens and Presumption in the Production of a 'Divine' Image," *JBL* 141, no. 2 (2022): 219–233.
125. Michael B. Hundley, "What is the Golden Calf?" *CBQ* 79, no. 4 (2017): 559–579. Carios Museum houses many reliefs and paintings featuring calves.

For instance, the chief Canaanite or Ugaritic god El was called "Bull El, our father." Some understand the symbolism of the calf in the context of Exodus 32 as representing might and victory in war rather than fertility, and the Exodus narrative supports this notion. For example, in Exodus 15:3, God is called a "warrior" or "a man of war" (ESV). The war against the Amalekites portrays Moses and Joshua as military leaders (17:9, 13).[126] The angel of God is said to "go before" or "go ahead of" Israel to drive out the Canaanites (23:20, 23). The phrase "go before" (23:23 NASB) connects the golden calf narrative to subsequent narratives that depict God as a warrior who goes before Israel to fight for them.[127]

After the creation of the golden calf, the narrative shifts once more to the people's perspective. They say, "These are your gods, Israel, who brought you up out of Egypt" (32:4).[128] Their words add to the ambiguity surrounding the symbolism of the golden calf. The calf is a single image, but the people use a plural form to refer to it. It is unclear whether they are referring to one God (god), multiple gods, or using the plural to indicate the multifaceted nature of the god or gods. In addition, in previous narratives, the phrase "who brought you up out of Egypt" is reserved for God.[129] Therefore, it is not surprising that some scholars argue that this golden calf represented God himself and that its creation directly violated the second commandment that prohibits the use of images to represent God.[130]

The narrative then shifts to Aaron's perspective – "when Aaron saw this" (32:5). However, it is unclear what exactly Aaron saw. Did Aaron see the behavior of the people? Did he see the calf? Did he see both? Did the narrator purposely omit the object in question and, if so, for what purpose?

The narrative moves on quickly to describe Aaron building an altar before the calf and proclaiming, "Tomorrow there will be a festival to the LORD" (32:5). Building an altar recalls Moses's building of an altar at the foot of Mount Sinai to prepare the people for worship (24:4). The phrase "a festival to the LORD" suggests that, from Aaron's perspective, the image of the golden

---

126. Though Jenzen considers Moses to be the war leader, I take Moses as both a war leader and an intercessor in Exodus 17:8–16.
127. For example, Exodus 32:34; 33:15–16, 19. See J. Gerald Janzen, "The Character of the Calf and Its Cult in Exodus 32," *CBQ* 52 (1990): 597–607.
128. The pronoun "they" appears to refer to the people mentioned in 32:1, but to whom were they talking? It seems that "they" refer to the leaders of the people speaking to the rest of the people.
129. For example, Exodus 6:7; 20:2.
130. For example, Hundley, "What is the Golden Calf?" 562.

calf was a symbol representing God. It is also possible that the calf functions as a substitute for the absent Moses, who, in the minds of the people, functions as a divine mediator. If these interpretations are correct, then the golden calf represents the "false images of the true God."[131] Due to the ambiguities in this story, we may infer that the golden calf represented either God or Moses as his meditator.

The incident ends with a feast, most likely a sacrificial ritual. The act of "play" or "laughing" (*tsakhaq*) – which the NIV renders as "indulge in revelry" – adds another layer of confusion. The term *tsakhaq* could refer to sexual rites as part of a ritual ceremony,[132] a ritual dance,[133] or simply laughing as in a joyful celebration, or even a combination of all these.

Although there is ambiguity on multiple levels in this section of the narrative, it is clear that the worship of the golden calf is completely opposed to what God intended for Israel. The crisis caused by Moses's absence once again places Israel in a liminal state, a situation fraught with danger and uncertainty. As the narrative unfolds, it becomes apparent that their worship of the golden calf comes at a great cost to Israel. This episode represents one of the darkest moments in Israel's national history, posing a threat to their very existence as the people of God (32:9–10) and a significant challenge to the process of their identity formation. As the story unfolds, the glorious descriptions of the tabernacle – given by God to Moses on Mount Sinai – and the dangerous state in which Israel now finds itself at the base of that very mountain create conflicting emotions of anticipation and anxiety.

Table 17: Proper Worship and False Worship Contrasted

Proper Worship – Tabernacle	**False Worship – Golden Calf**
God initiates (25:1)	People initiate (32:1)
Willing heart (25:2)	Aaron commands (32:2)
Detailed planning (Exodus 25–31)	Hasty actions (32:4)
Takes time (Exodus 36–40)	Instant (32:4)
Safeguards God's holiness (Exodus 25–31)	Makes God accessible (32:8)
Invisible God (Exodus 25–31)	Visible image (32:4)

---

131. I borrow the phrase from Rolf A. Jacobson, "Moses, the Golden Calf, and the False Images of the True God," *WW* 33, no. 2 (Spring 2013): 130–139.
132. The same word is used to describe Isaac caressing his wife in Genesis 26:8.
133. For example, Sarna, *Exodus*, 204, citing Judges 16:25 and Exodus 32:19.

In Asian contexts, broadly speaking, and specifically within Chinese settings, false worship often involves the veneration of celebrity pastors, dynamic speakers, and charismatic worship leaders. Some Chinese churches prioritize attendance and offerings over the spiritual growth of their congregations. While people may not construct a literal golden calf to represent God, the "golden calf" may take various forms and shapes, both within and outside the church. The tension between God's desire for proper worship and the human inclination toward false worship persists. The golden calf incident serves as a reminder that our identity is shaped by whom or what we worship.[134]

32:7–14 God's Anger and Moses's Intercession

What transpires at the foot of the mountain does not escape God's attention. Moses is immediately called down from the mountain, and God now suddenly refers to the Israelites as "your people" instead of "my people," signifying a great emotional distance between God and Israel. God no longer considers the Israelites the people of God who were brought out of the land of Egypt but, rather, as the people of Moses. In God's fury, he portrays Moses as their rescuer, reflecting his estrangement from the Israelites. God describes the people as "corrupt" (*shakhat*), which echoes the depraved condition of humanity and the earth in the Noahic story – where the same word "corrupt" is used to describe the people of Noah's time (Gen 6:11–13) – and connects with the themes of creation and de-creation.

God condemns the Israelites for making the golden calf and calls them "stiff-necked." There is a cultural correspondence in the Cantonese term *Neng Geng*, which describes a stubborn person as one who has a stiff neck. This illustrates the idea that "we become what we worship."[135] In God's anger, he asks to be left alone so that he can destroy the Israelites and then make Moses into a great nation. This represents a significant change in the original divine plan of "from Abraham to the nations" (Gen 12:1–3) to "from Abraham to Moses," revealing God's emotional turmoil toward Israel. Like the flood in Noah's time, God wants to be done with Israel and start over with Moses,

---

134. Shirley Ho relates the concept of *Li* to the worship of Yahweh in the Taiwanese Christian context and advocates for an embodied and ritualized worship of God as a way to turn away from pagan religious pluralism. Shirley S. Ho, "Taiwanese Christian *Li*: The Embodied Worship of the Lord," in *Exploring the Old Testament in Asia: Evangelical Perspectives*, eds. Jerry Hwang and Angukali Rotokha (Carlisle: Langham Global Library, 2022), 123–144.
135. "Those who make them will be like them, and so will all who trust in them" (Ps 115:8). Beale's study uses this verse as the book's title on idolatry. G. K. Beale, *We Become What We Worship: A Biblical Theology of Idolatry* (Downers Grove: IVP Academic, 2008), 78–86.

which implies a de-creation of God's original plan for Israel and the re-creation of a new nation through the line of Moses.

Moses's response is one of sorrow. He "sought the favor of the Lord his God," asking two rhetorical questions: "Why should your anger burn against your people, whom you brought out of Egypt with great power and a mighty hand?" and "Why should the Egyptians say, 'It was with evil intent that he brought them out, to kill them in the mountains and to wipe them off the face of the earth'?" (32:11–12). Moses's appeal is based on God's special relationship with Israel and God's reputation among the Egyptians. He then asks God to remember his covenant with the patriarchs. The previously "heavy-tongued" Moses turns out to be an eloquent speaker who puts forward persuasive arguments. Because of Moses's intercession, God relents and does not bring disaster upon Israel. Here, Moses functions as an intercessor and a mediator between God and Israel.

32:15–35 The Breaking of the Covenant

In verse 15, the narrative shifts to Moses's perspective, as he descends from the mountain with the two tablets of the testimony in his hand. The narrator elaborates on the nature of these two tablets – they are inscribed on both sides and are the work of God, written by God himself. This highlights the divine origin and authority of the tablets. Joshua, who is presumed to be near Moses but not with him on the summit of Sinai (24:13), tells Moses that he hears the sound of war in the camp.[136] Moses responds by saying that it is not the sound of either victory or defeat but the sound of singing.

As Moses approaches the camp at the foot of the mountain, he sees the calf and the dancing. The word "saw" forms a parallel as well as a contrast with the earlier descriptions where "the people saw" (32:1) and "Aaron saw" (32:5). Moses must have been stunned and shocked at the sight of the calf. The "dancing" refers to the "revelry" described earlier (32:6), and Moses perceives this as a ritual dance.[137] Then Moses's anger burns, mirroring God's anger referred to earlier on (32:10), and he throws the tablets, smashing them at the foot of the mountain – the place where the Israelites had entered into a covenant with

---

136. To sing (*'anot*) appears also in Miriam's singing in Exodus 15:21 ("Sing to the Lord!"), suggesting that when people sang to the golden calf, they perceived it as a representative of God. See Tigay, "Exodus," 176. When Joshua heard the "sound of war," judging by what Moses said in 32:18, Joshua might mean the "sound of victory."
137. In the later history of Israel, the prophets of Baal leaped about the altar as a form of ritual dance to spur Baal to action (1 Kgs 18:26).

God (24:3–4). Since the tablets represent the covenant between God and Israel, the smashing of the tablets signifies the breaking of the covenant because the Israelites have not kept their end of the agreement as earlier promised (19:8; 24:3, 7). Moses then takes the calf, burns it, grinds it to powder, and scatters the powder over the surface of the water. In the contemporary context, an equivalent action would be to tear up or shred a contract. Moses then makes the Israelites drink the water, an act known as drinking "the cup of judgment" as described later in Numbers 5:12–31.[138]

Then comes the conversation between Moses and Aaron. Moses confronts Aaron about his sin, but Aaron defends himself and places the blame on the Israelites. He claims that they were prone to evil and had asked him to make gods for them in Moses's absence. He adds, "Then they gave me the gold, and I threw it into the fire, and out came this calf!" (32:24). Aaron deliberately attempts to absolve himself of any wrongdoing and avoids taking any responsibility for his actions. Surprisingly, God seems to tolerate Aaron's actions. Later however, in Moses's own account in Deuteronomy, it becomes clear that God was indeed angry with Aaron and intended to destroy him. If not for Moses's intercession, Aaron would have suffered the consequence of his action (Deut 9:20).

When Moses sees that the people are "running wild"[139] because Aaron had let them get out of control, he stands at the entrance of the camp and calls for those who are loyal to God to come to him. The Levites rally to him, and Moses commands them to arm themselves with swords and go back and forth through the camp, from one end to the other, killing their brothers, friends, and neighbors (32:27). As a result, about three thousand men are killed that day.

Many Christians are troubled by this episode because it seems to portray the God of the OT as someone who is full of wrath. However, recognizing that God's nature is utterly holy and transcendent may enable us to view God's wrath as a relentless guarding of his holiness. "The wages of sin is death" (Rom

---

138. In Numbers 5:12–31, if a husband suspects his wife of committing adultery, he is to take the wife to a priest. The priest will take some holy water, mixed with some dust from the tabernacle floor into the water, and make the wife drink and swear. If she indeed commits adultery, the water will make her abdomen swell and she will have a miscarriage. If she is innocent, she will be clear of guilt and will bear children. We may call the cup of water she drinks a "cup of judgment."

139. Literally, "to let go" or "to let loose." The NASB translates it as "out of control." The same word appears in Numbers 5:18, thus drawing a connection between the idea of the "cup of judgment" in both texts.

6:23) rings true in stories like this. However, we must also acknowledge the severity of God's punishment of sin, which, from a human perspective, may sometimes seem to "go overboard," as in the case of Lamentations 1:5, 9, 11–17, which laments that God's punishment for sin is too much for anyone to bear. The killing of the three thousand men might be perceived as an act of cleansing and purgation or as a way to make an example of the few.[140]

Previously, the Levites had been assigned the role of serving in the context of worship within the sacred space of the tabernacle. Now, they are entrusted with the role of safeguarding God's holiness by destroying those who violate it. The Levites, having been set apart for God, are dedicated to God and, therefore, opposed to anyone who offends God's holiness, including their own brothers and neighbors. This episode reveals the ethical and theological complexities, dangers, and ambiguities of the liminal stage of Israel's journey in the wilderness. God's plan for Israel is to teach them about proper worship, yet Israel is unaware of what this means and is mindful only of their immediate need for a leader who will go before them on the journey toward their new home. The story of the golden calf is not primarily about a crisis that arose because of Moses's delay but, rather, focuses on the fundamental difference between human priorities and the divine agenda.

Verses 30–35 describe how Moses ascends the mountain to intercede for Israel once again. This ascent symbolizes humanity's attempt to repair the damage caused by Adam, who, because of his rebellion, was expelled from the garden of Eden. In this sense, Moses emerges as a new Adam.[141]

First, Moses confesses Israel's sin in making gods of gold. He then implores God to either forgive Israel's sin or blot Moses himself out of the book that God had written – the heavenly and divine book familiar to the people of the ancient Near East and the OT. Despite not being part of the sinful crowd, Moses selflessly identifies with them. However, God rejects Moses's proposal, declaring, "Whoever has sinned against me I will blot out of my book" (32:33). He then instructs Moses to lead the people to the place of which he has spoken, promising to send his angel ahead of them, which echoes Exodus 23:20–23. God also declares that Israel's sin would be dealt with at the appropriate time.

---

140. Kass, *Founding God's Nation*, 547–548.
141. The movement of descending and ascending the mountain of God is grounded in the gate liturgy where only the righteous person can ascend to meet God and be in God's presence. Morales, *The Tabernacle Pre-Figured*, 100–101.

The golden calf incident concludes with God punishing the people for their sinful actions in relation to the calf made by Aaron. Aaron's sin was letting the people convince him that they should have an idol, making the golden calf, building the altar, and letting the people worship the calf. The people's sin was not waiting patiently for Moses to return, insisting that Aaron make an idol for them, gathering the women's earrings, and worshiping the calf that Aaron built. This violation of the covenant by both Aaron and the Israelites leads to alienation between God and Israel and the withdrawal of the divine presence. The cost of false worship is the loss of God's presence, which proves detrimental to Israel.

Throughout the golden calf episode, the differing leadership styles of Moses and Aaron are apparent, offering insights and implications for ministry in the contemporary context. The table below contrasts their respective leadership styles.

Table 18: Right Leadership and Wrong Leadership Contrasted

Right Leadership – Moses	Wrong Leadership – Aaron
Listens to God's command (Exodus 25–31)	Listens to people's commands (32:1)
Dialogues with God	Does not consult God
Intercedes for his people (32:11–12, 31–32)	Does not intercede for his people
Takes responsibility for his people (32:11, 32)	Evades responsibility and blames others (32:24)

33:1–11 God's Presence Diminished

This scene highlights two changes in the divine-human relationship after the golden calf incident: the introduction of an angel (33:1–6) and the establishment of another "tent of meeting" (33:7–11). Both changes symbolize the withdrawal of divine presence from the Israelites. God now refers to the Israelites as "your people" (Moses's people) instead of "my people."[142] This change in pronoun from "my" to "your" echoes the same sentiment that was expressed when God considered destroying sinful Israel and making Moses a

---

142. For example, Exodus 3:7; 6:7; 8:22; 9:2, 13; 10:3.

great nation (32:10). God tells Moses that he will send an angel to lead him and to drive out the Canaanites and other nations, God himself will not go with Israel to the promised land because they are a stiff-necked people and God does not wish to destroy them on the way.

In Exodus 23:20–33, God had promised to send an angel to lead Israel into the land of the Amorites, the Hittites, and various other nations; he also said of this angel, "My Name is in him" (23:21). Here, although God sends the angel, God's name is no longer in him because God has separated himself from this angel. The only explanation for this change is the golden calf incident. As a result, the people are sad and go into mourning. They also strip off their ornaments as God instructs. "Stripped off" (*natsal*) is the same word used when the Israelites "plundered" the Egyptians as they were leaving Egypt (12:36). Now, due to their sin, the removal of what they had plundered represents a reversal and is perhaps also a symbol of mourning and repentance.

The diminishing of divine presence is further illustrated by the construction of another tent that Moses pitches outside the camp. This tent is not the tabernacle that is yet to be constructed but a private tent where Moses – and anyone else who wishes to – can meet with God. Compared to the tabernacle, this tent is smaller, located outside rather than at the center of the camp, and does not contain the ark. The functions Moses performs in this tent are similar to what Aaron would later do in the tabernacle, but God's presence in this tent of meeting is occasional rather than permanent.[143] This arrangement highlights Moses's elevated status in the eyes of the people. The people would rise, stand, and watch Moses until he entered the tent. The descent of the cloud whenever Moses entered the tent reinforces his special status with God. Whenever the people saw the pillar of cloud standing at the entrance to the tent, they would rise, stand at the entrance of their own tents, and worship. Verse 11, probably from the narrator's point of view, describes how "the LORD would speak to Moses face to face, as one speaks to a friend."[144] This suggests intimacy, mutuality, and even a sense of equality. This special relationship between God and Moses sets the stage for the subsequent negotiations between them regarding the divine presence.

---

143. Hamilton, *Exodus*, 561–562. Hamilton sums it well: "God does not pull a disappearing act; rather, he relocates." Hamilton, *Exodus*, 562.
144. Compare Numbers 12:8; Deuteronomy 34:10.

33:12–23 God's Presence Negotiated

In this conversation, Moses boldly addresses God as if they were equals, reflecting the narrator's portrayal of what true friendship means. The dialogue centers on negotiating divine presence through the use of verbs like "see," "find favor," "know," and "go," along with the repeated nouns "name" and "glory." God is depicted anthropomorphically, as possessing eyes, a face, hands, and a back. Moses is not speaking to an invisible spirit but conversing with a "visible God" who can see, speak, and move.

First, Moses quotes what God had said to him regarding his special status as someone known by God, who has found favor in God's eyes.[145] He then argues that he wants to know God and know his ways. Earlier, God had referred to the people as "the people you brought up out of Egypt" (33:1). Now, Moses reminds God that "this nation is your people" (33:13) – rather than Moses's people – with the aim of extending God's favor from Moses to the Israelites.

Moses continues to entreat God, asking how others will know that he has found favor in God's sight and arguing that it is God's presence with Israel that distinguishes his people from all other people on the earth. Moses's plea centers on God's reputation for fulfilling his promises. In response, God grants Moses's request. Moses then makes an even bolder request: "Now show me your glory" (33:18). "Glory" (*kabod*) is associated with heaviness, weightiness, and significance. It reflects the visible manifestation of God. Moses is asking God to manifest himself so that he can see God.

God's response is intriguing. It is neither "yes" nor "no" but both. God's glory is about his attributes and his character. God tells Moses that he will make all his goodness pass before Moses and proclaim his name – the Lord – in Moses's presence; God also reminds Moses that he reserves the right to show mercy and compassion to whomever he chooses. Then comes a caveat: "You cannot see my face, for no one may see me and live" (33:20). God wants to reveal his glory to Moses, but he does not want Moses to die because of this revelation. This idea of not being able to see God's face echoes the story of Jacob wrestling with an angel at Jabbok. After this struggle, Jacob said, "I saw God face to face, and yet my life was spared" (Gen 32:30). Both stories feature a face-to-face encounter with the divine presence and indicate the dire consequences of such an encounter.

---

145. Sarna points out that the phrase "I know you by name" (Exod 33:12, 17) is a Hebrew idiom and appears only here in the Old Testament with God as the subject. Sarna, *Exodus*, 213.

Nevertheless, God finds a way for Moses to see God without risking his life. God instructs Moses to stand on a rock near God, saying, "When my glory passes by, I will put you in a cleft in the rock and cover you with my hand until I have passed by. Then I will remove my hand and you will see my back; but my face must not be seen" (33:22–23). This act of concealing his face reflects God's transcendent nature, while the revealing of God's back points to his willingness to be vulnerable and visible to Moses. Both the concealing and revealing of God's presence highlight the divine tension in God's interaction with human beings.

This episode in Exodus raises a question: Can humans handle seeing the fullness of God's glory? If God were to show his glory in miraculous ways, could we handle it, or would we, like the Israelites (20:18–19), be terrified by his presence?

34:1–28 The Renewal of the Covenant

In Exodus 34, the focus shifts to the renewal of the covenant that Israel had breached. In this chapter, God takes the initiative to restore the relationship, proclaiming God's name and the significance of this name. This verbal proclamation, along with God's visible presence to Moses, reveals a God who desires to be known.[146] It is noteworthy that the proclamation of God's compassion and graciousness follows the golden calf incident, illustrating the tension and the delicate balance between God's wrath and his compassion. God will not leave the guilty unpunished, yet God also demonstrates great mercy to those who have sinned against him.

God summons Moses to ascend Mount Sinai once more and commands him to chisel out two new stone tablets, similar to the first ones. God promises to inscribe these tablets with the same words as on the first set of tablets. Moses obeys and goes up Mount Sinai the next morning carrying the two tablets of stone. God descends in the cloud and stands with Moses, proclaiming the name of God – the same name that God had revealed to Moses in Exodus 3 and 6 – that centers on God's character and attributes. God then passes in front of Moses and makes this proclamation:

---

146. Henrich notices the complex nature of divine visibility and invisibility in Exodus 25–40, where God's visibility is communicated through verbal proclamation, the tabernacle itself, and his presence to Moses, while God also conceals his full glory, and his face is not to be seen. Sarah S. Henrich, "Seen and Unseen: The Visibility of God in Exodus 25–40," *WW* (2006): 103–111.

> The LORD, the LORD, the compassionate and gracious God, slow to anger, abounding in love and faithfulness, maintaining love to thousands, and forgiving wickedness, rebellion and sin. Yet he does not leave the guilty unpunished; he punishes the children and their children for the sin of the parents to the third and fourth generation. (Exod 34:6–7)

The first part of the proclamation (34:6) focuses on God's compassion. The tetragrammaton of God's name – which means "to be" or "to become" – refers to the LORD as a God who is compassionate and gracious. "Compassionate" (*rakhum*) refers to warm feelings that arise from sympathy. "Gracious" (*khanun*) can be translated as merciful. Both adjectives amplify God's gracious compassion. "Slow to anger" is literally "long nose," providing a pictorial image of God as one who is patient since "nose" and "anger" come from the same root word in Hebrew. Slow to anger means slow to get angry. "Love" (*khesed*) refers to covenantal loyalty and steadfast commitment, often translated as loving-kindness. "Faithfulness" (*'emeth*) derives from the word "Amen," accentuating God's fidelity to his people. Together, the two pillars of love and faithfulness render God as one who is able to show compassion and mercy to sinful people.

This credal statement reverberates throughout the OT as the people of God learn to relate to their God. This is particularly evident in the Book of the Twelve (Joel 2:13; Jonah 4:2; Mic 7:18–19; Nah 1:2–3) and the Psalms (25:10; 86:5, 15; 103:8–9; 145:8). In his study of the divine name in Exodus, Austin Surls argues that the divine name is not revealed in full at the beginning of Exodus (3:13–15; 6:2–8) but is gradually unpacked throughout the narrative, with greater clarity in Exodus 33:12–23 and reaching a climax in Exodus 34:5–7.[147] Allusions to the divine name appear in various genres: narrative echoes in Moses's intercession (Num 14:13–19), homiletical echoes in Moses's speeches (Deut 1–4), petitionary echoes in Solomon's prayer at the temple dedication (1 Kgs 8:23; compare 2 Chr 6:14), Nehemiah's prayer (Neh 9:5–37), prophetic echoes, hymnic echoes in the Psalms, and sapiential echoes in Proverbs (Prov 3:3; 16:5–6).[148] His name – "the LORD, the LORD,

---

147. Austin Surls, *Making Sense of the Divine Name in the Book of Exodus: From Etymology to Literary Onomastics*, Bulletin for Biblical Research 17 (Winona Lake: Eisenbrauns, 2017), 13. Surls uses echoes, quotations, allusions, and appropriations when referencing the various uses of the divine name in later texts. However, he misses the echoes in laments (Lam 3:22–23).
148. Surls, *Making Sense of the Divine Name in the Book of Exodus*, 162–181.

the compassionate and gracious God" – reveals his personhood and his actions based on his personhood: "slow to anger, abounding in love and faithfulness, maintaining love to thousands, and forgiving wickedness, rebellion and sin" (34:6–7).

The second part of God's proclamation of his name (34:7) centers on his righteousness. Some Chinese Christians, interpreting this verse literally, believe in the concept of "generational sin," where sins against God by one generation are seen as having continuing consequences for the third and fourth generations. Therefore, they pray against the transmission of sin across generations. However, a closer look at verse 7 reveals that the numbers are not meant to be taken literally but symbolically, with "thousands" and "third and fourth generation" juxtaposed metaphorically to show a contrast. God will show his loyal love to thousands of generations – which represents a long time – but will only punish the guilty ones to the third and fourth generations – symbolizing a short time. This metaphorical reading emphasizes the importance of interpreting Scripture in its proper context. Upon hearing God's proclamation of his name, Moses responds by bowing to the ground and worshiping. In the presence of such a God, worship is the only appropriate response.

Identity formation within the diaspora involves a journey of knowing God and responding to him with appropriate worship. In Exodus 32–34, the correct worship of God is juxtaposed with the false worship of the golden calf. Similarly, in the Chinese diaspora, Christians may be susceptible to "worshiping" charismatic pastors who preach captivating sermons, relate interesting stories about their lives before conversion, or have impressive credentials. Without even being conscious of it, undue focus on such leaders can be a subtle form of worshiping the "golden calf."

Moses has been relying on his favor in the sight of God to negotiate on behalf of the Israelites. Now that God has revealed his glory, even if only partially, Moses begins to plead for God's mercy on behalf of Israel. He boldly asks that God's presence go with the Israelites and that he pardons their sin and takes them as his own possession (34:9). In response, God initiates the covenant renewal process. In Exodus 34:10–11, the twofold "behold" found in the Hebrew text (omitted in the NIV) stresses the solemnity of God's words as he commands Israel to carefully follow his instructions as he drives out the Amorites, Canaanites, Hittites, Perizzites, Hivites, and Jebusites. Israel must not make a covenant with these nations because doing so would ensnare them. Instead, they must tear down the altars of this people and worship God exclusively.

While similar warnings are found in Exodus 23:23–33, in chapter 34, these warnings become more severe. Nestled between a series of warnings, we find the first and second commandments (34:14, 17). God then addresses the matter of Israel's festivals or feasts (34:18–26), probably focusing specifically on this issue because of Aaron's proclamation of the worship of the golden calf as "a festival to the LORD" (32:5).[149] Festivals are often closely connected to group identity, as in the celebration of the Passover for ancient Israel or the Lunar New Year for Chinese people. What is in view here is the close affinity between festivals and idolatry. Therefore, God reiterates what festivals mean, specifying what these festivals are and explaining the reasons behind each of them.

God tells Moses to write down his words, which constitute the covenant he has made with Moses and Israel. This completes the renewal of the covenant. The narrator concludes this section by stating that Moses was with God for 40 days and 40 nights, fasting, while God inscribed on the tablets the covenant – that is, the Ten Commandments (34:27–28).[150]

34:29–35 Moses's Face Shines

The final section of the golden calf narrative focuses on the radiance or glory of Moses, which is essentially a reflection of God's glory. When Moses descends from Mount Sinai carrying the two tablets, his face shines because he has been in God's presence and spoken with God. Moses's "radiant" face is a reflection of divine glory and symbolizes the return of divine presence upon Israel, marking the transition from Israel's breach of the covenant to God's renewal of the covenant.[151]

When Aaron and the Israelites see Moses's radiant face, their response is one of fear – which mirrors their earlier reaction to seeing the glory of God (20:18). Therefore, Moses removes the veil from his face whenever he goes to speak with God and veils his face when he returns to the people to speak with them. The apostle Paul later refers to this episode to speak of the covenant of righteousness and the ministry of the Holy Spirit. Moses represented the covenant that brought condemnation. Yet, his face is shown with glory. So, "How much more would be the glory of those who preach the covenant that

---

149. In Exodus 23, the themes of festivals and foreign nations also appear together but in reverse order (festivals appear in 23:14–19 and the mention of the six nations appears in 23:20–33).
150. In Hebrew, "he wrote." Based on Exodus 34:1 and Deuteronomy 10:2, 4, the "he" is understood to be God.
151. Timmer, *Creation, Tabernacle, and Sabbath*, 131.

brings righteousness and those who receive that message?" Because of the Holy Spirit, their glory will be greater than Moses's. That was why the apostles and the believers should not cover their faces – their glories will keep on increasing unlike Moses's glory faded the longer he was away from God (2 Cor 3:7–18).

Exodus 32–34 begins with Israel's false worship and concludes with God's renewal of the covenant through Moses, who serves as a mediator and an intercessor. This paradigmatic story underscores Israel's pattern of unfaithfulness while highlighting God's faithfulness to his covenant.

EXODUS 35:1–40:38 RIGHT WORSHIP: THE CONSTRUCTION OF THE TABERNACLE

Identity formation involves a continuous process of construction and reconstruction. The false worship of the golden calf is contrasted with the proper worship of God, as illustrated in the construction of the tabernacle. In the context of the diaspora, people may worship "golden calves" in the form of pursuing an American (or European) dream apart from God or by seeking security through material means instead of rooting their identity in God. The inclusion of the golden calf story reflects the reality of human sinfulness and our ongoing liminal existence as we await redemption in, through, and by Jesus.

In the final section of the book of Exodus, the focus shifts from the detailed instructions on how to construct the tabernacle to its actual construction and completion. This shift suggests that Israel's journey with God is an ongoing process. The conclusion of one stage of identity formation marks the beginning of another new stage that requires further adjustments and readjustments. Thus, Israel is always on the move, always in transition between the old and new stages of their journey.

In the diaspora, building Chinese churches plays an important role in the identity formation of Chinese Christians. However, these sacred spaces require the ongoing presence of God among his people. The manifestation of this divine presence depends on the people's proper response to God, a response that is expressed through proper worship wherever they are in the world. As Israel is on the move, God is also on the move with the mobile tabernacle.[152]

This final section of the book of Exodus culminates in God's glory-filled portable dwelling place and his ongoing presence with Israel as they journey toward the promised land. The outline of this section is as follows:

---

152. Goldingay, *Old Testament Theology: Israel's Gospel*, 393.

35:1–3	The Sabbath command repeated
35:4–35	The call to construct
36:1–38:31	The construction
39:1–40:38	The construction completed

35:1–3 The Sabbath Command Repeated

This section resumes from where Exodus 31:12–18 left off, with the golden calf story in Exodus 32–34 appearing as an "interlude"[153] or "intrusion" in the sequence of events. The reiteration of the Sabbath command at this point in Israel's wilderness journey serves several functions. First, it functions as a conclusion to the divine instructions for building the tabernacle. Second, it frames the description of the covenant between God and Israel with the sign of the Sabbath. Third, it reminds Israel that the God who made a covenant with them is the same God who created the heavens and the earth since the six-seven-day pattern of work-rest reflects God's way of life.

35:4–35 The Call to Construct

Moses addresses the entire congregation of Israel, urging them to bring contributions to God (35:4–9). This call closely mirrors God's earlier call to Israel to build a tabernacle (25:1–9), with the command to build the tabernacle implied rather than explicitly stated. Moses then commands all those who are "skilled" – literally "wise of heart" – to come and participate in the building of the tabernacle, describing in detail the materials required for everything, from the exterior structure to the inner furnishings and even the priestly garments for Aaron and his sons.

The entire congregation of Israel responds, with the narrator emphasizing that these people are "willing" and that their hearts are "moved" (35:21, 22, 26, 29), which corresponds to Exodus 25:2. The repetition of "all" or "every" (*kol*) man[154] and the mention of both men and women (35:22, 29) expresses the total involvement of the people. It is also interesting to note the different roles of men and women (35:20–29). Moses then informs Israel that God has designated Bezalel and Oholiab as master craftsmen and endowed them with skills to perform "all kinds of work as engravers, designers, embroiderers in blue, purple and scarlet yarn and fine linen, and weavers" (35:35), an almost

---

153. Kaiser Jr., "Exodus," 478.
154. Exodus 35:20, 21, 22, 23, 24, 25, 26, 29.

verbatim repetition of Exodus 31:1–11. These craftsmen use their artistic gifts to build the dwelling place of God, illustrating the role of art in worship.[155] The verbatim repetition serves as "an obedience formula," stressing that the construction of the tabernacle conforms exactly to God's commands.

36:1–38:31 The Construction

The response from the people is overwhelmingly positive. Every morning, they bring freewill offerings for the construction of the tabernacle, far exceeding what is needed. In fact, Moses has to command the people to stop bringing contributions! The construction process begins with the exterior, with Bezalel making the 10 curtains. The details of how he makes these curtains illustrate his obedience to God's instructions and demonstrate how the full range of his artistic talents are used for God's work. Next, Bezalel makes 11 curtains of goat hair for the tent over the tabernacle. After this, he makes upright frames of acacia wood for the tabernacle. Again, the meticulous repetition of how he makes them reflects his obedience to God's instructions, reiterating that every detail conforms to God's pattern.

Bezalel[156] then makes crossbars – including the center crossbar – of acacia wood and overlays the frames with gold. He also makes a curtain of blue, purple, and scarlet yarn and finely twisted linen, with cherubim woven into it by a skilled worker. He also makes four posts of acacia wood, overlaying them with gold, and makes gold hooks for them and casts their four silver bases. For the entrance of the tent, he makes a curtain of blue, purple, and scarlet yarn and finely twisted linen, along with five posts with hooks, overlaid with gold, and five bases of bronze. The narrator's frequent repetition of "he made," along with details of what and how each item is made, emphasizes Bezalel's faithfulness in following orders as well as the integrity of the construction process.[157] Every detail of the construction of the tabernacle honors the divine design revealed by God to Moses on Mount Sinai (Exod 25:9, 40; see also 1 Chr 28:11–12,

---

155. This involvement of art in worship forms the basis for art in missions. Cornell, "Art on Mission with the Tabernacle Builders," 11.
156. The Hebrew text names Bezalel. NIV has "they," assuming Bezalel has recruited others to help him.
157. Other reasons for the repetition include showing the faithfulness of Moses in communicating God's message to the people, making a contrast between the making of the golden calf and the tabernacle, and following the pattern of "narrated twice" as God calls Moses to go to Egypt in Exodus 3:1–4:17 and 6:2–8, and God gives Israel the covenant and the tablets in Exodus 19–24 and chapter 34. Hamilton, *Exodus*, 611.

18–19), demonstrating its symbolic value as "a copy and shadow of what is in heaven" (Heb 8:5).

In Exodus 37, the narrative shifts from the construction of the exterior to the creation of the interior furnishings of the tabernacle. Bezalel and his team of workers make the ark, the mercy seat, the two cherubim on the mercy seat, the table of showbread, the lampstand with its branches and cups, the altar of incense, the sacred anointing oil, and the fragrant incense. In Exodus 38, having completed the furniture for the Holy of Holies and the Holy Place, Bezalel moves on to the Outer Court. He constructs the altar of burnt offerings – with horns overlaid with bronze on the four corners – and makes all its utensils of bronze, including pots, shovels, sprinkling bowls, meat forks, and firepans. He then builds the bronze basin and its stand, using the mirrors contributed by the women who served at the entrance to the tent of meeting.[158] The identity of these women is not clear. Some scholars suggest that they were cleaning ladies, while others propose that they were singers or musicians,[159] and still others associate these women with the women who served at the entrance to the tent of meeting (see 1 Sam 2:22b). What we do know is that these women played some role in ministering at the entrance to the tent of meeting. Comparative evidence from the ancient Near East supports the role of women in cultic practices, including the role of guards or praying at the foot of certain statues.[160]

Finally, Bezalel constructs the outermost area of the tabernacle, the Outer Court. He begins by making the curtains and bases for the posts, then creates the curtain for the entrance to the courtyard, which includes four posts, four bronze bases, and the tent pegs.

Exodus 38:21–31 notes that the cost of the construction is recorded by Ithamar, a son of Aaron. Ithamar accounts for the amounts of gold, silver, and bronze contributed and records how these are used in the construction of the tabernacle. Throughout the construction process, Bezalel and Oholiab

---

158. For the use of mirrors in antiquity, see Sarna, *Exodus*, 230. It is unclear why women were mentioned here. Perhaps as Sarna indicates even the lowest class of women were donating their mirrors for the work of the tabernacle. Sarna, *Exodus*, 230.
159. Durham, *Exodus*, 487–488. The suggestion of cultic prostitution is unlikely given the context of chapter 38. Other ancient versions attempt to interpret these women's activities as fasting, guarding, or praying. Hamilton, *Exodus*, 609.
160. Janet S. Everhart, "Serving Women and Their Mirrors: A Feminist Reading of Exodus 38:8b," *CBQ* 66 (2004): 46. The word "mirror" in Exodus 38:8 appears only here in the Old Testament. It comes from the root word "to see." Mirror is often associated with women, female power, and divinity in the ancient world.

serve as teachers of their artistic craft. God fills them with artistic skills and also enables them to guide others in using their gifts for the same purpose.[161] Conforming to God's way of building God's house does not, however, exclude individual creativity – for instance, God does not provide the designs for the shape of the loops and the clasps or specify exactly how the blue, purple, and scarlet are to be used in making the curtains.

39:1–40:38 The Construction Completed

In Exodus 39, the priestly garments are made in accordance with the instructions given earlier (Exod 28). These garments include the ephod, the breastpiece, the robe, the tunics, and other accessories. The repetition of "as the Lord commanded Moses" (39:1, 5, 7, 21, 26, 29, 31) creates a literary rhythm that echoes the creation narrative in Genesis 1. Moreover, in the concluding statement that Moses "inspected the work and saw that they had done it just as the Lord had commanded" (39:43), the comment that "Moses blessed them" serves as a fitting conclusion to Exodus 39 and also mirrors the pattern of creation in Genesis 1:1–2:3, where God saw that everything he had made was good. Just as God saw his creation and found it good, Moses saw the completion of the tabernacle and (we may presume) found it good. As God blessed the seventh day and made it holy, Moses blessed the people.

In chapter 40, the final chapter of Exodus, we read the introduction to the next chapter of Israel's history – worshiping God in his tabernacle while his glory dwells in it. If Exodus had ended in chapter 34, the story would have concluded with God's forgiveness and the renewal of the covenant. However, the book ends with the completion of the tabernacle filled with God's glory. This glorious divine presence continues with Israel throughout their wilderness journey toward the promised land, emphasizing God's continuing presence with his people.

Although this final chapter brings the Exodus story to an end, Israel's journey to the promised land continues; and most importantly, God's presence remains with his people throughout their journey. In this chapter, God speaks to Moses again, instructing him to set up the tabernacle that has just been constructed. Moses was the first to receive God's revelation about the tabernacle (24:18–25:9); and he is now given the responsibility of overseeing its erection and completion.

---

161. Cornell, "Art on Mission with the Tabernacle Builders," 11.

Exodus 25–40

In Exodus 40, God reiterates his previous instructions about the arrangement of the tabernacle's furnishings, beginning with its interior, which contains the holiest items such as the ark of the testimony and the curtain separating the Holy of Holies from the Holy Place. God then instructs Moses on how to place the less sacred items such as the table, the lampstand, the altar of incense, and the entrance curtain. Finally, God gives instructions about setting up the Outer Court, which includes the altar of burnt offerings, the basin, the courtyard, and the entrance curtain.

After dealing with the arrangement of the "hardware" – the tabernacle's furnishings – God turns to the "software" involved in setting up the tabernacle. He instructs Moses to anoint the tabernacle and its furnishings with the anointing oil. Moses must then bring Aaron and his sons to the entrance of the tabernacle, wash them with water, and dress them in the sacred priestly garments. Similarly, Moses is to dress the sons of Aaron in tunics and anoint them as priests – a priesthood that would continue throughout their generations. Moses does just as God had instructed, once again demonstrating his obedience.

The "tabernacle erection day" falls on the first day of the first month in the second year (40:17), which is New Year's Day. This day marks a new beginning and a new order, similarly to the way the Lunar New Year symbolizes the end of one year and the start of a new journey in the year ahead. In Exodus 40:18–33, Moses sets up everything according to God's instructions. The detailed description of what Moses did and the sevenfold phrase "as the Lord commanded him" (40:19, 21, 23, 25, 27, 29, 32) emphasize Moses's obedience to God's instructions and confirm that the tabernacle was indeed constructed according to God's design.

This completion narrative in Exodus echoes the creation of the world. Just as God finished the work of creation (Gen 2:1–2), Moses finished the work of building the tabernacle (Exod 40:33). The parallels extend further: Genesis speaks of a large world, whereas the tabernacle is a mini-world. Just as God's presence fills his entire world, it also fills the tabernacle. In this way, creation and redemption are held in profound harmony, reflecting God's purposes.

The following table shows the similarities between the construction of the tabernacle and the creation narrative.

Table 19: Construction of the Tabernacle and the Construction of the World

	Themes	Construction of the Tabernacle	Creation of the World
1	7th day	Moses receives the instructions for the tabernacle on the seventh day after the glory of the Lord has been on the mountain for six days (Exod 24:16).	God creates the world in six days and rests on the seventh day (Gen 1:1–2:3).
2	7 speeches	There are seven divine speeches in Exodus 25–31, culminating with the Sabbath command (31:12–17).	God creates the world in six days and concludes on the seventh day – the Sabbath (Gen 2:3).
3	7 summary formulas	The phrase "as the LORD commanded him" appears seven times (Exod 40:19, 21, 23, 25, 27, 29, 32).	The seven repetitions of "good" (*ki tob*) in creation (Gen 1:4, 10, 12, 18, 21, 25, 31).
4	Saw completion	Moses sees the work completed (Exod 39:32, 43; 40:33).	God sees that his creation is good (Gen 1:31).
5	Blessed the completion	Moses blesses the people (Exod 39:43).	God blesses the seventh day (Gen 2:3).
6	Creation, fall, re-creation	Construction of the tabernacle, the golden calf incident, and reconstruction of the tabernacle (Exod 25–31, 32–34, 35–40).	Creation of the world, the fall, and re-creation through Noah (Gen 1–2, 3–6, 6–9).

Based on the table above, the construction of the tabernacle parallels God's creation. As Levenson aptly remarks, building a tabernacle is akin to creating a "microcosm" – a small, ordered world within the larger "cosmos."[162] By constructing the tabernacle and performing the prescribed rituals, people actively participate in the divine ordering of the world and seek God's intervention in their lives and in the world around them.[163] Furthermore, Moses's role is analogous to God's role in creation.[164] Once again, these parallels emphasize

---

162. Levenson, *Creation and the Persistence of Evil*, 53–127.
163. Averbeck, "Tabernacle," in *DOTP*, 817–818.
164. Seth D. Postell, "Reading Genesis, Seeing Moses: Narrative Analogies with Moses in the Book of Genesis," *JETS* 65, no. 3 (2022): 437–455, especially 439.

the close connection between Genesis and Exodus and point to the strong link between creation and redemption.[165]

This final section of Exodus concludes with a powerful manifestation of God's presence (40:34–38). Without God's presence, the tabernacle would be merely a physical structure. It is the presence of God within the tabernacle that transforms it into a divine sanctuary. The cloud that once covered Mount Sinai (24:18) now envelops the tabernacle, and the glory that resembled a consuming fire on the summit of Mount Sinai now fills the tabernacle, signifying that God no longer descends upon Mount Sinai but, rather, dwells within his own house among the Israelites. Thus, the tabernacle becomes the "body" of God, filled with divine glory.[166] According to Sommer, God's image, *kabod*, and the ark are all forms of God's body.[167] This fluidity of the divine body leads to our understanding of the embodiment of God in the tabernacle as one form of God's body.

Interestingly, the Hebrew text employs body-related terminology to describe the tabernacle. For example, it refers to the sides of the ark and the altar of incense as ribs (*tselaʿ*, 25:12–14; 30:4; compare Gen 2:21), the rear side of the tabernacle as the thigh (*yerekah*, 26:22–23), the tenons or projections that connect the wooden boards as hands (*yadoth*, 26:17; 36:22), and the outer gate where the veils are hung as the *shoulder* (*katheph*, 27:14–15).[168] This use of anatomical terms might have been a figurative method employed by ancient people to describe the appearance of a building.

The way the different parts of the tabernacle fit together to form God's dwelling place offers profound insights into the nature of the church. As Paul says, "Just as a body, though one, has many parts, but all its many parts form one body, so it is with Christ" (1 Cor 12:12). It is fitting, then, that Paul uses both body and tabernacle imagery to describe the body of Christ – the church (Eph 4:15–16).

---

165. Morales concludes the tabernacle study this way: "The narrative arc from Gen 1–3 to Exod 40 may be traced as the expulsion from the divine presence to the gained re-entry into the divine presence via the tabernacle cultus." Morales, *The Tabernacle Pre-Figured*, 277.
166. Fretheim, *Exodus*, 315. Stephanie Dalley, "Temple Building in the Ancient Near East: A Synthesis and Reflection," in *From the Foundations to the Crenellations: Essays on Temple Building in the Ancient Near East and Hebrew Bible*, eds. Mark J. Boda and Jamie Novotny, AOAT 366 (Münster: Ugarit-Verlag, 2010), 241, 251.
167. Sommer argues that God's body also appears in different locations, in heaven, in the burning bush, and the standing stones. Sommer, *The Bodies of God and the World of Ancient Israel*, 47–49.
168. For the implications of the tabernacle and its body language, see Chloe Sun, *Coming from God* (Hong Kong: Tien Dao, 2014).

The fact that the glory of the LORD fills the tabernacle has profound implications for biblical theology. Since the creation of the world, God's desire has been to fill it with his presence. The tabernacle was constructed so that God could dwell with his people (Exod 25:8). God's glory filling the tabernacle also means that he restores his presence with his people after vowing to withdraw his presence from them due to the golden calf incident.[169] In the NT, Jesus himself dwells among humans by replacing the temple (John 1:14; 2:19). After Jesus's resurrection, the Holy Spirit dwells within the body of believers (1 Cor 6:19). In the eschaton (final days), God's presence will fill the whole world, and there will be no physical temple because God and the Lamb will be the temple, and the glory of God will illuminate the new creation (Rev 21:22–23).[170]

Because the cloud now rests (literally, "dwells") on the tabernacle, even Moses, a man of God, has only limited access to the tabernacle. The repeated emphasis on the glory of God filling the tabernacle amplifies its significance. The cloud functions as a visual symbol of God's presence and plans: whenever the cloud is lifted from above the tabernacle, the Israelites resume their journey; when the cloud does not lift, they remain where they were.

Throughout their wilderness journey, the cloud guided the Israelites by day, while the fire within the cloud was visible to the Israelites at night. The visual symbols of the tabernacle, the cloud, and the fire provide Israel with a tangible and direct experience of the divine presence in their journey toward the promised land. The threefold repetition of "all" (40:36, 38) stresses the completeness of God's presence and the inclusion of the entirety of God's people. The former divine absence in Exodus 1 is now replaced by the divine presence in all their journeys, emphasizing that the God who travels with Israel is a "God of all places."[171]

Although the promised land is still distant, God's enduring presence – manifested through the cloud, the fire, and the portable tabernacle – accompanies Israel in all their journeys toward this destination. As Israel journeys from Egypt to the promised land, from the familiar to the unknown, from what was to what will be, they are always a people on the move, in the in-between spaces. They are constantly learning, negotiating, and renegotiating their identity as God's people. They are always embracing the tension between their

---

169. Anderson, *That I May Dwell among Them*, 151.
170. For more on the biblical theology of God's presence, see Beale, *The Temple and the Church's Mission*. Beale and Kim, *God Dwells Among Us*. Duvall and Hays, *God's Relational Presence*, 13–38.
171. Volf and McAnnally-Linz, *The Home of God*, 68.

own religious frailty and God's covenant faithfulness. As the construction of the tabernacle demonstrates, Israel's identity formation depends on the proper worship of the one true God. Through their worship, Israel has forged a new identity as a Yahweh-worshiping community, seeing God as their true home. As Moses proclaims in Psalm 90:1, "Lord, you have been our dwelling place throughout all generations."

Just as God is the God of Israel, he is also the God of all people in their journeys toward their heavenly home. For Chinese Christians living in the diaspora, Chinese churches may serve as temporary spiritual homes that offer a sense of belonging until they reach their eternal home. The current diasporic condition is a new exodus – from everywhere to everywhere – for the worship of God. Along the way, they may experience periods of liminal existence and construct various forms of "golden calves," but these struggles are part of the journey of becoming. When employing the diasporic lens to read the experience of the Israelites in Exodus, Roth remarks: "Theirs is a story of journeying, not merely geographically, but also psychologically."[172] This psychological journeying implies an inward journey within the heart as well as an "upward" journey in one's interpretation of the spiritual journey. The sense of physical and social dislocation in new lands and one's perception of what God is doing in that journey together create a dialectical relationship in contemplating one's belonging and identity formation.

As diasporans living among different nations, there may be ambivalence toward the concept of home, a feeling of "homelessness," and the tensions of multiple homes, but all this creates a yearning for an eternal home where one can be with God and worship God endlessly with all creation.

The conclusion of Exodus marks the beginning of a new chapter in the Israelites' ongoing journey toward a permanent home and, ultimately, an eternal abode. We, like the Israelites, are also on an ongoing journey, where our experiences shape our character. The Israelites' identity formation process – from their deliverance from Egypt, through the in-between spaces – holds profound significance for all who journey with God. It inspires us to seek purpose and meaning in the grand narrative of redemption.

In conclusion, the interwoven themes of diaspora, identity formation, and the journey of becoming in Exodus will give readers a fresh perspective that informs and transforms them within their own unique contexts. May the experiences and lessons of the Israelites inspire us all on our own journeys

---

172. Roth, *Hyphenating Moses*, 194.

of becoming, and may the book of Exodus inform our understanding of the new exodus of our own times within the diaspora until the day when we all find our true home in the presence of God.

SELECTED BIBLIOGRAPHY

Alexander, T. Desmond. *Exodus*. AOTC 2. Series editors: David W. Baker and Gordon J. Wenham. London: Apollos, 2017.

———. *From Paradise to the Promised Land: An Introduction to the Pentateuch*. Grand Rapids: Baker Academic, 2002.

An, Hannah S. "A Canonical Reconsideration of the Song at the Sea (Exod 15:1–21): The Song of Moses or the Song of Miriam? *Canon & Culture* 10 (2016): 7–35.

Anderson, Bernhard W. *Contours of Old Testament Theology*. Minneapolis: Fortress, 1999.

Anderson, Gary A. *That I May Dwell among Them: Incarnation and Atonement in the Tabernacle Narrative*. Grand Rapids: Eerdmans, 2023.

Apple, Raymond. "*Shirat Hayam*: Miriam's Song?" *JBQ* 45, no. 2 (2017): 99–102.

Arnold, Bill T. "Pentateuchal Criticism, History of." *DOTP*, 622–631.

Assmann, Jan. *Moses the Egyptian: The Memory of Egypt in Western Monotheism*. Cambridge: Harvard University Press, 1997.

———. "Re." *DDD*, 689–692.

Augustine. *Confessions*. Translated by R. S. Pine-Coffin. New York: Penguin Classics, 1961.

Averbeck, Richard E. *The Old Testament Law of the Life of the Church: Reading the Torah in the Light of Christ*. Downers Grove: IVP Academic, 2022.

———. "Tabernacle." *DOTP*, 807–827.

———. "Slavery in the World of the Bible." In *Behind the Scenes of the Old Testament: Cultural, Social, and Historical Contexts*. Edited by Jonathan S. Greer, John W. Hilber, and John H. Walton, 423–430. Grand Rapids: Baker Academic, 2018.

Baker, David L. "The Figure of God and the Forming of a Nation: The Origin and Purpose of the Decalogue." *TB* 56, no. 1 (2005): 1–24.

Baker, D. W. "Source Criticism." *DOTP*, 798–805.

Barton, Assnat. *Reading Law as Narrative: A Study in the Casuistic Laws of the Pentateuch*. Atlanta: Society of Biblical Literature, 2010.

Baumann, Gerlinde. *Love and Violence: Marriage as Metaphor for the Relationship between YHWH and Israel in the Prophetic Books*. Translated by Linda M. Malony. Collegeville: Liturgical Press, 2003.

Beale, G. K. *The Temple and the Church's Mission: A Biblical Theology of the Dwelling Place of God*. NSBT 17. Downers Grove: InterVarsity Press, 2004.

———. *We Become What We Worship: A Biblical Theology of Idolatry*. Downers Grove: IVP Academic, 2008.

Bias, Mona P. "Old Testament Law and Ethics." In *Exploring the Old Testament in Asia: Evangelical Perspectives*. Edited by Jerry Hwang and Angukali Rotokha, 101–122. Carlisle: Langham Global Library, 2022.

Bills, Nathan. *A Theology of Justice in Exodus*. Siphrut 26. University Park: Eisenbrauns, 2020.

Blackburn, W. Ross. *The God Who Makes Himself Known: The Missionary Heart of the Book of Exodus*. NSBT 28. Downers Grove: InterVarsity Press, 2012.

Block, Daniel I. *Covenant: The Framework of God's Grand Plan of Redemption*. Grand Rapids: Baker Academic, 2021.

Booer, Suzanne. "Source and Redaction Criticism." In *Methods for Exodus*. Edited by Thomas Dozeman, Methods in Biblical Interpretation, 95–130. Cambridge: Cambridge University Press, 2010.

Botica, Aurelian. "The Tenth Commandment and the Concept of Inward Liability." In *Windows to the Ancient World of the Hebrew Bible: Essays in Honor of Samuel Greengus*. Edited by Bill T. Arnold, Nancy L. Erickson, and John H. Walton, 51–66. Winona Lake: Eisenbrauns, 2014.

Brown, William P. *Seeing the Psalms: A Theology of Metaphor*. Louisville: Westminster John Knox, 2002.

Brueggemann, Walter. *Sabbath as Resistance: Saying No to the Culture of Now*. Louisville: Westminster John Knox, 2017.

———. *The Book of Exodus*. New Interpreter's Bible, vol. 1. Nashville: Abingdon, 1994.

———. "The Doctor Will See You Now." *Word & World Supplement Series* 7 (2017): 3–13.

Budge, E. A. Wallis, trans. *The Egyptian Book of the Dead: The Complete Papyrus of Ani*. New York: Clydesdale, 2021. Originally published in 1895 by order of the Trustees of the British Museum.

Burke, Peter. "Identity." In *The Cambridge Handbook of Social Theory: Volume 2: Contemporary Theories and Issues*. Edited by Peter Kivisto, 63–78. Cambridge: Cambridge University Press, 2020.

Cao, Jian. *Chinese Biblical Anthropology: Persons and Ideas in the Old Testament and in Modern Chinese Literature; Contrapuntal Readings of the Bible in World Christianity*. Eugene: Pickwick, 2019.

Carmichael, Calum M. *The Origins of Biblical Law: The Decalogue and the Book of the Covenant*. Ithaca: Cornell University Press, 1992.

Carroll R., M. Daniel. *The Bible and Borders: Hearing God's Word on Immigration*. Grand Rapids: Brazos, 2020.

Chan, Kwok-bun. *Chinese Identities, Ethnicity and Cosmopolitanism*. London: Routledge, 2005.

Selected Bibliography

Chen, Diane G. "Filial Piety and Radical Discipleship in Matthew." In *T&T Clark Handbook of Asian American Biblical Hermeneutics*. Edited by Uriah Y. Kim and Sang Ai Yang, 340–350. London: T&T Clark, 2019.

Chen, Kevin. *Eschatological Sanctuary in Exodus 15:17 and Related Texts, Studies in Biblical Literature*. New York: Peter Lang, 2013.

Childs, Brevard S. *Introduction to the Old Testament as Scripture*. Philadelphia: Fortress, 1979.

———. *The Book of Exodus: A Critical, Theological Commentary*. OTL. Philadelphia: Westminster, 1974.

Clines, David, J. A. "The Ten Commandments, Reading from Left to Right." In *Interested Parties: The Ideology of Writers and Readers of the Hebrew Bible*. JSOTSup 205, 26–45. Sheffield: Sheffield Academic Press, 1995.

Confucius. *The Analects of Confucius*. Translated by James Legge. Bilingual Study edition. Las Vegas: Dragon Reader, 2016.

Cornell, Collin. "Art on Mission with the Tabernacle Builders." *Transformation* (2024): 1–16.

Cross, Frank Moore. *Canaanite Myth and Hebrew Epic: Essays in the History of The Religion of Israel*. Cambridge: Harvard University Press, 1973.

Currid, John D. *Ancient Egypt and the Old Testament*. Grand Rapids: Baker Books, 1997.

Dalley, Stephanie, trans. *Myths from Mesopotamia: Creation, the Flood, Gilgamesh, and Others*. Oxford: Oxford University Press, 1989.

———. "Temple Building in the Ancient Near East: A Synthesis and Reflection." In *From the Foundations to the Crenellations: Essays on Temple Building in the Ancient Near East and Hebrew Bible*. Edited by Mark J. Boda and Jamie Novotny. AOAT 366, 239–251. Münster: Ugarit-Verlag, 2010.

Devries, L. "Sheepskin." *ISBE* IV: 466.

Dharamraj, Havilah. *Ruth: A Pastoral and Contextual Commentary*. ABCS. Carlisle: Langham Global Library, 2019.

Douglas, Mary. *Purity and Danger : An Analysis of Concept of Pollution and Taboo*. London: Routledge & Kegan Paul, 1966.

Dozeman, Thomas B. *God at War: Power in the Exodus Tradition*. New York: Oxford University Press, 1996.

———. *Exodus*. ECC. Grand Rapids: Eerdmans, 2009.

———. "Creation and Environment in the Character Development of Moses." In *Character Ethics and The Old Testament: Moral Dimensions of Scripture*. Edited by M. Daniel Carroll R. and Jacqueline E. Lapsley, 27–36. Louisville: Westminster John Knox, 2007.

Dumbrell, William J. *Covenant and Creation: A Theology of Old Testament Covenants*. Nashville: Thomas Nelson, 1984.

Exodus

Durham, John I. *Exodus*. WBC 3. Waco: Word, 1987.
Duvall, J. Scott, and J. Daniel Hays. *Grasping God's Word: A Hands-On Approach to Reading, Interpreting, and Applying the Bible*. 3rd ed. Grand Rapids: Zondervan, 2012.
———. *God's Relational Presence: The Cohesive Center of Biblical Theology*. Grand Rapids: Baker Academic, 2019.
Edenburg, Cynthia. "The Book of the Covenant." In *The Oxford Handbook of Biblical Law*. Edited by Pamela Barmash, 157–175. Oxford: Oxford University Press, 2019.
Enns, Peter. *Exodus*. The NIV Application Commentary. Grand Rapids: Zondervan, 2000.
Estelle, Bryan D. *Echoes of Exodus: Tracing a Biblical Motif*. Downers Grove: IVP Academic, 2018.
Evans, John Frederick. "An Inner-Biblical Interpretation and Intertextual Reading of Ezekiel's Recognition Formulae with the Book of Exodus." ThD diss. University of Stellenbosch, 2006.
Everhart, Janet S. "Serving Women and Their Mirrors: A Feminist Reading of Exodus 38:8b." *CBQ* 66 (2004): 44–54.
Exum, J. Cheryl. "'You shall Let Every Daughter Live': A Study of Exodus 1.8–2.10." In *A Feminist Companion to Exodus to Deuteronomy*. Edited by Athalya Brenner, 37–61. Sheffield: Sheffield Academic Press, 1994.
———. "Second Thoughts About Secondary Characters: Women in Exodus 1.8–2.10." In *A Feminist Companion to Exodus to Deuteronomy*. Edited by Athalya Brenner, 75–87. Sheffield: Sheffield Academic Press, 1994.
Fentress-Williams, Judy. "Exodus." In *The Africana Bible: Reading Israel's Scripture from Africa and African Diaspora*. Edited by Hugh J. Page, Randall C. Bailey, Valerie Bridgeman, Stacy Davis, Cheryl Kirk-Duggan, Madipoane Masenya (ngwan'a Mphahlele), Nathaniel Samuel Murrell, and Rodney S. Sadler, 80–88. Minneapolis: Fortress, 2010.
Flory, Richard. "City of Dreams: Los Angeles as a Cradle for Religious Activism, Innovation, and Diversity." In *Migration, Transnationalism, and Faith in Missiological Perspective: Los Angeles as a Global Crossroads*. Edited by Kirsteen Kim and Alexia Salvatierra, 19–41. Lanham: Lexington, 2022.
Fokkelman, Jan P. *Reading Biblical Narrative: A Practical Guide*. Translated by Ineke Smit. Leiden: Deo, 1995.
Fretheim, Terence E. *God and World in the Old Testament: A Relational Theology of Creation*. Nashville: Abingdon, 2005.
———. *Exodus*. Louisville: John Knox, 1991.
Friedman, Richard Elliott. *The Exodus: How It Happened and Why It Matters*. New York: HarperOne, 2017.

Selected Bibliography

Fuller, Russell. "Exodus 21:22–23: The Miscarriage Interpretation and the Personhood of the Fetus." *JETS* 37, no. 2 (June 1994): 169–184.

Gane, Roy E. *Old Testament Law for Christians: Original Context and Enduring Application.* Grand Rapids: Baker Academic, 2017.

Garcia-Treto, Francisco. "Hyphenating Joseph: A View of Genesis 39–41 from the Cuban Diaspora." In *Interpreting Beyond Borders.* Edited by Fernando F. Segovia, 134–145. Sheffield: Sheffield Academic Press, 2000.

Geller, Stephen A. Geller. "Manna and Sabbath: A Literary-Theological Reading of Exodus 16." *Int* (Jan 2005): 5–16.

George, P. G., and Paul Swarup. "Exodus." In *South Asia Bible Commentary.* Edited by Brian Wintle, 75–134. Grand Rapids: Zondervan, 2015.

George, Sam. *Journeys of Asian Diaspora: Mapping Originations and Destinations,* vol. 1. Edited by Sam George. Minneapolis: Fortress, 2021.

———. "Diaspora: A Hidden Link to 'From Everywhere to Everywhere.'" *Missiology: An International Review* 39, no. 1 (January 2011): 45–56.

Gin, Debbie Hearn. "Ruth: Identity and Leadership from Multivocal Spaces." In *Mirrored Reflections: Reframing Biblical Characters.* Edited by Young Lee Hertig and Chloe Sun, 57–71. Eugene: Wipf & Stock, 2010.

Glanville, Mark R. *Freed to Be God's Family: The Book of Exodus.* Bellingham: Lexham Press, 2021.

Goldingay, John. *Old Testament Theology: Israel's Gospel.* Vol. 1. Downers Grove: IVP Academic, 2003.

Gong, Wenhui. *Mission Beyond: Chinese Diaspora Missions.* Paradise: Ambassadors for Christ, Inc., 2022.

Gordon, Cyrus H., and Gary A. Rensburg. *The Bible and the Ancient Near East.* New York: W. W. Norton & Company, 1997.

Gorospe, Athena E. *Narrative and Identity: An Ethical Reading of Exodus 4.* Leiden: Brill, 2007.

Gorospe, Athena E. with Charles Ringma. *Judges: A Pastoral and Contextual Commentary.* ABCS. Carlisle: Langham Global Library, 2016.

Gowan, Donald E. *Theology in Exodus: Biblical Theology in the Form of a Commentary.* Louisville: Westminster John Knox, 1994.

Greenberg, Moshe. *Understanding Exodus: A Holistic Commentary on Exodus 1–11.* Eugene: Cascade, 2013.

Hamilton, Victor P. *Exodus. An Exegetical Commentary.* Grand Rapids: Baker Academic, 2011.

Hanciles, Jehu J. *Migration and the Making of Global Christianity.* Grand Rapids: Eerdmans, 2021.

Harrell, James E., James K. Hoffmeier, and Kenton F. Williams. "Hebrew Gemstones in the Old Testament: A Lexical, Geological, and Archaeological Analysis." *BBR* 27, no. 1 (2017): 1–52.

Hart, George. *The Routledge Dictionary of Egyptian Gods and Goddesses*. 2nd ed. London: Routledge, 2005.

Hawkins, Ralph K. *Discovering Exodus: Content, Interpretation, Reception*, Discovering Biblical Texts. Grand Rapids: Eerdmans, 2021.

Hays, Christopher B. *Hidden Riches: A Sourcebook for the Comparative Study of the Hebrew Bible and Ancient Near East*. Louisville: Westminster John Knox, 2014.

Hendel, Ronald. "The Exodus in Biblical Memory." *JBL* 120, no. 4 (2001): 601–622.

Henrich, Sarah S. "Seen and Unseen: The Visibility of God in Exodus 25–40." *WW* (2006): 103–111.

Herring, Stephen L. "Moses as Divine Substitute in Exodus." *CTR* 9, no. 2 (Spring 2012): 53–68.

Heschel, Abraham Joshua. *The Sabbath: Its Meaning for Modern Man*. New York: Farrar, Straus and Giroux, 1951.

Ho, Shirley S. "Taiwanese Christian *Li*: The Embodied Worship of the Lord." In *Exploring the Old Testament in Asia: Evangelical Perspectives*. Edited by Jerry Hwang and Angukali Rotokha, 123–144. Carlisle: Langham Global Library, 2022.

Hoffmeier, James K. *Israel in Egypt: The Evidence for the Authenticity of the Exodus Tradition*. New York: Oxford University Press, 1997.

———. *Ancient Israel in Sinai: The Evidence for the Authenticity of the Wilderness Tradition*. New York: Oxford University Press, 2005.

Hoffmeier, James K., and Gary A. Rendsburg. "Pithom and Rameses (Exodus 1:11): Historical, Archaeological, and Linguistic Issues (Part I)." *Journal of Ancient Egyptian Interconnections* 33 (March 2022): 1–19.

Holbert, John C. "A New Literary Reading of Exodus 32: The Story of the Golden Calf." *QR* 10, no. 3 (Fall, 1990): 46–68.

Homan, Michael M. *To Your Tents, O Israel! The Terminology, Function, Form, and Symbolism of Tents in the Hebrew Bible and the Ancient Near East*, Culture & History of the Ancient Near East. Leiden: Brill, 2002.

Hornung, Erik. "Ancient Egyptian Religious Iconography." *CANE*, 1711–1730.

Huffmon, Herbert B. " 'An Eye for An Eye' and Capital Punishment." In *The Oxford Handbook of Biblical Law*. Edited by Pamela Barmash, 119–131. Oxford: Oxford University Press, 2019.

Hundley, Michael B. "What is the Golden Calf?" *CBQ* 79, no. 4 (2017): 559–579.

Hwang, Jerry. *Contextualization and the Old Testament: Between Asian and Western Perspectives*. Logia series. Carlisle: Langham Global Library, 2022.

Selected Bibliography

Imes, Carmen Joy. *Bearing God's Name: Why Sinai Still Matters.* Downers Grove: IVP Academic, 2019.

———. "Between Two Worlds: The Functional and Symbolic Significance of the High Priestly Regalia." In *Dress and Clothing in the Hebrew Bible: "For All Her Household Are Clothed in Crimson."* LHBOTS. Edited by Antonios Finites, 29–62. London: T&T Clark, 2019.

———. "Can I Get a Witness?: Miriam's Song in the Literary Design of Exodus." *BBR* 33, no. 4 (2023): 426–440.

Jacobson, Rolf A. "Moses, the Golden Calf, and the False Images of the True God." *WW* 33, no. 2 (Spring 2013): 130–139.

Janzen, J. Gerald. "Song of Moses, Song of Miriam: Who Is Seconding Whom?" *CBQ* 54 (1992): 211–220.

———. "The Character of the Calf and Its Cult in Exodus 32." *CBQ* 52 (1990): 597–607.

Johnstone, William. *Exodus 1–19.* S&HBC. Macon: Smyth & Helwys, 2014.

Kaiser, Jr., Walter. *The Messiah in the Old Testament; Studies in Old Testament Biblical Theology.* Grand Rapids: Zondervan, 1995.

Kaminsky, Joel S. *Yet I Loved Jacob: Reclaiming the Biblical Concept of Election.* Nashville: Abingdon, 2007.

Kang, Sa-Moon. *Divine War in the Old Testament and in the Ancient Near East.* BZAW 177. Berlin: W. de Gruyter, 1989.

Kass, Leon R. *Founding God's Nation: Reading Exodus.* New Haven: Yale University Press, 2021.

Keel, Othmar. *The Symbolism of the Biblical World: Ancient Near Eastern Iconography and the Book of Psalms.* Translated by Timothy J. Hallett. Winona Lake: Eisenbrauns, 1997.

Keel, Othmar, and Christopher Uelinger. *Gods, Goddesses, and the Images of God in Ancient Israel.* Translated by Thomas H. Trapp. Minneapolis: Fortress, 1998.

Kenny, Kevin. *Diaspora: A Very Short Introduction.* Oxford: Oxford University Press, 2013.

Kessler, John. *Between Hearing and Silence: A Study in Old Testament Theology.* Waco: Baylor University Press, 2021.

Kihlstrom, John F, Jennifer S. Beer, and Stanley B. Klein. "Self and Identity as Memory." In *Handbook of Self and Identity.* Edited by Mark R. Leary, and June Price Tangney, 68–90. New York: The Guilford Press, 2003.

Kim, Brittany, and Charlie Trimm. *Understanding Old Testament Theology: Mapping the Terrain of Recent Approaches.* Grand Rapids: Zondervan, 2020.

Kim, Koowon. "Yahweh and Other Gods." In *Exploring the Old Testament in Asia: Evangelical Perspectives.* Edited by Jerry Hwang and Angukali Rotokha, 25–40. Carlisle: Langham Global Library, 2022.

Kim, Rebecca Y. "Making Their Mark: Asian Americans and the Californian "Christian" Landscape." In *Migration, Transnationalism, and Faith in Missiological Perspective: Los Angeles as a Global Crossroads*. Edited by Kirsteen Kim and Alexia Salvatierra, 93–112. Lanham: Lexington, 2022.

Kling, David W. ""Let My People Go": Exodus in the African American Experience." In *The Bible in History: How the Texts Have Shaped the Times*. Edited by David W. Kling, 193–230. Oxford: Oxford University Press, 2004.

Klingbeil, Gerald A. "The Finger of God in the Old Testament." *ZAW* 112 (2000): 409–415.

Ko, Ming Him. *Leviticus: A Pastoral and Contextual Commentary*. ABCS. Carlisle: Langham Global Library, 2018.

Kuhn, Philip. *Chinese among Others: Emigration in Modern Times*. Translated by Li Ming Huan. Taiwan: Shang Wu Yin Shu Guan, 2019.

Landau, Ephraim. "Meat/Bread as a Parallel Word-Pair in Biblical Poetry: A Key to Understanding Exodus 16:1–15." *JBQ* 47, no. 1 (2019): 3–20.

Langston, Scott M. *Exodus through the Centuries*. Blackwell Bible Commentaries. Malden: Blackwell, 2006.

Lapsley, Jacqueline E. *Whispering the Word: Hearing Women's Stories in the Old Testament*. Louisville: Westminster John Knox, 2005.

Lau, Peter H. W. "Kinship, Patronage, and Corruption." In *Exploring the Old Testament in Asia: Evangelical Perspectives*. Edited by Jerry Hwang and Angukali Rotokha, 216–223. Carlisle: Langham Global Library, 2022.

Lee, Andrew Y. "The Future of English Ministry in Diaspora Chinese and Asian Churches." In *Reflections of Asian Diaspora: Mapping Theologies and Ministries*. Edited by Sam George, 181–203. Minneapolis: Fortress, 2022.

Lee, Archie C. C. "The Plague of Darkness and the Creation of Light: A Reading of Psalm 105:26–36 from the Notion of Calamities in Chinese Perspective." In *From Mari to Jerusalem and Back: Assyriological and Biblical Studies in Honor of Jack Murad Sasson*. Edited by Annalisa Azzoni, Alexandra Kleinerman, Douglas A. Knight, and David I. Owen, 439–452. University Park: Eisenbrauns, 2020.

Lee, Daniel D. *Doing Asian American Theology: A Contextual Framework for Faith and Practice*. Downers Grove: IVP Academic, 2022.

Lee, Helen. "Silent Exodus," *Christianity Today* (August 1996): 50–53.

Lee, Jung Young. *Marginality: The Key to Multicultural Theology*. Minneapolis: Fortress, 1995.

LeFebvre, Michael. *The Liturgy of Creation: Understanding Calendars in Old Testament Context*. Downers Grove: IVP Academic, 2019.

Lesko, Leonard H. "Death and the Afterlife in Ancient Egyptian Thought." *CANE*, 1763–1774.

Selected Bibliography

Leslie, Ben. "Ethical Perspectives on the Tenth Commandments." *RevExp* 113, no. 4 (2016): 538–545.

Leung Lai, Barbara M. *Through the 'I'- Window: The Inner Life of Characters in the Hebrew Bible*. Sheffield: Sheffield Phoenix, 2011.

Levenson, Jon D. *Sinai and Zion: An Entry into the Jewish Bible*. New York: Harper One, 1985.

Levy, David M. *The Tabernacle: Shadows of the Messiah: Its Sacrifices, Services, and Priesthood*. Bellmawr: The Friends of Israel Gospel Ministry, Inc., 1993.

Lewis, Theodore J. *The Origin and Character of God*. Oxford: Oxford University Press, 2020.

Lo, Chung Man Anna. *The Laws of the Imperialized: Understanding Exodus 19–24 as a Response to Imperial Legal Traditions*. Cumbria: Langham Academic, 2024.

Lo, Lung-Kwong. "The Nature of the Issue of Ancestral Worship among Chinese Christians." *Studies in World Christianity* 9, no. 1 (2003): 30–42.

Longman III, Tremper. *How to Read Exodus*. Downers Grove: IVP Academic, 2009.

———. *The Bible and the Ballot: Using Scripture in Political Decisions*. Grand Rapids: Eerdmans, 2020.

———. *Immanuel in Our Place: Seeing Christ in Israel's Worship*. Phillipsburg: P&R, 2001.

Longman III, Tremper, and Daniel G. Reid. *God is a Warrior*. Studies in Old Testament Biblical Theology. Grand Rapids: Zondervan, 1995.

Lunn, Nicholas P. " 'Raised on the Third Day According to the Scriptures': Resurrection Typology in the Genesis Creation Narrative." *JETS* 57, no. 3 (2014): 523–555.

Ma, Laurence J. C., and Carolyn Cartier, eds. *The Chinese Diaspora: Space, Place, Mobility, and Identity*. Lanham: Rowman & Littlefield Publishers, Inc., 2003.

Martens, Elmer A. *God's Design: A Focus on Old Testament Theology*. 4th ed. Eugene: Wipf & Stock, 2015.

Matthews, Victor H., and Don C. Benjamin, *Old Testament Parallels: Laws and Stories from the Ancient Near East*. 2nd ed. New York: Paulist, 2001.

McAfee, Matthew. "The Heart of Pharaoh in Exodus 4–15." *BBR* 20, no. 3 (2010): 331–354.

Meier, S. A. "Destroyer." *DDD*: 240–244.

Mendelsohn, Isaac. "On the Preferential Status of the Eldest Son." *BASOR* 156 (1959): 38–40.

Meyers, Carol. *Exodus*. The New Cambridge Bible Commentary. New York: Cambridge University Press, 2005.

———. "The Family in Early Israel." In *Families in Ancient Israel*. Edited by Leo G. Perdue et al., 32–33. Louisville: Westminster John Knox, 1997.

Miles, Steven B. *Chinese Diaspora: A Social History of Global Migration*. Cambridge: Cambridge University Press, 2020.

Miller, Geoffrey David. "Attitudes toward Dogs in Ancient Israel: A Reassessment." *JSOT* 32, no. 4 (2008): 487–500.

Miller, Patrick D., Jr. *The Divine Warrior in Early Israel*. HSM 5. Cambridge: Harvard University Press, 1973.

———. *The Ten Commandments*. Interpretation: Resources for the Use of Scripture in the Church. Louisville: Westminster John Knox, 2009.

Moberly, R. W. L. *Old Testament Theology: Reading the Hebrew Bible as Christian Scripture*. Grand Rapids: Baker Academic, 2013.

Morales, L. Michael Morales. *Exodus Old and New: A Biblical Theology of Redemption*, ESBT. Downers Grove: IVP Academic, 2020.

———. *The Tabernacle Pre-Figured: Cosmic Mountain Ideology in Genesis and Exodus*, Biblical Tools and Studies 15. Leuven: Peeters, 2012.

Mukujina, John. "Literary Solutions to Legal Problems: The Contribution of Exodus 2:13–14 to Exodus 21:22–23." *JSOT* 37, no. 2 (2012): 151–165.

Ndjerareou, Abel. "Exodus." In *Africa Bible Commentary*. Edited by Tokunboh Adeyemo, 85–128. Grand Rapids: Zondervan, 2006.

Ngwa, Kenneth N. *Let My People Live: An Africana Reading of Exodus*. Louisville: Westminster John Knox, 2022.

Noonan, Benjamin J. "Hide or Hue? Defining Hebrew taḥaš," *Biblica* 93 (4), (2012): 580–589.

Noth, Martin. *Exodus: A Commentary*. Philadelphia: Westminster, 1962.

Nysse, Richard W. "Retelling the Exodus." *WW* 33, no. 2 (2013): 157–165.

Oak Sung-Deuk. "Competing Chinese Names for God: The Chinese Term Question and Its Influence upon Korea," *Journal of Korean Religions* 3, no. 2 (2012): 89–115.

O'Mathuna, D. P. "Bodily Injuries, Murder, Manslaughter." *DOTP*, 93–94.

Palmer, Christine. "Israelite High Priestly Apparel: Embodying an Identity between Human and Divine." In *Fashioned Selves: Dress and Identity in Antiquity*. Edited by Megan Cifarelli, 117–128. Havertown: Oxbow Books, 2019.

Park, Esther HaeJin. "Women in Exodus and Asian Immigrant Women: Asian Female Immigrants' Bible Reading Strategy on Exodus 1–4." In *T&T Clark Handbook of Asian American Biblical Hermeneutics*. Edited by Uriah Y. Kim and Seung Ai Yang, 220–228. London: T&T Clark, 2019.

Parker, Simon B. "Aqhat" (CAT 1.17 column I: 26–33). In *Ugaritic Narrative Poetry*. Edited by Simon B. Parker. SBL Writings from the Ancient World Series, 49–80. Atlanta: Scholars Press, 1997.

Paulsell, Stephanie. *Honoring the Body: Meditations on a Christian Practice*. San Francisco: Jossey-Bass, 2002.

Selected Bibliography

Perdue, Leo G. "The Household, Old Testament Theology, and Contemporary Hermeneutics." In *Families in Ancient Israel*. Edited by Leo G. Perdue, Joseph Blenkinsopp, John J. Collins, and Carol Meyers, 223–257. Louisville: Westminster John Knox, 1997.

Phan, Peter C. *Christianity with an Asian Face: Asian American Theology in the Making*. Maryknoll: Orbis Books, 2003.

Pitkänen, Pekka. "Temple Building and Exodus 25–40." In *From the Foundations to the Crenellations: Essays on Temple Building in the Ancient Near East and Hebrew Bible*. Edited by Mark J. Boda and Jamie Novotny. AOAT 366, 255–280. Münster: Ugarit-Verlag, 2010.

Pixley, Jorge. "Liberation Criticism." In *Methods for Exodus*, Methods in Biblical Interpretation. Edited by Thomas B. Dozeman, 131–162. Cambridge: Cambridge University Press, 2010.

Poho, Rubin. "Slavery." In *Africa Bible Commentary*. Edited by Tokunboh Adeyemo, 89. Grand Rapids: Zondervan, 2006.

Postell, Seth D. "Reading Genesis, Seeing Moses: Narrative Analogies with Moses in the Book of Genesis." *JETS* 65, no. 3 (2022): 437–455.

Propp, William H. C. *Exodus 1–18: A New Translation with Introduction and Commentary*. AB. Vol. 1. New York: Doubleday, 1999.

———. *Exodus 19–40: A New Translation with Introduction and Commentary*. AB. Vol. 2. New York: Doubleday, 2006.

Prosic, Tamara. "Passover in Biblical Narrative." *JSOT* 82 (1999): 45–55.

Ritner, Robert K., trans. "The Great Cairo Hymn of Praise to Amun-Re." *COS* 1, no. 25: 37–40.

Roger, Syren. *The Forsaken Firstborn: A Study of a Recurrent Motif in the Patriarchal Narratives*. JSOTSup 133. Sheffield: Sheffield Academic Press, 1993.

Roth, Ann Macy. "Gender Roles in Ancient Egypt." In *A Companion to the Ancient Near East*. Edited by Daniel C. Snell, 227–334. Malden: Blackwell, 2007.

Roth, Federico Alfredo. *Hyphenating Moses: A Postcolonial Exegesis of Identity in Exodus 1:1–3:15*. Biblical Interpretation Series 154. Leiden: Brill, 2017.

Roth, Martha T. *Law Collections from Mesopotamia and Asia Minor*. 2nd ed. Writings from the Ancient World 6. Atlanta: Society of Biblical Literature, 1997.

———. "The Laws of Eshunna." *COS* 2, no.1 30: 332–335.

Rotokha, Angukali. "Exodus and Liberation: Naga Nationalism and the People of God." In *Exploring the Old Testament in Asia: Evangelical Perspectives*. Edited by Jerry Hwang and Angukali Rotokha, 185–204. Carlisle: Langham Global Library, 2022.

Sailhamer, John H. *The Pentateuch as Narrative*. Grand Rapids: Zondervan, 1992.

Sánchez M., Leopoldo A. "Theological Approaches to Migration: Their Impact on Missional Thinking and Action." In *Migration, Transnationalism, and Faith in Missiological Perspective: Los Angeles as a Global Crossroads*. Edited by Kirsteen Kim and Alexia Salvatierra, 177–194. Lanham: Lexington, 2022.

Santos, Narry F. "Exploring the Major Dispersion Terms and Realities in the Bible." In *Diaspora Missiology: Theory, Methodology, and Practice*. Edited by Enoch Wan, 21–38. Portland: Western Seminary, 2011.

Sarna, Nahum M. *Exploring Exodus: The Origins of Biblical Israel*. New York: Schocken Books, 1996.

———. *Exodus: The JPS Torah Commentary*. Philadelphia: The Jewish Publication Society, 1991.

Schafer, A. Rahel. "Rest for the Animals? Nonhuman Sabbath Repose in Pentateuchal Law." *BBR* 23, no. 2 (2013): 167–186.

Schlimm, Matthew Richard. *This Strange and Sacred Scripture: Wrestling with the Old Testament and Its Oddities*. Grand Rapids: Baker Academic, 2015.

Schmit, Konrad. *Genesis and the Moses's Story: Israel's Dual-Origins in the Hebrew Bible*. Translated by James D. Nogalski; Siphrut 3. Winona Lake: Eisenbrauns, 2010.

Scott, Marshall L. S. "Honor Thy Father and Mother: Scriptural Resources for Victims of Incest and Parental Abuse." *Journal of Pastoral Care* XLII, no. 2, Summer (1988): 139–148.

Segovia, Fernando F., ed. *Interpreting Beyond Borders*. Sheffield: Sheffield Academic Press, 2000.

———. "Toward a Hermeneutics of the Diaspora: A Hermeneutics of Otherness and Engagement." In *Reading from this Place: Social Location and Biblical Interpretation in the United States*. Edited by Fernando F. Segovia and Mary Ann Tolbert, 57–73. Minneapolis: Fortress, 1995.

Seibert, Eric A. *Disturbing Divine Behavior: Troubling Old Testament Images of God*. Minneapolis: Fortress, 2009.

Sexton, Jason S. "Borders and Barriers: Citizenship in California." In *Migration, Transnationalism, and Faith in Missiological Perspective: Los Angeles as a Global Crossroads*. Edited by Kirsteen Kim and Alexia Salvatierra, 131–150. Lanham: Lexington, 2022.

Shah, Sonia. *The Next Great Migration: The Beauty and Terror of Life on the Move*. New York: Bloomsbury Publishing, 2020.

Shao, Joseph. "Hybridity in the Old Testament." In *A Hybrid World: Diaspora, Hybridity, and Missio Dei*. Edited by Sadiri Joy Tira and Juliet Lee Uytanlet, 1–9. Littleton: William Carey, 2020.

Smedes, Lewis B. *Mere Morality: What God Expects from Ordinary People*. Grand Rapids: Eerdmans, 1983.

Selected Bibliography

Smith, Kay Huguera. "Diasporic Approaches." In *Reading the Bible around the World: A Student's Guide to Global Hermeneutics*. Edited by Federico Alfredo Roth, et al., 118–138. Downers Grove: IVP Academic, 2022.

Smith, Mark S. *The Pilgrimage Pattern in Exodus*, JSOTSup 239. Sheffield: Sheffield Academic Press, 1997.

———. *The Early History of God: Yahweh and the Other Deities in Ancient Israel*. 2nd ed. Grand Rapids: Eerdmans, 2002.

Sommer, Benjamin D. *The Bodies of God and the World of Ancient Israel*. Cambridge: Cambridge University Press, 2009.

Song, Angeline M. G. *A Postcolonial Woman's Encounter with Moses and Miriam*. New York: Palgrave Macmillan, 2015.

Stahl, Nanette. *Law and Liminality in the Bible*. JSOTSup 202. Sheffield: Sheffield Academic Press, 1995.

Steinberg, Naomi. "Feminist Criticism." In *Methods for Exodus*, Methods in Biblical Interpretation, ed. Thomas B. Dozeman, 163–192. Cambridge: Cambridge University Press, 2010.

Stienstra, Nelly. *YHWH is the Husband of His People: An Analysis of a Biblical Metaphor with Special Reference to Translation*. Kampen: Kok Pharos, 1993.

Stock, Augustine. *The Way in the Wilderness: Exodus, Wilderness and Moses Themes in the Old Testament and New*. Collegeville: Liturgical Press, 1969.

Stripling, Scott, James K. Hoffmeier, Gary A. Rendsburg, Peter Feinman, Ronald Hendel, and Mark D. Janzen. *Five Views on the Exodus: Historicity, Chronology, and Theological Implications*. Grand Rapids: Zondervan, 2021.

Suh, Myung Soo. *The Tabernacle in the Narrative History of Israel from the Exodus to the Conquest*. Studies in Biblical Literature 50. New York: Peter Lang, 2003.

Sun, Chloe T. *Attempt Great Things for God: Theological Education in Diaspora*. Theological Education between the Times Series. Edited by Ted A. Smith. Grand Rapids: Eerdmans, 2020.

———. *Conspicuous in His Absence: Studies in the Song of Songs and Esther*. Downers Grove: IVP Academic, 2021.

———. "Recent Research on Asian and Asian American Hermeneutics Related to the Hebrew Bible." *CurBR* 17, no. 3 (2019): 238–265.

———. "Reading Job as a Chinese Diasporian." In *T&T Clark Handbook of Asian American Biblical Hermeneutics*. Edited by Uriah Y. Kim and Sang Ai Yang, 295–305. London: T&T Clark, 2019.

———. "Elim." *EBR* 7:721–722.

———. "Dowry and Bride Price." *EBR* 6:1132–1133.

———. "Dance." *EBR* 6:65–66.

———. *Coming from God*. Hong Kong: Tien Dao, 2014.

———. "Bridging Past and Future: The In-Between Life of Moses." In *Logos for Life: Essays Commemorating Logos Evangelical Seminary's 20th Anniversary*, 217–237. Hong Kong: Tien Dao, 2009.

Surls, Austin. *Making Sense of the Divine Name in the Book of Exodus: From Etymology to Literary Onomastics*. Bulletin for Biblical Research 17. Winona Lake: Eisenbrauns, 2017.

Tan, Jonathan Y. *Introducing Asian American Theologies*. Maryknoll: Orbis Books, 2008.

Thomas, D. Winton. "Kelebh Dog: Its Origin and Some Usages of It in the Old Testament." *VT* 10, no. 4 (Oct 1960): 410–427.

Thomassen, Bjørn, *Liminality and the Modern: Living Through the In-Between*. London: Routledge, 2014.

Tigay, Jeffrey H. "Exodus." In *The Jewish Study Bible*, 2nd ed. Edited by Adele Berlin and Marc Zvi Brettler, 95–192. Oxford: Oxford University Press, 2014.

Timmer, Daniel C. *Creation, Tabernacle, and Sabbath: The Sabbath Frame of Exodus 31:12–17; 35:1–3 in Exegetical and Theological Perspective*. Band 227 Forschungen zur Religion und Literatur des Alten und Neuen Testaments. Gottingen: Vandenhoeck & Ruprecht, 2009.

Trimm, Charlie. "*YHWH Fights for Them!" The Divine Warrior in the Exodus Narrative*. Gorgias Biblical Studies 58. Piscataway: Gorgias, 2014.

———. *The Destruction of the Canaanites: God, Genocide, and Biblical Interpretation*. Grand Rapids: Eerdmans, 2022.

———. "God's staff and Moses's hand(s): The battle against the Amalekites as a turning point in the role of the divine warrior." *JSOT* 44 (2019): 198–214.

———. "Honor Your Parents: A Command for Adults." *JETS* 60, no. 2 (2017): 243–263.

Turner, Victor and Edith Turner, *Image and Pilgrimage in Christian Culture: Anthropological Perspective*. New York: Columbia University Press, 1978.

Twiss, Paul. "Learning God's Redemptive Good: Reading Genesis 50:15–21 as a Last Delay." *JETS* 66, no. 3 (2023): 405–419.

Uytanlet, Juliet Lee. "Hybridity and Chineseness: Finding Meaning in Theories." In *A Hybrid World: Diaspora, Hybridity, and Missio Dei*, eds., Sadiri Joy Tira and Juliet Lee Uytanlet, 102–105. Littleton: William Carey, 2020.

Van der Toorn, Karel. *Family Religion in Babylonia, Syria and Israel: Continuity and Change in the Forms of Religious Life*, Atlanta: Society of Biblical Literature, 2017.

Van Gennep, Arnold. *The Rites of Passage*. Chicago: The University of Chicago Press, 1960.

Van Houten, Christiana. *The Alien in Israelite Law*. JSOTSupp 107. Sheffield: Sheffield Academic Press, 1991.

Selected Bibliography

Van Voss, M. Heerma. "Hathor." *DDD*, 385–386.

Vandyke, Elizabeth. "Designing the Golden Calf: Pens and Presumption in the Production of a 'Divine' Image." *JBL* 141, no. 2 (2022): 219–233.

Velde, Herman Te. "Theology, Priests, and Worship in Ancient Egypt." *CANE* 3: 1731–1749.

Volf, Miroslav. *The End of Memory: Remembering Rightly in a Violent World*. Grand Rapids: Eerdmans, 2006.

Volf, Miroslav, and Ryan McAnnally-Linz, *The Home of God: A Brief Story of Everything*. Grand Rapids: Brazos, 2022.

Vos, R. L. "Apis." *DDD*, 68–72.

Walton, John H. *Chronological and Background Charts of the Old Testament*, revised. Grand Rapids: Zondervan, 1994.

———. "Exodus, Date of." *DOTP*, 258–272.

Walton, John H., and J. Harvey Walton. *The Lost World of the Israelite Conquest: Covenant, Retribution, and the Fate of the Canaanites*. Downers Grove: IVP Academic, 2017.

Wan, Enoch. *Diaspora Missiology: Theory, Methodology, and Practice*. Portland: Institute of Diaspora Studies, 2011.

Weems, Renita J. "The Hebrew Women are not Like the Egyptian Women: The Ideology of Race, Gender and Sexual Reproduction in Exodus 1." *Semeia* 59 (1992): 25–34.

Wells, Bruce. "What is Biblical Law? A Look at Pentateuchal Rules and Near Eastern Practice." *CBQ* 70, no. 2 (Apr 2008): 223–243.

Westbrook, Raymond, and Bruce Wells, *Everyday Law in Biblical Israel: An Introduction*. Louisville: Westminster John Knox, 2009.

White, Jon Manchip. *Everyday Life in Ancient Egypt*. Mineola: Dover Publications, 2002.

Widmer, Michael. *Standing in the Breach: An Old Testament Theology and Spirituality of Intercessory Prayer*. SIPHRUT 13. Winona Lake: Eisenbrauns, 2015.

Wong, Maria Liu. *On Becoming Wise Together: Learning and Leading in the City*. Grand Rapids: Eerdmans, 2023.

Wright, Christopher J. H. *The Mission of God: Unlocking the Bible's Grand Narrative*. Downers Grove: IVP Academic, 2006.

———. *Old Testament Ethics for the People of God*. Downers Grove: InterVarsity Press, 2004.

———. *Exodus*, The Story of God Bible Commentary. Grand Rapids: Zondervan, 2021.

Wright, David P. *Inventing God's Law: How the Covenant Code of the Bible Used and Revised the Laws of Hammurabi*. Oxford: Oxford University Press, 2009.

Wu, Jeanne. *Mission through Diaspora: The Case of the Chinese Church in the USA*. Carlisle: Langham Academic, 2016.
Wyatt, N. "Calf." *DDD*, 180–182.
Yang, Dominic Meng-Hsuan. *The Great Exodus from China: Trauma, Memory, and Identity in Modern Taiwan*. Cambridge: Cambridge University Press, 2021.
Yee, Gale A. "Postcolonial Biblical Criticism." In *Methods for Exodus*, Methods in Biblical Interpretation. Edited by Thomas B. Dozeman, 193–233. Cambridge: Cambridge University Press, 2010.
Yeh, Allen. *Polycentric Missiology: 21st-Century Mission From Everyone to Everywhere*. Downers Grove: IVP Academic, 2016.
Yep, Jeanette, Peter Cha, Paul Togunaga, Greg Jao, and Susan Cho Van Riesen. *Following Jesus without Dishonoring Your Parents*. Downers Grove: InterVarsity Press, 1998.
Zornberg, Avivah Gottlieb. *The Particulars of Rupture: Reflections on Exodus*. New York: Schocken Books, 2001.

Asia Theological Association
54 Scout Madriñan St. Quezon City 1103, Philippines
Email: ataasia@gmail.com Telefax: (632) 410 0312

OUR MISSION

The Asia Theological Association (ATA) is a body of theological institutions, committed to evangelical faith and scholarship, networking together to serve the Church in equipping the people of God for the mission of the Lord Jesus Christ.

OUR COMMITMENT

The ATA is committed to serving its members in the development of evangelical, biblical theology by strengthening interaction, enhancing scholarship, promoting academic excellence, fostering spiritual and ministerial formation and mobilizing resources to fulfill God's global mission within diverse Asian cultures.

OUR TASK

Affirming our mission and commitment, ATA seeks to:

- **Strengthen** interaction through inter-institutional fellowship and programs, regional and continental activities, faculty and student exchange programs.
- **Enhance** scholarship through consultations, workshops, seminars, publications, and research fellowships.
- **Promote** academic excellence through accreditation standards, faculty and curriculum development.
- **Foster** spiritual and ministerial formation by providing mentor models, encouraging the development of ministerial skills and a Christian ethos.
- **Mobilize** resources through library development, information technology and infra-structural development.

To learn more about ATA, visit www.ataasia.com or facebook.com/AsiaTheologicalAssociation

Langham Literature, along with its publishing work, is a ministry of Langham Partnership.

Langham Partnership is a global fellowship working in pursuit of the vision God entrusted to its founder John Stott –

> *to facilitate the growth of the church in maturity and Christ-likeness through raising the standards of biblical preaching and teaching.*

Our vision is to see churches in the Majority World equipped for mission and growing to maturity in Christ through the ministry of pastors and leaders who believe, teach and live by the word of God.

Our mission is to strengthen the ministry of the word of God through:
- nurturing national movements for biblical preaching
- fostering the creation and distribution of evangelical literature
- enhancing evangelical theological education

especially in countries where churches are under-resourced.

Our ministry

Langham Preaching partners with national leaders to nurture indigenous biblical preaching movements for pastors and lay preachers all around the world. With the support of a team of trainers from many countries, a multi-level programme of seminars provides practical training, and is followed by a programme for training local facilitators. Local preachers' groups and national and regional networks ensure continuity and ongoing development, seeking to build vigorous movements committed to Bible exposition.

Langham Literature provides Majority World preachers, scholars and seminary libraries with evangelical books and electronic resources through publishing and distribution, grants and discounts. The programme also fosters the creation of indigenous evangelical books in many languages, through writer's grants, strengthening local evangelical publishing houses, and investment in major regional literature projects, such as one volume Bible commentaries like the *Africa Bible Commentary* and the *South Asia Bible Commentary*.

Langham Scholars provides financial support for evangelical doctoral students from the Majority World so that, when they return home, they may train pastors and other Christian leaders with sound, biblical and theological teaching. This programme equips those who equip others. Langham Scholars also works in partnership with Majority World seminaries in strengthening evangelical theological education. A growing number of Langham Scholars study in high quality doctoral programmes in the Majority World itself. As well as teaching the next generation of pastors, graduated Langham Scholars exercise significant influence through their writing and leadership.

To learn more about Langham Partnership and the work we do visit **langham.org**

www.ingramcontent.com/pod-product-compliance
Lightning Source LLC
Chambersburg PA
CBHW050429240426
43661CB00055B/2316